FIFTH EDITION

DEVELOPMENT
and
SOCIAL CHANGE

A GLOBAL
PERSPECTIVE

PHILIP McMICHAEL
Cornell University

$SAGE

Los Angeles | London | New Delhi
Singapore | Washington DC

Los Angeles | London | New Delhi
Singapore | Washington DC

FOR INFORMATION:

SAGE Publications, Inc.
2455 Teller Road
Thousand Oaks, California 91320
E-mail: order@sagepub.com

SAGE Publications Ltd.
1 Oliver's Yard
55 City Road
London EC1Y 1SP
United Kingdom

SAGE Publications India Pvt. Ltd.
B 1/I 1 Mohan Cooperative Industrial Area
Mathura Road, New Delhi 110 044
India

SAGE Publications Asia-Pacific Pte. Ltd.
33 Pekin Street #02-01
Far East Square
Singapore 048763

Acquisitions Editor: David Repetto
Assistant Editor: Terri Accomazzo
Editorial Assistant: Lydia Balian
Production Editor: Laureen Gleason
Copy Editor: Anna Socrates
Typesetter: C&M Digitals (P) Ltd.
Proofreader: Rae-Ann Goodwin
Indexer: Molly Hall
Cover Designer: Gail Buschman
Marketing Manager: Erica DeLuca
Permissions Editor: Karen Ehrmann

Copyright © 2012 by SAGE Publications, Inc.

Printed in the United States of America.

Library of Congress Cataloging-in-Publication Data

McMichael, Philip.

Development and social change : a global perspective / Philip McMichael. —5th ed.

p. cm.

Includes bibliographical references and index.

ISBN 978-1-4129-9207-7 (pbk. : alk. paper)

1. Economic development projects—History.
2. Economic development—History.
3. Competition, International—History.
I. Title.

HC79.E44M25 2012
306.309—dc23   2011036148

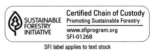

SFI label applies to text stock

14 15 16 17 10 9 8 7 6 5 4 3

Brief Contents

Detailed Contents

About the Author

Philip McMichael grew up in Adelaide, South Australia, and he completed undergraduate degrees in economics and in political science at the University of Adelaide. After traveling in India, Pakistan, and Afghanistan and doing community work in Papua New Guinea, he pursued his doctorate in sociology at the State University of New York at Binghamton. He has taught at the University of New England (New South Wales), Swarthmore College, and the University of Georgia, and he is presently International Professor of Development Sociology at Cornell University. Other appointments include Visiting Senior Research Scholar in International Development at the University of Oxford (Wolfson College), and Visiting Scholar, School of Political Science and International Relations at the University of Queensland. His book *Settlers and the Agrarian Question: Foundations of Capitalism in Colonial Australia* (1984) won the Social Science History Association's Allan Sharlin Memorial Award in 1985. McMichael edited *The Global Restructuring of Agro-Food Systems* (1994), *Food and Agrarian Orders in the World Economy* (1995), *New Directions in the Sociology of Global Development* (2005) with Frederick H. Buttel, *Looking Backward and Looking Forward: Perspectives on Social Science History* (2005) with Harvey Graff and Lesley Page Moch, *Contesting Development: Critical Struggles for Social Change* (2010), and *The Politics of Biofuels, Land and Agrarian Change* (2011) with Jun Borras and Ian Scoones. He has served as chair of his department, as director of Cornell University's International Political Economy Program, as chair of the American Sociological Association's Political Economy of the World-System Section, as president of the Research Committee on Agriculture and Food for the International Sociological Association, and as a board member of Cornell University Press. He has also worked with the Food and Agricultural Organization of the United Nations (FAO) and its Committee on Food Security, the UN Research Institute for Social Development (UNRISD), the international peasant coalition *Vía Campesina*, and the International Planning Committee for Food Sovereignty. He and his wife, Karen Schachere, have two children, Rachel and Jonathan.

Preface to the Fifth Edition

The fifth edition of this text updates the material in a world in substantial transition. The original framework and perspective of the first edition remain intact, although the attempt to organize development as a global project is fraught with instability and possibly planet-threatening trends. Accordingly, a new section outlining an emergent "sustainability project" has been added. The thread that weaves together this story of colonialism, developmentalism, globalization, and sustainability is that development is a project of rule, with environmental consequences. It takes different forms in different historical periods, and these have been laid out as changing sets of political-economic and political-ecological relations, animated by powerful discourses of discipline, opportunity, and sustainability. While this text may have the appearance of an economic argument, it is important to note that the framework is essentially political and world-historical in that it attempts to understand the intersection between the development enterprise and power relations in ordering the world and its ecological foundations. This account of development focuses on social and political transformations, and the various ways in which development is realized through social and spatial inequalities. It also considers these processes from the perspective of social movements, and how their resistances problematize the dominant vision of economism as a form of rule and as an increasingly evident threat to ecological stability.

The conceptual framework posits "development" as a political construct devised by dominant actors such as metropolitan states, multilateral institutions, and political and economic elites to order the world and contain opposition. Development and globalization are presented as projects with coherent organizing principles (e.g., economic nationalism, market liberalization), yet unrealistic in their vision and potential for accomplishment, since they are realized through inequality. The theoretical subtext of the development project is organized by extended Polanyian cycles of regulation and resistance. In the mid-twentieth century, a form of "embedded liberalism" (market regulation within a maturing nation-state system to contain labor and decolonization movements) informed social-democratic (developmentalist) goals within a Cold War context of economic and military aid to the Third World. This "development era" ended with a "countermobilization" of corporate interests dedicated to instituting a "self-regulating market" on a global scale from the 1970s onwards. The dominant discourse of neoliberalism proposed market liberalization, privatization, freedom of capital movement and access, and so on. This globalization project had a "test run" during the debt regime of the 1980s, and was institutionalized with the establishment of the World Trade Organization (WTO) in 1995. A *further* countermobilization—to the deprivations of the globalization project—has gathered momentum through maturing global justice movements in the 1990s, the Latin American and Arab rebellions of the new century, and a growing "legitimacy deficit" for the global development establishment. This is symbolized in the collapse of the Washington Consensus following the 1997 Asian-originating global financial crisis, recovery of the trope of "poverty reduction" in the Millennium Development Goals (MDGs) initiative of 2000, stalemate at the WTO, and growing antipathy toward the World Bank and the International Monetary Fund (IMF) among countries of the global South. Neoliberalism is at a crossroads, complicated by serious security concerns: with a social component—in mushrooming slums; an economic dimension—in both financial volatility and the casualization of employment; a political element—in acts of terrorism; and an ecological aspect—in the evidence of global climate change. How the current cycle of opposition and creative development alternatives will unfold is yet to be determined, but it is possible to see an emergent sustainability project which includes both security concerns—largely of those with political and economic power—and grassroots initiatives toward rethinking the values that define development.

The fifth edition has two major revisions. The first is the introduction of an explicit discussion of the origins and role of development theory. The purpose here is to (a) introduce basic theoretical concepts that organize our understanding of development, (b) situate these theoretical concepts in the era of decolonization and the optimism of the development decades, (c) examine how subsequent transformations in world ordering call such foundational development theory into question, and (d) indicate to the reader how the author has organized the narrative according to social change theory that allows transformation in conceptions of development.

The second major revision considers current events as indicative of fundamental transitions in development possibilities. These events, outlined in Chapter 8, include the conjunction of food, energy, financial, and climate crises, as well as a redistribution of political-economic power as registered in the rise of the Group of 21 (G-21)—in particular the BRICS—and the challenge to U.S. supremacy. Structural adjustment of states in the global North, combined with social rebellion in the Middle East and the aforementioned crises in several dimensions, call into question the assumptions and institutions associated with the "Globalization Project" and its neoliberal dictates. Chapter 9 provides the outlines of the "Sustainability Project" as an emergent set of practices and institutions governing the next iteration/ordering of "development," which is no longer about improving on the past so much as managing the future. The chapter considers the significance of a series of high-profile reports, initiatives, and green technologies—together these investigations and experiments reveal an array of disparate attempts to manage the future, and point toward a future ecological/climate regime.

The subject of development is difficult to teach. Living in relatively affluent surroundings, most university students understandably situate their society on the "high end" of a development continuum—at the pinnacle of human economic and technological achievement. And they often perceive the development continuum and their favorable position on it as "natural"—a well-deserved reward for embracing modernity. It is difficult to put one's world in historical perspective from this vantage point. It is harder still to help students grasp a world perspective that goes beyond framing their experience as an "evolved state"—the inevitable march of progress.

In my experience, until students go beyond simple evolutionary views, they have difficulty valuing other cultures and social possibilities that do not potentially mirror their own. When they do go beyond the evolutionary perspective, they are better able to evaluate their own culture sociologically and to think reflexively about social change, development, and global inequalities. This is the challenge we face.

Ancillaries

For the Instructor

The password-protected Instructor Site at **www.sagepub.com/mc michael5e** gives instructors access to a full complement of resources to support and enhance their courses. The following assets are available on the instructor site:

- An **essay test question bank** that provides a number of essay questions to test students' comprehension of the topics
- **PowerPoint** slides for each chapter that are integrated with the book's distinctive features and incorporate key tables, figures, and photos, for use in lecture and review

- **Chapter summaries and outlines** that provide valuable tools for use in handouts and lectures
- **Tables and figures from the book** in an easily downloadable format, for use in handouts and presentations
- **A timeline of globalization and development** from the printed text in a digital format

A Timeline of Development

WORLD FRAMEWORK	**Developmentalism (1940s–1970s)**
POLITICAL ECONOMY	State-Regulated Markets (Keynesianism) Public Spending
SOCIAL GOALS	Social Contract and Redistribution National Citizenship
DEVELOPMENT [Model]	Industrial Replication National Economic Sector Complementarity [Brazil, Mexico, India]
MOBILIZING TOOL	Nationalism (Post-Colonialism)
MECHANISMS	Import-Substitution Industrialization (ISI) Public Investment (Infrastructure, Energy) Education Land Reform
VARIANTS	First World (Freedom of Enterprise) Second World (Central Planning) Third World (Modernization via Development Alliance)

MARKERS

	Cold War Begins (1946)	Korean War (1950–53)	Vietnam War (1964–75)
Bretton Woods (1944)	Marshall Plan (1946)		Alliance for Progress (1961)
United Nations (1943)		Non-Aligned Movement Forum (1955)	Group of 77 (G-77) (1964) — World Economic Forum (1970)

FIRST DEVELOPMENT DECADE   SECOND DEVELOPMENT DECADE

```
|----●------------●------------●------------●------------●------------●-----|
  1940          1950          1960          1970
```

INSTITUTIONAL DEVELOPMENTS	World Bank, IMF, GATT (1944) US$ as Reserve Currency	PL-480 (1954)	UNCTAD (1964) Eurodollar/offshore $ market
	COMECON (1947)		

Globalism (1980s–2000s)

Self-Regulating Markets (Monetarism)
Public Downsizing

Private Initiative and Global Consumerism
Multi-Layered Citizenship and Recognition

Participation in World Market
Global Comparative Advantage
[Chile, South Korea; NAFTA]

Markets and Credit

Export-Orientation
Privatization
Entrepreneurialism
Public and Majority-Class Austerity

National Structural Adjustment (Opening Economies)
Regional Free Trade Agreements
Global Governance

Oil Crises (1973, 1979)		Cold War Ends (1989)	"New World Order"	Imperial Wars (2001–)		
	Debt Regime		WTO Regime		Climate Regime	
New International Economic Order Initiative (1974)			Chiapas Revolt (1994)	World Social Forum (2001)		
Group of 7 (G-7) (1975)	Earth Summit (1992)	Kyoto Protocol (1997)	Group of 20 (G-20) (1999)	MDGs (2000)	Stern Report (2006)	IAASTD Report (2008)

"LOST DECADE" "GLOBALIZATION DECADE"

1970	1980	1990	2000

GATT Uruguay
Round (1986–1994)
IPCC (1988)
UNFCCC (1988)

NAFTA (1994)
WTO (1995)

Offshore Banking   Structural Adjustment Loans   "Governance"/HIPC Loans

Glasnost/Perestroika

Acknowledgments

I wish to express my thanks to the people who have helped me along the way, beginning with the late Terence Hopkins (my graduate school mentor), and James Petras and Immanuel Wallerstein. The late Giovanni Arrighi played a critical role in encouraging me to cultivate "analytical nerve." For the first three editions, which include acknowledgment of the various people who were so helpful, special mention still goes to the original editor-in-chief, Steve Rutter, for his remarkable vision and his enthusiasm and faith in this project, as well as friends and colleagues who made significant contributions to improving this project—the late Fred Buttel, Harriet Friedmann, Richard Williams, Michelle Adato, Dale Tomich, Farshad Araghi, Rajeev Patel, Dia Da Costa, Gayatri Menon, and Karuna Morarji—and my undergraduate and graduate students (particularly my remarkable teaching assistants) at Cornell.

For this fifth edition, I have been fortunate to have the encouragement and understanding of publisher for sociology at SAGE, David Repetto, and the thoughtful guidance of editorial assistants for sociology, Maggie Stanley and Lydia Balian. Also, special thanks go to senior project editor, Laureen Gleason, and to editorial and marketing specialists Theresa Accomazzo and Erica DeLuca for their work behind the scenes, and especially to Anna Socrates, my fastidious copyeditor. Graduate student Ian Bailey provided much-needed and thorough research support when I needed it most and turned a critical eye on the first chapter. And Gary Hytrek prompted me to make more explicit my conceptual framework, despite my skepticism toward formal theorizing. Great thanks are also due to the reviewers of this edition: Pamela Altman, Dennis Canterbury, Julie Guthman, Robert Hard, Syndee Knight, and P. Pushkar.

Abbreviations

AfDB	African Development Bank
AGRA	Alliance for a Green Revolution in Africa
ALBA	Bolivarian Alternative for the Americas
AoA	Agreement on Agriculture (WTO)
APEC	Asia-Pacific Economic Cooperation
BAIR	Bureaucratic-Authoritarian Industrializing Regime
BIP	Border Industrialization Program
BRICS	Brazil, Russia, India, China and South Africa
CAFTA	Central American Free Trade Agreement
CBD	Convention on Biodiversity
CDM	Clean development mechanism
CEDAW	Convention on the Elimination of All Forms of Discrimination against Women
CGIAR	Consultative Group on International Agricultural Research
COMECON	Council for Mutual Economic Assistance
COP	conference of parties
ECA	Export Credit Agency
ECLA	Economic Commission for Latin America
EOI	export-oriented industrialization
EPZ	export processing zone
EU	European Union
FAO	Food and Agricultural Organization (UN)
FDI	foreign direct investment
FLO	Fairtrade Labelling Organizations International
FTA	Free Trade Agreement
FTAA	Free Trade Area of the Americas
GAD	gender and development
GATS	General Agreement on Trade in Services
GATT	General Agreement on Tariffs and Trade
GDI	Gender Development Index

GDL	global division of labor
GDP	gross domestic product
GEF	Global Environmental Facility
GEM	gender empowerment measure
GHG	greenhouse gas emissions
GLOBALGAP	Retailer Produce Working Group on Good Agricultural Practices
GNH	gross national happiness
GNP	gross national product
GPI	genuine progress indicator
HDI	Human Development Index
HIPC	heavily indebted poor countries
HYV	high-yielding variety
IAASTD	International Assessment of Agricultural Science and Technology for Development
ICT	information and communication technologies
IDS	Institute for Development Studies
IEA	International Energy Agency
IFI	international financial institutions
IFPRI	International Food Policy Research Institute
IIED	International Institute for Environment and Development
IMF	International Monetary Fund
IPCC	Inter-Governmental Plan on Climate Change
IPR	intellectual property rights
ISI	import-substitution industrialization
LDC	least developed countries
LDCF	less developed countries fund
MA	millennium ecosystem assessment
MDGs	millennium development goals
MNEA	Middle East North African states
MICs	middle-income countries
NAC	new agricultural country
NAFTA	North American Free Trade Agreement
NAM	Non-Aligned Movement
NAPA	National adaptation programme of action
NEPAD	New Partnership for Africa's Development
NGO	nongovernmental organization
NIC	newly industrializing country
NIDL	new international division of labor
NIEO	new international economic order
NTE	nontraditional export

OAU	Organization for African Unity
ODA	Overseas Development Assistance
OECD	Organisation for Economic Co-operation and Development
PRSP	poverty reduction strategy papers
RAI	Responsible agricultural investment
REDD	Reducing Emissions from Deforestation and Degradation
SAL	structural adjustment loan
SAP	structural adjustment policies
SEZ	special economic zone
TFN	Transnational Feminist Network
TIE	Transnationals Information Exchange
TNB	transnational bank
TNC	transnational corporation
TPN	Transnational Policy Network
TRIMs	trade-related aspects of investment measures
TRIPs	trade-related intellectual property rights
UNASUR	Union of South American Nations
UNCED	United Nations Conference on Environment and Development
UNCTAD	United Nations Conference on Trade and Development
UNDESA	United Nations Department of Economic and Social Affairs
UNDP	United Nations Development Program
UNEP	United Nations Environment Program
UNFCCC	United Nations Convention on Climate Change
WEEE	waste from electrical and electronic equipment
WEF	World Economic Forum
WHO	World Health Organization
WID	Women in Development
WSF	World Social Forum
WTO	World Trade Organization

1

Development

Theory and Reality

Development, today, is increasingly about how we survive the future, rather than how we improve on the past. While ideas of human progress, development stages, or visions of improvement will still guide social theory and policy making, how we manage "energy descent" and adapt to serious ecological deficits and climatic disruption will define our existence. How will this shift change our understanding and practice of development?

A central issue is how effectively policy makers (in states and development agencies) recognize the need for wholesale public coordination of planning to minimize and adapt to inevitable climatic changes. Plenty of new ideas, practices, and policies are surfacing, but more as a cacophony rather than a strategic endeavor to reverse our **ecological footprint**. (See Glossary/Index for bolded definitions.) While the Chinese government is strategic in promoting green technology, China—the major offshore assembly zone for global commodities—is now the leading source of global greenhouse gas emissions. China averages $150 billion worth of environmental damage annually, due to its breakneck economic growth. Climate summits have so far only confirmed the intransigence of governments held hostage to domestic growth policies—whether these governments are from the **global North** or the **global South**. This division, and which nation belongs to which "bloc"—and therefore is most responsible for emissions—only distracts authorities from substantive action. Another crisis also confronts twenty-first century nation-states, namely, the global crisis of unemployment and debt, which compounds the challenges of development futures.

Not only are there increasingly evident biophysical limits to development as we know it, but development is now compromised by mushrooming public austerity policies across the nation-state system. Such policies, tested in the global South from the 1980s, are now affecting the societies of the global North. All over, the development ideal of a social contract between governments and citizens is crumbling as hard-won social rights and entitlements erode—this is evident in contemporary European and U.S. political and social disorder as citizens protest cut-backs, as well as in the Middle Eastern uprisings against repressive regimes and joblessness (see Chapter 8). Arguably, "development" is not only in crisis but is at a significant turning point in its short history as a master concept of (Western-based) social science and cultural life.

This book is a guide to the rise and transformation of development as a vector of global social change over the last two centuries. From one (long-term) angle, it appears increasingly comet-like: a brilliant lodestar for the world, but perhaps destined to burn out as its energy-intensive foundations meet their limits. From another (immediate) angle, the energy dilemma forces renewed critical thinking about how humans might live sustainably on the planet. These perspectives are the subject of Chapter 9, "The Sustainability Project." Here we are concerned with the source and maturation of "development" as a master concept.

Development: History and Politics

Development had its origins in the colonial era, as Europeans began constructing systems of government—domestic and imperial—and concentrating within the emerging national states an industrial system fueled by the products of colonial labor regimes. As European political economies matured within this broader context, "development" emerged as the definitive concept. Global in its origins, the meaning of development nevertheless focused on European accomplishments. While such accomplishments came with massive social—and often violent—upheaval, they have been represented in theory as a set of idealized outcomes to be emulated by other countries. Accordingly, the "end" of development justifies the means of getting there, however disruptive socially and ecologically the process may be.

At this point it is helpful to work with Michael Cowan and Robert Shenton's distinction between development as an imminent and/or universal social *process,* and development as a political *intervention.* In the nineteenth century, development was understood *philosophically* as the improvement of humankind (in the form of knowledge-building, techno-logical change, wealth accumulation). European political elites interpreted development *practically*, as a way to socially engineer emerging national societies. Elites formulated government policy to manage the social trans-formations attending the rise of capitalism and industrial technologies, so development was identified with *both* industrialization *and* the regulation of its disruptive social impacts. These impacts began with the displacement of rural populations by land enclosures for cash cropping, a process that generated "undesirables," such as menacing paupers, restless proletarians, and unhealthy factory towns.[2] Development, then, meant balancing techno-logical change and class formation with social intervention, that is, manag-ing the citizen-subjects who experienced wrenching social transformations. At the same time, such transformations became the catalyst of competing political visions—liberal, socialist, conservative—of the ideal society.

In Europe's colonies, the inhabitants appeared undeveloped—by self-defined European standards. In this context, development (as "evolution") ideologically justified imperial intervention, whether to plunder or civilize. Either way, the social engineering impulse framed the European coloniza-tion of the non-European world. Not only did the extraction of colonial resources facilitate European industrialization, but European colonial administrators managed subject populations as they experienced their own version of wrenching social transformations. Thus development assumed an additional, normative meaning, namely, the "white man's burden"—the title of a poem by English poet Rudyard Kipling—imparting honor to an apparently noble task. The implied racism remains a part of the normative understanding (and world consequence) of development.

Under these circumstances, development extended modern social engi-neering to colonies incorporated into the European orbit. Subject popula-tions were exposed to a variety of new disciplines, including forced labor schemes, schooling, and segregation in native quarters. Forms of colonial subordination differed across time and space, but the overriding object was either to adapt or marginalize colonial subjects to the European presence. In this sense, development was a *power relationship*. For example, British colonialism introduced the English factory-model "Lancaster school" to the (ancient) city of Cairo in 1843 to educate Cairo's emerging civil service. Egyptian students learned the new disciplines necessary to a developing society that was busily displacing peasant culture with plantations of cotton for export to English textile mills and managing an army of migrant labor building an infrastructure of roads, canals, railways, telegraphs, and ports.[3] Through the colonial relation, industrialism was transforming both English and Egyptian society, producing new forms of social discipline among laboring populations and middle-class citizen-subjects. And, while industrialism produced new class inequalities within each society, colonialism racialized international inequality. In other words, development introduced new class and racial hierarchies within and across societies.

While development informed modern narratives in the age of industrialism and empire, it only became formalized as a *project* in the mid-twentieth century. This period was the high tide of decolonization, as the Western—British, Italian, German, French, Dutch, Portuguese, and Belgian—and Japanese empires collapsed, and when a standardizing concept, "development," as an emancipatory promise, became the new global ontology (a way of seeing/ordering the world).

In 1945, the United Nations, with the intent of expanding membership as colonies gained independence as sovereign states, institutionalized the System of National Accounts. A universal quantifiable measure of development, the Gross National Product (GNP), was born. At this point, the colonial rule of *subjects* under the guise of civilizing inferior races morphed into the **development project,** based on the ideal of self-governing states composed of *citizens* united by the ideology of nationalism. By the twentieth century's end, the global development project focused on market governance of and by self-maximizing *consumers*.

Development Theory

Specifying development as consumption privileges the market as the vehicle of social change. The underlying philosophy—deriving from a popular (but limiting) interpretation of Adam Smith's *The Wealth of Nations*[4] and formalized in neoclassical economic theory—is that markets maximize individual preferences and allocate resources efficiently. Whether this theory reflects reality or not, it is a deeply held belief that is now institutionalized in much development policy across the world. Why is this the case?

Naturalizing Development

There are two ways to answer this question. First, a belief in markets is a central tenet of liberal Western philosophy. Hungarian philosopher Karl Polanyi noted that modern liberalism rests on a belief in a natural propensity for self-gain, which translates in economic theory as the market principle—realized as consumer preference.[5] Self-gain, expressed through the market, drives the aspiration for improvement, aggregated as development.

Second, as Polanyi noted, to naturalize (competitive) market behavior a transhistorical attribute discounts other human attributes, or values—such as cooperation, redistribution, and reciprocity. For Polanyi, and other classical social theorists, economic individualism is quite novel in the history of human societies and specific to nineteenth-century European developments, rather than being an innate human characteristic.

While these other values are clearly evident today in human interactions, the aspiration for improvement, normalized now as a private motivation, informs development. That is, well-being and self-improvement are squarely centered on access to goods *and* services through the marketplace. Initial (dating from the mid-twentieth century) formulations of development paired private consumption with public provisions—infrastructure, education, health, water supply, commons, clean air, and so forth. The mid-twentieth century was the heyday of the welfare, or development, state. But from the last quarter of the twentieth century, increasingly all provisioning has been subjected to **privatization**, as the market becomes the medium through which we consume and develop. To this end, development has become synonymous with consumption.

This outcome was prefigured in one of the most influential theories of development emerging in the post–World War II world. In 1960, economist Walt Rostow published *The Stages of Economic Growth: A Non-Communist Manifesto*,[6] outlining a development theory that celebrates the Western model of free enterprise—in contrast to a state-planned economy. The "stages" traversed a linear sequence, beginning with "Traditional Society" (agrarian, limited productivity) and moving through "Preconditions for Take-off" (state formation, education, science, banking, profit-systematization), "Take-off" (normalization of growth, with investment rates promoting the expanded reproduction of industry), and "Maturity" (the second industrial revolution that moved from textiles and iron to machine-tools, chemicals, and electrical equipment)—and finally to the "Age of High Mass-Consumption," which is characterized by the movement from basic to durable goods, urbanization, and the rising level of white-collar versus blue-collar work.

This evolutionary sequence, distilled from the U.S. experience, represents the consumer society as the terminal stage of a complex historical process. Rostow also held out the U.S. model as the goal to which other (i.e., developing) societies should aspire, which partly explains Rostow's subtitle—expressing the Cold War rivalry between the United States and the Soviet Union at the time. The theorization of development as a series of evolutionary stages naturalizes the process, whether it occurs on a national (development era) or an international (globalization era) stage. Mass consumption was a final goal to be realized through membership of the "free world" at the time, and by implication, U.S. assistance would be available to spur the **Third World** of post-colonial, developing nations into progress along the stages.

However, note that Rostow's "development blueprint" depended on a political context. That is, markets were not so natural that they did not require creating, securing, and protecting (by a **development state**). Development was neither spontaneous or inevitable, rather it required an institutional complex on a world scale (a **development project**) to nurture it along, complete with trade, monetary, and investment rules, aid regimes, and a military umbrella—all of which were supplied through post-war multilateral institutions and bilateral arrangements led by the United States. In this way, theory came to imitate reality, which in turn is shaped by theory—informing public discourse and translating into policy implementation.

Global Context

Reality, of course, is more complicated than it first appears. Rostow's prescriptions artificially separated societies from one another. While this may have expressed the idealism of mid-twentieth century nationalism, to assign stages of growth to societies without accounting for their unequal access to offshore resources discounted a fundamental historic relationship between world regions that have been shaped by colonial and investment patterns. Not only did European powers once depend on their colonies for resources and markets, these patterns continued in the post-colonial era. Because of continuing **First World** dependence on raw materials from the **Third World**, some societies were more equal than others in their capacity to traverse Rostow's stages, as we shall see in Chapter 4.

It was this reality that stimulated **dependency analysis** and **world-system analysis**. The concept of "dependency" emerged in the mid-twentieth century from several quarters—an empirical observation by economist Hans Singer that "peripheral" countries were exporting more and more natural resources to pay for increasingly expensive manufactured imports; an argument by Singer's collaborator, Argentinean economist Raúl Prebisch, that Latin American states should therefore industrialize behind protective tariffs on manufactured imports; and earlier Marxist theories of exploitative imperialist relations between the European and the non-European world.[7] "Dependency" referred to the unequal economic relations between metropolitan societies and non-European peripheries—a factor accounting for the development of the former at the expense of the **underdevelopment** of the latter. As economist Andre Gunder Frank put it:

[H]istorical research demonstrates that contemporary underdevelopment is in large part the historical product of past and continuing economic and other relations between the satellite underdeveloped and the now-developed metropolitan countries. . . . When we examine this metropolis-satellite structure, we find that each of the satellites . . . serves as an instrument to suck capital or economic surplus out of its own satellites and to channel part of this surplus to the world metropolis of which all are satellites.[8]

World-system analysis, advanced by sociologist Immanuel Wallerstein, deepened the concept of dependency by elevating the scope of the modern social system to a global scale. States became political units competing for—or surrendering—resources within a **world division of labor.** Here regional labor forces occupy a skill/technological hierarchy associated with state strength or weakness in the capitalist world-economy.[9] From this perspective, the "core" concentrates capital-intensive or intellectual production and the "periphery" is associated with lower-skilled labor-intensive production, whether plantation labor or assembly of manufactured goods. As we shall see, this kind of geographical hierarchy is increasingly complicated by what journalist Thomas Friedman calls "flat world" processes (an example is India's Information Technology boom).[10]

While "dependency" broadens the analysis of development processes to world-scale relationships, challenging the assumption that societies are aligned along a self-evident spectrum of growth stages, it implies a "development-centrism"—where (idealized western) development is the term of reference. In this regard Wallerstein has argued that given the power hierarchy of the world-system, (idealized western) "development" represents a "lode-star" or master concept of modern social theory.[11] As such, the privileging of "development" denied many other collective/social strategies of sustainability or improvement in other cultures. Nevertheless, while measuring all societies against a conception of (industrial) development may have seemed the appropriate goal for modernization and dependency theory at mid-century, from the vantage point of the *twenty-first century* it is quite problematic. The growing recognition that the planet cannot sustain the current urban-industrial trends in China and India is one dramatic expression of this new reality.

Agrarian Questions

Urbanization is a defining outcome of development and the "stages of growth" metaphor, where "tradition" yields to "modernity" as industrialization deepens and nurtures it. Political scientist Samuel Huntington, writing about the process of modernization in *Political Order and Changing Societies* (1968), claimed, "Agriculture declines in importance compared to commercial, industrial, and other nonagricultural activities, and commercial agriculture replaces subsistence agriculture."[12] While this sequence is clearly in evidence, the way in which it has played out raises questions about the model of separate national development (leaving aside the problem of artificial boundary drawing of "nations" in the colonial world). Rather than commercial agriculture replacing subsistence agriculture in country by country, millions of small producers have been unable to survive because of foreign impact—in the form of colonialism, foreign aid, and unequal market relations—expressing the global power relations identified by dependency and world-system analysts. How we perceive these changes is the ultimate question: Even as social changes occur within nations, does that mean the change is "internally" driven? Thus, if subsistence agriculture declines or disappears, is this because it does not belong on a society's "development ladder"?[13] Or is it because of a deepening exposure of smallholders to unequal world market competition by agribusiness—where agricultural productivity ratios across high- and low-input farming systems have risen from 10 to 1 before 1940 to 2000 to 1 in the twenty-first century?[14]

Rather than simply developing "internally," Britain progressively outsourced its agriculture to the colonies, replacing subsistence agriculture there with plantations for commercial export. Such a global process played out in the North American continent as well, and partly accounts for the commercial dynamism of U.S. agriculture by the twentieth century (informing Rostow's model). Therefore, modeling the rise of commercial agriculture as a question of *domestic* transformation is only partially valid. Nevertheless, the absence of peasantries in the First World is a key register for development theory. A logical extrapolation (if not historical analysis) would therefore define peasant cultures elsewhere as remnants of "Traditional Society." As such, and according to this development model, peasant cultures are destined to disappear, whether because of urban gravitational pull, green revolution technologies, eviction by land grabs, or unequal competition from First World agribusiness exports.

Thus small farming cultures became development "baselines"—in theory, and in practice, given modern technology's drive to replace labor and control production. Unrecognized is the superior capacity or potential in surviving agrarian cultures for managing and sustaining their ecosystems than commercial agriculture, which overrides natural limits with chemicals and other technologies that deplete soil fertility, hydrological cycles, and biodiversity.[15] The current "global land grab" depends on representing small-holdings across the global South as "underutilized" land that would be better employed by conversion to commercial agricultural estates producing foods and biofuels largely for export.[16] Such activities raise the question as to whether and to what extent development—as modeled—is inevitable or intentional, and national or international?

Ecological Questions

In addition, this particular example of agricultural land usage also underscores a significant *ecological blindspot* in development theory. Where the passage from subsistence to commercial agriculture is represented as improvement (of single-crop productivity), it is an insufficient measure if it does not take into account the "externals." These are the significant social and environmental impacts such as disruption of agrarian cultures and eco-systems, the deepening of dependency on fossil fuel, and modern agriculture's responsibility for up to a third of greenhouse gas emissions (GHG). It is this consequence that challenges the veracity of linear projections of development, and also the wisdom of replacing a long-standing knowledge-intensive culture/ecology (farming) with an industrialized economic sector (agriculture).

One key example of this ecological blindspot is its reproduction in the **Human Development Index (HDI)**, constructed by the United Nations Development Programme (UNDP). The HDI overcame the singular emphasis on economic growth as development, but carried forward the absence of the ecological dimension:

> The concept of human development focuses on the ends rather than the means of development and progress. The real objective of development should be to create an enabling environment for people to enjoy long, healthy and creative lives. Though this may appear to be a simple truth, it is often overlooked as more immediate concerns are given precedence.[17]

While the HDI is known for its more robust measurement of (human) development, its data sources have lacked environmental content. This is particularly so given that humanity has now overshot the earth's biocapacity (see Figure 1.1). Focusing on the outcomes of development discounts how we live on the earth, that is, measuring what practices are sustainable or not. It was only in 2011 that the UNDP began to embrace an ecological

Figure 1.1   Humanity's Ecological Footprint

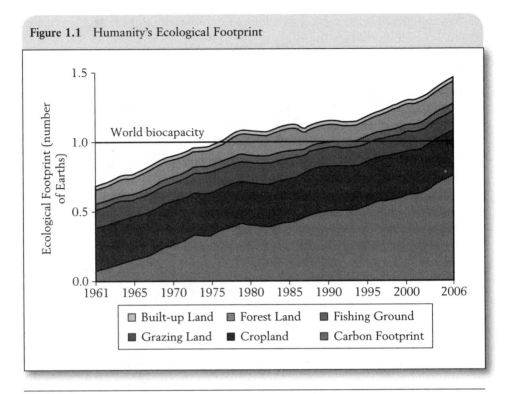

Source: Global Footprint Network 2010 National Footprint Accounts, see http://www.footprintnetwork
.org/en/index.php/newsletter/bv/humanity_now_demanding_1.4_earthsUS:official&channel=np&prmd
=ivns&tbm=isch&tbo=u&source=univ&sa=X&ei=aPv_TYmjEOqy0AHx7LGvDg&ved=0CDMQsA
Q&biw=1125&bih=821

sensibility. Thus the Human Development Report (2011) is "about the adverse repercussions of environment degradation for people, how the poor and disadvantaged are worst affected, and how greater equity needs to be part of the solution."[18]

Given the UNDP's reputation for questioning conventional wisdom, this new focus is a counterpoint to the *2005 Millennium Ecosystem Assessment,* which noted that the last half century of human action has had the most intensive and extensive negative impact on world ecosystems ever, and yet this has been accompanied by continuing global gains in human well-being.[19] Known as the **"environmentalist's paradox"** (since we might expect ecosystem degradation to negatively affect human well-being), researchers have noted that *average* measures of well-being may reduce the validity of this claim, but perhaps more significantly "technology has decoupled well-being from nature" and time lags will only tell.[20] In other words, mastery of nature may be effective in the short-term in generating rising consumption patterns, but also in masking the long-term implications of ecosystem stress. What such research suggests is that development needs a robust sustainability dimension. It is in this context that this book ends with an account of an emerging Sustainability Project.

DEVELOPMENT PARADOXES

The environmentalist's paradox, when inverted, is—in fact—a "development paradox." Former World Bank economist Herman Daly formulated this as an "impossibility theorem," namely, that the universalization of U.S.-style high mass consumption economy would require several planet Earths. Either way, the ultimate paradox here is that the environment is not equipped to absorb its unrelenting exploitation by the current growth model of endless accumulation. In other words, development as we know it is undermining itself.

Three of the nine planetary operational boundaries have been crossed already—climate change, biodiversity, and the nitrogen cycle—while others such as fresh water use and oceanic acidification are at serious tipping points. Meanwhile, the costs of ecological degradation are borne disproportionately by the poor—the very same people targeted by the development industry. Two paradoxical formulations follow: (1) development expands opportunity/prosperity but is realized through inequality; and (2) development targets poverty but often magnifies it. Related to these formulations is the notion (advanced by the World Bank in 1992) that economic growth is a condition for sustainable development, which the UK Stern Review of 2006 termed a paradox: since the cost of climate change adaptation would be far greater if we wait for higher future levels of wealth to address the problem.

Some subsidiary paradoxes include such questions as these: Are low-carbon cultures that live with rather than seek to master nature backward? Are non-western cultures judged poor in what makes western cultures rich? Is frugality poverty? Why is malnutrition common to western and non-western cultures (see Figure 1.2)? Are non-western cultures rich in what western cultures are now poor (non-monetized items such as open space, leisure, solidarity, ecological knowledge)? Should we measure living standards only in monetary terms?

Sources: Foster (2011), Stern (2006), Daly (1990).

Figure 1.2 Percentage of Population That Is Malnourished and Overweight

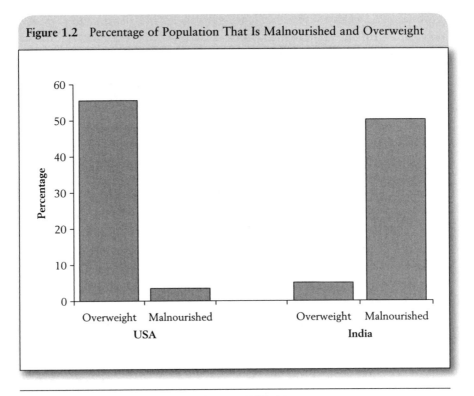

Source: Adapted from *New Internationalist* 353 (2003): 20.

Social Change

As we have seen, development theory provides a blueprint, and justification, for universalizing a process originating within Europe—but as "greater Europe," since European industrialization depended on displacing non-European industry and capturing non-European resources (minerals, raw materials, labor, and foodstuffs). Justification of this exploitation meant representing colonial intervention as a civilizing mission to those opposing colonialism on moral grounds. Of course colonial subjects resisted—for example, the successful late-eighteenth-century slave uprising in the French colony of Saint Domingue (forming the Haitian free state), but also the unsuccessful Amritsar rebellion put down savagely by British forces in India in 1919. Such uprisings marked a long-term politics of decolonization, with colonial subjects gaining moral and material power as **countermovements** to European empires, which in turn became increasingly costly to maintain. Resistance to colonialism—including substantial peasant mobilizations from China to Mexico to Kenya—was matched with labor uprisings and political organization during the late-colonial era. The British faced widespread labor strikes in their West Indian and African colonies in the 1930s, and this pattern continued over the next two decades in Africa as British and French colonial subjects protested conditions in cities, ports, mines, and on the railways.[21]

In other words, large-scale social changes accompanying industrial development involve definitive power struggles. Colonial rule generated a politics of decolonization, including class conflict, identity/cultural claims, and the desire for equality and sovereignty. The **colonial project** was certainly anchored in class relations as empires subordinated colonial labor forces and resources to service imperial needs. But this economic relation was accompanied by fundamental racial politics that both justified subjugation and fueled resistances across the colonial world. Added to the mix was the human rights dimension, whereby the desire for equality and sovereignty driving European social changes resonated in anti-colonial movements. While all three dimensions inform social struggles today, including gender and indigenous rights, they are all conditioned by the global development project that emerged in the mid-twentieth-century postcolonial era. Here, decolonization led to a universal realization of sovereignty in the (European-based) form of the nation-state, and expressed in the establishment of the United Nations organization in 1945.

The divided racial legacy of colonialism certainly did not disappear, but a very diverse world was bound together now by a universal principle: an international governmental structure enshrining the meaning and measurement of development as a *national standard*. This was institutionalized in the UN System of National Accounts by which monetized economic activity was recorded as Gross National Product (GNP). Outside of the Communist bloc (also known as the **Second World**), as national economic growth and income levels became the measure of development, so First- and Third-World societies came to be governed by the market (and its metrics), with varying degrees of public regulation.

The "market society" was the product of modern capitalism and its drive to commodify social relations, expressed in monetary exchanges. As Karl Marx pointed out, even human labor power came to be commodified via the wage contract, as villagers lost their means of livelihood and were forced to work for wages.[22] Karl Polanyi extended this observation to land and currency, noting that with the rise of nineteenth-century market society each of these substances came to be traded for a price. He argued that neither labor, land, nor money were *produced for sale,* and so were really "fictitious commodities." For this reason, when these substances are treated as commodities, workers, farmers, and businesses are exposed to exploitative or uncertain conditions. That is, their labor, farming, or entrepreneurship experience competitive relations beyond their control, by a market with seemingly independent authority. Under these circumstances, Polanyi proposed that social movements would inevitably arise to protect society from unregulated markets (a "double movement")—in effect, to re-embed markets within social controls. For Polanyi, the proof of this pudding was establishment of the twentieth-century welfare state, which became a model for the development state. It arose out of a European-wide social mobilization to protect the rights of workers, farmers, and businesses from the ill effects of unrestrained markets.[23]

The Projects as Framework

Within the terms of this broad social change theory, then, the postcolonial world order emerged from the combined force of decolonization politics and the new model of publicly regulated capitalist markets (as distinct from the communist model of a state-planned economy). Development as an ideal and as a policy carried forward the social welfare dimension, reinforced by the UN Declaration of Universal Human Rights (1948), through which governments were enjoined to protect civil rights through a **social contract** between state and citizen. This contract defined the era of the **development project** (1940s–1980), rooted in public regulation of markets as servants of states. The following era of the **globalization project** (1980s–through the present) saw markets regain ascendancy—with states as servants—and the incorporation of the "good market, bad state" mantra into public discourse. The tension between these poles continues in the emerging **sustainability project** (2000s onward) as the world transitions to a new project governed by a "climate regime."

This book frames the story of development around these three projects, as a clarifying method to underline the point that the meaning and practice of development changes with changing political-economic (and environmental) conditions. The transition from the development to the globalization project involved a political countermovement "from above" by powerful business and financial interests and their allies to reduce or eliminate public regulation of corporations and their ability to operate across national borders. Deregulation of markets has been the ultimate goal, legitimized by neo-liberal economic theory. And subsequent controversies over the impact of globalization at the turn of the twenty-first century have been generated by social mobilization "from below," driven by economic destabilization and intensification of social inequalities as markets have been disembedded from social controls.[24]

The **development paradox**, where poverty accompanies economic growth, is evident in the control of 50 percent of the world's income by the wealthiest 10 percent of the world's population, as well as in the deepening food crisis rendering over a billion people chronically hungry.[25] In India— with annual economic growth rates around 8 percent and projections of overtaking China's by 2013—almost half of its children under the age of five were malnourished in 2010. The paradox can be qualified by public action—when in 2009, child malnutrition was 42.5 percent in India, it was just 7 percent in China.[26]

The current market malaise and combination of crises—food, energy, climate, social—suggests the world is in transition toward another project, which I term the Sustainability Project. The dynamic that links these projects, and accounts for their succession, can be thought of as a series of Polanyian "double movements" (politicization of market rule via social mobilization). The colonial project accompanying the rise of capitalist markets yielded to the development project as social and decolonization countermovements challenged the ascendancy of the market in their respective territories. Then the development project yielded to a globalization project intent on restoring market sway and reducing the power of states and citizens to the status of servants and consumers respectively.

Currently, the crisis of the globalization project (addressed in Chapter 8) is stimulating a wide range of sustainability initiatives, from the global to the local scale, that are geared to containing or reducing environmental degradation and climate warming. How these may coalesce into some kind of world ordering is not yet clear. Whether we will see or make a more authoritarian world order built on energy and climate security claims, or some decentralized ecologically-based social organization, are some of the possibilities that are informing debate (see Chapter 9). In the meantime, it is important to situate our condition via some "development coordinates."

The Development Experience

Development is not an activity that other societies do to catch up to the "developed societies." That nomenclature is unfortunate, since it suggests there is a state of development enjoyed by a minority of the world's population that is the goal and envy of the rest of the world. It forgets that development is an endless process, not an end. Indeed, some argue that the West is busy "undeveloping" as jobs relocate to growth areas like China and India, as public infrastructure decays, and social services such as education and health care dwindle. From this perspective, development—at the national level—does not look like a linear process, nor is it a model outcome.

From a global perspective, development redistributes jobs to lower-wage regions. While transnational firms thereby enhance profitability, Northern consumers (at least those with incomes) enjoy access to low-cost products that are produced offshore. In this sense, development has been identified—for its beneficiaries—as consumption. This of course corresponds with Rostow's final growth stage, but not as a national characteristic—rather as a global relationship. Much of what we consume today has global origins. Even when a product has a domestic "Made in . . ." label, its journey to market probably combines components and labor from production and assembly sites located around the world. Sneakers, or parts thereof, might be produced in China or Indonesia, blue jeans assembled in the Philippines, a cell phone or portable media player put together in Singapore, and a watch made in Hong Kong. The British savor organic vegetables from western China, the Chinese eat pork fed with Brazilian soy, and North Americans consume fast foods that may include chicken diced in Mexico or hamburger beef from cattle raised in Costa Rica. And, depending on taste, our coffee is from Southeast Asia, the Americas, or Africa. We readers may not be global citizens yet, but we are certainly global consumers.

But global consumers are still a minority. While over three-quarters of the world's population can access television images of the global consumer, only half of that audience has access to sufficient cash or credit to consume. Television commercials depict people everywhere consuming global commodities, but this is just an image. We know that 20 percent of the world's population consume 86 percent of all goods and services, while the poorest 20 percent consume just 1.3 percent.[27] Distribution of, and access to, the world's material wealth is extraordinarily uneven. Almost half of the ex-colonial world dwells now in slums. Over 3 billion people cannot, or do not, consume in the Western style. Uruguayan writer Eduardo Galeano observes,

> Advertising enjoins everyone to consume, while the economy prohibits the vast majority of humanity from doing so. . . . This world, which puts on a banquet for all, then slams the door in the noses of so many, is simultaneously equalizing and unequal: equalizing in the ideas and habits it imposes and unequal in the opportunities it offers.[28]

And yet it is important also to note that while we may be accustomed to a commercial culture, and view it as the development "standard," other cultures and peoples are noncommercial, not comfortable with commercial definition, or are simply marginal to commercial life. Contrary to media images, global consumerism is neither accessible to—nor possible for—a majority of humans, nor is it a universal aspiration.

Nevertheless, the global marketplace binds consumers, producers, and even those marginalized by resource consumption. Consumers everywhere are surrounded, and often identified by, world products. One of the most ubiquitous, and yet invisible, world products is coltan, a metallic ore used in consumer electronics, such as computers and cell phones, in addition to nuclear reactors. It comes predominantly from the Congo, where militarized conflict over this valuable resource caused nearly 4 million deaths, and mining has negative environmental consequences for forests and wildlife. Such ethical issues, similar to those associated with "blood diamonds," have driven some electronics corporations to mine coltan elsewhere in Africa.[29]

The global marketplace is a matrix of networks of commodity exchanges. In any one network, there is a sequence of production stages, located in a number of countries at sites that provide inputs of labor and materials contributing to the fabrication of a final product (see Figure 1.3). These networks are called **commodity chains**. The chain metaphor illuminates the interconnections among producing communities dispersed across the world. And it allows us to understand that, when we consume a product, we often participate in a global process that links us to a variety of places, people, and resources. While we may experience consumption individually, it is a fundamentally social—and environmental—act.

Commodity chains enable firms to switch production sites for flexible management of their operations (and costs). Any shopper at The Gap, for example, knows that this clothing retailer competes by changing its styles on a short-term cycle. Such flexibility requires access through subcontractors to labor forces, increasingly feminized, which can be intensified or let go as orders and fashion changes. Workers for these subcontractors often have little security—or rights—as they are one of the small links in this global commodity chain stretching across an unregulated global workplace.

The world was shocked in 2010 when 18 Chinese migrant workers between 17 and 25 years old attempted suicide at Foxconn factories in three Chinese provinces. Foxconn recorded profits that year in excess of some of its corporate customers, such as Microsoft, Dell, and Nokia. Foxconn—responsible for producing iPhone 4, the iPod, and iPad 2—captures 50 percent of the world electronics market share in manufacturing and service.[30]

Figure 1.3   A Commodity Chain for Athletic Shoes

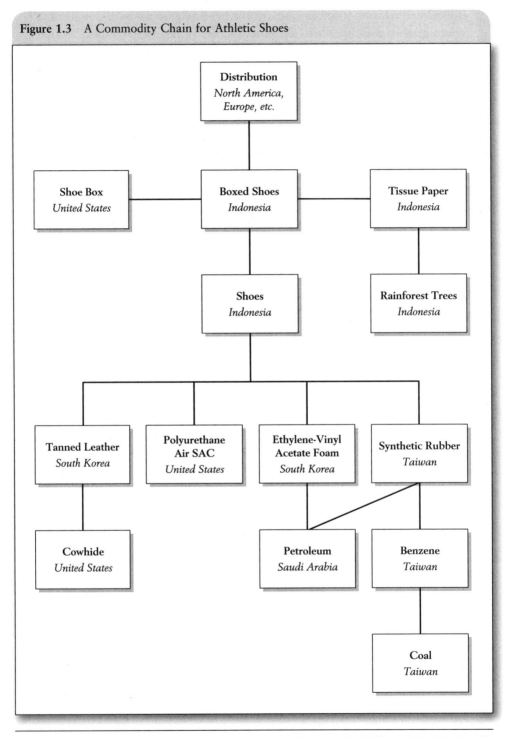

Source: Adapted from Bill Ryan and Alan During, "The Story of a Shoe," *World Watch*, March/April 1998.

CASE STUDY   Waste and the Commodity Chain

The disconnect between development theory and the environment is dramatized by the problem of waste, concealed in plain sight. The fact that consumption simultaneously produces waste is neither something consumers want to acknowledge, nor does it feature in measures of economic growth. And yet waste in general, and electronic waste (e-waste) in particular, are huge and problematic by-products of our lifestyle. The household electronics sector is now the fastest growing segment of municipal waste streams, as computing and communication technologies rapidly evolve. The UN estimates the annual global generation of waste from electrical and electronic equipment (WEEE) runs at a rate of between 20–50 million tons. In 2009, the UN Environment Programme (UNEP) reported that e-waste could increase by 500 percent over the next decade in rising middle-income countries. The toxicity of this waste is extraordinary: From 1994–2003, for example, disposal of personal computers released 718,000 tons of lead, 287 tons of mercury, and 1,363 tons of cadmium into landfills worldwide.

Cellular, or mobile, phones (1.2 billion sold globally in 2007) leach more than 17 times the U.S. federal threshold for hazardous waste. And yet the noxious ingredients (including silver, copper, platinum, and gold) are valued on second-hand markets, just as discarded e-waste may be recycled for reuse in poorer markets—sometimes by businesses such as Collective Good, which donate a portion of the profits to the Red Cross or the Humane Society. Refurbishing phones occurs from Ghana to India, where labor costs are lower and environmental regulations are less. About 70 percent of the world's discarded e-waste finds its way through informal networks to China, where it is scavenged for usable parts—often by children with no protection—and abandoned to pollute soil and groundwater with toxic metals. Africa is one of the largest markets for discarded phones, while China sells between 200–300 million phones annually to dealers in India, Mongolia, Vietnam, and Thailand, from where they may pass on to buyers in Laos, Cambodia, Bangladesh, and Myanmar. Just as water seeks its own level, unregulated markets enable toxic waste to leach into the global South. While there are regulations regarding hazardous waste, the 170-nation agreement called the Basel Convention is ambiguous on the question of restricting the movement of e-waste from North to South.

Why is the current fixation on the virtual, or "de-materialized" information economy unable to recognize the dependence on offshore manufacturing and disposal of waste—both of which pose social and environmental hazards?

Sources: Schwarzer et al. (2005); Widmer et al. (2005); Mooallem (2008); Leslie (2008); Salehabadi (2011).

Not everything we consume has such global origins, but the trend toward these worldwide supply networks is powerful. Our food, clothing, and shelter, in addition to other consumer comforts, have increasingly long supply chains. Take food, for example. Britain was the first nation to deliberately "outsource" a significant part of its food supply to its empire in the 1840s. In spite of the fact that the British climate is ideal for fruit production, 80 percent of pears and almost 70 percent of apples consumed by Britons now come from Chile, Australia, the United States, South Africa, and throughout the European Union.[31] The Dutch concept of "ghost acres" refers to additional land offshore used to supply a national diet. Britons are estimated to use about 4.1 million hectares of ghost acres to grow mainly animal feed.[32] Ghost acres include "food miles," prompting the remark, "This form of global sourcing . . . is not only energy-inefficient, but it is also doubtful whether it improves global 'equity,' and helps local farmers to meet the goals of sustainable development."[33] In other words, much commercial agriculture today is dedicated to supplying the global consumer rather than improving production for domestic consumers. It is extraverted, rather than introverted as in the Rostow schema. Thus,

> Half of all [Guatemala's] children under five are malnourished—one of the highest rates of malnutrition in the world. Yet the country has food in abundance. It is the fifth largest exporter of sugar, coffee, and bananas. Its rural areas are witnessing a palm oil rush as international traders seek to cash in on demand for biofuels created by U.S. and EU mandates and subsidies. But despite being a leading agro-exporter, half of Guatemala's 14 million people live in extreme poverty, on less than $2 a day.[34]

Globalization deepens the paradox of development by virtue of its sheer scale. Integrating the lives of consumers and producers across the world does not necessarily mean universalizing the benefits of development. The distance between consumers, and producers and their environments, means it is virtually impossible for consumers to recognize the impact of their consumption on people and environments elsewhere. At the other end, producers experience the social distance in the difficulty in voicing concerns about working conditions or the health of their habitats. Bridging this distance has become the focus of initiatives such as **fair trade**, or brand boycotts organized by activist movements or **nongovernmental organizations** (NGOs), to enhance transparency with information to support more responsible consumption.

CASE STUDY   Consuming the Amazon

In a recent report, *Eating Up the Amazon*, Greenpeace noted that "Europe buys half the soya exported from the Amazon state of Matto Grosso, where 90% of rainforest soya is grown. Meat reared on rainforest soya finds its way on to supermarket shelves and fast food counters across Europe." As the Greenpeace website claimed, "nuggets of Amazon forest were being served up on a platter at McDonald's restaurants throughout Europe." Following this dramatic report, McDonald's slapped a moratorium on purchasing soya grown in newly deforested regions of the rainforest, and entered into an alliance with Greenpeace, and other food retailers, to develop a zero deforestation plan, involving the government in monitoring the integrity of the forest and of its inhabitants, some of whom had been enslaved and subjected to violence. The global soy traders, Cargill, ADM, Bunge, Dreyfus, and Maggi, made a two-year commitment to the alliance.

What is all this about? Quite simply, like many nongovernmental organizations (NGOs) today, Greenpeace made the lifestyle connection and ecological relation embodied in chicken nuggets explicit. Documenting the ways in which the Brazilian soy boom—with all its social and environmental consequences—is a product of the fast food diet, Greenpeace made visible what is routinely invisibilized by an impersonal marketplace. By tracing the soy chain—with the aid of satellite images, aerial surveillance, classified government documents, and on-ground observation—Greenpeace reconstructed the geography of the soy trade, bringing the ethical dimensions of their diet to consumers' notice. While traders can escape the notice of the consuming public, retailers have become "brand sensitive" in an era in which information technology has created a new public space, and consumers have the ability to choose not to consume products that come with baggage.

What is the value of fast food compared with the value of preserving one of the richest and most biologically diverse rainforests on the planet—especially given that the scientific journal *Nature* recently warned that 40 percent of the Amazon rainforest will disappear by 2050 if current trends continue?

Source: Greenpeace, *Eating Up the Amazon*, 2006. Available at www.greenpeace.org.

With only 6 percent of the world adult population, North America holds 34 percent of household wealth (in monetary terms). Europe and high-income Asia-Pacific countries also have disproportionate wealth, whereas the overall share of wealth of Africans, Chinese, Indians, and other lower-income countries in Asia is substantially less than their population share, sometimes by a factor of more than ten.[35] Standardizing development measures reinforces the belief that there is a high correlation between GNP and social well-being. Clive Hamilton, executive director of the Australian Institute think tank, notes, "The evidence shows that, beyond a certain point, increased income does not result in increased well-being."[36]

CONCLUSION

Development, conventionally associated with economic growth, is a recent phenomenon. With the rise of European capitalism, state bureaucrats pursued economic growth to finance their needs for military protection and political legitimacy. But "development," as such, was not yet a worldwide strategy. It became so only in the mid-twentieth century, as newly independent states embraced development as an antidote to colonialism, with varying success.

The mid-twentieth-century **development project** (1940s–1970s) was an internationally orchestrated program of *nationally-sited* economic growth across the Cold War divide, involving superpower-provided financial, technological, and military assistance. Development was a United Nations ideal, as formerly colonized subjects gained political independence, and governments implemented a human rights–based social contract with their citizens. This book traces the implementation of this project, noting its partial successes and ultimate failure, in its own terms, to equalize conditions across the world, and the foreshadowing of its successor, the globalization project, in laying the foundations of a global market that progressively overshadowed the states charged with development in the initial post–World War II era.

The **globalization project** (1970s–2000s) superimposed open markets across national boundaries, liberalizing trade and investment rules, and privatizing public goods and services. Corporate rights gained priority over the social contract and redefined development as a private undertaking. The neoliberal doctrine ("market freedoms") underlying the globalization project has been met with growing contention, symbolized by the anti-neoliberal social revolt in Latin America over the last decade and the recent Middle-East rebellions, and the growing weight and assertiveness of China (and India) in the world political economy. Polanyi's double movement is alive and well.

Whether the global market will remain dominant is still to be determined. In the meantime an incipient **sustainability project**, heavily influenced by the climate change emergency, is forming, with China leading the green technology race and a myriad of environmental and justice movements across the world pushing states, business leaders, and citizens toward a new formulation of development as "managing the future" sustainably.

FURTHER READING

Crow, Ben, and Suresh K. Lodha. *The Atlas of Global Inequalities.* Berkeley: University of California Press, 2011.

Payne, Anthony, and Nicola Phillips. *Development.* Cambridge: Polity, 2010.

Perrons, Diane. *Globalization and Social Change: People and Places in a Divided World.* London: Routledge, 2004.

Sage, Colin. *Environment and Development.* London: Routledge, 2011.

Willis, Katie. *Theories and Practices of Development.* London: Routledge, 2011.

SELECT WEBSITES

Eldis Gateway to Development Information: www.eldis.org

Global Exchange: www.globalexchange.org

New Internationalist: www.newint.org

Raj Patel: www.RajPatel.org

UNDP Human Development Reports: http://hdr.undp.org/en/

World Bank Development Report: http://wdronline.worldbank.org/

PART I

The Development Project
(Late 1940s to Early 1970s)

2

Instituting the
Development Project

Development emerged during the colonial era. While it may have been experienced by nineteenth century Europeans as something specifically European, over time it came to be viewed as a universal necessity. Understanding why this was so helps to answer the question "what *is* development?"

As we have seen in Chapter 1, development (as social engineering) framed European colonization of the non-European world. Not only did the extraction of colonial resources facilitate European industrialization, but this process also required colonial administrators to manage subject populations adjusting to the extractive economy and monocultures, administering colonial rule for their masters, and experiencing physical, as well as psychic displacement. Under these circumstances, development assumed an additional meaning: the proverbial "white man's burden," a dimension that has persisted in various ways.

Non-European cultures were irrevocably changed through colonialism, and the postcolonial context was founded on inequality. When newly independent states emerged, political leaders had to negotiate an unequal international framework not of their making but through which their governments acquired political legitimacy. How that framework emerged is the subject of this chapter. But first we must address the historical context of colonialism.

Colonialism

Our appeal to history begins with a powerful simplification. It concerns the social psychology of European colonialism, built largely around stereotypes that have shaped perceptions and conflict for at least five centuries. (*Colonialism* is defined and explained in the box below, and the European colonial empires are depicted in Figure 2.1.) One such perception was the idea among Europeans that non-European native people or colonial subjects were "backward" and trapped in stifling cultural traditions. The experience of colonial rule encouraged this image, as the juxtaposition of European and non-European cultures invited comparison—but through the lens of Europe's powerful missionary and military-industrial apparatus. This comparison was interpreted—or misinterpreted—as European cultural superiority. It was easy to take the next step and view the difference as "progress," something the colonizers had, and could impart to their subjects.

WHAT IS COLONIALISM?

Colonialism is the subjugation by physical and psychological force of one culture by another—a colonizing power—through military conquest of territory and stereotyping the relation between the two cultures. It predates the era of European expansion (fifteenth to twentieth centuries) and extends to Japanese colonialism in the twentieth century and, most recently, Chinese colonization of Tibet. Colonialism has two forms: colonies of settlement, which often eliminate indigenous people (such as the Spanish destruction of the Aztec and Inca civilizations in the Americas); and colonies of rule, where colonial administrators reorganize existing cultures by imposing new inequalities to facilitate their exploitation. Examples of this are the British creation of local landlords, *zamindars*, to rule parts of India; the confiscation of personal and common land for cash cropping; depriving women of their customary resources; and the elevation of ethnoracial differences, such as privileging certain castes or tribes in the exercise of colonial rule. Outcomes are, first, the cultural genocide or marginalization of indigenous people; second, the introduction of new tensions around class, gender, race, and caste that continue to disrupt postcolonial societies; third, the extraction of labor, cultural treasures, and resources to enrich the colonial power, its private interests, and public museums; fourth, the elaboration of ideologies justifying colonial rule, including racism and notions of backwardness; and fifth, various responses by colonial subjects, ranging from death to submission and internalization of inferiority to a variety of resistances—from everyday forms to sporadic uprisings to mass political mobilization.

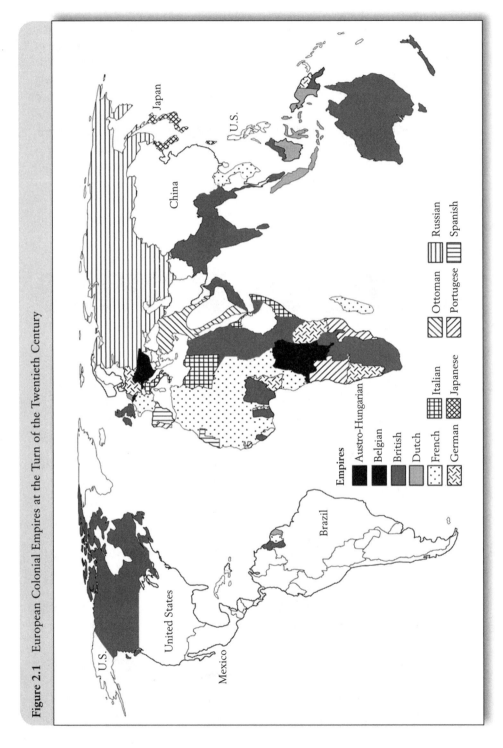

Figure 2.1 European Colonial Empires at the Turn of the Twentieth Century

Empires

Austro-Hungarian
Belgian
British
Dutch
French
German
Italian
Japanese
Ottoman
Portugese
Russian
Spanish

Such a powerful misinterpretation—and devaluing—of other cultures appears frequently in historical accounts. It is reflected in assumptions made by settlers about indigenous people they encountered in the Americas and Australasia. Europeans perceived the Native Americans and aboriginal Australians as people who did not "work" the land they inhabited. In other words, the native populations had no right of "property"—a European concept in which property is private and alienable. Their displacement from their ancestral lands is a bloody reminder of the combined military power and moral fervor with which the European powers pursued colonization. It also foreshadowed the modern practice of rupturing the unity of the human and natural world, a unity that characterized non-European cultures.

In precolonial Africa, communities relied on ancestral ecological knowledge and earth-centered cosmologies to sustain themselves and their environment. These methods were at once conservative and adaptive because, over time, African communities changed their composition, scale, and location in a long process of settlement and migration through the lands south of the equator. European colonists in Africa, however, saw these superstitious cultures as static and as only occupying—rather than improving—the land. This perception ignored the complex social systems adapted first to African ecology and then to European occupation.[1] Under these circumstances, Europeans viewed themselves as bringing civilization to the non-white races. French historian Albert Sarraut, ignoring non-European inventions such as gunpowder, the compass, the abacus, moveable type printing, and the saddle, claimed,

> It should not be forgotten that we are centuries ahead of them, long centuries during which—slowly and painfully, through a lengthy effort of research, invention, meditation and intellectual progress aided by the very influence of our temperate climate—a magnificent heritage of science, experience, and moral superiority has taken shape, which makes us eminently entitled to protect and lead the races lagging behind us.[2]

The ensuing colonial exchange was captured in the postcolonial African saying, "When the white man came he had the Bible and we had the land. When the white man left, we had the Bible and he had the land." Under colonialism, when non-Europeans lost control of their land, their spiritual life was compromised insofar as it was connected to their landscapes. It was difficult to sustain material and cultural integrity under these degrading extractive processes and conditions. At the same time, European colonization of natural resources converted land, water, cultivars, and food into economic categories, discounting their complex regenerative capacities and ecological interdependencies.

What Are Some Characteristics of Precolonial Cultures?

All precolonial cultures had their own ways of satisfying their material and spiritual needs. Cultures varied by the differentiation among their members or households according to their particular ecological endowments and social contact with other cultures. The variety ranged from small communities of subsistence producers, who lived off the land or the forest, to extensive kingdoms or states. Subsistence producers, organized by kin relations, usually subdivided social tasks between men, who hunted and cleared land for cultivation, and women, who cultivated and processed crops, harvested wild fruits and nuts, and performed household tasks. These cultures were highly skilled in resource management and production to satisfy their material needs. They generally did not produce a surplus beyond what was required for their immediate needs, and they organized cooperatively—a practice that often made them vulnerable to intruders because they were not prepared for self-defense. Unlike North American Indians, whose social organization provided leadership for resistance, some aboriginal cultures, such as those of Australia and the Amazon, lacked leadership hierarchies and were more easily wiped out by settlers. By contrast, the Mogul empire in seventeenth century India had a complex hierarchical organization based on local chiefdoms in which the chief presided over the village community and ensured that surpluses (monetary taxes and produce) were delivered to a prosperous central court and "high culture." Village and urban artisans produced a range of metal goods, pottery, and crafts, including sophisticated muslins and silks. Caste distinctions, linked to previous invasions, corresponded to divisions of labor, such as trading, weaving, cultivating, ruling, and performing unskilled labor. Colonizers typically adapted such social and political hierarchies to their own ends—alienating indigenous cultures from their natural ecologies, and their political systems from their customary social functions, incubating tensions that have been inherited by postcolonial states.

Sources: Bujra (1992); Rowley (1974).

Development thus came to be identified as the destiny of humankind. The systematic handicapping of non-Europeans in this apparently natural and fulfilling endeavor remained largely unacknowledged, just as non-European scientific, ecological, and moral achievements, and legacies in

European culture, were generally ignored. Being left holding the Bible was an apt metaphor for the condition of non-Europeans who were encouraged to pursue the European way—often without the resources to accomplish this task—of "development."

The Colonial Division of Labor

From the sixteenth century, European colonists and traders traveled along African coasts to the New World and across the Indian Ocean and the China seas seeking fur, precious metals, slave labor, spices, tobacco, cacao, potatoes, sugar, and cotton. The principal European colonial powers—Spain, Portugal, Holland, France, and Britain—and their merchant companies exchanged manufactured goods such as cloth, guns, and implements for these products and for Africans taken into slavery and transported to the Americas. In the process, they reorganized the world.

The basic pattern was to establish in the colonies specialized extraction and production of raw materials and primary products that were unavailable in Europe. In turn, these products fueled European manufacturing as industrial inputs and foodstuffs for its industrial labor force. On a world scale, this specialization between European economies and their colonies came to be termed the **colonial division of labor** (see Figure 2.2).

Figure 2.2   Distinguishing Between an International and a National Division of Labor

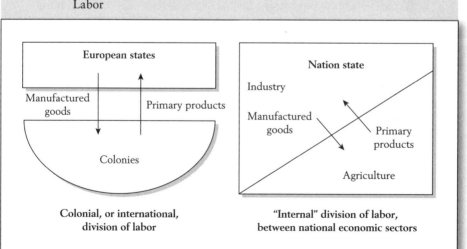

While the colonial division of labor stimulated European industrialization, it forced non-Europeans into primary commodity production. Specialization at each end of the exchange set in motion a transformation of social and environmental relationships, fueled by a dynamic relocation of resources and energy from colony to metropolis: an unequal ecological exchange.[3] Not only were the colonies converted into exporters of raw materials and foodstuffs, they also became "exporters of sustainability."[4]

CASE STUDY | **The Colonial Division of Labor and Unequal Ecological Exchange**

The ecological dimension of the colonial division of labor reminds us that industrialism is premised on transforming nature from a regenerative system to mere "raw material." Prior to industrial society and colonialism, the majority of humans depended on their local ecosystem to supply their various needs via a multiplicity of locally produced materials, harvesting just what was necessary. Overharvesting resources wastes energy, reducing an ecosystem's capacity and thereby threatening the sustainability of the human community. The colonial division of labor depended on overharvesting. Here, trade across ecosystemic boundaries focused extractive activities on those few resources profitable to the traders. Stephen Bunker and Paul Ciccantell, in their research on Amazonian ecology, observe, "Extractive economies thus often deplete or seriously reduce plants or animals, and they disrupt and degrade hydrological systems and geological formations [which] serve critical functions for the reproduction of other species and for the conservation of the watercourses and land forms on which they depend. Losses from excessive harvesting of a single species or material form can thus ramify through and reduce the productivity and integrity of an entire ecosystem."

The early Portuguese colonists, enslaving indigenous labor, extracted luxury goods from the Amazon such as cacao, rosewood, spices, caymans, and turtle eggs—all of which had high value to volume ratios in European markets. Wealthy Europeans prized turtle oil for perfume and lighting their lamps, but wasteful harvesting of turtle eggs for the oil severely depleted protein supplies and Amazonian aquatic environments on which populations depended for their material reproduction. English and French colonies of the eighteenth century imposed monocultures of sugar, tobacco, coffee, and tea. Mimi Sheller observes, "In consuming the Caribbean . . . Europe was itself transformed."

By the nineteenth century, European and North American extraction focused on industrial inputs such as rubber, further disrupting Amazonian habitats and ecology and exposing local industry to competition from commodities imported cheaply in the ample cargo space on the return leg of the rubber transport ships. As demand for rubber intensified later in the century, rubber plantations were established in Southeast Asia and Africa, by the British and the Americans respectively—in turn transforming those ecologies by introducing monocultures, and also impoverishing the Amazonian economy as feral rubber extraction declined.

Why does the developmentalist focus on human exchange through trade ignore the exchange with nature?

Sources: Bunker and Ciccantell (2005: 34–47); Sheller (2003: 81).

The colonial division of labor, as cause and consequence of economic growth, exposed non-European cultures and ecologies to profound disorganization, given the precipitous way in which colonies were converted into supply zones of labor and resources. Local crafts and mixed farming systems were undermined, alienating land and forests for commercial exploitation and rupturing the ecological balance. Not only did non-European cultures surrender their handicraft industries in this exchange, but also their agriculture was often reduced to a specialized **export monoculture**, where local farmers produced a single crop, such as peanuts or coffee, for export, or plantations (sugar, cotton, tea, rubber, bananas) were imposed on land appropriated from those who became plantation laborers. Systems of export agriculture interrupted centuries-old patterns of diet and cultivation, creating the all-too-familiar commercial food economy, in which "what was grown became disconnected from what was eaten, and for the first time in history, money determined what people ate and even if they ate."[5]

Handicraft decline was often deliberate and widespread. Perhaps the best-known destruction of native crafts occurred through Britain's conquest of India. Until the nineteenth century, Indian cotton muslins and calicos were luxury imports into Europe (as were Chinese silks and satins). By that time, however, the East India Company (which ruled India for the British Crown until 1858) undermined this Indian craft and, in its own words, "succeeded in converting India from a manufacturing country into a country exporting raw produce."[6] The company had convinced the British government to use tariffs of 70 to 80 percent against Indian finished goods and to permit virtually free entry of raw cotton into England. In turn, British traders flooded India with cheap cloth manufactured in Manchester. Industrial technology (textile machinery and the steam engine) combined with political power to impose the colonial division of labor, as British-built railway systems moved Indian raw cotton to coastal ports for shipment to Liverpool and returned across India with machine-made products, undermining a time-honored craft.

Social Reorganization under Colonialism

The colonial division of labor devastated producing communities and their craft- and agriculture-based systems. When the British first came to India in the mid-eighteenth century, Robert Clive described the textile city of Dacca as "extensive, populous, and rich as the city of London." By 1840, Sir Charles Trevelyan testified before a British parliamentary committee that the population of Dacca "has fallen from 150,000 to 30,000, and the jungle and malaria are fast encroaching upon the town. . . . Dacca, the Manchester of India, has fallen off from a very flourishing town to a very poor and small town."[7]

While native industries declined under colonial systems, local farming cultures lost their best lands to commercial agriculture supplying European consumers and industries. Plantations and other kinds of cash cropping proliferated across the colonial world, producing specialized tropical exports ranging from bananas to peanuts, depending on local agri-ecologies (see Table 2.1). Non-European societies were fundamentally transformed through the loss of resources and craft traditions as colonial subjects were forced to labor in mines, fields, and plantations to produce exports sustaining distant European factories. This was a *global* process, whereby slaves, peasantries, and laborers in the colonies provisioned European industrial classes with cheap colonial products such as sugar, tea, tropical oils, and cotton for clothing. European development was realized through a racialized global relationship, "underdeveloping" colonial cultures. The legacy of this relationship continues today—for example, Mali (ranked 160th out of 169 on the UN Human Development Index) derives half of its export revenues from cotton, with 40 percent of its population depending on this crop for their livelihoods, but the country is in unequal competition with highly subsidized cotton producers in the United States, the European Union, and China.[8]

Colonial systems of rule focused on mobilizing colonial labor. For example, a landed oligarchy (the *hacendados*) ruled South America before the nineteenth century in the name of the Spanish and Portuguese monarchies, using an institution called *encomienda* to create a form of native serfdom. Settler colonialism also spread to North America, Australasia, and southern Africa, where settlers used military, legal, and economic force to wrest land from the natives for commercial purposes using slave, convict, and

Table 2.1 Selected Colonial Export Crops

Colony	Colonial Power	Export Crop
Australia	Britain	Wool, wheat
Brazil	Portugal	Sugar, coffee
Congo	Belgium	Rubber, ivory
Egypt	Britain	Cotton
Ghana	Britain	Cocoa
Haiti	France	Sugar
India	Britain	Cotton, opium, tea
Indochina	France	Rice, rubber
Indonesia	Holland	Rubber, tobacco
Côte d'Ivoire	France	Cocoa
Kenya	Britain	Coffee, tea, sisal
Malaya	Britain	Rubber, palm oil
Senegal	France	Peanuts
South Africa	Britain	Gold, diamonds

indentured labor.[9] As the industrial era matured, colonial rule (in Asia and Africa) grew more bureaucratic. By the end of the nineteenth century, colonial administrations were self-financing, depending on military force and the loyalty of local princes and chiefs, tribes, and castes (note that the British presence never exceeded 0.5 percent of the Indian population).[10] Native rulers were bribed with titles, land, or tax-farming privileges to recruit male peasants to the military and to force them into cash cropping to pay the taxes supporting the colonial state.

Male entry into cash cropping disrupted patriarchal gender divisions, creating new gender inequalities. Women's customary land-user rights were often displaced by new systems of private property, circumscribing food production, traditionally women's responsibility. Thus British colonialism in Kenya fragmented the Kikuyu culture as peasant land was confiscated and men migrated to work on European estates, reducing women's control over resources and lowering their status, wealth, and authority.

In India, production of commercial crops such as cotton, jute, tea, peanuts, and sugar cane grew by 85 percent between the 1890s and the 1940s. In contrast, in that same period, local food crop production declined by 7 percent while the population grew by 40 percent, a shift that spread hunger, famine, and social unrest.[11] Using tax and irrigation policies to force farmers into export agriculture, Britain came to depend on India for almost 20 percent of its wheat consumption by 1900. Part of the reason that "Londoners were in fact eating India's bread" was the destruction of Indian food security by modern technologies converting grain into a commodity. New telegraph systems transmitted prices set by London grain merchants, prying grain reserves from villages along railway networks for export to Britain. Thus new global market technologies undermined the customary system of grain reserves organized at the village level as protection against drought and famine. For example, during the 1899–1900 famine, 143,000 peasants in Berar starved to death as the province exported tens of thousands of cotton bales in addition to 747,000 bushels of grain.[12]

Starvation in the colonies was not simply due to conversion of resources into export commodities. British rule in India, for example, converted the "commons" into private property or state monopolies. Forest and pasture commons were ecological zones of nonmarket resources to which villagers were customarily entitled—village economy across monsoonal Asia "augmented crops and handicrafts with stores of free goods from common lands: dry grass for fodder, shrub grass for rope, wood and dung for fuel, dung, leaves, and forest debris for fertilizer, clay for plastering houses, and, above all, clean water. All classes utilized these common property resources, but for poorer households they constituted the very margin of survival."[13] By the end of the 1870s, Britain had enclosed all Indian forests, previously communally managed. Ending communal access to grassland resources ruptured "the ancient ecological interdependence of pastoralists and farmers," and age-old practices of extensive crop rotation and long fallow, to replenish soils, declined with the expansion of cotton and other export monocrops.[14] Export monocultures displaced indigenous irrigation systems with canals, which blocked natural drainage, and thus exacerbating water salinity and pooling water in swamps, the perfect host environment for the dreaded malarial anopheline mosquito. A British engineer reported to the 1901 Irrigation Commission, "Canals may not protect against famines, but they may give an enormous return on your money."[15]

The colonial division of labor developed European capitalist civilization (with food and raw materials) at the same time that it undermined non-European cultures and ecologies. As European industrial society matured, the exploding urban populations demanded ever-increasing imports of sugar, coffee, tea, cocoa, tobacco, and vegetable oils from the colonies, and the expanding factory system demanded ever-increasing inputs of raw materials such as cotton, timber, rubber, and jute. The colonists forced more and more subjects to work in cash cropping, employing a variety of methods such as enslavement, taxation, land grabbing, and recruitment for indentured labor contracts.

As the African slave trade subsided, the Europeans created new schemes of forced, or indentured, labor. Indian and Chinese peasants and handicraftsmen, impoverished by colonial intervention or market competition from cheap textiles, scattered to sugar plantations in the Caribbean, Fiji, Mauritius, and Natal; to rubber plantations in Malaya and Sumatra; and to British East Africa to build the railways that intensified the two-way extraction of African resources and the introduction of cheap manufactured goods. In the third quarter of the nineteenth century alone, more than 1 million indentured Indians went overseas. Today, Indians still outnumber native Fijians; they also make up 50 percent of the Guyanese population and 40 percent of the residents of Trinidad. In the same period, 90,000 Chinese indentured laborers went to work in the Peruvian guano fields, and 200,000 went to California to work in the fruit industry, on the gold fields, and on the railways.[16] Displacement of colonial subjects from their societies and their dispersion to resolve labor shortages elsewhere in the colonial world have had a lasting global effect—most notably in the African, Indian, and Chinese diasporas. This cultural mosaic underlines modern expressions of race, ethnicity, and nationality—generating ethno-political tensions that shape national politics across the world today, and question the modernist ideal of the secular state.

THE COLONIAL PROJECT UNLOCKS A DEVELOPMENT PUZZLE

Colonialism was far-reaching and multidimensional in its effects. We focus here on the colonial division of labor because it isolates a key issue in the development puzzle. Unless we see the interdependence created through this division of *world* labor, it is easy to take our unequal world at face value and view it as a natural continuum, with an advanced European region showing the way for a backward, non-European region. But viewing world inequality as relational (interdependent) rather than as sequential (catch-up), calls the conventional

(Continued)

> **(Continued)**
>
> modern understanding of "development" into question. The conventional understanding is that individual societies experience or pursue development in sequence, on a "development ladder." If, however, industrial growth in Europe depended on agricultural monoculture in the non-European world, then development was more than simply a national process, even if represented as such. What we can conclude from the colonial project is that development historically depended on the unequal relationships of colonialism, which included an unequal division of labor and unequal ecological exchanges—both of which produced a legacy of "underdevelopment" in the colonial and postcolonial worlds. Persisting global inequality today, in material and governance terms, prompts the charge of "recolonization."

The secular-modernist ideal is contradicted by colonial racialized rule, where industrial and/or military techniques organized labor forces, schooling, and urban and rural surveillance, as well as supervised hygiene and public health.[17] European exercise of power in the colonies revealed the hard edge of power in the modern state, premised on class structuring via racial humiliation.[18] Such methods produced resistances among subject populations, whether laborers, peasants, soldiers, or civil servants. These tensions fed the politics of decolonization, dedicated to molding inchoate resistance to colonial abuses into coherent, nationalist movements striving for independence.

Decolonization

As Europeans were attempting to "civilize" their colonies, colonial subjects across the Americas, Asia, and Africa engaged the European paradox—a discourse of rights and sovereignty juxtaposed against their own subjugation. In the French sugar colony of Saint Domingue, the late-eighteenth-century "Black Jacobin" revolt powerfully exposed this double standard. Turning the rhetoric of the French Revolution successfully against French colonialism, the rebellious slaves of the sugar plantations became the first to gain their independence in the newly established nation of Haiti, sending tremors throughout the slaveholding lands of the New World.[19]

Resistance to colonialism evolved across the next two centuries, from the early-nineteenth-century independence of the Latin American republics (from Spain and Portugal) to the dismantling of South African apartheid in the early 1990s. Although decolonization has continued into the present day (with the independence of East Timor in 2002 and the Palestinians still struggling for a sovereign homeland), the worldwide decolonization movement peaked as European colonialism collapsed in the mid-twentieth century, when World War II sapped the power of the French, Dutch, British, and Belgian states to withstand anticolonial struggles. Freedom was linked to overcoming the deprivations of colonialism. Its vehicle was the *nation-state*, which offered formal political independence. Substantively, however, the sovereignty of independent states was shaped by the cultural and economic legacies of colonialism.

Colonial Liberation

Freedom included overcoming the social-psychological scars of colonialism. The racist legacy of colonialism penetrated the psyche of colonist and colonized and remains with us today. In 1957, at the height of African independence struggles, Tunisian philosopher Albert Memmi wrote *The Colonizer and the Colonized*, dedicating the American edition to the (colonized) American Negro. In this work (published in 1967), he claimed,

> Racism . . . is the highest expression of the colonial system and one of the most significant features of the colonialist. Not only does it establish a fundamental discrimination between colonizer and colonized, a *sine qua non* of colonial life, but it also lays the foundation for the immutability of this life.[20]

To overcome this apparent immutability, West Indian psychiatrist Frantz Fanon, writing from Algeria, responded with *The Wretched of the Earth*, a manifesto of liberation. It was a searing indictment of European colonialism and a call to people of the former colonies (the Third World) to transcend the mentality of enslavement and forge a new path for humanity. He wrote,

> It is a question of the Third World starting a new history of Man, a history which will have regard to the sometimes prodigious theses which Europe has put forward, but which will also not forget Europe's crimes, of which the most horrible was committed in the heart of man, and consisted of the pathological tearing apart of his functions and the crumbling away of his unity. . . . On the immense scale of humanity, there were racial hatreds, slavery, exploitation and above all the bloodless genocide which consisted in the setting aside of fifteen thousand millions of men. . . . Humanity is waiting for something other from us than such an imitation, which would be almost an obscene caricature.[21]

Decolonization was rooted in a liberatory upsurge, expressed in mass political movements of resistance. In Algeria (much as in Palestine today), the independence movement incubated within and struck at the French occupation from the native quarter. The use of terror, on both sides, symbolized the bitter divide between colonizer and colonized (portrayed in Gillo Pontecorvo's classic film *Battle of Algiers*).

CASE STUDY   **The Tensions and Lessons of the Indian Nationalist Revolt**

Mahatma Gandhi's model of nonviolent resistance to British colonialism affirmed the simplicity and virtue in the ideal-typical premodern solidarities of Indian village life. Rather than embrace the emerging world of nation-states, Gandhi argued, didactically, that Indians became a subject population not because of colonial force but through the seduction of modernity. Gandhi's approach flowed from his philosophy of transcendental (as opposed to scientific or historical) truth, guided by a social morality. Gandhi disdained the violent methods of the modern state and the institutional rationality of the industrial age, regarding machinery as the source of India's impoverishment, not only in destroying handicrafts but in compromising humanity:

> We notice that the mind is a restless bird; the more it gets the more it wants, and still remains unsatisfied. . . . Our ancestors, therefore, set a limit to our indulgences. They saw that happiness is largely a mental condition. . . . We have managed with the same kind of plough as existed thousands of years ago. We have retained the same kind of cottages that we had in former times and our indigenous education remains the same as before. We have had no system of life-corroding competition. . . . It was not that we did not know how to invent machinery, but our forefathers knew that if we set our hearts after such things, we would become slaves and lose our moral fibres.

Gandhi's method of resistance included wearing homespun cloth instead of machine-made goods, foreswearing use of the English language, and mistrusting the European philosophy of self-interest. Gandhi viewed self-interest as undermining community-based ethics, and advocated the decentralization of social power, appealing to grassroots notions of self-reliance, proclaiming,

Independence must begin at the bottom. Thus, every village will be a republic or panchayat having full powers. It follows, therefore, that every village has to be self-sustained and capable of managing its affairs even to the extent of defending itself against the whole world.

While Gandhi's politics, anchored in a potentially reactionary Hindu religious imagery, galvanized rural India, Indian nationalism actually rode to power via the Indian National Congress and one of its progressive democratic socialist leaders, Jawaharlal Nehru. Nehru represented the formative national state, viewing the Gandhian philosophy as inappropriate to the modern world but recognizing its mobilizing power. Infusing the national movement with calls for land reform and agrarian modernization to complement industrial development, Nehru declared, "It can hardly be challenged that, in the context of the modern world, no country can be politically and economically independent, even within the framework of international interdependence, unless it is highly industrialized and has developed its power resources to the utmost."

Together, Gandhi and Nehru are revered as fathers of independence and the Indian national state, respectively. Note that the struggle against empire was woven out of two strands: an *idealist* strand looking back and looking forward to a transcendental Hinduism anchored in village-level self-reliance, as well as a *realist* strand looking sideways and asserting that Indian civilization could be rescued, contained, and celebrated in the form of a modern state.

Did Gandhi and Nehru's opposing visions of development at the time of Indian independence foreshadow today's rising tension between sustainability and maximum economic growth?

Source: Chatterjee (2001: 86, 87, 91, 97, 144, 151).

Other forms of resistance included militarized national liberation struggles (e.g., Portuguese African colonies, French Indo-China) and widespread colonial labor unrest. British colonialism faced widespread labor strikes in its West Indian and African colonies in the 1930s, and this pattern continued over the next two decades in Africa as British and French colonial subjects protested conditions in cities, ports, mines, and on the railways. In this context, development was interpreted as a pragmatic effort to preserve the colonies by improving material conditions—and there was no doubt that colonial subjects understood this and turned the promise of development back on the colonizers, viewing development as an entitlement. British

Colonial Secretary MacDonald observed in 1940, "If we are not now going to do something fairly good for the Colonial Empire, and something which helps them to get proper social services, we shall deserve to lose the colonies and it will only be a matter of time before we get what we deserve."[22] In these terms, eloquent international appeals to justice in the language of rights and freedom by the representatives of colonized peoples held a mirror up to the colonial powers, in their demands for freedom.

A new world order was in the making. From 1945 to 1981, 105 new states joined the United Nations (UN) as the colonial empires crumbled, swelling UN ranks from 51 to 156. The extension of political sovereignty to millions of non-Europeans (more than half of humanity) ushered in the era of development.[23] This era was marked by a sense of almost boundless idealism, as governments and people from the First and Third Worlds joined together in a coordinated effort to stimulate economic growth; bring social improvements through education, public health, family planning, and transport and communication systems to urban and rural populations; and promote political citizenship in the new nations. Just as colonized subjects appropriated the democratic discourse of the colonizers in fueling their independence movements, so leaders of the new nation-states appropriated the idealism of the development era and proclaimed equality as a domestic and international goal, informed by the UN Universal Declaration of Human Rights (1948).

The UN declaration represented a new world paradigm of fundamental human rights of freedom, equality, life, liberty, and security to all, without distinction by race, color, sex, language, religion, political opinion, national or social origin, property, birth, or other status. The declaration also included citizenship rights—that is, citizens' rights to the **social contract**: everyone was "entitled to realization, through national effort, and international co-operation and in accordance with the organization and resources of each State, of the economic, social and cultural rights indispensable for his dignity and the free development of his personality."[24]

Decolonization and Development

Decolonization gave development new meaning, linking it to the ideal of sovereignty, the possibility of converting subjects into citizens, and the pursuit of economic development for social justice. Already independent Latin American states adopted similar goals, having been inspired by French and U.S. revolutionary ideologies of liberal-nationalism, which informed nineteenth-century European nation building via national education systems, national languages and currencies, and modern armies and voting citizens. These ideologies also informed the twentieth-century movements in Asia and Africa for decolonization, coinciding with the rise of the United States to global power and prosperity. Eager to reconstruct the post–World War II world to expand markets and the flow of raw materials, the United States led an international project, inspired by a vision of development as a *national* enterprise to be repeated across a world of sovereign states.

U.S. development modeled this vision, being more "inner-directed" than the "outer-directed" British imperial model (as "workshop of the world"). In spite of the relentless destruction of native American cultures as the continent was claimed (*internal colonialism*), U.S. origins in the revolt of the North American colonies against British colonialism in the late eighteenth century informed an "anticolonial" heritage. Once slavery was abolished, the New South was incorporated into a national economic dynamic articulating agricultural and industrial sectors. Figure 2.2 depicts the difference between the colonial and the national division between industry and agriculture.

The division of labor between industry and agriculture defining the global exchange between colonial powers and their colonies was now *internalized* within the United States. Chicago traders, for instance, purchased Midwestern farm products for processing, in turn selling machinery and goods to those farmers. This mutual prosperity of city and countryside is a *model*—that is, it *prescribes an ideal version,* even as foreign trade and investment continued. But it did industrialize agriculture. On the American plains, farmers "ripped open enormous areas of prairie grasslands" and enjoyed high yields so long as crops drew down the "vast storehouse of accumulated organic fertility just below the surface." As this rich topsoil was consumed, the land frontier was extended, until reaching its ecological limits in the "dustbowl" crisis of the 1930s. The solution was publicly supported agro-industrialization, centered on commodity stabilization programs. Specialized mono-cropping encouraged an excessive use of industrial inputs, such as chemical fertilizers, whose corrosive effect on soils generates the "fertilizer treadmill." The export of this model of capital-intensive industrial farming has defined agricultural modernization, with global ecological consequence.[25]

Postwar Decolonization and the Rise of the Third World

In the era of decolonization, the world subdivided into three geopolitical segments. These subdivisions emerged after World War II (1939–1944) during the Cold War, dividing the capitalist Western (First World) from the communist Soviet (Second World) blocs. The Third World included the postcolonial bloc of nations. Of course, there was considerable inequality across and within these subdivisions, as well as within their national units. The subdivision of the world is further explained in the box below.

In this era, the United States was the most powerful state economically, militarily, and ideologically. Its high standard of living (with a per capita income three times the West European average), its anti-colonial heritage, and its commitment to liberal domestic and international relations lent it the legitimacy of a world leader, and the model of a developed society.

HOW WE DIVIDE THE WORLD'S NATIONS

Division of the nations of the world is quite complex and extensive, and it depends on the purpose of the dividing. The basic division made (by French demographer Alfred Sauvy in 1952) was into three worlds: The First World was essentially the capitalist world (the West plus Japan), the Second World was basically the socialist world (the Soviet bloc), and the Third World was the rest—mostly former European colonies. The core of the Third World was the group of Nonaligned Countries steering an independent path between the First and Second Worlds, especially China, Egypt, Ghana, India, Indonesia, Vietnam, and Yugoslavia. In the 1980s, a Fourth World was named to describe marginalized regions. The United Nations and the development establishment use a different nomenclature: developed countries, developing countries, and least developed countries—this terminology echoes "modernization" theory, which locates countries on a continuum, or "development ladder," ascended as a country develops an industrial economy, rational-legal administrative structures, and a pluralist-representative political system.

Ranged against the United States were the Soviet Union and an assortment of Eastern European communist states. This Second World was considered the alternative to First World capitalism. The Third World, the remaining half of humanity—most of whom were still food-growing rural dwellers—was represented in economic language as impoverished or, in Fanon's politico-cultural language, as the "wretched of the earth."

Whereas the First World had 65 percent of world income with only 20 percent of the world's population, the Third World accounted for 67 percent of world population but only 18 percent of its income. While some believe the gap in living standards between the First and Third Worlds registers differential rates of growth, others believe that much of it was a result of colonialism.[26] Still others are skeptical of distinguishing cultures via a uniform standard based on income levels, since non-Western cultures value non-cash-generating practices.

Economic disparity between the First and Third Worlds generated the vision of development that would energize political and business elites in each world. Seizing the moment as leader of the First World, President Harry S. Truman included in a key speech on January 20, 1949, the following proclamation:

> We must embark on a bold new program for making the benefits of our scientific advances and industrial progress available for the improvement and growth of underdeveloped areas. The old imperialism—exploitation for foreign profit—has no place in our plans. What we envisage is a program of development based on the concepts of democratic fair dealing. . . . Only by helping the least fortunate of its members to help themselves can the human family achieve the decent, satisfying life that is the right of all people. Democracy alone can supply the vitalizing force.[27]

The following year, a Nigerian nationalist echoed these sentiments:

> Self-government will not necessarily lead to a paradise overnight. . . . But it will have ended the rule of one race over another, with all the humiliation and exploitation which that implies. It can also pave the way for the internal social revolution that is required within each country.[28]

Despite the power differential between the United States and the African countries, the shared sentiments affirmed the connection between decolonization and development, where sovereign states could pursue national economic growth with First World assistance. The program of development pursued by new nations, "dependence" in independence, marked the postcolonial experience.

President Truman's paternalistic proclamation confirmed this understanding in suggesting a new paradigm for the postwar era: the division of humanity into developed and undeveloped regions. This division of the world projected a singular destiny for all nations. Mexican intellectual Gustavo Esteva commented,

> Underdevelopment began, then, on January 20, 1949. On that day, two billion people became underdeveloped. In a real sense, from that time on, they ceased

being what they were, in all their diversity, and were transmogrified into an inverted mirror of others' reality: a mirror that defines their identity . . . simply in the terms of a homogenizing and narrow minority.[29]

In other words, the proclamation by President Truman divided the world between those who were modern and those who were not. *Development/ modernity* became the discursive benchmark. This was a way of looking at the world, a new paradigm, suggesting that the ex-colonial world was not only backward, but could also develop, with help.

This new paradigm inscribed First World power and privilege in the new institutional structure of the postwar international economy. In context of the Cold War between First and Second Worlds (for the hearts and resources of the ex-colonial world), "development" was simultaneously the restoration of a capitalist world market to sustain First World wealth, through access to strategic natural resources, and the opportunity for Third World countries to emulate First World civilization and living standards. Because development was both a blueprint for the world of nation-states *and* a strategy for world order, I call this enterprise the **development project**. The epithet *project* emphasizes the political content of development, as an organizing principle. It also underlines the subjective meaning of development, as defined by those with the means to make the rules.

The power of the new development paradigm arose in part from its ability to present itself as universal, natural, and therefore uncontentious—obliterating its colonial roots. In a postcolonial era, Third World states could not repeat the European experience of developing by exploiting the labor and resources of other societies. Development was modeled as a national process, initiated in European states. Its aura of inevitability devalued non-European cultures and discounted what the West learned from the non-European world. Gilbert Rist observed of postcolonial states, "Their right to self-determination had been acquired in exchange for the right to self-definition,"[30] suggesting that in choosing the Western-centered future for the world, they legitimized (or naturalized) it. Of course, each state imparted its own particular style to this common agenda, drawing on regional cultures such as African socialism, Latin American bureaucratic authoritarianism, or Confucianism in East Asia.

Ingredients of the Development Project

The development project was a political and intellectual response to the condition of the world at the historic moment of decolonization. Under these conditions, development assumed a specific meaning. It imposed an essentially economic (reductionist) understanding of social change. In this way, development could be universalized as a market culture common to all, driven by the nation-state and economic growth.

The Nation-State

The **nation-state** was to be the framework of the development project. Nation-states were territorially defined political systems based on the government–citizen relationship that emerged in nineteenth-century Europe. Colonialism exported this political model (with its military shell), framing the politics of the decolonization movement, even where national boundaries made little sense. The UN Economic Commission for Africa, for example, argued in 1989 that African underdevelopment derived from its arbitrary postcolonial geography, including 14 landlocked states, 23 states with a population below 5 million, and 13 states with a land mass of fewer than 50,000 hectares each.[31] The following insert illustrates the effects of these arbitrarily drawn boundaries.

HOW WAS AFRICA DIVIDED UNDER COLONIALISM?

The colonial powers inflicted profound damage on that continent, driving frontiers straight through the ancestral territories of nations. For example, we drew a line through Somalia, separating off part of the Somali people and placing them within Kenya. We did the same by splitting the great Masai nation between Kenya and Tanzania. Elsewhere, of course, we created the usual artificial states. Nigeria consists of four principal nations: the Hausa, Igbo, Yoruba, and Fulani peoples. It has already suffered a terrible war which killed hundreds of thousands of people and which settled nothing. Sudan, Chad, Djibouti, Senegal, Mali, Burundi, and of course Rwanda, are among the many other states that are riven by conflict.

Source: Quoted from Goldsmith (1994: 57).

During the 1950s, certain leading African anticolonialists doubted the appropriateness of the nation-state form to postcolonial Africa. They knew that sophisticated systems of rule had evolved in Africa before colonialism. They advocated a pan-African federalism whose territories would transcend the arbitrary borders drawn across Africa by colonialism. However, decisions about postcolonial political arrangements were made in London and Paris where the colonial powers, looking to sustain spheres of influence, insisted on the nation-state as the only appropriate political outcome of decolonization. Indeed, a British Committee on Colonial Policy advised the prime minister in 1957, "During the period when we can still exercise control in any territory, it is most important to take every step open to us to ensure, as far as we can, that British standards and methods of business and administration permeate the whole life of the territory."[32] An African elite, expecting gains from decolonization—whether personal or national—prepared to assume power in the newly independent states. The power its members assumed was already mortgaged to the nation-state system: a vehicle of containment of political desires and of extraction of resources via European military and economic aid, investment, and trade—the paradox of sovereignty.

Pan-Africanism was unsuccessful; nevertheless, it did bear witness to an alternative political and territorial logic. Some of Guinea's rural areas were in fact attached as hinterlands to urban centers in other states, such as Dakar in Senegal and Abidjan in the Côte d'Ivoire. Considerable cross-border smuggling today is continuing testimony to these relationships. Fierce civil wars broke out in Nigeria in the 1960s and in Ethiopia in the 1970s, states such as Somalia and Rwanda collapsed in the early 1990s and, in the twenty-first century, military conflict in the Congo threatened a repartition of Africa, and Sudan subdivided, creating a new state in 2011: South Sudan. Such eruptions all include ethnic dimensions, rooted in social disparities and cross-border realities. In retrospect, they suggest that the pan-African movement had considerable foresight. Ideas about the limits to the nation-state organization resonate today in new macro-regional groupings.

Economic Growth

The second ingredient of the development project was economic growth. A mandatory UN System of National Accounts institutionalized a universal quantifiable measure of national development. The UN Charter of 1945 proclaimed "a rising standard of living" as the global objective. This "material well-being" indicator is measured in the commercial output of goods and services within a country: capita gross national product (GNP), or the national average of per capita income. While per capita income was not the sole measure of rising living standards (health, literacy, etc.), the key criterion was measurable progress toward the "good society," popularized by U.S. presidential adviser Walt Rostow's idea of the advanced stage of "high mass consumption."[33]

In the minds of Western economists, development required a kind of jump-start in the Third World. Cultural practices of wealth sharing and cooperative labor—dissipating individual wealth, but sustaining the community—were perceived as a *traditional* obstacle to making the transition. The solution was to introduce a market system based on private property and accumulation of wealth. A range of modern practices and institutions designed to sustain economic growth, such as banking and accounting systems, education, stock markets and legal systems, and public infrastructure (transport, power sources) was required.

The use of the *economic growth* yardstick of development, however, is fraught with problems. Average indices such as per capita income obscure inequalities among social groups and classes. Aggregate indices such as rising consumption levels, in and of themselves are not accurate records of improvement in quality of life. Running air conditioners is measured as increased consumption, but it also releases harmful hydrocarbons into the warming atmosphere. Economic criteria for development have normative assumptions that often marginalize other criteria for evaluating living standards relating to the quality of human interactions, physical and spiritual health, and so on.

The emphasis on converting human interactions into measurable (and taxable) cash relations discounts the social wealth of nonmonetary activities (nature's processes, cooperative labor, people growing their own food, performing unpaid household labor, and community service). Wolfgang Sachs observed of early 1940s comparative statistical measurement of "economic growth,"

> As soon as the scale of incomes had been established, order was imposed on a confused globe: horizontally, such different worlds as those of the Zapotec people of Mexico, the Tuareg of north Africa, and Rajasthanies of India could be classed together, while a vertical comparison to "rich" nations demanded relegating them to a position of almost immeasurable inferiority. In this way, "poverty" was used to define whole peoples, not according to what they are and want to be, but according to what they lack and are expected to become. Economic disdain had thus taken the place of colonial contempt.[34]

Framing the Development Project

Perhaps the most compelling aspect of the development project was a powerful perception by planners, governmental elites, and citizens alike that development was destiny. Both Cold War blocs understood development in these terms, even if their respective paths of development were different.

Each bloc took its cue from key nineteenth-century thinkers. The West identified free-enterprise capitalism as the endpoint of development, based in Jeremy Bentham's utilitarian philosophy of the common good arising out of the pursuit of individual self-interest. Communist orthodoxy identified the abolition of private property and central planning as the goal of social development, deriving from Karl Marx's collectivist dictum: "from each according to their ability, and to each according to their needs."

Although the two political blocs subscribed to opposing representations of human destiny, they shared the same modernist paradigm. *National industrialization* would be the vehicle of development in each.

National Industrialization: Ideal and Reality

"National industrialization" had two key assumptions. First, it assumed that development involved the displacement of agrarian civilization by an urban-industrial society. For national development policy, this meant a deliberate shrinking of the agricultural population as the manufacturing and service sectors grew. It also meant the transfer of resources such as food, raw materials, and redundant labor from the agrarian sector as peasants disappeared and agricultural productivity grew. Industrial growth would ideally feed back into and technify agriculture. These two national economic sectors would therefore condition each other's development, as in the U.S. case discussed earlier in this chapter and illustrated in Figure 2.2.

Second, the idea of national industrialization assumed a *linear direction* for development—that is, playing catch-up with the West. Soviet dictator Joseph Stalin articulated this doctrine in the 1930s, proclaiming, "We are fifty or a hundred years behind the advanced countries. We must make good this distance in ten years. Either we do it or they crush us."[35] Stalin's resolve came from the pressures of military (and therefore economic) survival in a hostile world. The Soviet Union industrialized in one generation, "squeezing" the peasantry to finance urban-industrial development with cheap food.

Across the Cold War divide, industrialization symbolized success. Leaders in each bloc pursued industrial development to legitimize their power; the reasoning was that, as people consumed more goods and services, they would subscribe to the prevailing philosophy delivering the goods and support their governments. *Development is not just a goal; it is a method of rule.*

The competitive—and legitimizing—dynamic of industrialization framed the development project across the Cold War divide. Third World states climbed on the bandwagon. The ultimate goal was to achieve Western levels of affluence. If some states chose to mix and match elements from either side of the Cold War divide, well and good. The game was still the same: catch-up. Ghana's first president, Kwame Nkrumah, proclaimed, "We in Ghana will do in ten years what it took others one hundred years to do."[36]

Economic Nationalism

Decolonization involved a universal nationalist upsurge across the Third World, assuming different forms in different countries depending on the configuration of social forces in each national political system. Third World governments strove to build national development states—whether centralized like South Korea, corporatist like Brazil, or decentralized and populist like Tanzania. The **development state** organizes national economic growth by mobilizing money and people. It uses individual and corporate taxes, along with other government revenues such as export taxes and sales taxes, to finance public building of transport systems and to finance state enterprises such as steel works and energy exploration. And it forms coalitions to support its policies. State elites regularly use their power to accumulate wealth and influence in the state—whether through selling rights to public resources to cronies or capturing foreign aid distribution channels. As Sugata Bose remarked of the Indian state, "Instead of the state being used as an instrument of development, development became an instrument of the state's legitimacy."[37] Either way, the development state was a central pillar of the postwar development era.

Import-Substitution Industrialization

Just as political nationalism pursued sovereignty for Third World populations, so **economic nationalism** sought to reverse the colonial division of labor—as governments encouraged and protected domestic industrialization with tariffs and public subsidies, reducing dependence on primary exports ("resource bondage").

Economic nationalism was associated with Raul Prebisch, an adviser to the Argentine military government in the 1930s. During that decade's world depression, world trade declined and Latin American landed interests lost political power as shrinking primary export markets depleted their revenues. Prebisch proposed an industrial protection policy. Import controls reduced expensive imports of Western manufactured goods and shifted resources into domestic manufacturing.[38] This policy was adopted in the

1950s by the UN Economic Commission for Latin America (ECLA), under Prebisch's lead as executive secretary.

Import-substitution industrialization (ISI) framed initial economic development strategies in the Third World as governments subsidized "infant industries." The goal was a cumulative process of domestic industrialization. For example, a domestic automotive industry would generate parts manufacturing, road building, service stations, and so on, in addition to industries such as steel, rubber, aluminum, cement, and paint. In this way, a local industrial base would emerge. ISI became the new economic orthodoxy in the postwar era.[39] In formally promoting economic nationalism, ironically ISI substantively resulted in encouraging direct investment by foreign firms.

Development states like Brazil redistributed private investment from export sectors to domestic production, establishing a development bank to make loans to investors and state corporations in such central industries as petroleum and electric power generation. When the domestic market was sufficiently large, multinational corporations invested directly in the Brazilian economy—as they did elsewhere in Latin America during this period. Latin America characteristically had relatively urbanized populations with expanding consumer markets.[40]

By contrast, the South Korean state centralized control of national development and the distribution of industrial finance. South Korea relied less on foreign investment than Brazil and more on export markets for the country's growing range of manufactured goods. Comprehensive land reforms equalized wealth among the rural population, and South Korean development depended on strategic public investment decisions that more evenly distributed wealth among urban classes and between urban and rural constituencies.

FOREIGN INVESTMENT AND THE PARADOX OF PROTECTIONISM

When states erected tariffs in the development era, multinational corporations hopped over and invested in local, as well as natural resource, industries. For Brazil, in 1956, foreign (chiefly U.S.) capital controlled 50 percent of the iron and rolled-metal industry, 50 percent of the meat industry, 56 percent of the textile industry, 72 percent of electric power production, 80 percent of cigarette manufacturing, 80 percent of pharmaceutical production, 98 percent of the automobile industry, and 100 percent of oil and gasoline distribution. In Peru, a subsidiary of Standard Oil of New Jersey owned the oil that represented 80 percent of national production, and Bell Telephone controlled telephone services. In Venezuela, Standard Oil produced 50 percent of the oil, Shell another 25 percent, and Gulf one-seventh. In what Peter Evans has called the "triple alliance," states such as Brazil actively brokered relationships between foreign and local firms in an attempt to spur industrial development.

Sources: de Castro (1969: 241–242); Evans (1979).

To secure an expanding industrial base, Third World governments constructed political coalitions among different social groups to support rapid industrialization—such as the Latin American **development alliance**.[41] Its social constituency included commercial farmers, public employees, urban industrialists, merchants, and workers dependent on industrialization, organized into associations and unions. Policy makers used price subsidies and public services such as health and education programs, cheap transport, and food subsidies to complement the earnings of urban dwellers, attract them to the cause of national industrialization, and realize the *social contract.*

The development alliance was also a vehicle of *political patronage,* whereby governments could manipulate electoral support. Mexico's Institutional Revolutionary Party (PRI), which controlled the state for much of the twentieth century, created corporatist institutions such as the Confederation of Popular Organizations, the Confederation of Mexican Workers, and the National Confederation of Peasants to channel patronage "downward" to massage loyalty "upward." Political elites embraced the development project, mobilizing their national populations around the promise of rising living standards, and expecting economic growth to legitimize them in the eyes of their emerging citizenry.

In accounting for and evaluating the development project, this book gives greatest attention to the Western bloc, since Western affluence was the universal standard of development and modernity, and this has been extended under the guise of the globalization project to the ex–Second World following the collapse of the Soviet empire in 1989.

SUMMARY

The idea of development emerged during, and within the terms of, the colonial era. This global hierarchy informed the understanding of development as a European achievement. Meanwhile, colonialism disorganized non-European societies by reconstructing their labor systems around specialized, and ecologically degrading, export production, and disorganizing the social psychology of colonial subjects. Exposure of non-European intellectuals, workers, and soldiers to the European liberal discourse on rights fueled anticolonial movements for political independence.

The political independence of the colonial world gave birth to the *development project,* a blueprint for national political-economic development as well as a "protection racket," insofar as international aid, trade, and investment flows were calibrated to military aid from the West to secure Cold War perimeters and make the "free world" safe for business. Third World states become at once independent, but collectively defined as "underdeveloped."

The pursuit of rising living standards, via industrialization, inevitably promoted Westernization in political, economic, and cultural terms as the non-European world emulated the European enterprise. The influential terms of the development project undercut Frantz Fanon's call for a non-European way, qualifying the sovereignty and diversity that often animated the movements for decolonization. It also rejected the pan-African insight into alternative political organization. Both of these ideas have reemerged recently, and they have a growing audience.

The remainder of this book explores how these ideals have worked out in practice, and how they have been reformulated. The next chapter examines the development project in action.

FURTHER READING

Achebe, Chinua. *Things Fall Apart.* London: William Heineman, 1958.

Davis, Mike. *Late Victorian Holocausts: El Niño Famines and the Making of the Third World.* London: Verso, 2001.

Escobar, Arturo. *Encountering Development: The Making and Unmaking of the Third World.* Princeton, NJ: Princeton University Press, 1995.

Evans, Peter. *Dependent Development: The Alliance of Multinational, State, and Local Capital in Brazil.* Princeton, NJ: Princeton University Press, 1979.

Fanon, Frantz. *The Wretched of the Earth.* Harmondsworth, UK: Penguin, 1967.

Leys, Colin. *Underdevelopment in Kenya: The Political Economy of Neo-Colonialism.* Berkeley: University of California Press, 1975.

Memmi, Albert. *The Colonizer and the Colonized.* Boston: Beacon Press, 1967.

Mitchell, Timothy. *Colonizing Egypt.* Berkeley: University of California Press, 1991.

3

The Development Project

International Framework

When countries became independent nation-states, they joined the international relations of the development project. But how could a national strategy simultaneously be international?

- First, the colonial division of labor's legacy of "resource bondage" was embedded in Third World social structures, where trading classes of landowners and merchants, enriched by the exports of primary goods, would favor this relationship. And, of course, the First World still desired raw materials and agricultural imports and markets for its industrial products.
- Second, as newly independent states industrialized, they purchased First World technology, for which they paid with loans or foreign exchange earned from primary exports.
- Third, nation-states formed within an international framework, with the normative, legal, and financial relationships of the United Nations (UN) and the Bretton Woods institutions integrating states into universal political-economic relations.

National economic growth strategies depended, then, on the stimulus of these new international economic arrangements. The UN declared the 1960s and 1970s "Development Decades" to mobilize international development cooperation. In this chapter, we examine the construction of the Bretton Woods system and look at how its multilateral arrangements shaped national development strategies. We then examine the ways in which the development project reshaped the international division of labor.

WHAT ARE THE INGREDIENTS OF THE DEVELOPMENT PROJECT?

The development project was an internationally organized strategy for stimulating nationally managed economic growth. As colonialism collapsed, political elites of newly independent states embraced development as an enterprise for growth, revenue generation, and legitimacy. The Western experience offered a (partial) model, and an international institutional complex supplied financial and technical assistance for development across the world, protected by Cold War military relations. Some ingredients were

- an organizing concept with universal claims (e.g., development as rising living standards, rationality, and scientific progress);
- a national framework for economic growth;
- an international framework of aid (military and economic) binding the developing world to the developed world, and securing continuing access to its natural and human resources;
- a growth strategy favoring industrialization;
- an agrarian reform strategy encouraging agro-industrialization;
- development-state initiatives to manage investment and mobilize multi-class political coalitions into a development alliance supporting industrial growth; and
- realization of development through new inequalities, embedded in states and markets along regional, class, gender, racial, and ethnic lines.

The International Framework

The pursuit of national economic growth depended on international relations, both material and political-legal. Material supports included foreign aid, technology transfer, stable currency exchange, and international trade. Aid and trade relationships followed well-worn paths between ex-colonial states and their postcolonial regions. Complementing these historic relationships were the Bretton Woods institutions and the political, military, and economic relationships of the new superpower, the United States, as it sought to contain the rival Soviet empire.

Following the severe 1930s depression and the devastation of World War II (1939–1945), the United States spearheaded two initiatives to reconstruct the world economy: the bilateral Marshall Plan and the multilateral **Bretton**

Woods program. The development project emerged within the Marshall Plan and was formalized under the Bretton Woods program, but it did not become a fully fledged operation until the 1950s, the peak decade of Third World political independence.

U.S. Bilateralism: The Marshall Plan (Reconstructing the First World)

In the post–World War II years, the United States focused on European reconstruction as the key to stabilizing the Western world and securing capitalism. European grain harvests in 1946 would reach only 60 percent of prewar levels. Scarcity of labor skills and certain goods depleted transport and communication networks, and countless refugees posed enormous problems. There was also a growing popular desire for social reform.[1] Returning from Europe in 1947, U.S. Assistant Secretary of State for Economic Affairs Will Clayton stated,

> Communist movements are threatening established governments in every part of the globe. These movements, directed by Moscow, feed on economic and political weakness. . . . The United States is faced with a world-wide challenge to human freedom. The only way to meet this challenge is by a vast new programme of assistance given directly by the United States itself.[2]

In these political circumstances, the United States hoped to use financial aid to stabilize discontented populations and rekindle economic growth in strategic parts of the world. Central to this strategy was containing communism—primarily in Europe, where the Soviet Union had laid claim to territories east of Berlin, but also in the Far East, where communism had gained ground, first in China and then in North Korea. The United States courted nations' allegiance to the Western free enterprise system with financial assistance. In 1950, Secretary of State Dean Acheson proposed to concentrate assistance in Western Europe, to counter Soviet rule over Eastern Europe: "We cannot scatter our shots equally all over the world. We just haven't got enough shots to do that. . . . If anything happens in Western Europe the whole business goes to pieces."[3]

U.S. bilateral initiatives—increasingly important in the Cold War—complemented and sometimes contradicted these multilateral initiatives. The Marshall Plan was a bilateral transfer of billions of dollars to Europe and Japan, serving U.S. geopolitical goals in the Cold War. The plan restored trade and price stability, and expanded production, to undercut socialist movements and labor militancy. Dollar credits, allowing recipients to purchase U.S. goods, and a massive rearmament effort closely integrated these countries' economies with that of the United States, solidifying political loyalty to the Western "free world."

Europeans desired social peace and full employment, to be achieved through closely regulated national economies, but the U.S. government wanted an open world economy. The Marshall Plan solved this dilemma, using bilateral aid to facilitate international trade and encourage U.S. direct investment in European national economies. [4]

Multilateralism: The Bretton Woods System

The idea for an international bank was part of the plan to reconstruct the world economy in the 1940s. Trade was to be restored by disbursing credit to regions devastated by war or colonialism. The famous July 1944 conference of 44 financial ministers at Bretton Woods, New Hampshire, provided the opportunity to create such an international banking system. Here, the U.S. Treasury steered the conference toward chartering the foundation of the "twin sisters": the **World Bank** and the **International Monetary Fund (IMF)**.

Each institution was based on member subscriptions. The World Bank would match these subscriptions by borrowing money in international capital markets to raise money for development. The IMF was to disburse credit where needed to stabilize national currency exchanges. The conference president, Henry Morgenthau, foresaw

> the creation of a dynamic world economy in which the peoples of every nation will be able to realize their potentialities in peace . . . and enjoy, increasingly, the fruits of material progress on an earth infinitely blessed with natural riches. This is the indispensable cornerstone of freedom and security. All else must be built upon this. For freedom of opportunity is the foundation for all other freedoms.[5]

These were the key sentiments of the development project: multinational universalism, viewing nature as an unlimited resource, and a liberal belief in freedom of opportunity as the basis of political development and rising living standards.

The functions of the Bretton Woods agencies were as follows:

- to stabilize national finances and revitalize international trade (IMF);
- to underwrite national economic growth by funding Third World imports of First World infrastructural technologies; and
- to expand Third World primary exports to earn foreign currency for purchasing First World exports.

The World Bank's mandate was for large-scale loans to states for national infrastructural projects such as dams, highways, and power plants, complementing smaller scale private and public investments. In its first 20 years, two-thirds of the Bank's loans purchased inputs to build transportation and electric power systems. At the same time, the Bank invested in large-scale cash crop agriculture, such as cacao, rubber, and livestock, deepening the legacy of the colonial division of labor.[6]

The Bretton Woods institutions lubricated the world economy by moving funds to regions that needed purchasing power. Expanded trade stimulated economic growth across the First World–Third World divide. At the same time, these agencies disseminated the technologies of the development project, encouraging Third World states to adopt the capital-intensive methods of the West. Whereas Europe had taken several centuries to industrialize, Third World governments expected to industrialize rapidly with multilateral loans, substituting capital-intensive for labor-intensive production technologies despite substantial populations already displaced from customary habitats.

The Bretton Woods system was unveiled as a universal and multilateral attempt to promote rising living standards on a global scale. Of the 45 nations in attendance at Bretton Woods, 27 were from the Third World. Nevertheless, the institution had a First World imprint. First, control of the World Bank was dominated by the five biggest shareholders (beginning with the United States), whose representatives appointed their own executive directors to the board. The remaining seven directors represented the remaining member states. Such asymmetry, including overwhelming male representation, still exists. Second, the president of the World Bank is selected by the United States president, and the managing director of the IMF is appointed by the largest European nations (the United Kingdom, France, and Germany).[7] Third, the Bank finances foreign exchange costs of approved projects, encouraging import dependence (in capital-intensive technologies) in development priorities. Finally, the IMF adopted a "conditionality" requirement, requiring applicants to have economic policies that met certain criteria for them to obtain loans. International banks and other lenders inevitably adopted IMF conditionality as their criterion for Third World loans. In this way, Third World development priorities were tailored toward external (i.e., First World) evaluation.[8]

World Bank lending, however effective, reflected First World priorities. The Bank has emphasized "productive" investments, such as energy and export agriculture, rather than "social" investments, such as education, health services, water and sanitation facilities, and housing. In addition, as a global agency, the Bank finds it more convenient to invest in large-scale, capital-intensive projects that might, for example, have common techno-logical inputs and similar appraisal mechanisms.[9] Not only has the Bank sponsored Western **technology transfer**, but it has also established an *institutional presence* in Third World countries. When the Bank finances infra-structural projects, these are often administered through agencies with semi-autonomous financial and political power within host countries, as the case study shows.

In examining how the development project issued from the Bretton Woods institutions, we have focused on the World Bank as the key multi-lateral agency responsible for underwriting Third World development. In addition to its parastatal influence, the World Bank framed development priorities via onsite project agencies and by encouraging large-scale power generation and transport projects, stimulating industrialization on a Western scale. The World Bank also channeled loans into intensive agriculture, requir-ing fossil fuel, energy-dependent technical inputs such as chemical fertilizers, pesticides, and hybrid seeds. It catalyzed development project norms, creat-ing the Economic Development Institute in 1956 to train Third World officials (soon to be prime ministers or ministers of planning or finance in their own countries) in the theory and practice of development.[10]

In short, multilateralism, World Bank style, characterized the Bretton Woods system—World Bank policy set the parameters for development. Third World elites by and large embraced these parameters, since they were in no position to present an alternative to free enterprise. When govern-ments adopted socialist policies, loan funds would shrink.

Politics of the Postwar World Order

As the realm of free enterprise expanded, the political dynamics of the Cold War deepened. While the United States and the Soviet Union were busy dividing the world, the countries of the Third World came together to assert their own international presence. We explore the interplay of all these forces in the following sections.

Foreign Aid

An examination of the patterns of Western foreign aid shows that pat-terns of development assistance contradicted the universalism of the devel-opment project. All states could not be equal, as some were more significant than others in the maintenance of order in the world market system. Western aid concentrated on undercutting competition from states or political movements that espoused rival (i.e., socialist) ideologies of development. Economic and military aid and trade to stabilize geopolitical regions prioritized regionally powerful states such as South Korea, Israel, Turkey, and Iran. These states functioned as military outposts in securing the perimeters of the "free world" and in preventing a "domino effect" of defections to the Soviet bloc.

Cold War rivalry governed much of the political geography of the development project. The Soviet Union was expanding economic and political relations with Third World states, especially newly independent states in Asia and Africa. By 1964, the Soviet Union had extended export credits to about 30 states, even though eight received the most aid. Under the Soviet aid system, loans could be repaid in local currencies or in the form of traditional exports, a program that benefited states short of foreign currency. Not only was the Soviet Union offering highly visible aid projects to key states such as Indonesia and India, but aid policies also clearly favored states pursuing policies of central planning and public ownership in their development strategies.[11]

For the United States and its First World allies, then, the development project was more than a transmission belt for Western technology and economic institutions. So long as the Third World—a vital source of strategic raw materials and minerals—was under threat from a political alternative, First World security was at stake. In 1956, this view was articulated clearly by Walt Rostow, the influential development economist and presidential advisor: "The location, natural resources, and populations of the underdeveloped areas are such that, should they become effectively attached to the Communist bloc, the United States would become the second power in the world."[12]

The United States' foreign aid patterns between 1945 and 1967 confirm this view of the world. Yugoslavia, for instance, received considerable aid as the regional counterweight to the Soviet Union. Elsewhere, aid to geopolitically strategic states (including Iran, Turkey, Israel, India, Pakistan, South Vietnam, Taiwan, South Korea, the Philippines, Thailand, and Laos) matched the total aid disbursement to all other Third World countries.[13]

The Non-Aligned Movement

Against this world ordering was an emerging Third World perspective that advocated a more independent vision. As decolonization proceeded, the composition of the United Nations shifted toward a majority of non-European member states. In 1955, the growing weight of the Third World in international politics produced the first meeting of "nonaligned" Asian and African states at Bandung, Indonesia, forming the **Non-Aligned**

Movement (NAM) by 1961. Key players were the leaders of Yugoslavia (Tito), Indonesia (Sukarno), India (Nehru), Ghana (Nkrumah), North Vietnam (Ho Chi Minh), Egypt (Nasser), and China (Zhou Enlai). The NAM used its collective voice in international fora to forge a philosophy of noninterference in international relations. President Nyerere of Tanzania articulated this position in terms of economic self-reliance:

> By non-alignment we are saying to the Big Powers that we also belong to this planet. We are asserting the right of small, or militarily weaker, nations to determine their own policies in their own interests, and to have an influence on world affairs. . . . At every point . . . we find our real freedom to make economic, social and political choices is being jeopardized by our need for economic development.[14]

The subtext of this statement, following the final Bandung communiqué, involved questioning the legitimacy of the model of development embedded in the multilateral institutional order. The first bone of contention was the paucity of multilateral loans. By 1959, the World Bank had lent more to the First World ($1.6 billion) than to the Third World ($1.3 billion). Third World members of the UN pressed for expanded loans, with concessions. The First World's response was to channel this demand toward the World Bank, where the International Development Association (IDA) was established to make loans at highly discounted rates (called "soft loans") to low-income countries. In addition, several regional banks were established— including the Inter-American Development Bank (IDB) in 1959, the African Development Bank (AfDB) in 1964, and the Asian Development Bank (ADB) in 1966.[15]

The Group of 77

International trade remained contentious. The **General Agreement on Tariffs and Trade (GATT)**, founded in 1947, enabled states to negotiate reciprocal trade concessions, but without adjusting for the uneven effects of colonialism.[16] In fact, during the 1950s, the Third World's share of world trade fell from one-third to almost one-fifth, with declining rates of export growth associated with declining terms of trade.[17]

Third World pressure founded the **United Nations Conference on Trade and Development (UNCTAD)** in 1964—the first international forum in which Third World countries, caucusing as the **Group of 77 (G-77)**, collectively demanded world-economic reforms. They demanded stabilized and improved primary commodity prices, opening First World markets to

Third World manufactures, and expanding financial flows from the First World.

While UNCTAD had a limited world-economic impact, its scholar/planner members infused international agencies with a "Third Worldist" perspective. Perhaps its most concrete influence was on the World Bank under its president, Robert McNamara (1968–1981), who refocused development (for a time) on quality of life issues rather than simply income measures—the idea of "growth with equity"[18]

We now take leave of the institutional side of the development project to examine its impact on the international division of labor.

Remaking the International Division of Labor

If the development project was an initiative to promote Third World industrialization, then it certainly had some success. The result was uneven, however, and in some respects industrialization was quite incomplete. Nevertheless, by 1980 the international division of labor had been remade, if not reversed. Overall, exports from the Third World included more manufactured goods than raw materials, and the First World was exporting 36 percent more primary commodities than the Third World.[19]

The Newly Industrializing Countries (NICs)

The average growth rate for the Third World in the 1960s was 4.6 percent; however, six Third World **newly industrializing countries (NICs)**[20] grew at rates of 7 to 10 percent.[21] These six countries were Hong Kong, Singapore, Taiwan, South Korea, Brazil, and Mexico. The rise of the NICs revealed two sides of the development project. On one hand, NICs fulfilled the expectation of rising living standards and upward mobility in the international system, *legitimizing the development project, as showcases.* The other middle-income countries—especially Malaysia, Thailand, Indonesia, Argentina, and Chile—expected to follow the same path. On the other hand, the NICs also demonstrated the *selectivity* of the development project. They cornered the bulk of private foreign investment, and considerable (Cold War driven) military aid sustaining authoritarian regimes.[22] Much of this was concentrated in developing export production facilities in textiles and electronics in South Korea, Taiwan, Mexico, and Brazil. In 1969, for instance, most of the foreign investment in electronic assembly centered on the Asian NICs—Hong Kong, South Korea, Taiwan, and Singapore.[23] Between 1967 and 1978, the share of manufactured exports from the NICs controlled by transnational corporations (TNCs) was 20 percent in Taiwan, 43 percent in Brazil, and 90 percent in Singapore.[24] Distribution of industrial growth in the Third World was also highly concentrated. Between 1966 and 1975, more than 50 percent of the increase in value of Third World manufacturing occurred in only four countries, while about two-thirds of the increase was accounted for by only eight countries: Brazil, Mexico, Argentina, South Korea, India, Turkey, Iran, and Indonesia.[25]

Figure 3.1   Textiles, Clothing, and Footwear Exports from Newly Industrializing Countries

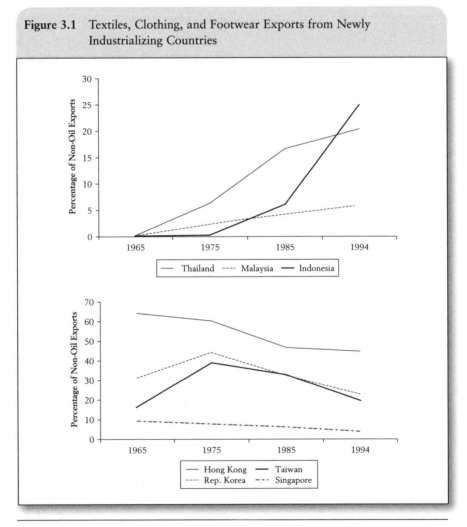

Sources: Adapted from graphs in Ransom (2001b:103); data retrieved from UNCTAD (1996: 118–119).

Across the Third World, countries and regions differed in their levels of industrialization. The manufacturing portion of the gross domestic product (GDP) in 1975 was 5 percent in Africa, 16 percent in Asia, and 25 percent in Latin America and the Caribbean.[26] By 1972, the Organisation for Economic Co-operation and Development (OECD) reported, "It has become more and more clear that measures designed to help developing countries as a group have not been effective for [the] least developed countries. They face difficulties of a special kind and intensity; they need help specifically designed to deal with their problems."[27] *The idea of a universal blueprint was clearly fading.*

The European First World lost its core manufacturing position in this period. Japan and a middle-income group of Third World states improved their share of world manufacturing, from 19 to 37 percent.[28] In agriculture, the Third World's share of world agricultural exports fell from 53 to 31 percent between 1950 and 1980, while the American granary consolidated its critical role in world agricultural trade.[29] By the 1980s, the United States was producing 17 percent of the world's wheat, 63 percent of its corn, and 63 percent of its soybeans; its share of world exports was 36 percent in wheat, 70 percent in corn, and 59 percent in soybeans.[30] On the other side of the globe, between 1961 and 1975 Third World agricultural self-sufficiency declined everywhere except in centrally planned Asian countries (China, North Korea, and Vietnam). In all regions except Latin America, self-sufficiency dropped below 100 percent. Africa's self-sufficiency, for instance, declined from 98 percent in 1961 to 79 percent in 1978.[31]

Two questions arise:

- Why did commercial agriculture concentrate in the First World, while manufacturing dispersed to the Third World?
- Is there a relation between these trends?

The answer lies in the political structures of the development project. While import-substitution industrialization (ISI) protected Third World "infant" industries, farm subsidies protected First World agriculture under the terms of the GATT. These policies complemented one another via American food surplus aid mechanisms, substantially reshaping the international division of labor. Central to this process was a "food-aid regime," which demonstrated the profoundly international character of the development project as a strategy of ordering the world under the guise of promoting development.

CASE STUDY   South Korea in the Changing International Division of Labor

South Korea is arguably the most successful of the middle-income NICs, transforming its economy and society in the space of a generation. In 1953, agriculture generated 47 percent of its gross national product (GNP), whereas manufacturing generated less than 9 percent. By 1981, these proportions had switched to 16 percent and 30 percent respectively. At the same time, the contribution of heavy and chemical industries to total industrial output matured from 23 percent in 1953–1955 to 42 percent in 1974–1976. How did this happen?

South Korea depended on injections of American dollars following the Korean War in the early 1950s, as it pursued the ISI strategy. By 1973, its government's Heavy Industry and Chemicals Plan encouraged industrial maturity in shipbuilding, steel, machinery, and petrochemicals, and complemented ISI with export-oriented industrialization, beginning with labor-intensive consumer goods such as textiles and garments. From the early 1960s to the early 1980s, manufactured goods rose from 17 to 91 percent of exports, as increasingly sophisticated electronics goods emerged, and as Korean manufacturers gained access to foreign markets.

South Korea exemplifies a development state whose success depended on a rare flexibility in policy combined with the unusually repressive political system of military ruler Park Chung Hee (1961–1979). Koreans worked extremely long hours only to find their savings taxed away to support government investment policies. Industrial labor had no rights. Confucianism promoted consensus, and the authority of education and the bureaucracy, providing a powerful mobilizing cultural myth. A frontline position in the Cold War helped, as the United States opened its markets to Korean exports.

Meanwhile, cheap U.S. food exports were key. Before 1960, virtually no Western-style bread was consumed in Korea—rice is cherished, and at that time, the country was self-sufficient in food. By 1975, however, South Korea was only 60 percent food self-sufficient, and by 1978 it belonged to what the U.S. Department of Agriculture calls "the billion dollar club." That is, South Korea was purchasing $2.5 billion worth of American farm commodities, primarily wheat. The government provided free lunch bread to schoolchildren, and thousands of Korean housewives attended sandwich-making classes, financed by U.S. "counterpart funds" from its food aid program.

The South Korean farming population fell by 50 percent as urban industry attracted rural migrants. From 1957 to 1982, more than 12 million migrated to work in industrial cities like Seoul and Pusan. Rural migration occurred, but not because rice farms consolidated—they remained extremely small scale, retaining an average farm size of 1 hectare (2.471 acres), closely husbanded by the state with farm credit and price supports.

Since the South Korean "miracle" depended significantly on the subsidy to its industrialization strategy provided by cheap American food (lowering wage costs), and on access to U.S. markets for its manufactured exports, was its development ultimately a domestic or an international process?

Sources: Chung (1990: 43); Evans (1995); Harris (1987: 31–36); Wessel (1983: 172–173).

The Food-Aid Regime

In the postwar era, the United States set up a food-aid program to channel food surpluses to Third World countries. Surpluses arose out of the U.S. agro-industrial model, protected by tariffs and subsidies (institutionalized in the GATT). Farmers specialized in one or two commodities (such as corn, rice, sugar, and dairy products) and, with technological support from the public purse, routinely overproduced. Farm subsidies set prices for farm goods above their price on the world market. The resulting surpluses were used to subsidize Third World wage bills with cheap food. It was a substantial transfer of agricultural resources to Third World urban-industrial sectors. This **food-aid regime**[32] set in motion the rural–urban prescriptions of development economists, with a difference: *operating on a global, instead of a national, scale.*

The Public Law 480 Program

To dispose of farm surpluses, the U.S. government instituted the Public Law 480 Program (PL-480) in 1954. It had three components: commercial sales on concessionary terms—discounted prices in local currency (Title I); famine relief (Title II); and food bartered for strategic raw materials (Title III). The stated goal was "to increase the consumption of U.S. agricultural commodities in foreign countries, to improve the foreign relations of the U.S. and for other purposes." In 1967, the U.S. Department of Agriculture reported, "One of the major objectives and an important measure of the success of foreign policy goals is the transition of countries from food aid to commercial trade."[33]

Title I sales anchored this food aid regime, accounting for 70 percent of world food aid (mostly wheat) between 1954 and 1977. By the mid-1960s, food aid accounted for one-quarter of world wheat exports, determining the prices of traded foods. Management of food surpluses stabilized prices, and this in turn stabilized two key, and mutually conditioning, parts of the development project: the American agricultural economy and Third World government industrial plans.

Food Dependency

Under the aid program, wheat imports provisioned rising Third World urban populations. Third World governments established distribution programs to channel aid to reward the so-called "development alliance" of manufacturers, labor unions, urban professionals, and middle classes. Cheap food thus supported consumer purchasing power and subsidized the cost of labor, stabilizing urban politics and improving the Third World environment for industrial investments.

The impact of food aid varied across the world, depending on the resources of particular countries and their development policies. South Korea was a success story largely because the government centralized management of its rice culture and the supply of labor to the industrial centers. By contrast, urbanization in Colombia followed the collapse of significant parts of its unprotected farm belt under the competitive impact of food aid and commercial imports of wheat. Stimulated by the food aid program, imports of discounted wheat grew tenfold between the early 1950s and 1971, reducing by half the prices obtained by Colombian farmers. Displaced peasants contributed to the characteristic urban underemployment and low-wage economy of Third World countries.[34]

Between 1954 and 1974, major recipients of U.S. food aid were India, South Korea, Brazil, Morocco, Yugoslavia, South Vietnam, Egypt, Tunisia, Israel, Pakistan, Indonesia, Taiwan, and the Philippines (see Figure 3.2). Usually, it was cheaper and easier for governments to import wheat to feed their growing urban populations than to bankroll long-term improvements in the production, transportation, and distribution of local foods.[35] Food aid allowed governments to purchase food without depleting scarce foreign currency, but it built "food dependency."

Shipments of food were paid for in counterpart funds—that is, local currency placed in U.S. local bank accounts as payment—in India, for example, the United States owned over one-third of the rupee supply by the 1970s.[36] These funds could be spent only by U.S. agencies within the recipient country, on a range of activities such as infrastructural projects,

Figure 3.2   Food Shortage Regions and Food Aid Recipients

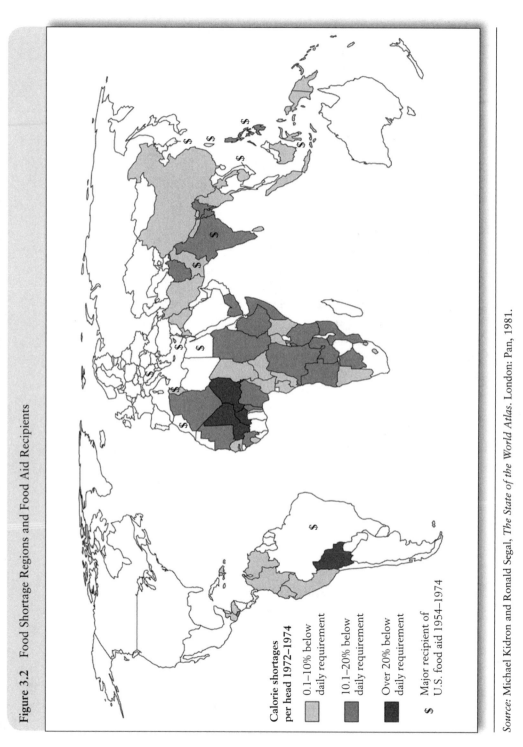

Calorie shortages
per head 1972–1974

☐ 0.1–10% below
   daily requirement

■ 10.1–20% below
   daily requirement

■ Over 20% below
   daily requirement

$ Major recipient of
   U.S. food aid 1954–1974

Source: Michael Kidron and Ronald Segal, *The State of the World Atlas.* London: Pan, 1981.

supplies for military bases, loans to U.S. companies (especially local agribusiness operations), locally produced goods and services, and trade fairs. Counterpart funds were also used to promote *new diets* among Third World consumers in the form of school lunch programs and the promotion of bread substitutes. U.S. Senator George McGovern predicted in 1964,

> The great food markets of the future are the very areas where vast numbers of people are learning through Food for Peace to eat American produce. The people we assist today will become our customers tomorrow. . . . An enormous market for American produce of all kinds will come into being if India can achieve even half the productivity of Canada.[37]

By 1978, the Third World was receiving more than three-quarters of American wheat exports. At the same time, Third World per capita consumption of wheat rose by almost two-thirds, and per capita consumption of all cereals except wheat increased 20 percent while per capita consumption of traditional root crops declined by more than 20 percent.[38] In Asian and Latin American urban diets, wheat progressively replaced rice and corn. Wheat (and rice) imports displaced maize in Central America and parts of the Middle East and millet and sorghum in West Africa. Subsidized grain imports also undercut the prices of traditional starches (potatoes, cassava, yams, and taro). Thus, traditional "peasant foods" were replaced by the new "wage foods" of grains and processed foods consumed by urban workers.[39]

The rising consumption of imported wheat in Third World countries was linked to two far-reaching changes:

- the erosion of peasant agriculture, urban food rations enabled subsidized wage foods to outcompete peasant foods; and
- the expansion of an industrial labor force, as small producers left the land for low-wage jobs in the rapidly growing cities.

In the conventional development model, these social trends occur within a national framework. In reality, via the development project, they occurred within an international political-economic framework as First World farmers supplied Third World industrial workers, thus remaking the international division of labor.

Remaking Third World Agricultures

The intent of the PL-480 program was to create future markets for commercial sales of U.S. grains as consumers shifted to wheat-based diets.

Consumption of final products (bread) was complemented by expanding consumption of other surplus agricultural goods, such as feed grains and agricultural technology. Behind this stood the massive state-sponsored expansion in American agricultural productivity, which outstripped manufacturing from the 1950s to the 1970s. Disposal of surpluses was a matter of government policy. At this point, it is important to reflect on the longer-term consequences of a short-term "food-empire" strategy. Such public support of "petro-farming"—where petroleum fuels industrial agriculture via mechanization, inorganic fertilizers, pesticides, herbicides and seed varnishes, abandoning agriculture's natural biological base— undermines nature's intrinsic ecological qualities over time. In the process, intensive agriculture annually loses 2 million acres of farm land to erosion, soil salinity, and flooding, in addition to consuming groundwater 160 percent faster than it can be replenished.[40] Marc Reisner, referring to the American West in *Cadillac Desert*, wrote, "Westerners call what they have established out here a civilization, but it would be more accurate to call it a beachhead. . . . And if history is any guide, the odds that we can sustain it would have to be regarded as low."[41] This agribusiness model remains one of the key exports stemming from the era of the development project.

The Global Livestock Complex

During the food-aid regime, surplus grain was sufficiently cheap and plentiful to feed livestock rather than people. Expanding supplies of feed grains stimulated the growth of commodity chains linking specialized feed producers with specialized animal protein producers across the world. Beyond a wheat-based diet, more affluent Third World consumers shifted up the food chain, from grain to animal protein (beef, poultry, pork, and shrimp). Such "dietary modernization" is as much the result of policy as it is the consequence of rising incomes. The hamburger commodity chain has its counterpart to petro-farming's ecological impact in deforestation. For example, between 1960 and 1990, over 25 percent of the Central American rainforest was converted to pasture for cattle in turn, converted into hamburgers for an expanding fast-food industry in the United States. The contributions of beef production to global warming, via carbon dioxide, nitrous oxide, and methane, are significant, as Jeremy Rifkin reminds us: "Altered climates, shorter growing seasons, changing rainfall patterns, eroding rangeland, and spreading deserts may well sound the death knell for the cattle complex and the artificial protein ladder that has been erected to support a grain-fed beef culture."[42]

American grain-processing industries followed the movement of cattle from open-range feeding to grain feeding (75 percent by the early 1970s).

The grain companies that formerly sold and processed wheat diversified into processed feeds (corn, barley, soybeans, alfalfa, oats, and sorghum) for cattle and hog feedlots as well as poultry motels. Consumption of animal protein became identified with "the American way of life," as meat accounted for one-quarter of the food bill by 1965.[43] Beef consumption roughly doubled between the turn of the century and 1976, and poultry consumption more than tripled between the 1930s and 1970.[44] Looking ahead, factory farms in the United States today annually produce well over 1 billion tons of manure, laden with chemicals, antibiotics, and hormones, which leach into rivers and water tables.[45] The animal protein culture is also symbolic of the problematic chemical technology enabling modern development.

Through the food aid program, exports of feed grains also flourished as animal protein consumption spread among Third World middle classes. The U.S. Feed Grains Council routinely channeled counterpart funds, via over 400 agribusinesses, into the development of local livestock and poultry industries.[46] In 1969, four South Korean firms entered into joint ventures with U.S. agribusinesses (including Ralston-Purina and Cargill) to acquire technical and marketing expertise. The 1970 PL-480 annual report stated these enterprises would use counterpart funds "to finance construction and operation of modern livestock feed mixing and livestock and poultry production and processing facilities. As these facilities become fully operational, they will substantially expand the market for feedgrain and other feed ingredients."[47]

CASE STUDY   Food and Class Relations

The growing feed grains trade traces changing social diets as societies transform.

Animal protein consumption reflects rising affluence as middle-class Third Worlders embraced First World diets beyond those staple (grain, primarily wheat) diets promoted directly through food aid. (Ernst) Engel's law correlated the dietary move from starch to grain to animal protein and fresh vegetables with rising incomes. Rather than reflecting individual choice, however, dietary differentiation reflects who controls production of certain foods, and how consumption patterns distribute among social classes.

Consider Egypt, where, in 1974–1975, the richest 27 percent of the urban population consumed four times as much animal protein as the poorest 27 percent. Rising incomes, complemented by U.S. and Egyptian government subsidies, fostered a switch from legumes and maize to wheat and meat products. From 1970 to 1987, livestock production outstripped crop production on an order of ten to one. Egypt's grain imports exploded as it became the world's largest importer after Japan and China. Timothy Mitchell notes that dependence on imported grain stems from a government-sponsored shift to meat consumption, remarking,

> Egypt's food problem is the result not of too many people occupying too little land, but of the power of a certain part of that population, supported by the prevailing domestic and international regime, to shift the country's resources from staple foods to more expensive items of consumption.

Engel's law appears to operate globally, as different classes dine on different parts of the food chain, but the difference is an effect of the development project. As wealthy consumers dine "up" on animal protein, the working poor dine either on food aid grains or the low end of the food chain: low-protein starchy diets, or little at all.

While it seems *natural* for those with rising incomes to consume animal protein, can we separate meat consumption from the political mechanisms and social inequalities that support such indirect consumption of feed grains, displacing direct consumption of grains and other staple foods?

Sources: Gardner and Halweil (2000); Mitchell (1991).

A global livestock complex formed, with livestock production expanding across the Third World, and specialized feed grain supply zones concentrating in the First World and in "middle-income" countries such as Brazil and Argentina. Between the late 1940s and 1988, world production of soybeans increased sixfold. At the same time, maize production was revolutionized as a specialized, capital-intensive agro-industry, outstripping the value of the world wheat trade by a factor of six.[48]

The Green Revolution

The other major contribution to the remaking of Third World agriculture was the **green revolution**, associated with a "package" of plant-breeding agricultural technologies originally developed by the Rockefeller Foundation in Mexico—increasing production of corn, wheat, and beans in the two decades after 1943 by 300 percent—and, in a combined venture with the Ford Foundation in the Philippines in the 1960s, then in tropical centers in Nigeria and Colombia. In 1971 it culminated in the formation of the Consultative Group on International Agricultural Research (CGIAR), sponsored by the Food and Agricultural Organization (FAO), the United Nations Development Program (UNDP), and the World Bank, with research facilities and gene banks across the world.[49] The green revolution was also the principal medium through which the U.S. model of chemical agriculture was introduced into the Third World—a technology transfer involving specific political choices and consequences.

Green revolution advocacy symbolized the idealized prescriptions of the development project, with its focus on output, despite known social and ecological consequences.[50] In the development narrative, rural population shrinkage is inevitable as agriculture "modernizes." The question is, why shrink huge rural populations where industry was either capital-intensive or not extensive, and slumdwellers comprise 50 percent of Third World populations?

"Productivism" has been a central development theme. It was promoted heavily by the U.S. land-grant university system, with an extension program geared to a model of commodity-specific research, supporting large, capitalized farmers.[51] Within the development project, the "entire argument for increasing yields was framed by the specter of increasing population." This argument lent moral and political legitimacy to a technological solution (despite the consequences), it represented population as an independent variable (we have seen how the case study of Egypt questions this) and, finally, the green revolution program appealed to "economic nationalism," a central ingredient of developmentalism at the time.[52]

Even more compelling were the political implications of the Chinese model where, following the 1949 communist revolution, about 45 percent of total cultivated land monopolized by landlords was redistributed to small and landless peasants. Collectivization of land mobilized underemployed surplus labor and investment in water management and local enterprises, and extended basic health and rural education through a decentralized process supplemented with central government assistance—albeit with a goal of squeezing agriculture to finance industrial growth and centralized administration.[53] Whether or not this vast social experiment ultimately succeeded, the Chinese model loomed large in countries like India, where Prime Minister Nehru was determined to match the Chinese.[54] However, Indian national institutional reforms required compliance by state governments, generally dominated by landlords and merchants unfavorable to land reform and labor cooperatives. The revolution would thus change color, from red to green.

Meanwhile, the United States, with the leverage of its counterpart funds in India, was encouraging India to substitute green revolution technology for land redistribution.[55] Pressure to extend chemical agriculture stemmed from the conversion of wartime nitrogen production (for bombs) to inorganic fertilizer, displacing nitrogen-fixing legumes and manure, and the development of insecticides, stemming from World War I nerve gases, with advances in petroleum refining and organic chemistry.[56]

"Petro-farming"—marrying the chemical industry with the energy sector—both enabled and encouraged proliferation of green revolution technology, with the FAO providing extension services for the disposal of synthetic fertilizer across the Third World, intensifying agricultural dependence on the energy sector.[57] Vandana Shiva remarks, "The Green Revolution seeds were designed to overcome the limits placed on chemically intensive agriculture by the indigenous seeds."[58]

The new high-yielding varieties (HYVs) of hybrid seeds were heavily dependent on disease- and pest-resisting chemical protections in the form of fungicides and pesticides. Intensive irrigation and fertilization were necessary to optimize macro-nutrient yields, eliminating traditional leafy greens (micro-nutrients such as vitamin A) now redefined as "weeds" and targeted by herbicides. The HYVs produced "wage foods" for urban consumers, displacing "peasant foods" produced with methods of crop-rotation to maintain soil fertility. In 1984, an Indian farmer commented on the stronger, healthy soils promoted by manure-based fertilizer: "chemical fertilizer makes the crop shoot up . . . whereas organic manure makes for strength. Without strength, no matter how much fertilizer you put, the field won't give output."[59] The hybrid seed ruptured the ecological cycle of natural regeneration and renewal, replacing it with linear flows of purchased inputs and commodified outputs, and incorporating farmers into the "chemical treadmill."[60] Long-term economic and ecological impacts have been blamed for as many as 100,000 farmer suicides in India between 1993 and 2003.[61]

The expansion of green revolution agriculture embodied the two sides of the development project: the national and the international. From a *national* perspective, governments sought to improve agricultural productivity and the delivery of maize, wheat, and rice to urban centers. In the context of the food-aid regime, this *import-substitution* strategy either supplemented food aid or complemented its competitive effects on local farmers. The green revolution produced dramatic yields, but highly concentrated in a few ecologically advantaged regions of the Third World. Asia and, to a much lesser degree, Latin America have captured the benefits from the new grain varieties, while Africa—lacking an expansive commercial wheat or rice culture—has charted few gains. The major wheat-producing countries in the Third World—India, Argentina, Pakistan, Turkey, Mexico, and Brazil—planted the bulk of their wheat acreage in the new hybrid varieties, accounting for 86 percent of the total green revolution wheat area by the 1980s. Meanwhile, six Asian countries—India, Indonesia, the Philippines, Bangladesh, Burma, and Vietnam—were cultivating more than 87 percent of the rice acreage attributed to the green revolution by the 1980s.[62]

From an *international* perspective, the food aid program helped to spread green revolution technology. Counterpart funds routinely promoted agribusiness and green revolution technologies, complemented with loans from institutions such as the United States Agency for International Development (USAID) and the World Bank.[63] These agencies aimed to weave First World agricultural technologies into Third World commercial farming.

The green revolution was realized through the increase of rural income inequalities. In parts of Latin America, such as Mexico, Argentina, Brazil, and Venezuela, as well as in irrigated regions of India (Punjab and Haryana), this high-input agriculture promoted economic differentiation among—and often within—farming households. Within households, typically women have less commercial opportunity. Hybrid seeds and supporting inputs had to be purchased; to buy them, participants needed a regular supply of money or credit. Women tended to be excluded—not only because of the difficulty of obtaining financing but also because of agricultural extension traditions of transferring technology to male heads of households.

Among farming households, the wealthier ones were more able to afford the package—and the risk—of introducing the new seed varieties. They also prospered from higher grain yields—often with easier access to government services than their poorer neighbors, who lacked the political and economic resources to take full advantage of these technologies. Rising land values often hurt tenant farmers by inflating their rent payments, forcing them to rent their land to their richer neighbors or to foreclose to creditors. Finally, the mechanical and chemical technologies associated with the green revolution either reduce farmhand employment opportunities for poor or landless peasants (where jobs were mechanized) or degrade working conditions where farmhands are exposed to toxic chemicals, such as pesticides and herbicides.[64]

Anti-rural Biases of the Development Project

Within the framework of the development project, Third World governments strove to feed growing urban populations cheaply, for political support, for lowering wages, and for national security. The term **urban bias** has been coined to refer to the systematic privileging of urban interests, from health and education services through employment schemes to the delivery of food aid.[65] This bias was central to the construction of development alliances based in the cities of the Third World. But it also expressed the modernist belief in peasant redundancy.

Urban bias did not go unnoticed in the countryside. Growing rural poverty, rural marginalization, and persistent peasant activism over the question of land distribution put **land reform** on the political agenda in Asia and Latin America. When the Cuban Revolution redistributed land to poor and landless peasants in 1959, land reforms swept Latin America. Between 1960 and 1964, Brazil, Chile, Costa Rica, the Dominican Republic, Ecuador, Guatemala, Nicaragua, Panama, Peru, and Venezuela all enacted land reforms. The Alliance for Progress (1961)—a program of nationally planned agrarian reform coordinated across Latin America—provided an opportunity for the United States to use land reforms to undercut radical insurgents and stabilize rural populations via a U.S.-inspired family farming model.[66]

The land reform movement exempted commercialized farmland, redistributing what was left, including frontier lands. Indeed, considerable "re-peasantization" occurred during this period. In Latin America, two-thirds of the additional food production between 1950 and 1980 came from frontier colonization, and the number of small farmers with an average of two hectares of land grew by 92 percent. Overall, arable land increased by as much as 109 percent in Latin America and 30 percent in Asia but possibly declined in Africa.[67] Resettlement schemes on frontiers, including forests, were typically financed by the World Bank, especially in Indonesia, Brazil, Malaysia, and India, and they usually privileged males, as household heads—"one of the principal mechanisms of exclusion of women as direct beneficiaries."[68] These strategies sometimes simply relocated rural poverty. In Brazil between 1960 and 1980 roughly 28 million small farmers were displaced by industrial farming for export to enhance foreign exchange earnings. The displaced farmers spilled into the Amazon region, burning the forest for new and often infertile land.[69]

Persistent rural poverty through the 1960s highlighted the urban bias of the development project. At this point, the World Bank (under Robert McNamara) devised a new poverty alleviation program—a multilateral scheme to channel credit to smallholding peasants and stabilize rural populations where previous agrarian reforms failed, with quite mixed success. Outcomes included leakage of credit funds to more powerful rural operators, displacement of hundreds of millions of peasants, and the incorporation of surviving peasant smallholders via credit into commercial cropping at the expense of basic food farming.[70]

The lesson we may draw from this episode of reform is that neither the resettlement of peasants nor their integration into monetary relations is always a sustainable substitute for supporting agro-ecological methods that preserve natural cycles of regeneration of land, water, and biodiversity. The assumptions of the development project heavily discriminated against the survival of peasant culture, as materially impoverished as it may have seemed.

Through a combination of food dumping, and institutional support of commercial and export agriculture, the long-term assault on peasant agriculture begun in the colonial era has intensified. Priority given to import and production of "wage foods"—compromising soil fertility and hydrological cycles—undermines the viability of household food production as a livelihood strategy for peasants and a subsistence base for the rural poor. The result has been a swelling migration of displaced peasants to overcrowded urban centers of Latin America, Asia, and Africa, creating a "planet of slums."[71]

SUMMARY

The development project was multilayered, as national strategies of economic growth dovetailed with international programs of multilateral and bilateral assistance. The Third World *as a whole* was incorporated into a *singular* project, despite national and regional variations in available resources, starting point, and ideological orientation.

Military and economic aid programs shaped the geopolitical contours of the "free world," integrating Third World countries into the Western orbit. They also shaped patterns of development through technological transfer and food subsidies to industrialization programs. Food aid was significant in securing geopolitical alliances as well as in reshaping the international division of labor via support of Third World manufacturing. As development economists predicted, Third World industrialization depended on the transfer of rural resources. But this transfer was not confined to national arenas, as exports of First World food and agricultural technology constituted a *global* rural–urban exchange.

The international dimension is as critical to our understanding of the development processes during the postwar era as is the variety of national forms. We cannot detail such variety here, and that is not the point of this story. Rather, the focus is on understanding how the development project set in motion a *global* dynamic that embedded national policies within an international institutional and ideological framework. This framework was theoretically in the service of national economic growth policies, but proved to be ultimately internationalizing. Social changes within Third World countries put their own local face on what was ultimately a common global process of development embedded in unequal relations, and technology transfer, between the First and Third Worlds.

In this chapter, we have examined one such example of these transfers, and we have seen how they condition the rise of new social structures. First World agricultural expansion was linked with the rise of new industrial classes in the Third World. At the same time, the export of green revolution technology to Third World regions stimulated social differentiation among men and women and among rural producers, laborers, and capitalist farmers. Those peasants unable to survive the combined competition of cheap foods and high-tech farming in the countryside migrated to the cities, further depressing wages. Not surprisingly, this scenario stimulated a massive relocation of industrial tasks to the Third World, reshaping the international division of labor. This is the subject of Chapter 4.

FURTHER READING

Chang, Ha-Joon. *Kicking Away the Ladder: Development Strategy in Historical Perspective.* London: Anthem Press, 2002.

Gupta, Akhil. *Postcolonial Developments: Agriculture in the Making of Modern India.* Durham, NC: Duke University Press, 1998.

Kloppenburg, Jack R., Jr. *First the Seed: The Political Economy of Plant Biotechnology, 1492–2000.* Cambridge, UK: Cambridge University Press, 1988.

Rich, Bruce. *Mortgaging the Earth: The World Bank, Environmental Impoverishment and the Crisis of Development.* Boston: Beacon, 1994.

SELECT WEBSITES

Consultative Group on International Agricultural Research (CGIAR): www.cgiar.org

Food and Agriculture Organization (FAO), UN: www.fao.org

International Monetary Fund (IMF): www.imf.org

United Nations Conference on Trade and Development (UNCTAD): www.unctad .org

The World Bank: www.worldbank.org

4

Globalizing Developments

R ecall that the "economic nationalism" of the development project was an
ideal, not a guarantee. The conversion of segments of domestic production to export production deepened the participation of national economies in
the world market. This chapter focuses on the socioeconomic dimensions of
this transformation, anticipating the process and politics of globalization, as
the development project was replaced by the globalization project.

The development project depended on postwar reconstruction of the
world market, albeit subordinated to the development concerns of nation-
states. The Cold War marked the rise of a U.S.-centered world economy in
which the U.S. government deployed military and economic largesse to
secure an informal empire as colonialism receded. With the West focused on
containing Soviet and Chinese power, the development project settled on
the twin economic foundations of *freedom of enterprise* and the U.S. dollar
as the *international currency*. Bilateral disbursements of dollars wove
together the principal national economies of the West and Japan and, as the
dollar source, the U.S. Federal Reserve System led those countries' central
banks in regulating an international monetary system.[1]

Within this arrangement, Third World political elites pursued national
development targets assisted by substantial military and financial aid pack-
ages. Countries differed in their resource endowments and their political
regimes—ranging from military dictatorship to one-party states to parliamentary rule. Nonetheless, despite expectations of convergence through development, divergent forces soon appeared. These included a growing, rather than
diminishing, gap between First and Third World living standards and a substantial differentiation among states within the Third World, as the newly

industrializing countries "took off." *In combination,* these divergent developments signaled a deepening integration of production relations *across,* rather than within, nation-states. The development "fast track" was emerging in the web of economic relations across national borders as a new form of global economy emerged, leaving the national experiment behind.

Third World Industrialization in Context

The rise of the **newly industrializing countries (NICs)** appeared to confirm that the colonial legacy was in retreat and that industrialization would inevitably expand into the Third World. Each of the NICs, with some variation, moved through low-value industries (processed foods, clothing, toys) to higher-value industries (steel, autos, petrochemicals, machinery). Whereas the Latin American NICs (Mexico and Brazil) began the early phase in the 1930s, graduating to the more mature phase in the 1950s, the Asian NICs (Taiwan and South Korea) began manufacturing basic goods in the 1950s and did not upgrade until the 1970s. The other regional variation was that the Asian NICs financed their import-substitution industrialization (ISI) via the export of labor-intensive products because they lacked the resource base and domestic markets of the Latin NICs.[2]

With the exception of Hong Kong, most of the NICs had strong development states guiding public investment into infrastructure development and industrial ventures with private enterprise. The South Korean development state virtually dictated national investment patterns.[3] Industrialization depended on the size of domestic markets as well as access to foreign exchange for purchasing First World capital equipment technologies. As technological rents rose, Latin NICs adopted the **export-oriented industrialization (EOI)** model of the Asian NICs to earn foreign exchange.

Widespread EOI signaled a significant change in strategies of industrialization, increasingly organized by transnational corporation (TNC) investment and marketing networks. For First World firms, EOI became a means of relocating the manufacturing of consumer goods, and then machinery and computers, to the Third World. Third World states welcomed the new investment with corporate concessions and a ready supply of cheap, disorganized labor. At the same time, First World consumption intensified with easy credit and a mushrooming of shopping malls and fast food outlets in the 1970s. The *global consumer* and the *global labor force* became mutually dependent.[4]

Third World manufacturing exports outpaced the growth in world manufacturing trade during this period, increasing their share of world trade from 6 to 10 percent between 1960 and 1979. The NICs accounted for the bulk of this export growth, its composition broadening from textiles, toys, footwear, and clothing in the 1960s to more sophisticated exports of electronics and electrical goods bound for the First World, as well as machinery and transport equipment bound for the Third World, by the 1970s.[5] Asian NIC development was achieved by rooting industrialization in the world economy. Thus,

> Mexico, Brazil, Argentina, and India . . . accounted for over 55% of all Third World industrial production but only about 25% of all Third World manufactured exports (narrowly defined). Hong Kong, Malaysia, Singapore and South Korea . . . were responsible for less than 10% of Third World production but 35% of all Third World manufactured exports (narrowly defined).[6]

The Asian NICs' export orientation was exceptional for geopolitical reasons. First, the East Asian perimeter of the Pacific Ocean was a strategic zone in the Cold War security system. Military alliances opened U.S. markets to exports, often of goods assembled for U.S. corporations. Second, Japan's historic trade and investment links with this region deepened as Japanese firms invested in low-wage assembly production offshore. In each case, the Asian NICs reaped the benefits of access to the near-insatiable markets of the United States and Japan. The global and regional contexts have been as influential in their growth as domestic policy measures and national economic cultures.

The World Factory

The expanding belt of export industries in the Third World, led by the NICs, provides a clue to a broader transformation occurring within the world at large. There was a new "fast track" in manufacturing exports, superseding the traditional track of exporting processed resources. It heralded the rise of the **world factory**: proliferating manufacturing export platforms producing world, rather than national, products. Often, the production steps are separated and distributed among geographically dispersed sites in assembly-line fashion, producing and assembling a completed product. World products—including automobiles, cell phones, computers, jeans, or electronic toys—emerge from a single site or a global assembly line of multiple sites (commodity chains) organizing disparate labor forces of varying skill, cost, and function.[7]

The phenomenal growth of export manufacturing using labor-intensive methods in the East Asian region, as well as regions such as Mexico's border-industrial zone, signaled the rise of *a global production system*. In Asia, the stimulus came from the relocation of the Japanese industrial model of hierarchical subcontracting arrangements to sites across the region. The Mexican Border Industrialization Program (BIP) paralleled this "decentralization" of industrial production, importing unfinished components to this new industrial enclave for assembly as a world market product. In 1965, the Mexican government implemented the BIP to allow entirely foreign-owned corporations to establish labor-intensive assembly plants (known as *maquiladoras*) within a twelve-mile strip south of the border. Concessions to firms employing Mexican labor at a fraction of U.S. wages and paying minimal taxes and import duties to the Mexican government were part of a competitive world factory strategy. In 1967, the Mexican minister of commerce stated, "Our idea is to offer an alternative to Hong Kong, Japan, and Puerto Rico for free enterprise."[8] The *maquiladoras* have earned about one-third of Mexico's scarce foreign currency income.

U.S. firms establishing assembly plants in the BIP concentrated on garments, electronics, and toys. By the early 1970s, 70 percent of the operations were in electronics, following a global trend of U.S. firms relocating electronic assembly operations to southern Europe, South Korea, Taiwan, and Mexico, seeking low-cost labor in response to Japanese penetration of the transistor radio and television market. The 168 electronics plants established by 1973 on the Mexican border belonged to firms such as General Electric, Fairchild, Litton Industries, Texas Instruments, Zenith, RCA, Motorola, Bendix, and National Semiconductor. There were also 108 garment shops, sewing swimsuits, shirts, golf bags, and undergarments; some subsidiaries of large companies such as Levi Strauss; and other small sweatshops (unregulated workplaces) subcontracted by the large retailers.[9]

The cost calculus driving the relocation of manufacturing to the Third World includes avoidance of stringent environmental regulations. Over a quarter of factory operators in the city of Mexicali, close to the California border, cited Mexico's lax environmental enforcement as a condition of relocation. The impact is both physical and environmental. Electronics factories commonly include open and toxic fume-emitting containers of carcinogenic acids and solvents; this results in chronic illness, such as headaches, sore throat, and drowsiness, among the workforce documented in the Mexican film *Maquilopolis*. Even with more stringent U.S. environmental regulation, California's Silicon Valley includes 29 sites listed on the Environmental Protection Agency's Superfund list of most contaminated toxic dumps—such environmental hazards accompany the proliferation of semiconductor manufacturing. Chemical discharges from *maquiladoras* into open ditches adjacent to shantytowns have been linked to cancer, birth defects, and brain damage, and factories in **export-processing zones (EPZs)** have been associated with the dumping of pollutants into local waters, affecting drinking water and fisheries.[10]

CASE STUDY   The Chinese World Factory

Looking ahead to the present, China has become perhaps the prime location for the "world factory." The government anticipated this development by establishing "special economic zones" (SEZs) in coastal regions in the 1980s to attract foreign investment. By the mid-1990s, when the East Asian NICs had emerged as "middle-income countries" with relatively high-skilled labor forces, China was the preferred site for foreign investors—especially Korean and Taiwanese investors, with rising labor costs at home. In 1995, the ratio of factory wages in China to South Korea/Taiwan to Japan was approximately 1:30:80.

In her investigations of shoe factories (such as Reebok and Nike) in Dongguan City, sociologist Anita Chan notes the vast concrete industrial estates mushrooming on former rice paddies. Local farmers live off the rents from the factories, while tens of thousands of migrants from China's poorer hinterland swell the low-wage workforce. Twelve-hour shifts—with enforced overtime—and seven-day workweeks are common, with managers using militaristic methods to break in and control the migrant labor force—in addition to requiring a deposit of two to four weeks' wages and confiscation of migrant ID cards. Between 1980 and 2001, 380,000 foreign-owned exporting plants were established in China, as the Chinese proportion of world exports from such plants grew from 1 percent to almost 50 percent, and China became synonymous with the "world factory."

Today China produces about half of the world's shoes and a proliferating array of electronic items, toys, and garments for the global economy. While this may appear to be China's "industrial revolution," to the extent that a substantial portion is export manufacturing, it is also a global industrial revolution. And, to the extent that this global industrial revolution depends on a moving belt of world factories (from Hong Kong to Mexico, to China, and now to Vietnam, India, and Bangladesh), including labor and capital-intensive work, the notion of a national "development ladder" is rendered increasingly problematic.

Even if some foreign manufacturers integrate with local firms, surpassing simple processing, how can we square such development with the human casualties from the sweatshops along the way?

Sources: Boyd (2006); Chan (1996: 20); Faison (1997: D4); Greider (2001); Myerson (1997); Perrons (2005); Sachs (2005).

The global proliferation of low-wage assembly marked the strategic use of export platforms chiefly in the Third World by competing TNCs from the United States, Europe, and Japan and, later, from some Third World countries. As these companies seek to reduce their production costs to enhance their global competitiveness, so export platforms have spread. Thus the NICs' strategy of export-oriented industrialization sparked the world factory phenomenon: from sweatshops in Los Angeles to subcontractors in Bangladesh, Ireland, Morocco, and the Caribbean.

The Strategic Role of Information Technologies

The world factory system is nourished by the technologies of the "information age." Especially important in the latest of these revolutions is the semiconductor industry. Semiconductors—notably the integrated computer chip—are the key to the new information technologies that undergird the accelerating globalization of economic relations. Advances in telecommunication technologies enable firms headquartered in global cities such as New York, London, or Tokyo to coordinate production tasks distributed across sites in several countries. Information technologies allow rapid circulation of production design blueprints among subsidiaries, instructing them in retooling their production to accommodate changing fashion or reorganize production methods in their offshore plants. Thus we find global assembly lines stretching from California's Silicon Valley or Scotland's Silicon Glen to assembly sites in Taiwan, Singapore, Malaysia, or Sri Lanka.[11] What appears to be an expansion of industrial exporting, from a national (accounting) perspective, is increasingly a globally organized production system. As participants in global assembly lines, national economic sites may specialize in producing just airplane wings, or automobile dashboards, or shoe soles, or buttonholes. Since export platforms are substitutable, nationally located production loses permanence.

How has this come about? Microelectronics. This was a leading industry in establishing the world factory, given the low skill in much electronic assembly and the dispersion of electronics *production* to export platforms across the world. In turn, high-tech electronic *products* such as computers and digital telecommunications technology enable the global dispersion and coordination of production and circulation in other industries, from banking to textiles to automobiles. Thus information technology globalizes the production of goods and services, in both senses. In particular, it has enabled the proliferation of EPZs.

The Export-Processing Zone

Export-processing zones, or free trade zones (FTZs), are specialized manufacturing export estates with minimal customs controls, and they are usually exempt from labor regulations and domestic taxes. EPZs serve firms seeking lower wages and Third World governments seeking capital investment and foreign currency to be earned from exports. The first EPZ appeared at Shannon, Ireland, in 1958; India established the first Third World EPZ in 1965 and, as early as the mid-1980s, roughly 1.8 million workers were employed in a total of 173 EPZs around the world. By 2006, there were 3,500 EPZs in 130 countries, employing 66 million workers (40 million of which were in China).[12]

The dynamics of EPZs contradict the economic nationalism of the development project in favoring export markets over domestic market development, which features local production capacity and consumption. Export-processing zones typically serve as *enclaves*—in social as well as economic terms. Often physically separate from the rest of the country, walled in with barbed wire, locked gates, and special security guards, EPZs are built to receive imported raw materials or components and to export the output directly by sea or air. Workers are bused in and out daily or live in the EPZ under a short-term labor contract. Inside the EPZ, whatever civil rights and working conditions exist in the society at large are usually denied to the workforce. As noted in 1983, "Free trade zones . . . mean more freedom for business and less freedom for people."[13] It is a workforce assembled under conditions analogous to those of early European industrialization, enhancing the profitability of modern, global corporations.

Export-processing zones provided an early portal for Third World women to enter the global workforce, just as English and American farm girls staffed the early textile mills. The new "factory girls" earned in one week approximately what their First World counterparts earned in one hour. In the early 1980s, 80–90 percent of zone workers were females between 16 and 25 years old. Women were regarded as best suited to the tasks because of their "natural patience" and "manual dexterity"—a personnel manager of a Taiwanese assembly plant claimed, "Young male workers are too restless and impatient to be doing monotonous work with no career value. If displeased, they sabotage the machines and even threaten the foreman. But girls, at most they cry a little."[14] Appealing to Orientalist stereotypes, a Malaysian investment brochure stated, "The manual dexterity of the oriental female is famous the world over. Her hands are small and she works fast with extreme care. Who, therefore, could be better qualified by nature and inheritance to contribute to the efficiency of a bench-assembly production

Figure 4.1   Number of EPZs by Selected Country, 2003

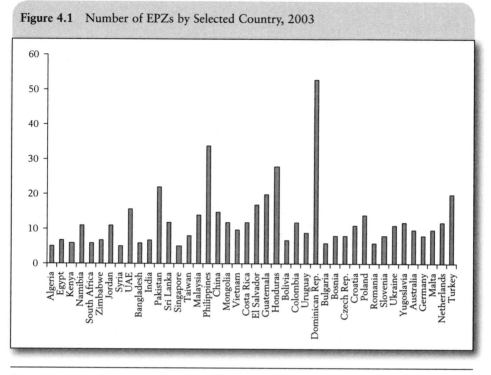

Source: International Labor Organization (ILO, 2003).

line than the oriental girl."[15] On balance, much of the world's now 27 million strong EPZ labor force has comprised women.[16] Between 1975 and 1995, garment production spawned 1.2 million jobs in Bangladesh, with women taking 80 percent—this imbalance has considerable impact on Islamic culture. In 1998, the International Labor Organization estimated 2,000 EPZs employed 27 million workers, 90 percent of whom were female. In Mexico, young women accounted for roughly 78 percent of the *maquiladora* workforce in 1979, some 85 percent in the mid-1990s, and 54 percent in 2004.[17] The shifting gender proportions of the labor force (here, "defeminization") mark the generalization of the *maquila* system throughout Mexico, at the point when the work upgraded beyond simple assembly; higher proportions of female workers occur in simple assembly zones such as Indonesia, Mauritius, Tunisia, Sri Lanka, and the Philippines.[18] The construction of global assembly work on the foundation of a feminized labor force remains a constant, as sweatshops cycle through countries in search of lower wages and appropriate locations. The absence of rights and regulations renders such labor vulnerable to super-exploitation, with employees often being forced to work overtime—sometimes up to 48 hours—to meet rush orders, under debilitating conditions (as in the film *China Blue*). The following description of a worker at an electronics *maquiladora* near Tijuana captures the conditions of sweatshop labor.

> Her job was to wind copper wire on to a spindle by hand. It was very small and there couldn't be any overlap, so she would get these terrible headaches. After a year, some of the companies gave a bonus, but most of the girls didn't last that long, and those that did had to get glasses to help their failing eyes. It's so bad that there is constant turnover.[19]

While sweatshops may register on some indicators of development, Raquel Grossman notes that retirement due to failing eyesight leaves such young women betwixt and between the factory culture and their previous life; many of these are compelled to work in the "entertainment industry," whether in bars and restaurants, or the sex trade.[20]

The foreign companies that employ EPZ workers obtain concessions, such as free trade for imports and exports, infrastructural support, tax exemptions, and locational convenience for re-export. For example, for *maquila* investment in Sonora, one of the poorest border states, the Mexican government's most favorable offer was 100 percent tax exemption for the first ten years and 50 percent for the next ten.[21] In short, the EPZ is typically an island in its host country, separated from domestic laws and contributing little to the host economy, other than mostly dead-end jobs and foreign currency earned via export taxes levied by host states. The EPZ belongs instead to an archipelago of production sites across the world—concentrated in Latin America, the Caribbean, and Asia—that serve world markets.

The Rise of the New International Division of Labor (NIDL)

The formation of a global labor force began during the development project. The effects of urban bias, agrarian class polarization accelerated by the green revolution, and cheap food imports combined to expel peasants from the land. From 1950 to 1997, the world's rural population decreased by some 25 percent, and now over half of the world's population dwells in and on the margins of sprawling cities.[22] European depeasantization was spread over several centuries, with the pressure on cities relieved through immigration to settlement colonies in the Americas and Australasia. But for Third World societies, this process has been compressed into a few generations, slightly longer for Latin America. Rural migrants overwhelm the cities, generating what has been termed a "planet of slums."[23]

Depeasantization does not by itself create a global labor force; it simply swells the ranks of displaced people lacking means of subsistence and needing wage work. Wage work for a global labor force stems from the *simplification* of First World manufacturing work and *relocation* of these routine tasks as low-cost jobs to form a global assembly line linking sites across the world.

Initially, First World mass production developed around large production runs using assembly lines of work subdivided into specialized tasks. Simplification *deskills* assembly work, anticipating the global assembly line. As the world factory emerged, such tasks as cutting, sewing, and stitching in the garment or footwear industries or assembly, machine tending, or etching in the electrical, automobile, or computer chip industries relocated to cheap labor regions. At the same time, the technologies to coordinate those tasks generated a need for new skilled labor, such as managerial, engineering, or design labor, tasks often retained in the First World. This produced a *bifurcation of the global labor force,* with skilled labor concentrating in the First World, and unskilled labor concentrating in the Third World. TNCs coordinated this bifurcation via their "internal" labor hierarchies as early as the 1970s, for example,

> Intel Corporation is located in the heart of California's "Silicon Valley." . . . When Intel's engineers develop a design for a new electronic circuit or process, technicians in the Santa Clara Valley, California plant will build, test, and redesign the product. When all is ready for production of the new item, however, it doesn't go to a California factory. Instead, it is air freighted to Intel's plant in Penang, Malaysia. There, Intel's Malaysian workers, almost all young women, assemble the components in a tedious process involving hand soldering of fiber-thin wire leads. Once assembled, the components are flown back to California, this time for final testing and/or integration into a larger end product. And, finally, they're off to market, either in the United States, Europe, or back across the Pacific to Japan.[24]

In the 1970s, the relocation of deskilled tasks to lower-wage regions of the world was so prevalent that the concept of a **new international division of labor (NIDL)** was coined to describe this development. NIDL referred to an apparent *decentralization of industrial production* from the First to the Third World. The conditions for this movement were defined as endless supplies of cheap Third World labor, the new technical possibility of separating and relocating deskilled manufacturing tasks offshore, and the rise of transport and informational technologies to allow coordination of global production systems.[25]

CASE STUDY   Gendering the Global Labor Force

"Endless supplies of cheap Third World labor" needs definition. Much labor-intensive work is feminized, depending on complex patriarchal and subcontracting hierarchies. Labor-intensive export platform industries prefer young, unmarried, and relatively educated women. While employers argue that women are suited to the jobs because of their dexterity and patience, these qualities are required as much by the jobs themselves as by patriarchal assumptions and practices reproduced within the factories, sweatshops, and home work units. Job construction changes with conditions; as Laura Raynolds shows for Dominican Republic plantations—in times of recession unemployed men may displace women via the use of local patronage networks, with work regendered to reward masculine competition.

Women are typically subjected to long work-days and lower wages compared with men. High turnover, lack of union rights, sexual harassment, and poor health characterize the female workforce that has mushroomed across the Asian, Central American, and Middle Eastern regions. Under these conditions, patriarchal states—competing for foreign investment—encourage women to enter the workforce at the same time as the new female workforce may be under official (especially Islamic) scrutiny for loose morals, and governments withhold maternity benefits, child care, and education opportunities on the grounds that they are "secondary workers" in a male-dominated labor market. Rural families propel—and sometimes sell—their teenage girls into labor contracts, viewing their employment as a daughterly duty or a much-needed source of income. Fuentes and Ehrenreich quote Cynthia Enloe: "the emphasis on family is absolutely crucial to management strategy. Even recruitment is a family process. Women don't just go out independently to find jobs. . . . Discipline becomes a family matter since, in most cases, women turn their paychecks over to their parents. Factory life is, in general, constrained and defined by the family life cycle."

Where young women and children work in family production units (a widespread practice), subcontractors rely on patriarchal pressures to discipline the workers. In the workplace, teenage girls are often forced to take birth control pills to eliminate maternity leave and payments or are forced to have abortions if they get pregnant. Labor contractors and managers routinely demand sexual favors from young women for awarding jobs, giving rise to a "factory harem mentality." The endless nature of the supply of female labor comes from their short working life in many of these jobs—because of the eye-hand coordination of girls that peaks at age 16; the physical deterioration from low wages, poor health, and nutrition; the high turnover due to harassment; the steady experience of having the life sucked out of them by long working hours and no advancement in skills; and the steady stream of new cohorts of younger women to follow, whether from the countryside, the children of the working poor, or international traffickers in labor. These are the compelling conditions that enable a particular kind and scale of casual labor to form around the world to supply the brand owners the brands to sell to the insatiable global consumer.

What kind of development is realized through the manipulations of gender inequalities?

Sources: Agarwal (1988); Fernandez-Kelly (1983:129); Fuentes and Ehrenreich (1983); Kernaghan (1995); Ong (1997); Pyle (2001); Raynolds (2001).

With global bifurcation of labor skills, skilled labor became concentrated in the First World, extending to enterprising states such as the East Asian NICs (South Korea, Taiwan, Singapore, and Hong Kong), which used public investment to upgrade workforce skills. The upgrading was necessary as their wage levels were rising in relation to other countries hosting export production, such as Malaysia, Indonesia, and the Philippines. In 1975, if the hourly wage for electronics work in the United States was measured at 100, the relative value for equivalent work was 12 in Hong Kong and Singapore, 9 in Malaysia, 7 in Taiwan and South Korea, 6 in the Philippines, and 5 in Indonesia and Thailand.[26] This wage differentiation forced the East Asian NICs to upgrade their segment of the global labor force. What may appear as national development has specific world-historical origins.

East Asian countries improved their competitiveness by specializing in more sophisticated export manufacturing for First World markets, using skilled (more male) labor rather than semiskilled and unskilled labor. After upgrading their labor force, the NICs attracted skilled labor inputs as a regional growth strategy. As the skilled work came, these states became headquarters, or cores, of new regional divisions of labor patterned on the production hierarchy between Japan and its East and Southeast Asian neighbors.

By 1985, an East Asian division of labor developed in the semiconductor industry for U.S. firms through the upgrading of the production hierarchy. Final testing of semiconductors (capital-intensive labor involving computers with lasers) and circuit design centers were located in Hong Kong, Singapore, and Taiwan; wafer fabrication in Malaysia; and assembly in

Malaysia, Thailand, the Philippines, and Indonesia. In the 1970s, semiconductors were assembled in Southeast Asia and then flown back to the United States for testing and distribution, but by the 1980s Hong Kong imported semiconductors from South Korea and Malaysia to test them for re-export to the First World and for input in Hong Kong's fabled watch assembly industry.[27]

Patterns of global and regional sourcing have since mushroomed across the world, particularly under the stimulus of informatics. Firms establish subsidiaries offshore or extensive subcontracting arrangements in labor-intensive consumer goods industries such as garments, footwear, toys, household goods, and consumer electronics. The Nike Corporation produces most of its athletic shoes through subcontracting arrangements in South Korea, China, Indonesia, and Thailand; product design and sales promotion are reserved for its U.S. headquarters, where the firm "promotes the symbolic nature of the shoe and appropriates the greater share of the value resulting from its sales."[28] In these senses, the legacy of the world factory revolution has been an initial global bifurcation of labor skills—made increasingly complex by global subcontracting arrangements, as firms have entered into joint ventures to organize their supplies, reduce their costs, and position their final assembly operations for global and/or regional marketing.

From the NIDL to a Global Labor Force

The rise of global subcontracting transformed the tidy bifurcation of labor between the First World (skilled) and the Third World (unskilled labor), captured in the NIDL concept, into a *bifurcation of labor everywhere*. Why did this shift take place? First, it occurred because of skill upgrading by firms in the NICs. The second reason is that global subcontracting threatens (by relocation) organized labor in the First World, weakening some unions and casualizing some labor. Bifurcation is the separation of a core of relatively stable, well-paid work from a periphery of casual, low-cost labor, irrespective of location. We see it occurring in tertiary education, across and within institutions, where teaching is divided between tenured professors and part-time lecturers. This relationship has no particular geography, although its most dramatic division remains a North–South one.

Bifurcation encourages subcontracting, which often has a dark side in the exploitation commonly experienced by unprotected labor throughout the world. In 1999, the United Nations estimated there were about 20 million bonded laborers worldwide, with half that number in India. Similarly, the International Labor Organization estimates about 80 million children younger than age 14 work across the world in conditions hazardous to their

Figure 4.2   Percentage of Workforce Involved in Making Products, Provisions, and Services Exported From Selected EPZ Host Countries, 1994

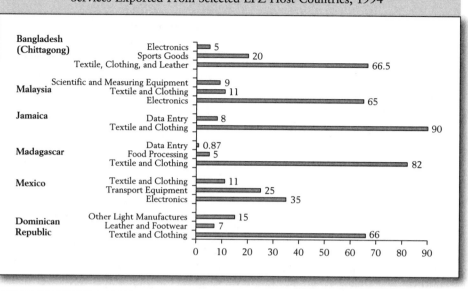

Sources: International Confederation of Free Trade Unions (1995, www.cftu.org); International Labor Organization (1995, www.ilo.org).

health—in farming, domestic labor, drug trafficking, fireworks manufacturing, fishing, brick making, carpet weaving, sex work, stone quarrying, and as soldiers. Many of these children work 14-hour days in crowded and unsafe workplaces.[29] Regardless of whether transnational corporations offer better conditions than local firms, the global subcontracting system severely weakens and/or eliminates regulation of employment conditions.

As firms restructure and embrace **lean production**, they may trim less-skilled jobs and fulfill them through subcontracting arrangements that rely on casual labor, often overseas. The U.S. automobile sector outsourced so much of its components production from the late 1970s that the percentage of its workforce belonging to unions fell from two-thirds to one-quarter by the mid-1990s. Not only did outsourcing bifurcate auto industry labor, but the expansion of this nonunion workforce also eroded wages, such that between 1975 and 1990, the low-wage workforce grew by 142 percent, from 17 to 40 percent of the automobile workforce. And for the U.S. workforce as a whole, industrial restructuring reduced real average weekly earnings by 18 percent from the mid-1970s to the mid-1990s. Meanwhile, union density fell from 25 to 14.5 percent across the period 1980 to 1995.[30]

First World **de-industrialization** occurred from 1970 to 1994: manufacturing employment fell 50 percent in Britain, 8 percent in the United States, 18 percent in France, and 17 percent in Germany, with many of these being "low-tech" jobs, such as footwear, textiles, and metals. In 1995 alone, the U.S. apparel industry lost 10 percent of its jobs; jobs lost in the fabrics industry accounted for 40 percent of manufacturing jobs lost that year. More than 50 percent of the U.S. clothing market is accounted for by cheap imports from Asia and Latin America. Around 65,300 U.S. footwear jobs disappeared in the 1980s—for example, Nike ceased making athletic shoes in the United States and relocated most of its production to South Korea and Indonesia. In the early 1990s, a worker—usually female—in the footwear industry in Indonesia earned $1.03 per day compared with an average wage in the U.S. footwear industry of $6.94 per *hour*.[31] The gap left by the relocation of manufacturing to the Third World has partially been filled by postindustrial work (retailing, health care, security, finance, restaurants), some of which is performed by migrant labor—creating cycles of ethnic tension during times of economic downturn. Temporary and part-time employment—accounting for one-third of U.S. employees in 1995—and multiple jobs have become a common pattern for low-skilled workers.

Manufacturing labor has lost considerable organizational, as well as numerical, power to corporate strategies of restructuring, leading to the qualitative restructuring of work. After a decade of conservative government restructuring of the British labor force (weakening union rights, eliminating minimum wages, reducing jobless benefits), Britain in the 1990s became a new site for offshore investment from Europe—mostly in part-time jobs (electronic assembly, apparel, clerical tasks) undertaken by women at considerably lower wages than would be paid in Europe.[32] Typically, "Third World" working conditions are just as likely to appear in the global North via the practice of lean production. Garment sweatshops are a recurring phenomenon—for example, in New York City—and a range of "Third World" jobs has spread in First World cities over the past two decades. In other words, the *global labor force*—including working conditions—is well entrenched everywhere, however tenuous.

Global integration habitually marginalizes people and their communities, as jobs are automated, shed, or relocated by corporations under global competitive pressures. Competition compels firms not only to go global but also to keep their sourcing flexible, and therefore their suppliers—and their workers—guessing. The women's wear retailer Liz Claiborne, which divides its sources mainly among the United States, Hong Kong, South Korea, Taiwan, the Philippines, China, and Brazil, claims, "The Company does not own any manufacturing facilities: all of its products are manufactured through arrangements with independent suppliers. . . . The Company does not have any long-term, formal arrangements with any of the suppliers which manufacture its products."[33] As the world market has been corporatized, firms that once organized paternalistic "company towns," have shed that responsibility as they have reached out to the more abstract (i.e., flexible and expendable) global labor force.

CASE STUDY   The Corporatization of World Markets

Export markets concentrate in the global North, where markets are much denser than Southern markets and consumer culture is well entrenched. Export, or world, markets are typically organized by TNCs. UN data reveal that transnational corporations account for two-thirds of world trade. Fifty of the largest 100 economies are run by TNCs—for instance, General Motors and Toyota are larger (by revenue) than Malaysia, Nigeria, Pakistan, Egypt, and Peru. TNCs control most of the world's financial transactions, (bio)technologies, and industrial capacity—including oil and its refining, coal, gas, hydroelectric and nuclear power plants, mineral extraction and processing, home electronics, chemicals, medicines, wood harvesting and processing, and more.

The top five TNCs in each major market (such as jet aircraft, automobiles, microprocessors, and grains) typically account for 40–70 percent of all world sales, with the 10 largest corporations in their field controlling 86 percent of telecommunications and 70 percent of the computer industry. UNCTAD in 2002 reported that sales by foreign subsidiaries were twice the value of world exports of goods and services, and that 60,000 TNCs owned over 820,000 subsidiaries, with about 45.5 million employees (compared with 17.5 million in 1982). The combined annual revenues of the 200 largest corporations exceeded those of the 182 states with 80 percent of the world's population. Corporate tax rates have declined significantly in most Northern states—from 30 to 7 percent of U.S. government funds since the early 1950s—shifting tax burdens to lotteries, personal income, and sales.

Most of the largest 350 TNCs are headquartered in France, Germany, Japan, the United Kingdom, and the United States, accounting for 70 percent of all transnational investment and about 50 percent of all the companies themselves. Walmart is now the largest corporation in the world and the largest importer of Chinese-made products, with more than 1 million nonunionized employees (three times the number of General Motors), a large proportion of whom are employed part-time with minimal benefits.

(Continued)

(Continued)

Under these circumstances of globalization, the framework and content of development appear to have been redefined—not as governments pursuing social equity for national citizens, but as corporations pursuing choice for the global consumer-citizen.

If the consumer-citizen represents at most two-fifths of the world's population, what kind of development (and globalization) do we have?

Sources: Alperovitz (2003: 15); Baird and McCaughan (1979: 135–136); Beams (1999); Brown (1993: 47); Daly and Logan (1989: 67); Ellwood (1993: 5; 2001: 55–63); Hightower (2002); Karliner (1997: 5); Korten (1995: 323); Martin and Schumann (1997: 12); Perrons (2005: 69); *The Economist* (July 16, 1994); Global Policy Forum (2011): http://www.globalpolicy.org/component/content/article/221/47176.html

As corporations shuffle the global employment deck, residents of the global North experience declining real wages (a trend since 1972), rising poverty rates, increased family stress and social disorder, rising public health care costs, and so on. The feminization of work involves lowering wages and job conditions and, in addition to declining social services, has overstressed mechanisms of social reproduction—for which women typically take most responsibility.[34] Proposed retraining schemes to help workers adjust to a shifting employment scene are often ineffectual, as most replacement jobs are low paid and low- or no-benefit service work.[35]

The loss of jobs is not simply an offshoring of production ("global sourcing"); it "hollows out" a nation's economic base and erodes social institutions that stabilize the conditions of employment and habitat associated with those jobs. A century of institution-building in labor markets, in corporate/union relations, and in communities can disappear overnight, when the winds of the market are allowed to blow across uneven national boundaries. Those who have work find they are often working longer hours to make ends meet, despite remarkable technological advances. Development has become a game of snakes and ladders.

Global Sourcing

Global sourcing is a strategy used by transnational corporations and host governments alike to improve their world market position and secure predictable supplies of inputs. Because of the formation of an infinitely available global labor force, firms reorganize marketing strategies to segment consumer markets. This means substituting flexible production for standardized mass production, using smaller and less specialized (multi-tasking) labor forces. In fact, flexible—or lean—production reorganizes mass production to segment or differentiate consumer markets, often endlessly: the sneaker industry is a clear example.

Figure 4.3 Comparison of the World's 25 Largest Corporations with GDPs of Selected Countries (2007)

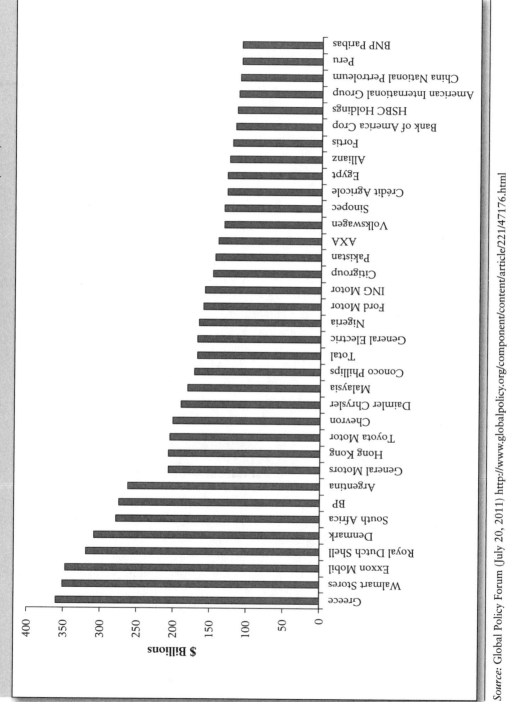

Source: Global Policy Forum (July 20, 2011) http://www.globalpolicy.org/component/content/article/221/47176.html

The size of market segments depends on social class incomes, corresponding to a considerable stratification of consumer products. With a global market, firms are increasingly under pressure to respond to changing consumer preferences as the life span of commodities declines (with rapidly changing fashion and/or technologies). Shifting consumer tastes require greater flexibility in firms' production runs, use of inputs, use of inventory, and selling strategies. In the 1980s, the Toyota Company introduced the just-in-time (JIT) system of "flexible mass production."[36] With JIT (via informatics), simultaneous engineering replaces the sequencing of mass production—the "just-in-case" system in which materials are produced on inflexible assembly lines to supply standardized consumer markets. By contrast, simultaneous engineering allows quicker changes in design and production, so firms can respond to volatile consumer markets.

The JIT system promotes both global *and* regional corporate strategies. Changing fashions favors subcontracting cheapened global labor forces. In more capital-intensive sectors, where automated technologies are less transferable, firms tend to invest in regional sites so they can respond quickly to local/regional market signals as fashions change.[37] The recent concentration of investment flows in the denser regions of the world market reflects this corporate strategy. Thus, countries such as Mexico and Malaysia become important investment sites precisely because of the new regional complexes of the North American Free Trade Agreement (NAFTA) and the Asia-Pacific Economic Cooperation (APEC). A current instance is the *Plan Puebla de Panama* complex: an industrial corridor linking the south of Mexico to Panama to mobilize the pool of displaced, cheap, indigenous labor to produce for North American markets.[38]

CASE STUDY   Global/Regional Strategy of a Southern Transnational Corporation

We tend to think of TNCs as Northern in origin. The Charoen Pokphand (CP) Group was formed in Bangkok in 1921 by two Chinese brothers to trade in farm inputs. In the 1960s, CP expanded into animal feed production, and from there to vertically integrated poultry production, providing inputs (chicks, feed, medicines, credit, extension services) to farmers and in turn processing and marketing poultry regionally in East Asia. In the 1980s, CP entered retailing, acquiring a Kentucky Fried Chicken (KFC) franchise for Thailand, and now controls about one-quarter of the Thai fast-food market as an outlet for its poultry, including 715 7-Eleven convenience stores. By the mid-1990s, CP was Thailand's largest TNC and Asia's largest agro-industrial conglomerate, with 100,000 employees in 20 countries. It was an early investor in China, establishing a feed mill in Shenzhen in 1979, in a joint venture with Continental Grain. In 1995, CP was operating 75 feed mills in 26 of China's 30 provinces; controlled the KFC franchise rights for China, operating in 13 cities; and its poultry operations accounted for 10 percent of China's broilers, producing 235 million day-old chicks per annum.

Today, CP has investments in fertilizers, pesticides and agro-chemicals, vehicles, tractors, supermarkets, baby foods, livestock operations in poultry and swine, milk processing, crop farming and processing, seed production, aquaculture, and jute-backed carpets, as well as in telecommunications, real estate, retailing, cement, and petrochemicals. CP produces poultry in Turkey, Vietnam, Cambodia, Malaysia, Indonesia, and the United States, as well as animal feed in Indonesia, India, and Vietnam. CP is now involved in shrimp farming, controlling 65 percent of the Thai market, and is the world's largest producer of farmed shrimp, with sites in Indonesia, Vietnam, China, and India, as Thai farms experience ecological stress.

When we see the extent of a TNC's concentration of power over regional or global economic activity, where is this kind of development going, and whose future does it serve?

Source: Goss et al. (2000).

Agricultural Globalization

With the food aid regime and the green revolution both incorporating Third World countries into international circuits of food and agribusiness technologies, the "**world farm**" emerged alongside the "**world factory**." In this process, many Third World country development profiles switched from a focus on modernizing agriculture as a domestic industry toward developing agriculture as a world industry. A second green revolution facilitated this switch.

As we saw in Chapter 3, beginning in the 1960s, the green revolution encouraged agribusiness in the production of wage foods for urban consumers in the Third World. Beyond that *national* project, agribusiness technology has spread from basic grains to other grains—especially feedstuffs—to livestock, and to horticultures of fresh fruits and vegetables. Further, agribusiness has created feed-grain substitutes such as cassava, corn gluten feed, and citrus pellets, and biotechnology is creating plant-derived "feedstocks" for the chemical industry. This kind of agriculture depends on hybrid seeds, chemical fertilizers, pesticides, animal antibiotics, and growth-inducing chemicals, specialty feeds, and, most recently, genetically modified plants. It is a specialized, high-input agriculture servicing high-value markets, in addition to food processing and agrochemical firms. It extends green revolution technology from basic to consumer foods and agro-industrial inputs, and has been termed the second **green revolution**.[39] A distinguishing feature is that whereas the first green revolution was a *public* initiative geared to *national* markets (for staples), its successor is a *private* initiative increasingly geared to *global* markets with dietary inequalities.

The second green revolution also contributes to the globalization of markets for high-value foods such as off-season fresh fruits and vegetables. This market is one of the most profitable for agribusinesses. As global markets have deepened and transport technologies have matured, "cool chains" maintain chilled temperatures for transporting fresh fruit and vegetables grown in the Third World to supermarket outlets across the world. U.S. firms such as Dole, Chiquita, and Del Monte moved beyond their traditional commodities such as bananas and pineapples into other fresh fruits and vegetables. By coordinating producers scattered across different climatic zones, these firms reduce the seasonality of fresh fruits and vegetables. Year-round produce availability is complemented with exotic fruits, vegetables, and salad greens.[40]

In this new division of world agricultural labor, transnational corporations typically subcontract with or hire smallholders to produce specialty horticultural crops and off-season fruits and vegetables for export processing (canning, freezing, gassing, boxing, juicing, and dicing) to supply expanding consumer markets located primarily in Europe, North America, and the Asia-Pacific. As the conversion of agriculture into a global, increasingly feminized industry proceeds, it impinges on women's livelihoods, their food security, and that of their families. Most food consumed across the world is produced by women, accounting for 30–40 percent in Latin America, 50–60 percent in Asia, and 80–90 percent in Sub-Saharan Africa.[41] Women's lack of security and rights in land means that commercialization easily erodes women's role in and control of food production. As small farming is destabilized, women must work in the agribusiness sector on plantations and in processing plants, as planters, pickers, and packers, feminizing the global agricultural labor force, and adding to women's workday, despite income benefits and associated "empowerment."

CASE STUDY   **Global Labor in Agriculture and the Question of Food Security**

The global fruit and vegetable industry depends on flexible contract labor arrangements. Coordination of multiple production sites, for a year-round supply of fresh produce, is achieved through information technologies. These supply chains disconnect producers and consumers with interesting consequences: consumers are ignorant of the conditions (especially gender inequities) under which their goods are produced, while producers increasingly grow food for distant consumers rather than for their own communities.

Deborah Barndt's research retraces the journey of the tomato from Mexico to the ubiquitous fast-food and retailing outlets of North America. Naming it "Tomasita," to underline its ethnic and gendered labor origins, she describes a plant of one of Mexico's largest agro-exporters, Santa Anita Packers, which in peak season employs more than 2,000 pickers and 700 packers. The improved seed varieties need heavy doses of pesticides, but health and safety education and the required protective gear are lacking. Perhaps a more visually striking indicator of monocultural production is the packing plant, employing hundreds of young women whom the company moves from one site to another as a kind of "mobile *maquiladora* . . . the only Mexican inputs are the land, the sun, and the workers. . . . The South has been the source of the seeds, while the North has the biotechnology to alter them . . . the workers who produce the tomatoes do not benefit. . . . They now travel most of the year—with little time to grow food on their own plots in their home communities . . . with this loss of control comes a spiritual loss, and a loss of a knowledge of seeds, of organic fertilizers and pesticides, of sustainable practices such as crop rotation or leaving the land fallow for a year—practices that had maintained the land for millennia."

The food security of northern consumers depends on Mexican food *in*security. Displaced *campesinas* (especially indigenous women) work in the *agromaquilas* or in North American orchards or plantations, earning in a day what takes a week to earn in Mexico.

What are the long-term consequence of a global food system that destabilizes peasant communities and exacerbates southern food dependency for no good reason other than profit and a year-round supply of tasteless tomatoes?

Source: Barndt (1997: 59–62).

The New Agricultural Countries (NACs)

As with manufacturing, agribusiness investments first concentrated in select Third World countries (e.g., Brazil, Mexico, Argentina, Chile, Hungary, and Thailand), known as the **new agricultural countries (NACs)**.[42] They were analogous to the NICs insofar as their governments promoted agro-industrialization for urban and export markets. As the development project has receded, agro-exporting has intensified. Such agro-exports have been called nontraditional exports (NTEs) because they either replace or supplement the traditional tropical exports of the colonial era. Nontraditional exports tend to be high-value foods such as animal protein products and fruits and vegetables, or low-value feed grains and biofuels.

Thailand's traditional role in the international division of labor as an exporter of rice, sugar, pineapples, and rubber is now complemented with an expanding array of nontraditional primary exports: cassava (feed), canned tuna, shrimp, poultry, processed meats, and fresh and processed fruits and vegetables. Former exports such as corn and sorghum are now mostly consumed domestically in the intensive livestock sector. Raw agricultural exports, which accounted for 80 percent of Thailand's exports in 1980, now represent 30 percent; processed food makes up 30 percent of manufactured exports. Thailand is a model NAC.[43] Viewed as "Asia's supermarket," Thailand expanded its food processing industry on a foundation of rural smallholders under contract to food processing firms. Food companies from Japan, Taiwan, the United States, and Europe use Thailand as a base for regional and global export-oriented production. For example, to promote poultry agro-exporting, the Thai government organized a complex of agribusinesses, farmers, and financial institutions with state ministries to promote export contracts, distributing land to landless farmers for contract growing and livestock farming.[44] The feed industry, coupled with low-cost labor, helped Thai poultry producers compete with their U.S. (and now Chinese) counterparts in the Japanese market. Thailand is the world's largest producer of farmed shrimp[45]—a symbol of how consumer affluence and the NAC phenomenon reproduce one another.

Just as the NICs served as platforms for global supply chains in manufacturing, so the NACs have served **global sourcing**. Three U.S. agribusiness firms have worldwide meat-packing operations, raising cattle, pigs, and poultry on feedstuffs supplied by their own subsidiaries. Cargill, headquartered in Minnesota, is the largest grain trader in the world, operating in 70 countries with more than 800 offices or plants and more than 70,000 employees. It has a joint venture with Nippon Meat Packers of Japan, called Sun Valley Thailand, from which it exports U.S. corn-fed poultry products to the Japanese market. ConAgra, headquartered in Nebraska, owns 56 companies and operates in 26 countries with 58,000 employees. It processes feed and animal protein products in the United States, Canada, Australia, Europe, the Far East, and Latin America. Tyson Foods, headquartered in Arkansas, runs a joint venture with the Japanese agribusiness firm C. Itoh, which produces poultry in Mexico, supplied with U.S. feedstuffs, for both local consumption and export to Japan.[46]

Second green revolution technologies, and nontraditional exporting, have reorganized agriculture across the world as a "world farm," serving the global market rather than the national project. Increasing quantities of fruits and vegetables are being grown under corporate contract by peasants and agricultural laborers around the world. The global fruit and salad bowl is seemingly bottomless. In an era when much of this production is organized by huge food companies and global supermarkets (e.g., Walmart, Tesco, Carrefour, Ahold) that subcontract with growers and sell in consumer markets across the world, growers face new conditions of work.

From the early 1990s, the average share of supermarkets in food retailing in much of South America and East Asia (other than China and Japan), Northern-Central Europe, and South Africa rose from roughly 10–20 percent (1990) to 50–60 percent by the early 2000s. By comparison, supermarkets had a 70–80 percent share in food retail in the United States, United Kingdom, and France in 2005. A "second wave" spread to parts of Southeast Asia, Central America, and Mexico, and Southern-Central Europe, where supermarket shares of food retailing rose from 5–10 percent in 1990 to 30–50 percent by the early 2000s. A "third wave," reaching 10–20 percent of food retailing by 2003, occurred in parts of Africa (especially Kenya), the remaining parts of Central and South America, and Southeast Asia, as well as China, India, and Russia—these last three being the current frontrunner destinations.[47]

As discussed in Chapter 2, New World farmers (in the Caribbean and the Americas) and non-Europeans (Asians and Africans) have been producing specialized agricultural products for export for some time, but the scale and profitability of export food production have expanded greatly in recent decades as the number and concentration of world consumers have grown, carefully nurtured nowadays by global supermarket chains. This means that the producers must meet high, and increasingly privatized (i.e., corporate), standards of quality and consistency for marketing purposes. Contract farmers, mostly women, are thus vulnerable to changing standards of competition. On agro-industrial estates, women are considered more reliable and attentive as workers than men; and are trained to monitor plant health and growth and to handle fruit and work efficiently. Employers

presume women are more suited to the seasonal and intermittent employ-
ments (e.g., harvesting, processing, and packing) necessary for flexibility.[48]

Global Finance

The globalization of finance accompanies the deepening of transnational
production and consumption relationships. Transnational banks (TNBs)
formed in the 1970s via a burgeoning *offshore capital market*. The TNBs
were banks with deposits outside the jurisdiction or control of any
government, usually in tax havens in places such as Switzerland, the
Bahamas, or the Cayman Islands. TNBs made massive loans from these
deposits to Third World governments throughout the 1970s.[49] To understand
why this financial globalization occurred, we need to look at the duality of
the Bretton Woods system, where *national* economic growth depended on
the *international* circulation of American dollars.

Bretton Woods maintained stable exchanges of currency between trading
states. Fixed currency exchanges stabilized domestic interest rates and,
therefore, national economies. Governments could thus implement macroeconomic policy "without interference from the ebb and flow of international capital movements or flights of hot money," said John Maynard
Keynes, the architect of the postwar world economic order.[50] Within this
stable monetary framework, Third World countries pursued development
programs with some predictability.

The Offshore Money Market

Foreign aid and investment underwrote national economic growth during the 1950s and 1960s, breeding a growing offshore dollar market (that
was accessed also by the Soviet Union). This was the Eurocurrency market,
initially centered in London's financial district. Depositing earnings in this
market, TNCs evaded Bretton Woods currency stabilizing controls on
cross-border movements of capital.

Eurodollar deposits ballooned as U.S. military and economic spending
expanded abroad during the Vietnam War. As overseas dollar holdings
dwarfed U.S. gold reserves, they became a U.S. liability if cashed in for gold.
President Nixon avoided this catastrophe by declaring the dollar noncon-
vertible in 1971—ending the gold-dollar standard by which all currencies
were *fixed* to a gold value through the U.S. dollar. From then on, national
currencies would *float* in relative value (but with the dollar as the dominant
reserve currency). At the same time, the United States liberalized international financial relations (against European and Japanese wishes). Removal

of exchange controls protected the autonomy of U.S. policy, separating it from offshore financial claims. Floating exchange rates allowed the United States to shift the adjustment problems of its large deficits on to other investors and states via their speculative purchases of dollars or American assets, or revaluation of their own currencies.

The deregulation of the international financial system signaled a change in the balance of forces. *Internationally,* U.S. power was waning as rival economies emerged, and financial deficits from the Vietnam war and overseas corporate investments mounted. *Domestically,* conservative forces— including an increasingly coherent neoliberal coalition—and multinational corporate interests favored financial liberalization—to reassert U.S. power in the post–Bretton Woods era.[51]

Deregulation introduced an era of uncontrolled—and heightened—capital mobility as currency speculators bought and sold national currencies. Financial markets, rather than trade, began to determine currency values, and speculation on floating currencies destabilized national finances. By the early 1990s, world financial markets traded roughly $1 trillion daily in various currencies, all beyond the control of national governments.[52] The loss of currency control by governments threatens their political-economic sovereignty, meaning financial, rather than social, priorities discipline policy content.

Banking on Development

Fueled by the 1973 spike in oil prices engineered by the Organization of the Petroleum Exporting Countries (OPEC), the offshore capital market grew from $315 billion in 1973 to $2,055 billion in 1982. The seven largest U.S. banks saw their overseas profits climb from 22 to 60 percent of their total profits in the same time period.[53] By the end of the 1970s, trade in foreign exchange was more than 11 times the value of world commodity trade. The instability of currencies, and therefore of profitability conditions, forced TNCs to diversify their global operations to reduce their risk.[54] In this way, the financial revolution, combined with a flood of petrodollars, consolidated *a global production system.* With the First World in an oil price-induced recession, global banks turned to Third World governments, eager to borrow and considered unlikely to default. By encouraging massive borrowing, the banks brokered the 1970s expansion in the middle-income Third World countries, now the world-economic growth engine.

In the early 1970s, bank loans accounted for only 13 percent of Third World debt, while multilateral loans made up more than 33 percent. At the end of the decade, the composition of these figures had reversed, with banks holding about 60 percent of the debt.[55] The departures from the original development model are summarized in the following box.

DEPARTURES FROM THE DEVELOPMENT MODEL IN THE 1970S

The 1970s was a decade of transition, as the development project unwound. First, financial deregulation challenged national sovereignty by opening national markets to cross-border capital flows, destabilizing macroeconomic planning. Second, unregulated private bank lending displaced official, multilateral lending to Third World states, but such debt financing was unsound—too much money was lent on the assumption that countries could not go bankrupt. When the debt crisis hit, austerity measures undid many of the gains of the development project. Third, TNCs produced more and more manufactured goods and agricultural products for world, rather than domestic, markets. Fourth, by the 1980s, the discourse switched to "world market participation" as the key to development.

Willing private lenders represented a golden opportunity for Third World states to exercise some autonomy from the official financial community. By 1984, all nine of the largest U.S. banks were lending more than 100 percent of their shareholders' equity in loans to Mexico, Brazil, Argentina, and Venezuela, while Lloyds of London lent a staggering 165 percent of its capital to such countries.[56]

Loans typically served several functions. Political elites sought to legitimize rule with grand public development projects represented in nationalist terms, to strengthen their militaries, and to enrich their patronage networks with lucrative contracts resulting from loans. In Brazil, between 1964 and 1985, a string of military generals pursued the characteristic Latin American nationalist model, using loans to build the public sector in steel, energy, and raw material production. With debt financing, Brazil transformed itself from a country earning 70 percent of its export revenue from one commodity—coffee—into a major producer and exporter of a multiplicity of industrial goods—including steel, aluminum, petrochemicals, cement, glass, armaments, and aircraft—and processed foodstuffs such as orange juice and soybean meal. Rio de Janeiro and São Paulo have new subway systems, railroads take ore from huge mines deep in the interior to new ports, and major cities are linked by a modern telecommunications network.[57]

Between 1976 and 1984, the rise in public foreign debt roughly matched a parallel outflow of private capital to banks in New York, the Cayman Islands, and other financial havens.[58] The composition of Latin American borrowing shifted dramatically between the 1960s and the late 1970s, as official loans fell from 40 to 12 percent, private foreign direct investment fell from 34 to 16 percent, and foreign bank and bond financing rose from 7 to 65 percent.[59] Between 1970 and 1982, the average share of gross domestic investment in the public sector of 12 Latin American countries rose from 32 to 50 percent. State managers borrowed heavily to finance the expansion of public enterprise, sometimes as a counterweight to the foreign investor presence in these economies.

During the 1970s, public foreign debt grew twice as fast as private foreign debt in Latin America. By 1978, foreign loans financed 43 percent of the Mexican government's budget deficit and 87 percent of state-owned companies. As public foreign debt grew in the Third World, regimes reached beyond the ideals of the development project, borrowing to enrich their patronage networks, strengthen power through militarization or grand projects, or simply make up lost ground. During the 1970s, state enterprises across the Third World enlarged their share of the gross domestic product (GDP) by almost 50 percent. Because it was so uncontrolled, *debt financing inflated the foundations of the development state.* The ensuing debt crisis deepened the vulnerability of Third World development states to banks and multilateral managers, who appeared on the scene in the 1980s.

CASE STUDY   Containment and Corruption—Incubating the Debt Crisis

Assigning blame for the debt crisis is complicated. Certainly the old colonial tactic of surrogate rule died hard—for much of the development era, military control was the rule rather than the exception in the Third World, where the West bankrolled dictators as client regimes in the Cold War. Powerful military leaders, such as Ferdinand Marcos of the Philippines, Chile's Augusto Pinochet, and Iraq's Saddam Hussein, ruled through fear as they squandered the national patrimony. An estimated 20 percent of loans by non-oil-exporting countries went to imports of military hardware—in essence, militarizing the development project.

In the Congo, the CIA helped bring President Mobutu to power in 1965 for a rapacious 31-year rule. Mobutu renamed his country Zaire, authenticating his rule in African nationalist terms, but he traded away Zaire's vast natural resources, including a quarter of the world's copper and half its cobalt, for bank

(Continued)

(Continued)

loans totaling billions of dollars and half of U.S. aid to Sub-Saharan African in the late 1970s. From the spoils, he stashed $4 billion by the mid-1980s, in addition to a dozen European estates to which he traveled on chartered Concorde flights. Under his rule, Zaire gained 500 British double-decker buses, the world's largest supermarket, and an unwanted steelworks. After the president was deposed in 1996, Mobutu's family inherited his fortune, and the country inherited his $12 billion debt.

Two years later, when General Suharto was forced to resign, his severance pay was estimated at $15 billion—13 percent of Indonesia's debt—owed mostly to the World Bank. During Suharto's dictatorship of 30 years, the World Bank loaned more than $30 billion, some of which went into constructive literacy programs, while more than $630 million underwrote the regime's infamous "transmigration" program to colonize the archipelago, including massacres in East Timor. In 1997, a secret World Bank memorandum from Jakarta disclosed a monumental development scandal: that "at least 20 to 30 percent" of the Bank's loans "are diverted through informal payments to GOI [Government of Indonesia] staff and politicians."

If Cold War containment encouraged military rule and corruption was rife, how did it serve development, and why should the burden of debt repayment be borne disproportionately by the citizen-subjects of these Third World states?

Sources: Pilger (2002: 19–20); Roodman (2001: 5–6, 27).

SUMMARY

This chapter has examined the emergence of a global production system. Specialization in the world economy, rather than replication of economic activities within a national framework, has emerged as the new criterion of "development." NICs and NACs have served increasingly as export platforms for TNCs, which bring technologies of flexible manufacturing and the second green revolution, respectively. As a result, the "world factory" and the "world farm" phenomena have proliferated across the Third World, producing world products for the global consumer class. As jobs have relocated from First World factories to Third World EPZs, a process of labor casualization has occurred, as organized labor in the former has been forced to yield to the competitive low-cost and unorganized labor of the latter, via the exploitation of information technology by TNCs. The formation of a global labor force has involved political decisions that unravel the social compact with First World labor, and cycle Third World labor into sweatshops. Women predominate in the low-skill, low-paid jobs, but "defeminization" occurs as labor organizes, wages rise, and/or industrial upgrading takes place in the NICs and their immediate followers. This patterning represents a transition between state-managed national economic growth in the development project and the international market networks anticipating the globalization project.

In effect, a new global economy was emerging, beyond trade among national economies. Global financial organization mapped on to global production systems emerging via Third World export strategies. Offshore money markets redistributed private capital to governments as loans, and transnational corporations invested in export production. A frenzy of development initiatives ensued, as Third World states sought to emulate the NICs. Public investments complemented and underwrote private enterprise, nevertheless rendering states vulnerable to a debt crisis. As we shall see in the following chapter, when credit dried up in the 1980s, the debt crisis reversed the original reliance on the development state, laying the foundations for the globalization project.

FURTHER READING

Bonnano, Alessandro, Lawrence Busch, William Friedland, Lourdes Gouveia, and Enzo Mingione, eds. *From Columbus to ConAgra: The Globalization of Agriculture and Food.* Lawrence: University Press of Kansas, 1994.

Gereffi, Gary, and Miguel Korzeniewicz, eds. *Commodity Chains and Global Capitalism.* Westport, CT: Praeger, 1994.

Hoogvelt, Ankie. *Globalization and the Postcolonial World: The New Political Economy of Development.* London: Macmillan, 1987.

Nash, June, and Maria Patricia Fernández-Kelly, eds. *Women, Men, and the International Division of Labor.* Albany: State University of New York Press, 1983.

Sklair, Leslie. *Assembling for Development: The Maquila Industry in Mexico and the United States.* Boston: Unwin Hyman, 1989.

SELECT WEBSITES

Gender Equality and Development (UNESCO): www.unesco.org/shs/gender

Global Policy Forum: http://www.globalpolicy.org/home.html

Institute for Agriculture and Trade Policy (USA): www.iatp.org/

International Labor Organization (UN): www.ilo.org/

Multinational Monitor (USA): www.multinationalmonitor.org

PART II

The Globalization Project
(1980s to 2000s)

5

Instituting the Globalization Project

The globalization project succeeded the development project—not because development is dead but because its coordinates have changed. Development, formerly a public project, was redefined as a private, global project. Why not just "globalization" (without the project)? Isn't globalization inevitable? Maybe so, but as a vehicle of development, it is sobering to realize that, despite the promise of prosperity with "free markets," material benefits are largely confined to only about two-fifths of the world's population. The remainder toil in highly exploitative work settings, or struggle to survive on marginal lands or urban slums, as markets capture resources for the global minority with purchasing power. To call it a project emphasizes the politics of globalization. Markets are neither natural nor free. They are institutional constructs, managed by powerful players, including international financial institutions, banks, corporations, states, and even nongovernmental organizations (NGOs). The distinctiveness of the globalization project is its political intervention to overcome the limits of the development project.

Intervention involved more than two decades of military and financial disciplining of Third World policies restricting foreign corporate access to Third World resources and markets, beginning, perhaps, with the installation of General Suharto in Indonesia (1965), as below. Within the Third World, export-oriented industrialization fueled economic growth, legitimizing a new "free market" model of development. Development, which had been defined as nationally managed economic growth, was redefined in the World Bank's *World Development Report 1980* as "participation in the world market."[1] The redefinition prepared the way for superseding economic nationalism and embracing globalization. *The global economy was emerging as the unit of development.*

Securing the Global Market Empire

In 1965, Indonesian President Sukarno and his brand of economic nationalism were overthrown in a bloody coup led by General Suharto. Declassified documents reveal that a 1964 British Foreign Office file called for the defense of Western interests in Southeast Asia because it is "a major producer of essential commodities. The region produces nearly 85 percent of the world's natural rubber, over 45 percent of the tin, 65 percent of the copra, and 23 percent of the chromium ore." Two years earlier, a CIA memo recorded an agreement between British Prime Minister Harold Macmillan and U.S. President John F. Kennedy to "liquidate president Sukarno, depending on the situation and available opportunities."[2]

Time-Life, Inc., sponsored a 1967 meeting in Geneva between General Suharto, his economic advisers, and corporate leaders representing "the major oil companies and banks, General Motors, Imperial Chemical Industries, British Leyland, British-American Tobacco, American Express, Siemens, Goodyear, the International Paper Corporation, and US Steel." With Ford Foundation help, General Suharto reformulated a development partnership with foreign investment. James Linen, president of Time-Life, Inc., expressed the *birth of this new global order* when he observed in his opening remarks, "We are here to create a new climate in which private enterprise and developing countries work together . . . for the greater profit of the free world. This world of international enterprise is more than governments. . . . It is the seamless web of enterprise, which has been shaping the global environment at revolutionary speed."[3]

These events marked a turning point, forging a new discourse of *global development partnership* between states and corporations. Intervention was consistent with U.S. President Eisenhower's containment policy articulated for that region in 1959:

> One of Japan's greatest opportunities for increased trade lies in a free and developing Southeast Asia. . . . The great need in one country is for raw materials, in the other country for manufactured goods. The two regions complement each other markedly. By strengthening Vietnam and helping insure the safety of the South Pacific and Southeast Asia, we gradually develop the great trade potential between this region . . . and highly industrialized Japan to the benefit of both.[4]

The war waged in Vietnam by a United States–led coalition during the next decade confirmed this policy, followed by strategic interventions in Chile, El Salvador, Nicaragua, Panama, Granada, and Iraq, as well as disbursements of military and economic aid to secure the perimeter of the "free world" and its resource empire. Militarization was critical, securing and prying open the Third World to an emerging project of global development orchestrated by the United States as the dominant power.

The Third World was unruly during this prelude to the globalization project. Between 1974 and 1980, national liberation forces came to power in 14 different Third World states, perhaps inspired by the Vietnamese resistance. The collusion among the members of the Organization of the Petroleum Exporting Countries (OPEC) in hiking oil prices in 1973 threatened economic stability in the West. Then in 1974 the Group of 77 (G-77) proposed to the UN a **New International Economic Order (NIEO)** involving reform of the world economic system to improve the position of Third World states in international trade and their access to technological and financial resources. The NIEO initiative offered a "dependency" perspective, namely, that First World structural power stunted Third World development. Despite exceeding the UN growth target of 5 percent growth per annum for the second development decade, economic and social indices showed that most Third World countries had not achieved the rising living standards promised by the development project. In 1974 the World Bank reported,

> It is now clear that more than a decade of rapid growth in underdeveloped countries has been of little or no benefit to perhaps a third of their population. Paradoxically, while growth policies have succeeded beyond the expectations of the first development decade, the very idea of aggregate growth as a social objective has increasingly been called into question.[5]

Algerian president Houari Boumedienne told the UN General Assembly in 1974,

> Inasmuch as [the old order] is maintained and consolidated and, therefore, thrives by virtue of a process which continually impoverishes the poor and enriches the rich, this economic order constitutes the major obstacle standing in the way of any hope of development and progress for all the countries of the Third World.[6]

The NIEO was a charter of economic rights and duties of states, designed to codify global reform along neo-Keynesian lines (public initiatives). Widely perceived as "the revolt of the Third World," the NIEO initiative was a culmination of collectivist politics growing out of the Non-Aligned Movement (NAM). But it was arguably a movement for reform at best, its prime movers being the presidents of Algeria, Iran, Mexico, and Venezuela— all oil-producing nations distinguished by their very recently acquired huge oil rents, as opposed to the impoverished "least developed countries" (LDCs) and the newly industrializing countries (NICs).[7] The Third World united front strategy unraveled—in large part because of growing divergence between middle-income and poorer states.

Coinciding with the NIEO episode was a strengthening of a First World core: the formation of the **Group of Seven (G-7)** states. The finance ministers of the United States, the United Kingdom, France, West Germany, Japan, Italy, and Canada held secret meetings annually, performing crisis management, including containing the NIEO and its politics of economic nationalism.[8] The debt regime of the 1980s provided the perfect opportunity.

The Debt Regime

The 1980s debt crisis instituted a new era of *global governance* in which individual national policies were subjected to external, rule-based procedures that strengthened the grip of the First World through the international financial institutions (the IMF and the World Bank). In other words, the debt crisis spawned a **debt regime**. The divisions in the Third World enabled global political and economic elites to argue that debt stress stemmed from failure to copy the NICs' strategy of export diversification in the world market.[9] Although represented as examples of market virtue—to justify neoliberal ideology—the NICs were in fact state-managed economies.

The debt crisis began in 1980 when the U.S. Federal Reserve Board moved to stem the fall in the dollar's value from its over-circulation in the 1970s lending binge—reducing dollar circulation with an aggressive monetarist policy.[10] The contraction of credit raised interest rates as banks competed for dwindling funds. Lending to Third World states slowed, and shorter terms were issued—hastening the day of reckoning on higher cost loans. Some borrowing continued, nevertheless—partly because of rising oil prices. Higher oil prices actually accounted for more than 25 percent of the total debt of the Third World.[11]

Third World debt totalled $1 trillion by 1986. Even though this amount was only half of the U.S. national debt in that year, it was significant because countries were devoting new loans entirely to servicing previous loans.[12] Unlike the United States, cushioned by the dollar standard (the *de facto* international reserve currency preferred by countries and traders),

Third World countries were unable to continue debt servicing—their dollar reserves lost value as real interest rates spiked, First World recession reduced consumption of Third World products, and Third World export revenues collapsed as primary export prices declined 17 percent relative to First World manufactured exports.[13]

The World Bank estimated the combined average annual negative effect of these "external" shocks in 1981–1982 to be 19.1 percent of GDP in Kenya, 14.3 percent in Tanzania, 18.9 percent in the Côte d'Ivoire, 8.3 percent in Brazil, 29 percent in Jamaica, and more than 10 percent in the Philippines.[14] Third World countries were suddenly mired in a *debt trap*: debt was choking their economies. To repay the interest (at least), they had to drastically curtail imports and drastically raise exports. But reducing imports of technology jeopardized growth. Expanding exports was problematic, as commodity prices were at the lowest in 40 years—a result of the expansion of commodity exports to reduce debt. The market alone could not solve these problems.

Debt Management

The chosen course of action was debt management. The Bretton Woods institutions were back in the driver's seat, even though 60 percent of Third World debt was with private banks. The IMF assumed a supervisory status, implementing Structural Adjustment Policies (SAPs) in the mid-1980s: a comprehensive restructuring of production priorities and government programs in a debtor country. Working with the World Bank and its structural adjustment loan (SAL), the IMF levied restructuring conditions on borrowers in return for loan rescheduling—demanding *policy restructuring*, whereby debtor states received austere prescriptions for political-economic reforms.

In 1989, the executive director of UNICEF, James P. Grant, observed,

> Today, the heaviest burden of a decade of frenzied borrowing is falling not on the military or on those with foreign bank accounts or on those who conceived the years of waste, but on the poor who are having to do without necessities, on the unemployed who are seeing the erosion of all that they have worked for, on the women who do not have enough food to maintain their health, on the infants whose minds and bodies are not growing properly because of untreated illnesses and malnutrition, and on the children who are being denied their only opportunity to go to school. . . . It is hardly too brutal an oversimplification to say that the rich got the loans and the poor got the debts.[15]

Under this regime, debt was defined as an individual liquidity problem (i.e., the shortage of foreign currency) rather than a systemic problem. That is, the debt managers blamed debtor policies rather than the financial system.

Mexico was the first "ticking bomb" in the global financial structure, with an $80 billion debt in 1982. Over 75 percent of this was owed to private banks. Mexican political forces were divided between a "bankers' alliance" and the "Cárdenas alliance"—representing a nationalist coalition rooted in the labor and peasant classes.[16] The outgoing president, José López Portillo, allied with the latter group, opposed debt management proposals by nationalizing the Mexican banking system and installing exchange controls against capital flight, shocking the international financial community when he declared in his outgoing speech,

> The financing plague is wreaking greater and greater havoc throughout the world. As in Medieval times, it is scourging country after country. It is transmitted by rats and its consequences are unemployment and poverty, industrial bankruptcy, and speculative enrichment. The remedy of the witch doctors is to deprive the patient of food and subject him to compulsory rest. Those who protest must be purged, and those who survive bear witness to their virtue before the doctors of obsolete and prepotent dogma and of blind hegemoniacal egoism.[17]

Portillo's conservative successor, Miguel de la Madrid, agreed to a bailout, in which the IMF put up $1.3 billion, foreign governments $2 billion, and the banks $5 billion in "involuntary loans." In 1986, Mexico was rewarded for resisting a regional effort to form a debtors' club.[18]

The Mexican bailout became a model. In other middle-income nations (e.g., Brazil, Thailand, Turkey) as in Mexico, development alliance constituencies—particularly ruling elites and middle classes benefiting from the original loans—used their power to shift repayment costs on to the working poor via austerity cuts in social services. As World Bank chief economist Stanley Fischer noted in 1989, "Most of the burden has been borne by wage earners in the debtor countries."[19]

Reversing the Development Project

As countries adopted debt regime rules and restructured their social economies, they reversed the development project, institutionalizing development as "participation in the world market," focusing on export intensification and "shrinking the state." Social protections evolved from line-item subsidies in national policies to the status of "emergency funds"—pioneered by the World Bank as "Social Funds" to soften the impact of austerity in the Caribbean, Latin America, and Africa. These "social safety nets," such as the Bolivian *Fondo de Emergencia Social* and the Egyptian Social Fund, were administered by NGOs through decentralized feeding and microcredit programs that often bypassed communities with the least resources to propose programs, and neglected gender differences.[20] In the meantime, rescheduling bought time for debt repayment, but it came at a heavy cost.

Adjustment measures included the following:

- drastic reduction of public spending (especially on social programs, including food subsidies);
- currency devaluation (inflating prices of imports and reduce export prices, to improve the balance of trade);
- export intensification (to earn foreign exchange);
- privatization of state enterprises (to "free" the market); and
- reduction of wages to attract foreign investors and reduce export prices.

Most of these measures fell hardest on the poorest and least powerful social classes—those dependent on wages and subsidies. While some businesses and export outfits prospered, poverty rates climbed. Governments saw their development alliances crumble with deindustrialization and shrinking funds for subsidizing urban constituencies.

In Mexico, the debt regime eliminated food subsidies for basic foods such as tortillas, bread, beans, and rehydrated milk. Malnourishment grew. Minimum wages fell 50 percent between 1983 and 1989, and purchasing power fell to two-thirds of the 1970 level. By 1990, the basic needs of 41 million Mexicans were unsatisfied, and 17 million lived in extreme poverty.[21] Meanwhile, manufacturing growth rates plummeted, from 1.9 in 1980–1982 to 0.1 in 1985–1988, depleting formal employment opportunities.[22] With state financial support, Mexico became a significant agro-exporter—by 1986, exporting to the United States more than $2 billion worth of fresh fruits, vegetables, and beef .[23]

In Africa, the severity of the debt burden meant that Tanzania, Sudan, and Zambia were using more than 100 percent of their export earnings to service debt in 1983. In Zambia, the ratio of debt to gross national product (GNP) increased from 16 to 56 percent in 1985. African economies were particularly vulnerable to falling commodity prices during the 1980s, individual commodities comprising 40–85 percent of export earnings. Thus African coffee exporters had to produce 30 percent more coffee to pay for one imported tractor and then produce more coffee to pay for the oil to run it.[24]

IMF/World Bank adjustment policies in Africa reduced food subsidies and public services, leading to urban demonstrations and riots in Tanzania, Ghana, Zambia, Morocco, Egypt, Tunisia, and Sudan. In Zambia, for

Figure 5.1 Locations of Riots against Austerity Programs

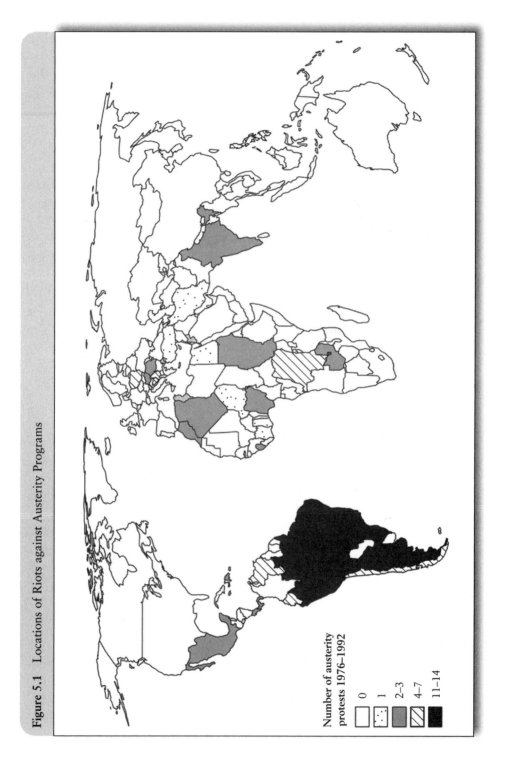

Number of austerity
protests 1976–1992

☐	0
⋯	1
▨	2–3
▨	4–7
■	11–14

example, the price of cornmeal—a staple—rose 120 percent in the mid-1980s following adjustment. Between 1980 and 1986, average per capita income declined by 10 percent, and unemployment almost tripled.[25] In effect, all the "development" indicators, including infant mortality, took a downturn under the impact of adjustment policies. The NGO Oxfam reported in 1993 that World Bank adjustment programs in Sub-Saharan Africa were largely responsible for reductions in public health spending and a 10 percent decline in primary school enrollment.[26]

CASE STUDY   **IMF Riots—Citizens Versus Structural Adjustment**

The so-called "IMF riots" swept across the Second and Third Worlds, representing the demise of the development project. Between 1976 and 1992, some 146 riots occurred in 39 of the approximately 80 debtor countries, including Romania, Poland, Yugoslavia, and Hungary. These large-scale, often coordinated, urban uprisings protested the public austerity measures, with rioters often breaking into food banks. The rioters contested the unequal distribution of the means of livelihood, targeting policies that eroded the social contract. Collapsing social entitlements included a range of subsidized services to members of hyperurbanized environments, including food, health care, education, transportation, and housing. Riots sought to restore basic mechanisms of social reproduction. They also targeted the IMF as the source of policies undermining national public capacity, and therefore, popular sovereignty. Björn Beckman claimed that the logic of the structural adjustment program was to "further weaken the motivation of the state to respond to the popular demands that have been built into the process of postcolonial state formation."

Given the profound transition underway across the structurally adjusted Third World, should this series of protests be understood as being about more than shrinking material resources—such as the shrinking democratic space, or even the demise of the promise of development?

Sources: Beckman (1992: 97); Kagarlitsky (1995: 217); Walton and Seddon (1994).

During the "lost decade" of the 1980s, the poorer regions of the world economy lost considerable ground. From 1978–1992, more than 70 countries undertook 566 stabilization and SAPs to manage their debt.[27] The debtor countries collective entered the 1990s with 61 percent more debt than they held in 1982.[28]

As a consequence of growing debt, many countries found themselves under greater scrutiny by global managers, in addition to surrendering greater amounts of their wealth to global agencies. The turning point was 1984. In that year, the direction of capital flows reversed—that is, the inflow of loan and investment capital into the former Third World was replaced by an *outflow* in the form of debt repayment (see Figure 5.2). The (net) extraction of financial resources from the Third World during the 1980s exceeded $400 billion.[29] The debt crisis opened up the Third World—now recategorized as the global South[30]—to Northern-imposed disciplines, foreign investment, and unsustainable export production to defray debt.

Challenging the Development State

As neoliberalism consolidated its orthodoxy in the 1980s, debt managers demanded a *shrinking* of states of the former Third World, through reductions in social spending and the **privatization** of state enterprises. As a condition of

Figure 5.2   Net Transfers of Long-Term Loans to Third World States

Source: UN, Human Development Report (1997: 64).

debt rescheduling, governments sold off their public assets. As a result, the average number of privatizations in this region of the world expanded tenfold across the decade. From 1986 to 1992, the proportion of World Bank SALs demanding privatization rose from 13 to 59 percent, and by 1992 more than 80 countries had privatized almost 7,000 public enterprises—mostly public services such as water, electricity, or telephones.[31]

Although there is no doubt that some development state elites had pursued excessive public financing, privatization accomplished two radical changes:

- It reduced public capacity in developmental planning and implementation, thereby privileging the corporate sector.
- It extended the reach of foreign ownership of assets in the global South—precisely the condition that governments had tried to overcome in the 1970s (see Figure 5.3).

Figure 5.3   Select Private Foreign Direct Investment Flows in the 1990s

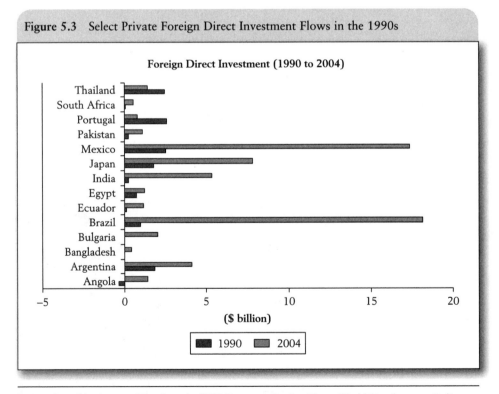

Source: http://devdata.worldbank.org/wdi2006/contents/Section6.htm, World Development Indicators 2006

Rather than losing the money they had loaned in such excessive amounts, banks earned vast profits on the order of 40 percent per annum on Third World investments alone.[32] Foreign investment in the Third World resumed between 1989 and 1992, increasing from $29 billion to $40 billion (especially in Mexico, China, Malaysia, Argentina, and Thailand).[33] The restructured global South was now quite profitable for private investment: wages were low, governments were not competing in the private capital markets, and an export boom in raw materials, manufactures, and foodstuffs was underway.

During the debt regime, the World Bank established local agencies (known as parastatals) to administer its SAPs. Structural adjustment loans (SALs) restructure national economies and redistribute power within the state—that is, privileging the central bank and trade and finance ministries over program-oriented ministries (social services, agriculture, education), and thus weakening the political coalitions and goals of the national development state.[34] This power shift removes resources from state agencies that support and regulate economic (e.g., import-substitution industrialization [ISI]) and social sectors affecting the majority of the citizenry, especially the poorer classes. These resources are shifted to the agencies more directly connected to global enterprise: global economic criteria override national social criteria (see Figure 5.4).

The World Bank's premise for the policy shift was that development states were overly bureaucratic and inefficient on one hand, and unresponsive to their citizenry on the other. In the Bank's Sub-Saharan Africa report, it reinterpreted "shrinking" the state to mean a reorganization of state administration to encourage popular initiatives. Some of these observations were credible, confirmed by authoritarian government, corruption, and "hollow" development financing—such as Zaire President Mobutu's lavish global–jet set lifestyle and Côte d'Ivoire President Félix Houphouët-Boigny's construction in his home village of a larger-than-life-size replica of St. Peter's basilica in the Vatican. Nevertheless, the solutions proposed and imposed by the Bank substituted growing external control of these countries in the name of financial orthodoxy.[35] Noting the revival of "trusteeship" in the 1990s, Jeffrey Sachs observed,

> Not unlike the days when the British Empire placed senior officials directly into the Egyptian and Ottoman finance ministries, the IMF is insinuated into the inner sanctums of nearly 75 developing-country governments around the world—countries with a combined population of some 1.4 billion. These governments rarely move without consulting the IMF staff, and when they do, they risk their lifelines to capital markets, foreign aid, and international respectability.[36]

When states become unaccountable, citizens may withdraw into a "shadow" economy and society, as illustrated in the Tanzanian case study.

Figure 5.4   Government Spending on Foreign Debt and Social Services (Selected Countries, 1995)

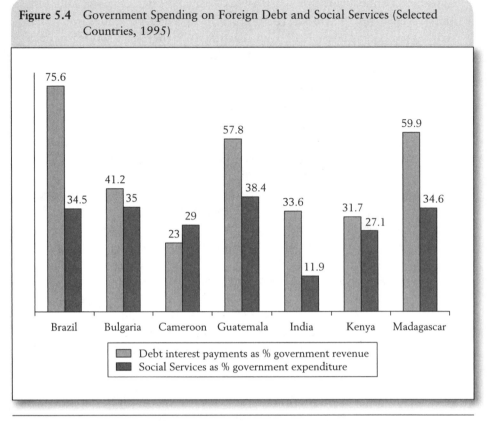

Source: World Bank, *World Development Report*, 1998–1999.

Note: Social Services includes health, education, social security, welfare, housing, and community services.

CASE STUDY   **Tanzanian Civil Society Absorbs Structural Adjustment**

Political democratization may be one outcome of urban grassroots resistance to their government's betrayal of the development alliance's social pact by implementing austerity measures. Another may involve depending on the "informal economy" as a survival strategy. Between 1974 and 1988, with real wages falling by 83 percent, Tanzanians intensified their income-generating activities "off the books"—with crop sales on parallel markets in the agricultural sector; sideline incomes for wage workers such as baking, carpentry, or tailoring; schoolchildren absenteeism so that children could work for family income; supplementary tutorials by school teachers; moonlighting physicians; and so forth. As Aili Maria Tripp remarks, austerity "was somewhat softened by the fact that more than 90 percent of household income was coming from informal businesses, primarily operated by women, children, and the elderly. By providing alternatives to the state's diminishing resource base, these strategies diverted demands that otherwise might have overwhelmed the state. . . . In the end, little was demanded of a state that had placed itself at the center of the nation's development agenda and had established itself as the guarantor of society's welfare."

Does this kind of self-organizing activity offer us a glimpse of an alternative, sustainable conception of development, or is it simply an intensified form of feminized social reproduction?

Sources: Rist (1997: 130–132); Tripp (1997: 3–6, 13).

In summary, the debt regime reformulated the terms of economic management, relocating power within states to open them up to growing influence over their policies by global agencies and markets. The World Bank and IMF programs of adjustment imposed standard rather than tailored remedies on indebted states. Governments and business elites in the former Third World countries often collaborated in this enterprise, being well placed to benefit from infusions of foreign capital, some of which is used for patronage. Meanwhile, the debt burden was and is still borne disproportionately by the poor.

The Globalization Project

Alongside the debt regime, during the 1980s the United States led an attempt to build a free market global consensus—focusing on breaking down the resistance of the Soviet empire (the Second World) to market capitalism. This was a central geopolitical strategy of the emerging globalization project.

As it happened, Eastern European countries, borrowing from the West to finance consumer items demanded by restive citizens, came under IMF supervision. By 1986 Soviet President Mikhail Gorbachev was formulating plans for *perestroika* (restructuring) in exchange for membership in the Bretton Woods institutions. IMF policies required replacement of central planning by "market-responsive" enterprises, and reduced food, transport, heating fuel, and housing subsidies (i.e., economic rights of the socialist systems). Social equality was redefined as the equality of private opportunity, which was exploited by former public officials, who enriched themselves as public property was privatized. Once the Soviet Union and empire fell in 1989, Western shock treatment methods were deployed, leading to a precipitous decline in Russian living standards and an explosion of organized crime. But the world was now unipolar—instead of the bipolarity of the Cold War era—and cleared for the globalization project proper.[37]

The key principle of the globalization project was the implementation of a free world market. The economic nationalism associated with the development project was viewed as limiting development because it obstructed the transnational mobility of goods, money, and firms in the service of efficient (i.e., private) allocation of global resources. As early as 1971, at the inception of the (corporate-based) World Economic Forum, its first publication declared, "Nationalism is economically indefensible."[38] The world market took its place, organized by TNCs (as opposed to states organizing national markets).

Representing TNCs are institutions such as the World Trade Organization (WTO) that have governed this global project. The founding director-general of the WTO, Renato Ruggiero, expressed this in the following way:

It is a new world. . . . The Cold War is over. Even more significant is the rise of the developing world as a major power in the international economy as a result of the shift to freer markets and open trade—an event that could rank with the industrial revolution in historical significance. All this is taking place against the backdrop of globalization—the linking together of countries at different levels of development by technology, information, and ideas, as well as by economics.

In this vision, the future of development lies with the world market, linked by the rules of neoclassical economic discourse. Ruggiero continued,

If we want real coherence in global policymaking and a comprehensive international agenda, then coordination has to come from the top, and it must be driven by elected leaders . . . progress in resolving the challenge of the new century will hinge on our ability not just to build a coherent global architecture, but to build a political constituency for globalization. . . . Without the WTO, we will go back to a world of national barriers, protectionism, economic nationalism, and conflict.[39]

In this way, he articulated the vision of the globalization project: the implementation of "market rule" via the restructuring of policies and standards across the nation-state system. The globalization project did not begin on any particular date, but it signifies a new way of thinking about development. Global management of capitalism emerged in the 1980s when the Bretton Woods institutions made explicit claims about *managing a global economy*, brought into being via the debt regime. Among the political and economic elites, a consensus emerged, redefining development in private terms as "trade not aid." Backed with the financial coercion of multilateral institutional debt management, it assumed the name of the **Washington Consensus**. Thus the globalization project was born.

With the advent of the globalization project, development did not disappear; rather, its meaning changed. Global elites reframed development as the deepening of markets (as resource allocators). The globalization project involved political choices to (re)define the bearings and future of states and their civic responsibilities. If competing in the world market requires policies of cutting public expenditures that may reduce safeguards and standards of employment, health care, and education, then globalization is a decision, not an inevitability. And it centers on "governance," which overrides and reformulates government.

Global Governance

In the shift from development to globalization projects, governments faced a world order in which global institutions assumed a more powerful governing role. This role is by no means absolute, and it requires compliance from the states themselves, guaranteed by consensus or coercion (which can backfire as the Arab Spring of 2011 demonstrated).

Ultimately, the most effective way of guaranteeing compliance is to institutionalize market rule, where individual governmental functions are recomposed as global governance functions and enforced through multilateral protocols. Indeed, at the first ministerial meeting of the WTO in December 1996, Director-General Ruggiero remarked that preparing a global investment treaty was similar to "writing the constitution of a single global economy." The debt regime was the prelude for this powerplay, and it had demonstratively political origins, as expressed in 1990 by the newly formed South Commission (an organ of the global South):

> What is abundantly clear is that the North has used the plight of developing countries to strengthen its dominance and its influence over the development paths of the South. . . . While adjustment is pressed on them, countries in the North with massive payments imbalances are immune from any pressure to

adjust, and free to follow policies that deepen the South's difficulties. *The most powerful countries in the North have become a de facto board of management for the world economy*, protecting their interests and imposing their will on the South. The governments of the South are then left to face the wrath, even the violence, of their own people, whose standards of living are being depressed for the sake of preserving the present patterns of operation of the world economy.[40]

In other words, the World Bank/IMF partnership in structurally adjusting particular states is a *method of governing* and an attempt to resolve instability in a deregulated global money market. Ongoing management of global financial relations has become a practical necessity to stabilize economies and open or "denationalize" them in the process, with support from the WTO.

CASE STUDY   **Mexican Sovereignty Exposed—From Above and Below**

Mexico's admission into the Organisation for Economic Co-operation and Development (OECD) via its participation in NAFTA precipitated the 1994 *Zapatista* uprising in Chiapas, a region of intensive resource extraction by foreign companies. Protesting President Salinas's decision, *Zapatista* spokesperson Subcomandante Marcos claimed it was a "death sentence for indigenous peoples." The *Zapatistas* declared, "When we rose up against a national government, we found that it did not exist. In reality we were up against great financial capital, against speculation and investment, which makes all decisions in Mexico, as well as in Europe, Asia, Africa, Oceania, the Americas—everywhere." Having questioned Mexican sovereignty, the uprising unsettled regional financial markets. The *Zapatistas* suggested that NAFTA was a confidence trick of the globalization project:

> At the end of 1994 the economic farce with which Salinas had deceived the Nation and the international economy exploded. The nation of money called the grand gentlemen of power and arrogance to dinner, and they did not hesitate in betraying the soil and sky in which they prospered with Mexican blood. The economic crisis awoke Mexicans from the sweet and stupifying dream of entry into the first world.

The Mexican *peso* lost 30 percent of its value in December 1994, generating a negative "tequila effect" throughout Latin American financial markets.

International financiers hastily assembled a financial loan package of $18 billion to stabilize the *peso*. The United States committed over $9 billion, while the European Central Banks provided $5 billion. Canada also contributed $1 billion, and a dozen global banks, including Citibank, added a $3 billion line of credit. Finally, the IMF was called in to lend both money *and* its stamp of approval to restore investor confidence in the Mexican economy. U.S. president Clinton remarked in 1995, "Mexico is sort of a bellwether for the rest of Latin America and developing countries throughout the world." Confidence in NAFTA was also at stake.

If the Mexican bailout was to stabilize the global economy and legitimize the globalization project, the question remains why Chiapas has been occupied by the Mexican federal army ever since. What is it about the globalization project that makes it value foreign investment over human rights?

Sources: Bradsher (1995: D6); Starr (2000).

Global circuits (of debt, money, investment, and pension funds) are so embedded in national economies (and vice versa) that stabilizing these destabilizing financial relations (as evidenced by domino-like financial crises: Asia in the late-1990s, Europe in the late 2000s) dominated national policy making. While adopted by countries (in varying fashion), governance protocols favoring open markets reflect requirements of, or conditions favored by, the **global managers**—officials of the international financial institutions of the IMF and the World Bank, G-7 political elites, executives of TNCs, and global bankers. Indebted states restructure their political-economic priorities to obtain creditworthiness in the eyes of the global financial community. An agro-export priority, which may negatively affect national food security, nonetheless conforms to the requirements of sound financial policy. It may enhance foreign exchange earnings for a time, but it reorients agriculture to supplying foreign consumers. Thus global governance essentially deepens global market relations within states, compromising their sovereignty and accountability to citizens.

Under these conditions, the World Bank, now the principal development (financing) agency, has played a definite governing role. It "dictate[s] legal and institutional change through its lending process" since its 1989 report, in which it asserted that governance evaluation in debtor countries is within its jurisdiction[41]—in spite of the fact that citizens do not elect the World Bank, nor the IMF, nor have they formally consented to WTO protocols, broadly termed "liberalization."

Liberalization and the Reformulation of Development

Liberalization downgrades the social goals of national development, while upgrading participation in the world economy through such means as tariff reduction, export promotion, financial deregulation, and relaxation of foreign investment rules. Together, these policies reformulate development as a global project—implemented through liberalized states incorporated into a world market constructed by transnational banks and firms, informatics, and multilateral institutions. While liberalization privileges a corporate development model, its proponents claim it facilitates capital transfer, competition, and trade expansion as methods of increasing economic growth and general well-being. As suggested in the following case study of Chile, liberalization is also realized through new forms of social inequality.

CASE STUDY | **Chile—The Original Model of Economic Liberalization**

Chile is perhaps the founding model of economic liberalization. A military coup in 1973 eliminated the democratically elected socialist president Salvador Allende, implementing detention, torture, and execution of thousands of Chileans as part of an eight-year period of debilitating authoritarian rule. General Augusto Pinochet pursued a radical free market reform, otherwise known as "shock treatment," masterminded by economists trained at the University of Chicago, a center of neoclassical economics. Over the next two decades, 600 of the country's state enterprises were sold; foreign investment expanded into strategic sectors such as steel, telecommunications, and airlines; trade protection dwindled; and the dependence of the Chilean gross domestic product (GDP) on trade grew from 35 percent in 1970 to 57.4 percent in 1990. In other words, *Chile was structurally adjusted before structural adjustment became fashionable.* Sergio Bitar, Allende's minister of mining, remarked that privatization was "the greatest diversion of public funds that has occurred in our history, without the consultation of public opinion or accountability to a congress."

Chile was one of the most democratic of Latin American nations prior to the assault on its parliamentary and civil institutions. Debt restructuring in the 1980s increased social polarization. Social spending continued to fall, wages were frozen, and the *peso* was seriously devalued. Deindustrialization set in, unemployment levels rose to between 20 and 30 percent, and real wages suffered a 20-percent reduction. Meanwhile, an export boom occurred, retiring debt and earning the Chilean experiment a reputation as a miracle. U.S. president George H. W. Bush declared in Chile in 1990, "You deserve your reputation as an economic model for other countries in the region and in the world. Your commitment to market-based solutions inspires the hemisphere."

By 1990, about 40 percent of the 13 million Chilean people were impoverished in a country once known for its substantial middle class. The pursuit of global efficiency had weakened the domestic fabric of social security and local production. In consequence, a sustained grassroots movement, centered in the *poblaciones* (slums) and active from the mid-1970s, succeeded in regaining elections in 1988, when Pinochet was defeated.

As the original laboratory for neoliberalization policies, what does the Chilean experience suggest about the construction of the globalization project?

Sources: Bello (1994: 42, 44–45, 59); Collins and Lear (1996: 157, 162); George (1988: 131–132); Schneider, quoted in Chomsky (1994: 184); Schneider (1995: 3, 194, 201).

Theoretical justification for the governing strategy of market opening/liberalization derives from nineteenth century English political economist David Ricardo's concept of **comparative advantage**—linking economic growth to optimizing trading advantage through economic specialization, reflecting a nation's relative resource endowments. The theorem stated that when countries exchange their most competitive products on the world market, national and international economic efficiency results.[42] This theorem contradicts the development project's ideal of a series of integrated national economies, while affirming the globalization project's focus on the global economy as the unit of development. But the theorem did not allow for capital mobility, which today is central to the construction of a corporate-based comparative advantage.

Even here, "capital mobility" is often leveraged by export credit agencies (ECAs), whose loans to Southern countries help finance and guarantee foreign investment by Northern corporations. The British ECA's goal is to "help exporters of UK goods and services to win business and UK firms to invest overseas by providing guarantees, insurance, and reinsurance against loss."[43] The U.S. ECA favors AT&T, Bechtel, Boeing, General Electric, and McDonnell Douglas. During the 1990s, development loans from ECAs averaged about twice the amount of the world's total development assistance.

Until the 1970s, "comparative advantage" represented a minority strand of economic thought, being out of step with mid-twentieth century social history. As the welfare state's wage and social program costs ate into profits, a corporate countermovement resuscitated neoclassical market theory, relegating Keynesian ideas of state intervention and public investment to the background. The political form of neoclassical economic theory, **neoliberalism**, took universal shape in welfare reform/reversal, wage erosion, relaxing trade controls, and privatization schemes—the underpinnings of the globalization project.

The doctrine of comparative advantage legitimizes the relationships between liberalization's downward pressure on social rights and its export regime. It is evident in the enlargement of the global labor force at the base of ubiquitous supply chains (foodstuffs, manufactures, services), and in the deepening of natural resource extraction. Where the latter threatens habitats, displaced peasants, fisherfolk, and forest dwellers join the swelling pool of labor, some of whom find work in export production. This doctrine, represented as the new development strategy for countries as they find their world market niche, has been interpreted as a *selective development* device, where local and global firms mobilize cheap land and labor for export production to provision distant consumers, thus: "millions of acres once used to feed poor families in poor countries are now used to grow kiwis, asparagus, strawberries, and baby carrots for upper-middle-class consumers who can now eat what was once the fare of kings—365 days a year."[44] The consequence is a selective realization of "high mass consumption," an expanding consumer class, and its "insatiable appetite for energy, private automobiles, building materials, household appliances, and other resource-intensive commodities."[45]

Under these circumstances, fueled by "freeing" markets to supply relatively cheap resources, commercial extraction of natural resources has intensified globally, threatening environments and resource regeneration. The close correlation between debt, export liberalization, and high rates of deforestation, as depicted in Figure 5.5, is well known.[46] In Chile, timber exports doubled in the 1980s, reaching beyond industrial plantations to the logging of natural forests. Chile's export boom overexploited the country's natural resources beyond their ability to regenerate.[47] In Ghana, the World Bank's African *model* of structural adjustment, the exports of mining, fishing, and timber products were accelerated to close the widening gap between cocoa exports and severely declining world prices of cocoa. From 1983 to 1988, timber exports increased from $16 million to $99 million, reducing Ghana's tropical forest to 25 percent of its original size.[48] The NGO Development GAP (Group for Alternative Policies) reported that deforestation, threatens household and national food security now and in the future. Seventy-five percent of Ghanaians depend on wild game to supplement their diet. Stripping the forest has led to sharp increases in malnutrition and disease. For women, the food, fuel, and medicines that they harvest from the forest provide critical resources, especially in the face of decreased food production, lower wages, and other economic shocks that threaten food security.[49]

After 70 countries underwent structural adjustment, the resulting glut of exports produced the lowest commodity prices seen on the world market since the 1930s. The NGO Oxfam calls this the "export-led collapse."[50] Across the world today, 20 million households produce coffee, but the overproduction has brought the price of beans to a 30-year low. For a $2.70 cup of coffee, farmers receive on average 2.3 cents, while the transnationals (such as Proctor & Gamble, Philip Morris, and Nestlé) receive around $1.33.[51]

Contrary to neoclassical theory, export reliance often puts regions in the global South at a *comparative disadvantage*. Liberalization substitutes reliance on the world market for self-reliance as the organizing principle of development. The flow of credit to debt-stressed nations typically depends on renunciation of national development norms, including public investment, protection of local producers, labor forces, communities, environments, the commons, and social entitlements. All of these norms are viewed as impediments to the market, which is why the globalization project begins with market liberalization as the path to "efficiency." The globalization project includes an explicit vision of global order, quite distinct from that of the era of the development project:

- In the development project era, the slogan was "Learn from, and catch up with, the West." Now, under comparative advantage, the slogan is "Find your niche in the global marketplace."
- While the development project held out *replication* as the key to national development, the project of globalization presents *specialization* as the path to economic prosperity.

But specialization in monoculture, or the global assembly line, does not alter the reality that the mechanisms of specialization—wage cutting, ecological homogenization, privatization, and reduction of social entitlements—are repeated everywhere, intensifying market competition. Short-term competition/efficiencies are sought at the long-term expense of the social contract and the environment. In theory, this may produce greater productivity, but at the cost of considerable and irreversible economic and social marginalization, impoverishment, environmental stress, and displacement.

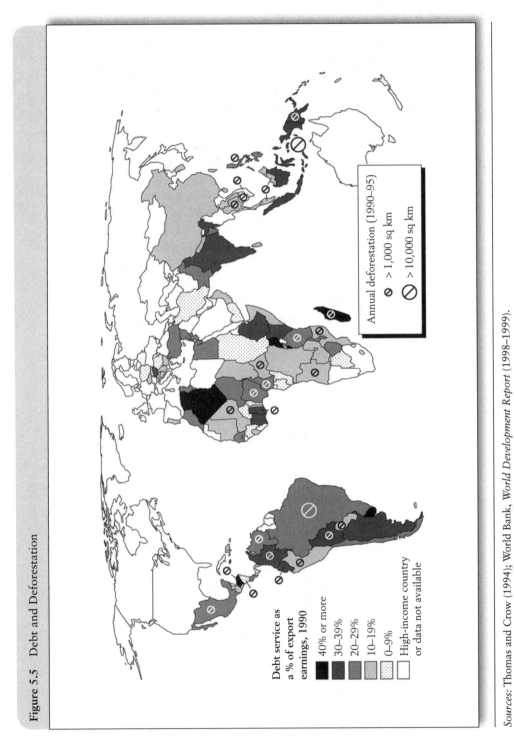

Figure 5.5 Debt and Deforestation

Annual deforestation (1990–95)

⊘ > 1,000 sq km

⊘ > 10,000 sq km

Debt service as
a % of export
earnings, 1990

40% or more
30–39%
20–29%
10–19%
0–9%
High-income country
or data not available

Sources: Thomas and Crow (1994); World Bank, *World Development Report* (1998–1999).

**NEOLIBERALISM DISPLACES
THE DEVELOPMENT STATE**

Sociologist Emir Sader (University of Sao Paulo) characterizes the shift from the development state model to neoliberalism: "The state was displaced by the market, workers and citizens by consumers, rights by competition, work and electoral documents by credit cards, public squares by shopping centres, human companionship by television, social policies by private corporate welfare, the national by the global, social integration by social exclusion, equality by discrimination, justice by inequality, solidarity by selfishness, humanism by consumerism, social parties and movements by NGOs and volunteer organizations."

Source: Sader (2009: 171).

The Making of a Free Trade Regime

The debt regime elevated the Bretton Woods institutions to a governance role, targeting the global South. From 1986 to 1994, the whole world became the target of the Uruguay Round of the General Agreement on Trade and Tariffs (GATT). The Uruguay Round was to establish a set of new and binding rules concerning free trade, freedom of investment, and protection of intellectual property rights. Once formulated, these rules framed the WTO.

The United States engineered the creation of the GATT in 1948 as an alternative to the International Trade Organization (which included provisions from the UN Declaration of Human Rights concerning full employment, working conditions, and social security).[52] Through GATT, trade expansion was *delinked from the social contract.* From 1948 through 1980, GATT reduced tariff rates on trade in manufactured goods by more than 75 percent.[53] Agriculture was excluded from the GATT. In the 1980s, at a time of recession and declining industrial leadership, the United States initiated the Uruguay Round, with the aim of liberalizing agriculture and services (such as banking, insurance, telecommunications), in which the North held a competitive advantage. Northern pressure and the promise of open markets for southern products, including agricultural goods, won acceptance from the South.[54]

The liberalization movement was supported by an activist lobby of "free trader" agro-exporting states (the Cairns Group), TNCs like IBM and American Express, and agribusinesses such as Cargill, Ralston-Purina,

General Mills, Continental Grain, RJR Nabisco, and ConAgra, looking to reduce trade barriers, domestic price supports, and supply-management policies restricting demand for farm inputs such as fertilizer and chemicals. Corporations produce and sell farm products across the world—they take advantage of seasonal variation and dietary variation. Alternatively, family farmers are spatially fixed and depend on national farm policy—input and price subsidies, farm credit, risk insurance, and import controls—for their economic viability.

Given the competitive dumping of surplus foods by the United States and Europe, depressing agricultural prices by 39 percent (1975–1989),[55] GATT proposed an "urgent need to bring more discipline and predictability to world agricultural trade."[56] Southern farm sectors were adversely affected by dumping, deepening food import dependency, especially in Sub-Saharan Africa. However, while liberalization was expected to stabilize markets, it has not stabilized farming in the global South, since markets are controlled by huge agribusiness corporations, which dictate prices at the expense of family farmers. The United States challenged GATT's Article XI food security provisions, arguing for comparative advantage:

> The U.S. has always maintained that self-sufficiency and food security are not one and the same. Food security—the ability to acquire the food you need when you need it—is best provided through a smooth-functioning world market.[57]

In short, the making of a free trade regime reconstructed "food security" as a market relation, privileging and protecting corporate agriculture and placing small farmers at a comparative disadvantage. Food security would now be "governed" through the market by corporate, rather than social, criteria.

The World Trade Organization

The singular achievement of the GATT Uruguay Round was the creation of the World Trade Organization (WTO) on January 1, 1995. The WTO, with over 150 voting members, assumes unprecedented power to enforce GATT provisions. It is unprecedented because, as discussed below, the WTO is arguably less about trade rule consistency than about governing member states via liberalization. *Free trade* is a misnomer for the reach of WTO rules. In combination, they challenge national democratic processes, removing decision making to nontransparent tribunals located in Geneva, Switzerland, using "market logic" to override individual government policy where it interferes with "free trade."

Unlike the GATT (a trade treaty only), the WTO has independent jurisdiction similar to the United Nations. That is, it has the power to enforce its rulings on member states, and these include rulings going beyond simply cross-border trade into the realm of "trade-related" issues. This means setting rules regarding the movement of goods, money, and productive facilities across borders—rules that restrict countries from enacting legislation or policies discriminating against such movement. WTO rules, in advancing trade freedoms, privilege corporate rights to compete internationally. This means ensuring that TNCs receive treatment equal to that received by domestic firms and reducing or removing local restrictions (e.g., labor, health, environmental laws) on trade and investment that might interfere with corporate competitiveness in the global marketplace. The WTO staff are unelected bureaucrats and its proceedings are secret, thus denying citizen participation in making and evaluating policy. In 1994, World Bank economist Herman Daly warned that establishing rules to override national governments' capacity to regulate commerce "is to wound fatally the major unit of community capable of carrying out any policies for the common good."[58]

The WTO has an *integrated dispute settlement* mechanism. If a state is perceived to be distorting trade obligations in one area, such as curbing investments in timber cutting to protect a forest, it can be disciplined through the application of sanctions against another area of economic activity, like some of its manufactured exports. Member states can lodge complaints through the WTO, whose decision holds automatically unless every member of the WTO votes to reverse it. Should states refuse to comply, the WTO can authorize the plaintiff to take unilateral action. Martin Khor, director of the Third World Network, suggests that, in claiming to reduce "trade-distorting" measures, the WTO becomes "development-distorting."[59] The very *threat* of such challenges has already had the effect also of diluting national laws protecting human and environmental health.

The WTO, in enforcing market freedoms, *depoliticizes* their profound social impact. Thus the 1996 Singapore Ministerial Declaration invites objection to labor rights laws: "We reject the use of labor standards for protectionist purposes, and agree that the comparative advantage of countries, particularly low-wage developing countries, must in no way be put into question."[60] And, as the outgoing director-general of GATT, Peter Sutherland, declared in 1994, "Governments should interfere in the conduct of trade as little as possible."[61] This implies a *general* challenge to national laws and regulations regarding the environment, health, preferential trade relations, social subsidies, labor legislation, and so on. While the challenge does not eliminate all laws, it seeks to *harmonize* regulation internationally, lowering the ceiling on democratic initiatives within the national polity. As we shall see, the goal of depoliticizing the economy can backfire, and this explains in large part the mushrooming global social justice movement.

In this sense, although implementation is uneven, the WTO expresses the essence of the globalization project. That is, global managers assume extraordinary powers to govern the web of global economic relations lying across nation-states, privileging corporate over democratic rights. We now examine four of the principal and mutually reinforcing protocols of the WTO: the Agreement on Agriculture (AoA), Trade-Related Investment Measures (TRIMs), Trade-Related Aspects of Intellectual Property Rights (TRIPs), and the General Agreement on Trade in Services (GATS).

The Agreement on Agriculture (AoA)

The 1995 Agreement on Agriculture advocated universal reductions in trade protection, farm subsidies, and government intervention. Many Southern farmers have been unable to recover the cost of their production in the face of a 30 percent or more collapse of world prices for farm goods in the first half-decade since the AoA was instituted.[62] Countries with the capacity to pay (the United States and European states) retained concealed subsidies, at the expense of much larger Southern farm populations who are threatened daily with imports (i.e., "dumping") of cheap farm commodities from the North.

With liberalization, farmers everywhere are under pressure to compete by selling cheap. Corporate farmers survive by subsidized "scale economy." Between 1998 and 1999, UK farm income fell by about 75 percent, driving 20,000 farmers out of business, and U.S. farm income declined by almost 50 percent between 1996 and 1999. In the global South, conservative estimates are that in the 1990s between 20 and 30 million people lost their land from the impact of AoA trade liberalization.[63]

CASE STUDY   **Global Comparative Disadvantage—The End of Farming as We Know It?**

A report from Public Citizen's *Global Trade Watch* documents the elimination of small farmers across the whole North American region as the legacy of NAFTA. While about 2 million Mexican *campesinos* have lost their maize farms to cheap and heavily subsidized corn exports from the North, U.S. farmers are also faced with an intensification of competitive imports from Mexico and Canada, replacing crops grown in the United States, such as fruit, vegetables, and other labor-intensive foodstuffs. Since 1994, some 33,000 U.S. farms with under $100,000 annual income have disappeared (six times the decline for 1988–1993). In Mexico, half of the rural population earns less than $1.40 a day (insufficient to feed themselves), with about 500 people leaving the countryside daily.

Policy changes such as these enhance agribusiness power. Public Citizen notes with respect to U.S. policy,

> Proponents of the legislation contended it would make farming more efficient and responsive to market forces; in reality it essentially handed the production of food to agribusiness. . . . Congress has had to appropriate emergency farm supports—in massive farm bailout bills—every year since the legislation went into effect.

But 56 percent of U.S. emergency taxpayer assistance went to the largest 10 percent of the farms. Once NAFTA opened Mexico to 100 percent foreign investor rights, Pillsbury's Green Giant subsidiary relocated its frozen food processing from California to Mexico to access cheap wages, minimal food safety standards, and zero tariffs on re-export to the United States. Cargill purchased a beef and chicken plant in Saltillo, and Cargill de Mexico invested nearly $200 million in vegetable oil refining and soybean processing in Tula. Anticipating continent-wide liberalization; Tyson Foods has operations in Mexico, Brazil, Argentina, and Venezuela; ConAgra processes oilseed in Argentina; Archer Daniels Midland crushes and refines oilseed, mills corn and flour, and bioengineers feeds in Mexico, Central America, and South America; and Walmart is in Mexico, Argentina, and Brazil. Public Citizen remarks,

> Multinational agribusinesses were positioned uniquely to take advantage of trade rules that force countries to accept agricultural imports regardless of their domestic supplies. The companies utilized their foreign holdings as export platforms to sell imported agriculture goods in the United States, and by thus increasing supply put negative pressures on U.S. agriculture prices.

When liberal policy and northern subsidies enable corporations to *construct* comparative advantages, rendering family/peasant farming "inefficient" and rural populations food insecure, how can "market-based allocation" retain credibility?

Sources: Davis (2006); Jordan and Sullivan (2003: 33); Public Citizen (2001: ii–iv, 10, 13, 16, 19–21).

Liberalization is evidently less about freeing trade than about consolidating a corporate food regime.[64] Through the AoA, the WTO institutionalized the private form of food security. Under the AoA, states no longer have the right to self-sufficiency as a national strategy. Rather, the minimum market access rule guarantees the "right to export" (therefore the requirement to import), even under conditions of subsidized exports. "Food security," then, is not food self-reliance but rather food import dependency for a large minority of southern states. By the mid-1990s, half of the foreign exchange of the 88 low-income food deficit countries went to food imports.[65]

In the absence of public capacity in the South, unprotected farmers are at a comparative disadvantage. In 2000, Oxfam asked, "How can a farmer earning US$230 a year (the average per capita income in LDCs [least developed countries]) compete with a farmer who enjoys a subsidy of US$20,000 a year (average subsidy in OECD countries)?"[66] In India, Devinder Sharma observes, "Whereas for small farmers the subsidies have been withdrawn, there is a lot of support now for agribusiness industry. . . . The result is that the good area under staple foods is now shifting to export crops, so we'll have to import staple food."[67] Forty percent of Kenya's children work on plantations, which export pineapple, coffee, tea, and sugar. While these foodstuffs supply European markets, 4 million Kenyans face starvation.[68]

Trade-Related Investment Measures (TRIMs)

The TRIMs effort is an attempt to reduce "performance requirements" imposed on foreign investment by host governments. Such requirements might include expecting a TNC to invest locally, hire locally, buy locally, and transfer technology as a quid pro quo for investment access.[69] The WTO uses TRIMs to manage the cross-border movement of goods and services production, especially—the WTO website explains—since trade follows investment, and a third of world trade in 1995 was internal to companies. The point of TRIMs is to secure investor rights, as if they have no political impact. One proponent argues, "The multinational corporate community would then be able to rationalize their regional and global sourcing strategies on the basis of productivity, quality, and cost considerations in place of the political dictates that now disrupt their operations."[70]

CASE STUDY   Evolving Corporate Property Rights

TRIMs laid the foundations for corporate property rights, allowing foreign investors to challenge a government for imposing "performance requirements." Under NAFTA's Chapter 11, corporations can bypass domestic courts and directly sue governments when municipal, state, or national legislation threatens their profits. Thus the U.S. Metalclad Corporation successfully sued Mexico over environmental protection. The municipality of Guadalacazar (San Luís Potosí state) had refused a construction permit to Metalclad to develop a toxic waste landfill in an ecologically protected zone. The company had secured a permit from the federal and state governments, but the municipal government stood firm, as it had with a Mexican owner of the site, and was required to compensate Metalclad to the tune of $16.6 million. Because of these extended rights in regional trade agreements, there is mounting pressure for a new WTO agreement that would extend TRIMs to allow corporations to sue governments for restriction of profits.

Why would states sign on to protocols that subvert their sovereign power and ability to represent their citizens?

Sources: McBride (2006); Wallach and Woodall (2004: 270).

The argument in favor of TRIMs is they reduce domestic content requirements that misallocate local resources, raise costs, penalize competitive investment, and burden consumers, in addition to slowing technological adoption, reducing quality, and retarding management practices.[71] In other words, the role of TRIMs is to enhance conditions for transnational investment by reducing the friction of local regulations. Greater freedom for investors under TRIMs is justified by evidence of "higher-than-average wages and benefits, advanced technology, and sophisticated managerial and marketing techniques," as well as a stronger "integration effect" with the local economy. It is exemplified in the Mexican auto industry, where parent firms invested in local supply firms for self-interest and not because of local content requirements, resulting in the creation of globally competitive Mexican auto part suppliers. Also, in the Malaysian semiconductor industry, an indigenous machine tool firm matured from supplying parts to foreign investors to supplying high-precision computer-numeric tools and factory automation equipment to international and domestic markets.[72] But the "integration effect" favors integration the other way: of local producers into the world market, rather than foreign investors integrating into a program of domestic industrialization.

Trade-Related Intellectual Property Rights (TRIPs)

The WTO website defines intellectual property rights as "rights given to persons over the creations of their minds. They usually give the creator an exclusive right over the use of his/her creation for a certain period of time." The TRIPs protocol was defined by a coalition of 12 major U.S. corporations, a Japanese federation of business organizations, and the agency for European business and industry. Based on a synthesis of European and U.S. patent laws, intellectual property rights protection is to be administered by the WTO. Advocates claim that it simplifies the protection of property rights across national borders and protects and promotes innovation for everyone by guaranteeing profits from technological developments, such as computer software, biotechnological products and processes, and pharmaceuticals. But critics contest this corporate definition of intellectual rights, arguing that biodiverse and generic knowledge should remain available to humankind as a global "commons."[73]

Many commercial drugs these days derive from chemicals found in tropical flora and fauna. The Northern lifestyle is directly connected to the extraction of these sorts of resources, such as drugs from the rosy periwinkle of Madagascar to fight childhood leukemia and testicular cancer; Brazzein, a powerful sweetener from a West African berry; biopesticides from the Indian neem tree; and human cell lines to identify genes causing illnesses such as Huntington's disease and cystic fibrosis.[74]

It seems rational that the world's biodiversity should service humankind. This is why so much attention is being paid to preserving the tropical rainforests, for example, given their rich biological variety. At issue is the question of control of resources, and the relationship between Northern lifestyle and the rights of indigenous peoples in the developing nations, mostly in the global South.

The global South contains 90 percent of global biological wealth, and scientists and corporations of the North hold 97 percent of all patents. Patents on biological wealth give patent holders exclusive control over the use of the genetic materials. Corporations have often patented genetic material obtained from a Southern country without payment or obligation, turned it into a commodity such as a medicine, and then charged a fee for use of the genetic resource in local production or high prices for the commodity—even to the country where the material originated, often over centuries. Critics view this appropriation of genetic material by foreigners as **biopiracy**.[75]

The entire living world is up for grabs in this particular vision of commodifying natural endowments and resources. TRIPs grew out of an attempt to stem intellectual property pirating of Western products (watches, CDs, etc.) in the global South but, ironically, it now appears to sanction a reverse biological form of piracy on a disproportionate scale, threatening livelihood, rather than commodity rights. About 1.4 billion people in the global South depend primarily on farm-saved seeds and on crop genetic diversity as the basis of cultural and ecological sustainability. Farmers express concern that if firms can patent traditional seed stock, planting of traditional crops may be liable for patent infringement.[76] This concern arises because firms such as I.C. Industries and Pioneer Hi-bred sought licensing rights to use a gene from an African cowpea. When inserted into crops such as corn and soybeans, the gene increases pest resistance. As the Rural Advancement Foundation International (RAFI, now ETC) asked, "The question is, who are the inventors? [The scientists] who isolated the gene? Or West African farmers who identified the value of the plant holding the gene and then developed and protected it?"[77] The IPR regime privileges governments and corporations as legal entities, disempowering villagers by disavowing their experimental knowledge rights.[78]

The TRIPs protocol establishes uniform standards, globally, for intellectual property rights protection, allowing exclusion of plants and animals from patent laws, but insisting on intellectual property rights for "inventors" of micro-organisms, microbiological processes and products, and plant varieties, which must be either patentable or subject to an effective *sui generis* system, which states interpret to mean plant variety protection—as in the 1992 Convention on Biological Diversity, which confirmed national sovereignty over genetic resources and affirmed that nations are entitled to "fair and equitable sharing of the benefits." The significance of the *sui generis* system is that one premised on collective rights to biodiversity would recognize diverse cultural knowledge and practices—but the extent that it is used in this way is another matter.

CASE STUDY | **Big Pharma and the Question of Intellectual Property Rights**

Perhaps the most visible controversy over IPRs has centered on the question of generic antiretroviral drugs to treat HIV/AIDS patients, of whom there are over 40 million worldwide. Brazil produced generic versions prior to the TRIPs agreement in 1996, sidestepping royalties to the pharmaceutical companies, and reducing the price by 80 percent. The government saved about $250 million a year on the drugs, and also on hospital care for untreated patients. Government labs, researching the composition of pharmaceutical company drugs to produce lower cost generics locally, were threatened with a WTO dispute. UNCHR and WHO intervention on the grounds of human rights secured an outcome with the Health Ministry negotiating price reductions of over 50 percent with the drug companies. Meanwhile, South Africa's Treatment Action Campaign (TAC), spearheading the struggle for affordable medicine for HIV-related illnesses (joined by *Médecins Sans Frontières* and Oxfam), helped to shame 39 pharmaceutical transnational corporations (TNCs) into settling a suit they brought against the South African government to stop its purchase of generic drugs from third parties (like Brazil).

The typical antiretroviral AIDS drug cocktail costs US$10,000–$15,000— fees well beyond the reach of a large proportion of HIV carriers in the global South. Large countries, such as India, Egypt, Thailand, Argentina, and Brazil, manufacture cheap generic drugs (around $600) to reduce public health costs, becoming targets for challenges by the big pharmaceutical companies, citing infringements of the TRIPs protocol's protection of patent rights. A loophole, allowing countries to manufacture or import generic drugs for national health emergencies, challenged for several years by the companies and the United States, was ratified by the WTO in August 2003.

In times of health crises—or indeed at any time—should intellectual property rights be used to subordinate public rights to corporate rights?

Sources: Ayittey (2002); Becker (2003: 14); Booth (1998); Boseley (2007); Central Intelligence Agency (2000); De Waal (2002: 23); Dugger (2007:6); Elliott (2001: 12); Flynn (2002); Gevisser (2001: 5–6); Le Carre (2001: 13–13); *Médecins Sans Frontières* website: www.msf.org; Perlez (2001: A12); Stuart (2003: 21).

General Agreement on Trade in Services (GATS)

Services, unlike goods, are defined as "anything you cannot drop on your foot."[79] They include public and financial services. The 1994

GATS regime opened markets for trade in services by establishing the rights to corporate "presence" in member countries for the delivery of a service in the areas of finance, telecommunications, and transport. "GATS 2000" is a fundamentally more far-reaching protocol to compel governments to provide unlimited market access to foreign service providers, without regard for social and environmental impacts of the service activities.[80] As Tony Clarke notes, GATS 2000 involves the following:

- Imposing severe constraints on the government's ability to protect environmental, health, consumer, and other public interest standards. A "necessity test" requires government proof that regulations on service provision are the "least trade restrictive," parallel with WTO rules on trade in goods.
- Restricting government funding of public works, municipal services, and social programs. Using WTO "national treatment" protocols on government procurement and subsidies, it would impede the role of government funds for public services, making them equally available to foreign-based private service corporations.
- The guaranteed access of private service corporations to domestic markets in all sectors, including health, education, and water, is accelerated by permitting commercial presence in GATS member countries.
- "Every service imaginable is on the table, including a wide range of public services in sectors that affect the environment, culture, energy and natural resources, plus drinking water, health care, K–12 education, postsecondary education, and social security; along with transportation services, postal delivery, prisons, libraries, and a variety of municipal services."
- Finally, access provisions are more profound, applying to most government measures affecting "trade-in-services," such as labor laws, consumer protection, subsidies, grants, licensing standards and qualifications, market access restrictions, economic needs tests, and local content provisions.

In other words, GATS threatens to replace the social contract between state and citizen with a private contract between corporation and consumer. The democratic claims of the citizen-state (expressed in municipal contracts for construction, sewage, garbage disposal, sanitation, and water services) would yield to the private capacities of the consumer-citizen, at the expense of the public interest and its development expressions. In this proposal, we see the elimination of all vestiges of the development state and its replacement by corporate services globally.

CASE STUDY   **Water, Water, Everywhere? Unless It's a Commodity . . .**

When a service is commodified, it becomes the property of only those who can afford to buy it. Its availability on the market for some makes it scarce for others. Water is understood to be the last infrastructure frontier for private investors. Only 5 percent of water services are in private hands, and expansion opportunities are estimated at a trillion dollars. Water privatization is dominated by two French TNCs: Vivendi SA and Suez Lyonnaise des Eaux. Other TNCs involved include Bechtel, Enron, and General Electric. The GATS protocol favors privatization of this public good, and implementation is anticipated by a provision in NAFTA forbidding a country from discriminating in favor of its own firms in the commercial use of its water resources. Meanwhile, the IMF and the World Bank demand privatization of water services as a funding condition.

A case in point is Ghana, where an IMF loan tranche in 2002 was only released on condition that the government required "full cost recovery" in all public utilities, including water. Vivendi, Suez, and Saur of France and Biwater of Britain used this condition to cherrypick lucrative contracts, leaving sewerage, sanitation, urban poor, and rural water provision for local authorities and communities. While the national budget is downsized to save money for loan repayment, a public service disappears, and water prices go through the roof. One community member exclaimed, "The rain does not fall only on the roofs of Vivendi, Suez, Saur and Biwater, neither does it fall only on the roofs of the World Bank and the IMF; it falls on everyone's roof. Why are they so greedy?"

Should the availability and distribution of a basic and precious resource such as water or food be governed by market forces, which tend to favor only those with purchasing power and compromise human rights?

Sources: www.corpwatchindia.org/issues/PID.jsp?articleid=1603; Amenga-Etego (2003: 20–21); Barlow (1999: 2, 7, 14, 18, 27, 33, 38); Godrej (2003: 12); Vidal (2003: 24).

The strategy used by the proponents of GATS 2000 is, to term it appealingly, a *trade agreement*, and it demands openness to "cross-border" provision of services (by TNCs) as a condition for opening EU and U.S. markets in garments, textiles, and agricultural products.[81] Oxfam's Kevin Watkins notes that this is a replay of the Uruguay Round, when the global North offered to open its markets in return for protection of TNC patents (which cost the global South $40 billion in increased technology costs), and suggests that, while the game has changed, the rules are the same: "The West buys your bananas and shirts if you give its banks and insurance companies unrestricted access to your markets."[82] GATS advocates argue that the conversion of public entities into privately owned, profit-making concerns eliminates bureaucratic inefficiency and government debt, providing superior services on a user-pays basis.

WHAT ARE THE INGREDIENTS OF THE GLOBALIZATION PROJECT?

The globalization project combines several strands:

- a (Washington-based) consensus among global managers/policymakers favoring market-based rather than state-managed development strategies;
- centralized management of global market rules by the G-7 states;
- implementation of these rules through multilateral agencies (World Bank, IMF, and WTO);
- concentration of market power in the hands of TNCs and financial power in TNBs;
- subjection of all states to economic disciplines (trade, financial), varying by geopolitical position, global currency hierarchy, debt load, resource endowments, and so forth;
- realization of global development via new class, gender, race, and ethnic inequalities; and
- resistance at all levels, from marginalized communities to state managers to factions even within multilateral institutions, contesting unbridled market rule.

SUMMARY

The development project incubated an economic nationalism that became increasingly limiting to TNCs. At the same time a rising debt crisis enabled new direction in world ordering, via the debt regime. The new direction was the globalization project, an alternative way of organizing economic growth corresponding to the growing scale and power of the transnational banks and corporations. The increasing volume of economic exchanges and the greater mobility of money and firms required forms of regulation beyond the reach of the nation-state even if imposed through the system of nation-states. The WTO represents one such form of regulation.

The new global regulatory system subordinated states' social protections to liberalization. Overall, despite differences among states, they became surrogate managers of the global economy (or "market states"). The standardized prescriptions for liberalization reorganize regions and locales: from the removal of Mexican *campesinos* from long-held public lands to the rapid dismantling of public ownership of the economies of Eastern Europe to the proliferation of export processing zones and agro-export platforms. Many of these mushrooming export sites suffer the instability of flexible strategies of "footloose" firms, as they pick and choose their way among global sourcing sites. Social protections decline as communities lose their resource bases (declining social subsidies, dwindling forests) or their employment bases (as firms downsize or move offshore).

Under these conditions, globalization is everything but universalist in its consequences. It assigns communities, regions, and nation-states new niches or specialized roles (including marginalization) in the global economy. The development project proposed social integration through national economic growth under individual state supervision and according to a social contract between government and citizenry. Alternatively, the globalization project offers new forms of authority and discipline governed by the market.

FURTHER READING

George, Susan. *The Debt Boomerang: How Third World Debt Harms Us All.* Boulder, CO: Westview Press, 1992.

Mgbeoji, Ikechi. *Global Biopiracy: Patents, Plants, and Indigenous Knowledge.* Ithaca, NY: Cornell University Press, 2006.

Payne, Anthony. *The Global Politics of Unequal Development.* New York: Palgrave Macmillan, 2005.

Rosset, Peter M. *Food Is Different: Why We Must Get the WTO Out of Agriculture.* Halifax, NS: Fernwood, 2006.

Soederberg, Susanne. *Global Governance in Question: Empire, Class, and the New Common Sense in Managing North–South Relations.* London: Pluto, 2006.

Wallach, Lori, and Patrick Woodall, eds. *Whose Trade Organization? A Comprehensive Guide to the WTO.* London: New Press, 2004.

Woods, Ngaire. *The Globalizers: The IMF, the World Bank and Their Borrowers.* Ithaca, NY: Cornell University Press, 2006.

SELECT WEBSITES

Bretton Woods Project (USA): www.brettonwoodsproject.org
International Forum on Globalization (USA): www.ifg.org
Millennium Development Goals (MDGs): www.un.org/millenniumgoals
Public Citizen Global Trade Watch (USA): www.citizen.org/trade
Structural Adjustment Participatory Review International Network: www.saprin.org
UN Capital Development Fund: www.uncdf.org
World Health Organization (WHO): www.who.int/en
World Trade Organization (WTO): www.wto.org

6

The Globalization Project in Practice

The globalization project is about market integration, legitimacy management, and resistance. At the turn of the twenty-first century, the United Nations reported that the richest 20 percent of the world's population enjoyed 30 times the income of the poorest 20 percent in 1960, but by 1997 the difference was of the order of 74.[1] The exacerbation of global inequality via market integration made *legitimacy management* a priority for the development establishment to justify staying the course with liberalization and the corporate agenda. Food riots, poverty stabilization schemes, and a dramatic uprising in the Chiapas province of southern Mexico underscored the 1994 statement by the Inter-American Development Bank on the eve of the World Trade Organization (WTO)'s formation: "The resumption of economic growth has been bought at a very high social price, which includes poverty, increased unemployment, and income inequality, and this is leading to social problems."[2] Five years later, the WTO Seattle Ministerial (1999) registered a threshold in "anti-globalization" protest, as a variety of justice movements from across the world blocked the proceedings, giving voice to a widespread discontent with the neo-liberal model of global development. The following year, the United Nations offered the world "globalization with a human face" in the **Millennium Development Goals,** dedicated to addressing the key challenges of the new century: persistent poverty, pandemic disease, environmental damage, gender inequality, and Southern debt. And all this occurred during an explosion of the "fast world," driven by the internet boom, corporate mergers, and healthy-looking national accounts, as rates of

150

foreign investment and trade ballooned. As we shall see, in Chapter 8, this economic expansion did not last.

The globalization project has two faces: the face of unprecedented prosperity for the world's minority of investors and consumers; and the face of poverty, displacement, job and food insecurity, health crises (AIDS), and a widening band of informal activity (over 1 billion slumdwellers) as people make do in lieu of stable jobs, government supports, and sustainable habitats. This will be the subject matter of this chapter.

Here, we consider some key practices of globalization as a project. These are poverty governance, outsourcing, displacement, informalization, and recolonization. They provide the stimulus to the global justice movements examined in Chapter 8.

Poverty Governance

Under the umbrella of global governance in the globalization project, the World Bank and IMF play a central role. Structural adjustment policies (SAPs) spawned in the 1980s preceded the universal adoption of liberalization policies through the WTO from the mid-1990s. But the international financial institutions (IFIs), recognizing that SAPs increased the poor's vulnerability, were compelled to create a Social Emergency Fund (World Bank) and a new Compensatory and Contingency Financing Facility (IMF) in 1988 to target those who fell through the cracks. In the 1990s, the IFIs evolved "humanizing" global policies, starting with the Heavily Indebted Poor Countries (HIPC) Initiative of 1996, to provide exceptional assistance to countries with unsustainable debt burdens.[3] The IFIs' goal was to stave off a legitimacy crisis by elaborating "governance" mechanisms that continue to this day as poverty elimination remains unfulfilled. And legitimacy is crucial, since both institutions depend increasingly on loan repayment by borrowing from countries to bankroll their operations, as northern countries have significantly reduced their contributions.

Securing legitimacy involved "democratizing" SAPs, encouraging countries and NGOs to take "ownership" of policy formation and implementation. By 1999, an enhanced HIPC was created with African debtor states in mind, defining "conditionality" by a broad, participatory poverty reduction strategy.[4] The Bank director spoke of a "civil society revolution," basing development on "inclusion and participation, bringing together civil society, local competition, NGOs, the private sector, and the poor themselves . . . in order to foster trust and sustainability."[5] In this context, the World Bank commissioned a *Voices of the Poor* project: gathering testimony from

60,000 poor women and men in 50 countries, who overall expressed deep dissatisfaction with government corruption and a preference for World Bank involvement—although participating researchers suggested this was largely a legitimacy exercise.[6] While this exercise was underway, the hard truth was that, from 1996–1999, HIPC-eligible country debt had quadrupled, from $59 billion to $205 billion, mobilizing activists in the North, in particular the Jubilee 2000 organization, dedicated to debt forgiveness.[7]

Under these circumstances, the IFIs, still committed to debt repayment, repackaged neoliberal policies in participatory rhetoric, and incorporated NGO leaders into the World Bank's networks. Unpopular SAPs were refashioned as "partnerships," with states required to author their own development plans, subject to IFI approval, on which loans, debt rescheduling, and debt forgiveness can be made. These plans, known as **Poverty Reduction Strategy Papers (PRSPs)**, are compiled as "performances": "to meet the charge that imposing conditions is undemocratic, the IFIs now insist that other stakeholders, such as NGOs, churches, unions, and business, rather than just governments, are involved in writing the plans."[8] The PRSPs are a form of crisis management, marking a new phase of IFI management of the global South. The Bank's initial Bretton Woods focus on *project* loans for public infrastructure shifted to *policy* loans geared to structural adjustment in the global South during the 1980s, as market reforms redefined IFI development philosophy. Now PRSPs focus on new *process* conditions.[9]

The World Bank and the IMF characterized the PRSP program in 2002 as "a new approach to the challenge of reducing poverty in low-income countries based on country-owned poverty reduction strategies."[10] These procedures, in holding states accountable for poverty reduction, embed public priorities in private relationships—in effect fashioning "governance states."[11] Here, private commercial law adopted as public policy at the national level embraces WTO prescriptions for countries to "trade themselves out of poverty." At the global level, the project of poverty reduction—paralleling the 2000 Millennium Development Goals (MDGs)—entails policy coordination between the WTO, the IMF, and the World Bank.[12]

Poverty governance also involves coordinating international NGOs with access to information and resources, enabling them to leverage initiatives within states. Thus World Vision International and *Médicins sans Frontières* are pervasive in Africa today, organizing local schools and clinics in lieu of failed states, respectively.[13] As Oxfam, for example, observes, "PRSPs offer Oxfam and other NGOs major opportunities to influence policy and practice at local, national, and international levels, both at the formulation and implementation stage."[14] The privatization of states is also shaped by

Transnational Policy Networks (TPNs)—in Africa through the African Policy Institutes Forum, created by the World Bank to serve as professional training program centers, and serving as sites for preparation of PRSPs.[15] Privatization no longer means simply selling off public assets, but integrating states into TPNs as global market intermediaries—with the IFIs and the international NGO community acting as "surrogate representative(s) of . . . civil society in the state-donor partnership."[16]

Promoting market access reconstructs the state-civil society relation by complementing (or compromising) the state's authority with the authority of "civil society," using "budget monitoring" to secure conditionality, and establishing "a surveillance architecture capable of disciplining democracy."[17] This surveillance includes extending microloans through NGO intermediaries to the poor.[18] The rationale is that microlending will redirect existing survival networks, viewed by the World Bank as "social capital," into entrepreneurial activities.[19] Poverty governance enhances institutional legitimacy at the same time as it subjects societies to the market calculus.

Outsourcing

Outsourcing relocates goods and services production as a cost-reduction strategy and a means to increase operational flexibility of an organization. It includes offshoring, as firms shift production overseas. Outsourcing has become significant for two reasons: (1) the hypermobility of capital in an era of deregulation and expanding access to cheap/flexible labor and (2) the privatization of states. Under neoliberalism, in addition to corporate outsourcing, governments outsource service contracts to reduce public expenditure and/or privilege the private sector. GATS and IFIs promote such outsourcing, often with the effect of transferring monopoly power over the management of utilities to corporations, and outsourcing "governance" functions to NGOs.

Thus when the South African government outsourced Telkom, the state telephone company, in 2003, it completed the privatization of this essential service, which already had increased tariffs for poor households while slashing rates for rich families and firms, and cut 80 percent of new land lines because of the inability of poor subscribers to pay.[20] And in 2001, Philippines president Arroyo broke up and outsourced the state-owned National Power Corporation, following threats from the IMF and the Asian Development Bank to withhold credits worth nearly $1 billion. Here, "legislation, which privatizes the state distribution system, does not privatize the associated debt. Filipino taxpayers will continue to shoulder the burden."[21]

Meanwhile, in health care, the World Bank has maintained a policy that public sector inefficiencies hinder service delivery and made loans to outsource public health to private managed care initiatives. In Latin America, TNCs such as Aetna, CIGNA, the American International Group (AIG), and Prudential have invested heavily in Argentina, Chile, Brazil, and Ecuador. There are three characteristic effects of neoliberal policy: (1) Access to health care for the poor shrinks while investments grow—"between 1996 and 1999, revenues of multinational health care corporations grew much faster in Latin America than in the United States." (2) Outsourcing and cutbacks in public sector budgets reduce preventative programs, allowing banished diseases such as cholera, dengue fever, and typhus to reemerge as epidemics. (3) As has happened in a dozen states in the United States, after profiting through the privatization of public health care systems, managed care organizations and health insurance companies move on when profit margins fall.[22]

CASE STUDY   Sourcing Outsourcing in the Philippines

Challenging the homogenizing imagery of globalization, Steven McKay shows how corporate outsourcing of high-tech electronics production is not only about accessing cheap labor. It is also about local labor relations shaping global industry. In this case, the Philippine state partners with firms (such as Intel, Texas Instruments, Philips, Toshiba, and Hitachi) to help circumvent unions, and recruit along gendered and ethno-racial lines to gain labor-force loyalty and labor skills necessary to the demands of technology-intensive assembly and test manufacturing of semiconductors and computer hard disk drives. Regularizing, rather than casualizing, high-tech jobs, McKay notes that firms "invest in particular places and strategically localize elements of their work regimes in order to lower production costs, and/or better secure labor control and worker commitment."

When states privatize, they outsource public services. How does this differ from host states privatizing their citizens' sovereignty by assisting TNC access to labor forces segmented along gender and ethno-racial lines?

Source: McKay (2006: 13–14, 39, 130, 170, 188–189, 197, 217).

Corporate outsourcing has become virtually synonymous with globalization. We have seen how the "world factory" emerged on a foundation of the NIDL, as a forerunner of the era of global integration. This pattern, amplified by TRIMs, has consolidated as the **"global division of labor,"** now extending to high- and low-paid services and perishable agricultural commodities. Outsourcing of production has depended on the deepening of information and communication technologies (ICTs), especially microprocessing power and developments in fiber optics—for example, "e-mailing a 40-page document from Chile to Kenya costs less than 10 cents, faxing it about $10 and sending it by courier $50." By the twenty-first century, "more information was sent over a single cable in a second than over the entire Internet in a month in 1997."[23] This compression of space by time enhances the ability of firms to manage far-flung and fragmented outsourcing operations—coordinating movement of components through the supply chain, and of foods shipped across seasonal and time zones.

On top of a steady movement offshore of manufacturing jobs from the 1970s, *service jobs* began migrating from North to South in the 1990s. For instance, between 1996 and 2000, U.S. corporate outsourcing grew from $100 billion to $345 billion, concentrating in call centers, graphic design, computer programming, and accountancy.[24] Many of the new jobs in the Caribbean, for example, are data processing positions that large U.S. insurance, health industry, magazine subscription renewal, consumer credit, and retailing firms have shifted offshore at a lower cost. Swissair, British Airways, and Lufthansa relocated much of their reservations operations to Indian subcontractors in Bangalore, where "the staff are well educated at English-speaking universities, yet cost only a fraction of what their counterparts are paid in the North." Swissair claims, "We can hire three Indians for the price of one Swiss." The relocation of revenue accounts preparation saved 8 million francs and 120 jobs in Zurich. Eastern Europe has become an increasingly competitive site for labor-intensive computer programming, as well as "virtual sweatshops" where Romanians provide computer gaming services for wealthy Western players.[25] The Delhi telecomputing firm Selectronic receives doctors' dictation from a U.S. toll-free number, transcribing and transmitting transcriptions as texts to an American HMO, while America Online employs 600 Filipinos to answer over 10,000 technical and billing inquiries per day, mainly from the United States (80 percent of AOL's customer e-mail)—paying its customer-service representatives a daily rate equivalent to an hour's pay for an unskilled American worker. With outsourcing upgrades in India into product R&D, financial analysis, and handling insurance claims and payrolls, call center employee wages have increased by 50 percent, providing an opportunity for the Philippines, where call center jobs rose 100 percent over five years to 200,000 in late 2006.[26] India now outsources outsourcing in order to capture an expanding back office industry, as Indian wages rise, and China, Morocco, and

Mexico challenge India's successful model. Tata Consultancy Service has offices in Mexico, Brazil, Chile, and Uruguay. Cognizant Technology Solutions is in Phoenix and Shanghai, and Infosys is even outsourcing outsourcing to the Philippines, Thailand, Poland, China, and Mexico.[27]

IT services have been expanding in India at a rate of between 30 and 60 percent annually, with new frontiers of "virtual services" beyond customer-service centers beckoning to TNCs—"health care, where a scan may be carried out in one country, processed in another, and sent to a third for another opinion before being sent back home again, is one example."[28] The economics profession may be another mobile "virtual service." Thomas Friedman refers to this as the "democratization of technology," a conceptual forerunner of his "flat world," implying that technological capability enables the South to participate on a leveled global playing field.

CASE STUDY   **High Heels and High Tech in Global Barbados**

In an innovative study of "pink-collar" work and identities in the Caribbean, Carla Freeman explores how an Afro-Caribbean workforce has embraced the global division of labor in the informatics industry. Disadvantaged by Mexico's stranglehold on trade preferences with North America, the export-oriented countries of Barbados, Jamaica, and Trinidad offer their English-speaking tradition to the outsourcers.

Barbados, with a literacy rate of 98 percent and a reputation for order and polite service, turned itself into a haven for offshore information-based data-processing work, globally sourced by subsidiaries of British and U.S. telecommunication corporations:

On a typical shift . . . between about fifty and one hundred Barbadian women sit in partitioned computer cubicles of a given production floor from 7:30 in the morning until 3:30 in the afternoon, taking a half-hour break for lunch and sometimes a fifteen-minute stretch in between. Their keystrokes per hour are monitored electronically as they enter data from airline ticket stubs, consumer warranty cards, or the text of a potboiler novel for top U.S. airlines, appliance houses, and publishers. In each case, the surveillance of the computer, the watchful eye of supervisors, and the implementation of double-keying techniques are all aspects of the production process integral to the companies' guarantee of 99 percent accuracy rates.

> While such work is deskilled and clearly gendered, Freeman found that, despite better pay in the sugar cane fields, these women find "pink-collar" jobs attractive because of the identification with office work and informatics technology, because the Barbados Development Plan—development via information-based exports—includes guarantees of basic employment benefits, such as maternity and sick leave and paid vacations, and because differentiation from field and factory work through dress codes and consumption styles enables them to "experience class as gendered Afro-Caribbean subjects within a distinctly feminized arena."
>
> How should we understand the distinction between the discourse of global capitalism as an objective "economic" order with income hierarchies and its actual realization through cultural filters, where the development subject—such as these Barbadian women, for instance—embodies a complex local combination of global class and gender relations?
>
> *Source:* Freeman (2000: 23–48, 65).

India, in particular, is "blessed" with an English-speaking tradition, and, as with parts of the Caribbean, South Africa, Pakistan, and the Philippines, language has become a comparative advantage for this kind of service outsourcing. At the Delhi call center Spectramind, in addition to a two-hour seminar on the royal family, one set of "recruits receive a 20-hour crash course in British culture. They watch videos of British soap operas to accustom them to regional accents. They learn about Yorkshire pudding. And they are taught about Britain's unfailingly miserable climate." Another set of recruits, exposed to American TV shows and sporting slang, are "trained in the nuances of baseball, and Blue 'Tennessee Titans' pennants fly above their desks."[29] Following liberalization in 1991, foreign corporations established subsidiaries in India to outsource jobs in IT, financial services, business processes, pharmaceuticals, and automotive components, generating thousands of new jobs and annual rates of growth that are twice those in the North. Bangalore, Hyderabad, Delhi, and Mumbai displayed their newfound wealth as emerging "global cities."[30] While one-third of Bangalore's population are slumdwellers, half "lack piped water, much less cappuccino, and there are more ragpickers and street children (90,000) than software geeks (about 60,000)."[31] Not only are two-thirds of the populace (230 million) still residing in publicly neglected and deteriorating rural habitats, but the IT sector generates less than 2 percent of national income and employs

1 million in an economy where 8 million join the labor force annually.[32] Outsourcing generates clusters of prosperity networked more often across national borders than within them.

Rural land appropriation for outsourcing industries is routine (though not without resistance).[33] In China where, in Dongguan City (site of Reebok and Nike shoe manufacturers), local farmers now live off factory rents, while tens of thousands of migrants from the hinterland swell the workforce.[34] Datang, a rice-farming village in the late 1970s, with a cottage industry in socks, now produces 9 billion socks annually: "Signs of Datang's rise as a socks capital are everywhere. The center of town is filled with a huge government-financed marketplace for socks. The rice paddies have given way to rows of paved streets lined with cookie-cutter factories. Banners promoting socks are draped across buildings."[35] Renamed "Socks City," Datang is one of many new coastal cities: southeast is Shenzhou, the world's necktie capital; west is Sweater City and Kids' Clothing City; and to the south, in the low-rent district, is Underwear City.[36] In one of these cities, *China Blue* (2006) was filmed in a blue jeans factory—portraying the manufacturer's reliance on labor of teenage girls fresh from the rural hinterland. With an ethnographic approach, the film documents how pressures to cut costs are passed down from the English buyer, through the factory owner, to his vulnerable workforce, who are also forced to work shifts lasting sometimes more than 40 hours to meet "just in time" orders. Buyers, under pressure to ensure ethical brands, send inspectors who focus on product quality and turn a blind eye to the duplicate time cards and employee coaching organized by factory owners.

The global supermarket revolution is founded on an outsourcing model of "buyer-driven commodity chains," linking contract farmers with centralized food processing and retailing operations.[37] Transnational firms such as Ahold, Carrefour, and Walmart comprise 70–80 percent of the top five supermarket chains in Latin America, centralizing procurement from farmers across the region (and their own processing plants) and, together with Nestlé and Quaker, supplying regional consumer markets throughout the Mercosur trading bloc in the eastern part of Latin America. In Guatemala, where supermarkets control 35 percent of food retailing, "their sudden appearance has brought unanticipated and daunting challenges to millions of struggling, small farmers," lacking binding contractual agreements, rewarded only if they consistently meet new quality standards, and facing declining prices as they constitute a virtually unlimited source for retailers.[38]

"Standards" are critical to the outsourcing revolution, especially with perishables. WTO regulation of trade relations is complemented by extensive private regulation of production standards, regarding quality, safety, packaging, and convenience. The new "audit culture" generates certification schemes such as GlobalGAP (Good Agricultural Practices), an association of European supermarket chains concerned with regulating quality, safety, environment, and labor standards (in crop, livestock, and aquaculture production) surpassing publicly required standards.[39] Risk management encourages production consolidation—UK supermarkets are doing this to reduce their exposure to risk by expanding control over production and distribution.[40] In Kenya, where about 90 percent of horticulture is destined for Europe (especially the United Kingdom), the shift from smallholder-contract production to centralized employment on farms and in packing houses in the mid-1990s has in turn transformed farming women into a migrant labor force, as a household survival strategy.[41] Likewise, in Brazil's São Francisco Valley, "new agricultural districts" exporting mangoes, grapes, tomatoes, and acerola must meet specific quality controls and design, as well as setting parameters for labor and environmental conditions.[42]

Displacement

In the shadow of globalization lurks a rising dilemma: the casualization of labor and the redundancy of people.[43] Despite, and perhaps because of, an expanding global economy, numbers of unemployed (including hard-to-count long-term unemployed) in the global North have risen from 10 to almost 50 million between 1973 and the early twenty-first century.[44] This is the dilemma of structural unemployment, where automation and/or outsourcing of work sheds stable jobs and where redundant workers cease rotating into new jobs. It is matched across the world by other forms of displacement, including SAP-mandated dismantling of ISI sectors and privatization of public enterprise, forced resettlement by infrastructural projects (e.g., 1.2 million peasants resettled in China's Three Gorges Dam project),[45] civil wars, and the destabilization of rural communities by market forces (dumping of cheap food, land concentration, and decline of farm subsidies). At the turn of the twenty-first century, 1 billion workers (one-third of the world's labor force, mainly Southern) were either unemployed or underemployed.[46]

Displacement begins with depeasantization, even though agriculture is the main source of food and income for the majority of the world's poor. While about 3.8 billion people directly depend on the agricultural sector, more than half of the south's population is agrarian, rising to 85 percent in some of the poorest countries. The FAO notes, "Agriculture is also of great social, cultural, and environmental significance for rural communities. It

tends to be particularly important for women, who have the main responsibilities for feeding their families and are estimated to produce 60–80% of
food grown in most developing countries."[47] Long-term food security
depends on diversity of crop species, in contrast to industrial agriculture's
dependence on 15 crop species for 90 percent of its food calories,[48] nevertheless the subordination of agriculture everywhere to agribusiness and
global retailing is steadily driving peasants into an exploding global slum in
an era of jobless growth.

As we saw in Chapter 5, neoliberal food security means privileging food
importing over local farming for many southern states. The transnational
peasant coalition *Vía Campesina* notes, "the massive movement of food
around the world is forcing the increased movement of people."[49] Under the
WTO's Agreement on Agriculture, decoupling of (Northern) subsidies from
prices removes the price floor, establishing a *low* "world price" for agricultural commodities, and favoring traders and processors in the global food
industry at the expense of farmers everywhere.

Liberalization policies are rooted in IMF-World Bank structural adjustment measures, which have routinely required "free markets" in grain—for
example, in formerly self-sufficient countries like Malawi, Zimbabwe,
Kenya, Rwanda, and Somalia. In India, following a decade of neoliberalism, the Ministry of Agriculture stated in 2000, "The growth in agriculture
has slackened during the 1990s. Agriculture has become a relatively unre-
warding profession due to an unfavorable price regime and low value addition, causing abandoning of farming and migration from rural areas."[50]
The neoliberal paradox is that "free" markets exclude populations dispossessed by their implementation.[51]

Global economic integration intensifies displacement as the global
economy stratifies populations across, rather than simply within, national
borders. With provocative imagery, Jacques Attali, former president of the
European Bank for Reconstruction and Development, distinguishes *rich
nomads* ("consumer-citizens of the privileged regions") from *poor nomads*
("boat people on a planetary scale"):

> In restless despair, the hopeless masses of the periphery will witness the spec-
> tacle of another hemisphere's growth. Particularly in those regions of the South
> that are geographically contiguous and culturally linked to the North—places
> such as Mexico, Central America, or North Africa—millions of people will be
> tempted and enraged by the constant stimulation of wants that can't be satis-
> fied. . . . With no future of their own in an age of air travel and telecommuni-
> cations, the terminally impoverished will look for one in the North. . . . The
> movement of peoples has already begun; only the scale will grow: Turks in

Berlin, Moroccans in Madrid, Indians in London, Mexicans in Los Angeles, Puerto Ricans and Haitians in New York, Vietnamese in Hong Kong.[52]

Such fears, founded in latent stereotypes, underlie the concern of the global managers and many Northern consumer-citizens to stem the tide of global labor migration, and fears of associations with terrorism. Consequences range from the spread of "gated communities" and the Hummer to a rollback of civil rights in the global North, and the Norwegian tragedy of 2011.

A cursory glance at the newspapers in the global North confirms a broad anxiety about the ethnic composition of the underground global labor force, often manifested in outbreaks of racist violence toward "guest workers." This attitude has spread in Europe, where millions of "illegal" migrants (from Eastern Europe, Turkey, Central Asia, China, and Francophone West Africa) work in restaurants, construction, and farming—they "enjoy none of the workers' rights and protections or social benefits of the state . . . are paid less than the legal wage, and are often paid late, with no legal recourse." Advocates argue that legalizing the status of the "*sans papiers*" would reduce xenophobia.[53] The guest worker phenomenon is not unique to the twenty-first century, and the cycles of attraction and expulsion mirror economic cycles in host countries.

In the global North, continuing immigration is in the interests of firms needing cheap labor and of privileged people needing servants. The *displacement of love* via the feminization and export of care workers from the South to care for children of working women in the North has been termed the "global heart transplant," and linked to the "care drain" from the South via "chains of love," whereby migrant women work as "global nannies" at considerable emotional cost to their own children, who in turn are cared for by relatives or teenage girls at home.[54]

MIGRANT LABOR IN THE GLOBAL ECONOMY: ECONOMIC AND ENVIRONMENTAL REFUGEES

In the early twenty-first century, as many as 175 million people were estimated to be living as expatriate laborers around the world. Asian women are the fastest growing group of foreign workers, increasing by about 1 million each year.

(Continued)

(Continued)

Environmental migration is increasingly significant, with reports that 1 billion people could be displaced by climate change by 2050. Current sources include:

- 135 million people whose land is being transformed into deserts (desertification);
- 900 million of the world's poorest, existing on less than a dollar a day and living in areas vulnerable to soil erosion, droughts, desertification, and floods;
- 200 million people facing rising sea levels due to climate change;
- 50 million people in famine-vulnerable areas subject to climate change; and
- 550 million people already suffering from chronic water shortage.

Sources: Baird (2002: 10); Boyd (1998: 17); Perrons (2005: 211); Vidal (2007a).

Labor: The New Export

The mobility rights for capital guaranteed by neoliberalism do not extend to labor. Nevertheless, labor increasingly circulates, seeking employment opportunities—whether "legal," "illegal," or slave/bonded labor. Migration is not new to this century. The separation of people from the land is etched into the making of the modern world. Colonialism propelled migrations of free and unfree people. Between 1810 and 1921, 34 million people, mainly Europeans, emigrated to the United States alone. The difference today is the feminization of global migration: 75 percent of refugees and displaced persons are women and children.[55]

During the 1980s, spurred by debt regime restructurings, there was an internal migration in the former Third World of between 300 and 400 million people.[56] This pool of labor has contributed to global migration from overburdened cities to Northern regions as migrants seek to earn money for families back home. In excess of 100 million kinfolk depend on remittances of the global labor force. In the 1990s, for example, two-thirds of Turkey's trade deficit was financed by remittances from Turks working abroad.[57]

The World Bank estimates remittances totalling US$414 billion in 2009, of which US$316 billion went to the South, from some 192 million migrants or 3.0 percent of world population—"For some individual recipient countries, remittances can be as high as a third of GDP. Remittances also now account for about a third of total global external finance; moreover, the flow of remittances seems to be significantly more stable than other forms of external finance."[58]

The influx of foreign exchange not only supplies much-needed hard currency but, in an era of structural adjustment and privatization, remittance money supplements or subsidizes public ventures. Thus, in Indonesian villages, remittances finance schools, roads, and housing in lieu of public funding. Migrants invested $6 million in new roads, schools, churches, water systems, and parks in Zacatecas, Mexico, and President Vicente Fox (2002) commented, "The families that receive the money use it to buy shoes or beans, clothes, or books for their children. Now we want to channel part of that money for production for projects that generate jobs," matching, peso for peso, money remitted by migrant workers for public works projects in their home communities.[59] Then there is Kerala, an exceptionally socially progressive state in southern India and recognized by the UN in 1975 as having an impressive record of health and education expenditure, with life expectancy and literacy rates considerably higher than the Indian average. The "Kerala model," with its social priorities trumping the market-driven development model, nevertheless depends for 25 percent of its revenues on remittances from its almost 2 million expatriate workers in the Persian Gulf.[60]

Spurred by debt, labor export has become a significant foreign currency earner: Filipino overseas earnings are estimated to amount to $5.7 billion, for example. About 6 million Filipinos—increasingly from rural areas—work overseas in 130 countries as contract workers (seamen, carpenters, masons, mechanics, or maids).[61] The government of the Philippines includes labor in its export-led development strategy.[62] In addition to products, labor is exported—mainly to the oil-rich Middle East, where contractors organize the ebb and flow of foreign labor. One contractor, Northwest Placement, a privately run recruiting agency, receives 5,000 pesos ($181)—the maximum allowed by the Labor Department—from Filipino applicants on assurance of a job; this covers the costs of a medical check, visas, and government clearance fees. Not surprisingly, there are also plenty of unlicensed agencies operating.[63]

Figure 6.1   Remittance Trends for Top 10 Southern Recipients, 2006–2010

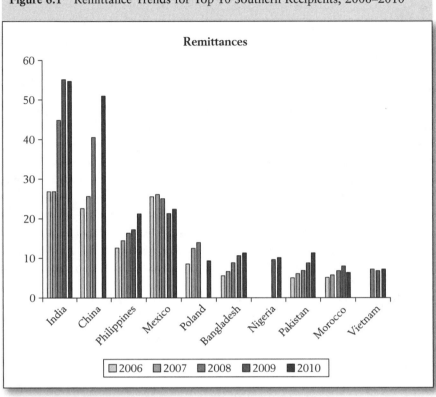

Source: http://en.wikipedia.org/wiki/Remittance

CASE STUDY   **Trafficking in Women—The Global Sex Trade Versus Human Rights**

Human trafficking is the fastest-growing form of bonded labor in today's global market, and the leading human rights violation. It is estimated that between 700,000 and 2 million women and children are trafficked annually, and that there are about 10 million trafficked people working at risk. After drug smuggling and gun running, human trafficking is the third largest illegal trade (with an annual profit of about $6 billion). Child trafficking dwarfs the trans-Atlantic slave trade at its peak, by a magnitude of 10. Some destinations are farming, restaurant labor, domestic servitude, fishing, mail-order brides, market stall labor, shop work, and the sex trade.

Human rights exploitation of trafficked people, who lack legal status and language skills, is easy and widespread. Since 1990, about 30 million women and children have been trafficked for prostitution and sweatshop labor. The rise in trafficking is directly related to the feminization of global poverty and the use of the Internet as a sex forum.

In Thailand, female emigration took off in the 1980s, as the East Asian boom disrupted cultural traditions and family livelihoods. Young women flooded into Bangkok from the Thai countryside, looking for income to remit to their villages, many ending up in Europe, the United States, Japan, South-East Asia, Australia, South Africa, or the Arabian Gulf in the burgeoning sex industry by deceit or by choice (sex work being a relatively high-income trade open to uneducated women). Thai sex tourism contributed to the demand for Thai women overseas. Research in northern Thailand has shown that about 28 percent of household income was remitted by absent daughters. A common motive is relieving poverty and debt, and often parents sell their daughters for a cash advance to be paid off by work in the global sex industry. Alternatively, individual women pay an agent's fee of around $500. From then on, women are devoid of rights: working as bonded labor; subject to arrest for illicit work and illegal residence; lacking rights to medical or social services overseas; forced to sell sex; at high risk of contracting HIV; and targets of racial discrimination and public humiliation if arrested.

Action against trafficking is hampered by collusion between source families and agents; by the lifestyle of the women, trapped by underground employers; and by governments interested in suppressing information to avoid adverse publicity.

How can global human rights agencies address the trafficking tragedy when governments are reluctant to intervene for fear of loss of foreign exchange or tourist dollars?

Sources: Pyle (2001); Skrobanek et al. (1997: 13–31, 68, 103); "Slavery in the 21st Century" (2001: 18); Worden (2001).

International labor circulation combines formal policies with decidedly informal working conditions. Migrant workers routinely lack human rights. Workers in the Gulf States, for example, are indentured, with no civic rights, no choice of alternative jobs, and no recourse against poor employment conditions and low wages—which are determined by the income levels of the country of origin. Migrant workers must surrender their passports on arrival; they reportedly work 12 to 16 hours a day, seven days a week. Governments in the migrant workers' home countries in Asia, dependent on foreign currency earnings, are reportedly resigned to the exploitation of their nationals. International labor union organizations have been ineffectual, especially as Middle Eastern states have united to suppress discussion in international forums of working conditions inside their countries.[64]

Labor migrates from all over the world into the United States. The scale is such that immigrants retain their cultural and linguistic traditions rather than assimilate. The juxtaposition of distinct cultures in countries to which labor migrates creates a *multicultural* effect—not necessarily benign, as a New York City Labor Department Official noted: "In the underground economies of the ethnic enclaves of Vietnamese, Cuban, Dominican, Central American, and Chinese, it is a case of immigrants exploiting immigrants."[65] Neoliberal restructuring and rising economic uncertainty has amplified "ethnicism," including "nativism." In a backlash against immigration. U.S. political discourse, for example, is polarized around the issue of undocumented Mexican workers, forgetting about the 2 million *campesinos* displaced by corn imports from the United States and withdrawal of rural credit under the terms of NAFTA.[66]

The conditions in which labor circulation has intensified have made multiculturalism a fragile ideal. Labor export arrangements deny rights and representation to migrant workforces, and deteriorating economies and communities in global-economic centers spark exclusionist politics that scapegoat cultural minorities. Development project ideals informed a politics of inclusion, rooted in broad-based class movements and political coalitions more committed to assimilation and the redistribution of resources. Under neoliberalism, inclusion is threatened by separatist politics stemming from economic restructuring. The "race to the bottom" is not just about wage erosion, it is also about tensions around difference.

Informalization

The globalization project is Janus-faced. It exaggerates the market culture at the same time as it intensifies its opposite—a growing culture of informal, or marginal, activity. This culture involves people working on the fringes of the market, performing casual and unregulated (often outsourced) labor, working in cooperative arrangements, street vending, or pursuing what are deemed illegal economic activities. Those who are bypassed or marginalized by development often form a culture parallel to the market culture. The question of whether informal culture is a real alternative or simply an unrecognized or impoverished margin of the formal culture depends on the context. For example, revival of subsistence farming may improve living standards over working as a rural laborer or existing on the urban fringe, as long as land is available. Marginalization is closely associated with forms of displacement—for example, cycles of expansion and contraction of formal economic activity, or the concentration of resources in fewer corporate hands, generate informalization.

Informalization is a politico-cultural process. With the rise of market societies, the boundaries of the formal economy were identified and regulated by the state for tax purposes, but they have always been incomplete and fluid, often by design and certainly by custom. An army of servants and housecleaners, for example, routinely works "off the books." Casual labor has always accompanied small-scale enterprise and even large-scale harvesting operations where labor use is cyclical. Also, a substantial portion of labor performed across the world every day is unpaid labor—such as housework and family farm labor.

Distinguishing between a formal economy with its legal/moral connotations, and an informal sector with its illegal or immoral connotations, is either artificial or political. We make the distinction here as it reveals the limits of official, formal development strategy, and identifies alternative, informal livelihood strategies—often intimately connected and mutually conditioning. Economists and governments make the distinction because national accounting measures legal cash transactions. By ignoring informal activity, development policy discounts and marginalizes substantial mechanisms of social reproduction, on which the formal "productive economy" depends. The consequences of this artificial distinction illuminate the crisis of structural adjustment, spotlighting the gendered foundations of material life. Bharati Sadasivam notes that the language of SAPs focuses

> overwhelmingly on the "productive economy," on making profits and covering costs. In the process, it takes for granted the "reproductive economy," which meets needs and sustains human beings. Macro models of mainstream economics assume that the process of reproduction and the maintenance of human resources will continue regardless of the way resources are reallocated. These models conceal the large contribution to the economy provided by the production and maintenance of the labor supply through childbirth and childcare, shopping, cooking, and housework. Economic reforms such as structural adjustment policies that call for cutbacks in state services and the free play of market forces fail to consider how such changes affect the relation between the "productive economy" and the "reproductive economy." Because the latter is sustained by unpaid nonmarket work mostly undertaken by women, macroeconomics also assumes an unlimited supply of female labor. It expects this

labor to adjust to and compensate for any changes in the "reproductive economy" brought about by macroeconomic policy measures such as withdrawals in state subsidies and services as well as rises in prices and taxes.[67]

The "informal economy" comprises two related domains: forms of social reproduction complementing production (as above); and informal "productive" activity off the books. For example, one of the world's largest slums, Dharavi, has an "informal" output of $1.25 billion a year, largely from the work of 250,000 people recycling the discarded waste of Mumbai's 16 million citizens. Before celebrating such ingenious microentrepreneurship among Dharavi's 1 million slumdwellers, note that most "workshops are constructed illegally on government land, power is routinely stolen, and commercial licenses are rarely sought. There is just one lavatory for every 1,500 residents, not a single public hospital, and only a dozen municipal schools. Throughout the slum, chicken and mutton stalls dump viscera into open drains thick with human and industrial waste; cholera, typhoid, and malaria are common. Taps run dry most of the time."[68]

Slumdwellers now comprise *a third* of the global urban population, and almost 50 percent of the population of the global South. UN-HABITAT estimates that the world's highest percentages of slumdwellers are in Ethiopia (99.4 percent of the urban population), Chad (99.4 percent), Afghanistan (98.5 percent), and Nepal (92 percent). Mumbai is the global slumdwellers' capital, with 10–12 million, Mexico City and Dhaka (9–10 million each), followed by Lagos, Cairo, Karachi, Kinshasa-Brazzaville, São Paulo, Shanghai, and Delhi (6–8 million each).[69]

In effect, neoliberal development and the generation of a "planet of slums" go together. Of course, these *peri-urban* communities, as they are known, have been expanding throughout the twentieth century, as the world's urban population surpassed that of the countryside in 2006.

Cities have absorbed nearly two-thirds of the global population explosion since 1950, and are currently growing by a million babies and migrants each week. . . . The global countryside, meanwhile has reached its maximum population and will begin to shrink after 2020. As a result, cities will account for virtually all future world population growth, which is expected to peak at about 10 billion in 2050. Ninety-five percent of this final buildout of humanity will occur in the urban areas of developing countries. . . . Indeed, the combined urban population of China, India, and Brazil already roughly equals that of Europe and North America.[70]

With global integration, the lines are drawn even more clearly, on a larger scale, and possibly more rapidly. There are professional and managerial classes—the Fast World elite—who participate in global circuits (involved with products, money, electronic communications, high-speed transport) linking enclaves of producers/consumers across state borders. Many of these people increasingly live and work within corporate domains, linked to the commercial and recreational centers, which are, in turn, delinked from national domains.[71] And there are those whom these circuits bypass or indeed displace. These are the redundant labor forces, the structurally unemployed, and the marginals, who live in shantytowns and urban ghettos or circulate the world.

Figure 6.2   Growth of World's Largest Cities, 1950 and 2007

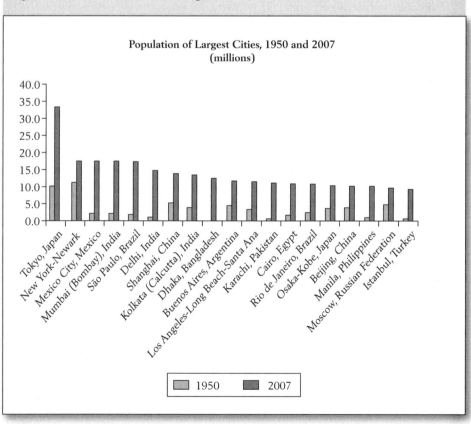

Source: Earth Policy Institute, 2008. Available at http://www.earth-policy.org/

Informalization as a process has two related *aspects:* the casualization of labor via corporate restructuring, and new forms of individual and collective livelihood strategies. The distinctive feature of corporate globalization is the active informalization of labor cascading across the world, as it is flexible, cheap, and depresses wages everywhere. Beginning with Export Processing Zones (EPZs), labor has been progressively *dis*organized via weakening and dismantling of labor regulations, incorporating vulnerable first-generation labor forces as depeasantization has proceeded. ILO estimates show some variation in the percentage of informalization of nonagricultural employment: 48 percent in North Africa, 51 in Latin America, 65 in Asia, and 72 in Sub-Saharan Africa.[72]

China shows an interesting variation on labor informalization. Given the draconian agricultural tax system in China, and an urban/rural differential greater than anywhere else, between 1996–2000 over 176 million peasants migrated to cities for work, but without the social benefits extended to urban residents. This itinerant labor force works mainly in newly zoned export factories and costing foreign corporations one-third the wage of city-born workers, itself a fraction of Northern wage costs. During this migration, the female percentage of informal workers rose from 45 to over 65 percent.[73] Sociologist Li Quiang's study of Beijing migrants (2002) revealed that one quarter were unpaid, almost two-thirds worked over 10 hours a day, with a sizable percentage working over 16 hours a day (over and above rush order episodes), and health care was non-existent.[74]

Meanwhile, in export agriculture from the global South, millions of women, comprising between 50 and 90 percent of workers employed in producing, processing, and retailing high-value horticultural crops (roses, apples, snowpeas, green beans, and avocados) experience informalization. TNCs organize these global supply chains, using their market power to pass business costs and risk on to suppliers, who in turn displace these on to their workforce. The ILO reports that rights violations of agricultural workers are "legion," and that women suffer weak labor rights, casualization, low wages, long hours, lax health and safety practices, gender stereotyping, and sexual harassment. Human rights violations of informal agricultural labor extend to child labor—for example, in 2003–2004, almost 83,000 children worked on cotton seed farms in India's Andhra Pradesh state, some supplying subsidiaries of TNCs such as Advanta, Bayer, Monsanto, Syngenta, and Unilever. NGOs report that many of these workers are under 10 years old, 85 percent are girls, and many are migrants from low castes, sold into debt bondage to pay off family loans: the "children's job is usually to cross-pollinate cotton flowers by hand for up to 13 hours a day; in the process they are exposed to toxic pesticides . . . and complain of headaches, nausea, and convulsions."[75]

The other face of informalization is the expanding range of activities of production and social reproduction occurring in the "shadow economy," comprising over 50 percent of the population of the global South. Commercial agriculture and habitat degradation routinely expel peasants and laborers from rural livelihoods; they migrate to urban centers where—as they hear on the radio and through migrant networks—jobs and amenities are available. As Hernando de Soto observes,

> Peru's legal institutions had been developed over the years to meet the needs and bolster the privileges of certain dominant groups in the cities and to isolate the peasants geographically in rural areas. . . . Once the peasants settled in the cities, however, the law began to lose social relevance. The migrants discovered that they were excluded from the facilities and benefits offered by the law . . . that they must compete not only against people but also against the system. Thus it was, that in order to survive, the migrants became informals.[76]

Complementing that image, Kalpana Sharma's *Rediscovering Dharavi* (the Mumbai slum) observes,

- It is a story of ingenuity and enterprise; it is a story of survival without subsidies or welfare; it is a story that illustrates how limited is the term "slum" to describe a place that produces everything from suitcases to leather goods, Indian sweets, papads, and gold jewelry.
- Every square inch of Dharavi is being used for some productive activity. This is "enterprise" personified, an island of free enterprise not assisted or restricted by the state, or any law. It brandishes its illegality. Child labor, hazardous industries, adulteration, recycling, popular products from cold drinks to toothpaste produced in Dharavi—it is all there for anyone to see. . . .
- If you want to eat the best *gulab jamuns* in town, buy the best *chiki*, acquire an export quality leather handbag, order World Health Organization (WHO) certified sutures for surgery, see the latest design in ready-made garments being manufactured for export, get a new suitcase or an old one repaired, taste food from the north and the south, see traditional south Indian gold jewelry—there are few better places in all of Mumbai than Dharavi.[77]

While such positive accounts restore perspective on life in "informal" areas, slumdwellers face recurring violence through demolition of their shacks. Sociologist Gayatri Menon's research on Dharavi notes, "Despite their careful selection of sites, because they live on public thoroughfares, pavement dwellers are routinely subjected to violent evictions and demolitions of their homes."[78] Reframing the notion of "invisibility," Fantu

Cheru represents the active withdrawal of African peasants from a failing formal economy, including paying taxes, as a "silent revolution": "the resuscitation of rural cooperatives, traditional caravan trade across borders, catering services and other activities that had once fallen into disuse, depriving the state of the revenue that traditionally financed its anti-people and anti-peasant development policies."[79] Here, exit is a strategic solution for producers and workers consistently bypassed by state policies. Serge LaTouche views the informal as

> comprehensive strategies of response to the challenges that life poses for displaced and uprooted populations in peri-urban areas. These are people torn between lost tradition and impossible modernity. The sphere of the informal has, incontestably, a major economic significance. It is characterized by a neo-artisanal activity that generates a lot of employment and produces incomes comparable to those of the modern sector.[80]

CASE STUDY   **Informalization Versus the African State—The Other Side of "Globalization"**

Aili Mari Tripp views the burgeoning informal sector across Africa as a form of resistance. Viewing informalization as more than a passive outcome of state or corporate restructuring, she focuses on the creative ways in which Africans have responded to the failure of development states, exacerbated by more than a decade of structural adjustment. Urban farming has proliferated in the absence of food subsidies, such that 68 percent of families in Dar es Salaam, Tanzania, grow their own vegetables and raise livestock. Noncompliance with the state has generated new institutional resources in Tanzania:

> Hometown development associations became visible in the late 1980s as urban dwellers sought to provide assistance to the rural towns from which they originated. They used these associations to build schools, orphanages, libraries, roads, and clinics; to establish projects to conserve the environment; to provide solar electricity and water; to disburse soft loans to women's groups engaged in business; and to raise funds for flood relief and other such causes. These new associations resemble the early, ethnically based welfare and burial societies that formed in Dar es Salaam in the early 1900s to help new migrants adjust to city life, except that their focus today is to assist people in their rural towns and villages.

In addition to these new resources, traditional resources such as midwifery and craftwork are revived, often undertaken by women. And new activities—from street vending, pastry selling, and hairbraiding to exporting seaweed—have sprung up. In some cases, informal businesses have become so successful in monetary terms that they have moved into the formal sector (e.g., in flour milling, dry cleaning, and prawn farming). The phenomenon of informalization combines individual enterprise as well as "moral economy," where community interests, rather than markets, define the values shaping economic activity. In Tanzania, the significance of informalization led to the 1991 Zanzibar Declaration, which acknowledged the legitimacy and social necessity of informal activities, outside of official corruption.

Is informalization one of today's problems to which there is no modern solution? Or is it simply a solution to modern problems?

Sources: O'Meara (1999: 34); Santos (2002); Tripp (1997: 13, 127, 188).

The "lost decade" intensified pressures to consolidate new livelihood strategies in already overburdened cities. Among Mexico's urban poor, collective pooling of resources to acquire land, shelter, and basic public services (water, electricity) was one widespread strategy for establishing networks among friends and neighbors to build their own cheap housing.[81] In 1992, Mexican intellectual Gustavo Esteva observed of the culture of the "new commons": "Peasants and grassroots groups in the cities are now sharing with people forced to leave the economic center the ten thousand tricks they have learned to limit the economy, to mock the economic creed, or to refunctionalize and reformulate modern technology."[82]

This culture, embedded in dense social networks among informals, has emerged as a new "safety valve" for the development establishment. An expanding sector of socially excluded people became embarrassing to the agents of structural adjustment, since traditional/collective forms of mutual aid and livelihood strategies among informals were considered modern anachronisms. To address this legitimacy crisis, and stabilize the poor (through the market, beyond the state), the culture of informality, serving as a survival mechanism for the poor, was redefined by the World Bank as an economic resource, as **social capital**, to be targeted by microlending. While microcredit has had some success in supporting low-income women, research in Nepal shows that it can also reinforce gender hierarchies, where women's work burden intensifies and husbands gain control of their business income—which means individual empowerment needs complementing with gender relations transformation.[83]

On top of the privations of structural adjustment, microcredit schemes also deplete mutual aid networks essential to survival of the poorest: women and children. Mercedes de la Rocha warns that, in Mexico, "persistent poverty over two decades has effectively brought the poor to their knees," and an NGO worker in Haiti claims the "tradition of mutual giving that allowed us to help each other and survive—this is all being lost."[84] Under these conditions, regions of informality become anomic, deepening human exploitation such as child prostitution and organ selling, with Chennai (India) having become world renowned for its "kidney farms."[85]

According to UN-HABITAT, slum populations now expand annually by 25 million. Consequently, countries like India are developing secondary cities to absorb informals—as India's chief economic planner, Montek Singh Ahluwalia, observes: "One hundred million people are moving to cities in the next 10 years, and it's important that these 100 million are absorbed into second-tier cities instead of showing up in Delhi or Mumbai."[86] *Planet of Slums* author Mike Davis notes that with "high-tech border enforcement blocking large-scale migration to the rich countries, only the slum remains as a fully franchised solution to the problem of warehousing this century's surplus humanity."[87]

Global Recolonization

The globalization project is realized through quite selective mechanisms of accumulation, dispossession, and neglect within a global field of power that retains the colonial imprint.[88] In Africa, postcolonial states, overly centralized and militarized, have generally served as instruments of wealth extraction.[89] Urban bias was amplified in Africa by state patronage systems constructed during colonialism on the basis of artificial tribal hierarchies.[90] The African one-party state arose out of the difficulties in securing power in and administering nation-states with artificial political boundaries. Such bifurcated power, between the centralized modern state and a "tribal authority which dispensed customary law to those living within the territory of the tribe," conditioned the current debility of African states.[91] This structure of power has facilitated the exploitation of rural areas by urban elites, enriched by foreign investment in resource extraction.[92]

Nobel laureate Wangari Maathai observes that the "modern African state is a superficial creation: a loose collection of ethnic communities or micro-nations" lumped together into a nation-state by the colonial powers: "some countries include hundreds of micro-nations within their borders; others only a few. Kenya has forty-two, Nigeria, two hundred and fifty . . . Zimbabwe, fewer than ten, and Burundi and Rwanda, three. . . . Most Africans didn't understand or relate to the nation-states created for them by the colonial powers; they understood, related to, and remained attached to the physical and psychological boundaries of their micro-nations."[93] Access to power and wealth operates through these filters, often at the expense of national coherence. The neoliberal era, combining austerity with extractive policies, has exacerbated these internal tensions. Either states serve as transmission belts between their hinterlands and the global economy, or subnational (ethnic) forces exploit political divisions and incapacities for similar purposes.

In the twenty-first century, anthropologist James Ferguson observes that deepening inequality stems from the condition where "capital 'hops' over 'unusable Africa,' alighting in mineral-rich enclaves that are starkly disconnected from their national societies." Ferguson continues, "it is worth asking whether Africa's combination of privately secured mineral-extraction enclaves and weakly governed humanitarian hinterlands might constitute not a lamentably immature form of globalization, but a quite 'advanced' and sophisticated mutation of it."[94] The model, restoring a colonial division of labor at the expense of coherent national institutions and societies, represents a form of "recolonization."

The contrast between Zambia's formerly paternalistic copper mining industry—with extensive social investment in housing, schools, hospitals, social workers, and sports clubs, and contemporary oil mining in Angola—is instructive. Whereas the former industry shed its social amenities under the glare of neoliberal reforms, the Angolan oil industry has been private from the start, where "nearly all of the production occurs offshore . . . and very little of the oil wealth even enters the wider society. In spite of some 25 years of booming oil production, Angolans today are among the most desperately poor people on the planet."[95] The dominant model emerging across the African oil states, similar to that of Angola, is characterized by "enclaved mineral-rich patches efficiently exploited by flexible private firms, with security provided on an 'as needed' basis by specialized corporations while the elite cliques who are nominal holders of sovereignty certify the industry's legality and international legitimacy in exchange for a piece of the action."[96] John Le Carré's 2006 novel *The Mission Song* fictionalizes this pattern.

African inequality expresses the selectivity of neoliberal development. Debates about Africa's marginality to the globalization project forget that Sub-Saharan Africa's foreign trade accounted for 52.7 percent of GDP in 2003, compared with a global average of 41.5 percent—one might argue that these countries' general "wealth is inversely proportional to their integration."[97] The 20 lowest-ranked countries in a 2004 UNDP ranking of "human poverty" (economic and well-being measures) are in Africa, which accounts for 39 of the 50 lowest-ranked countries.[98] The augmentation of the HIPC initiative in 2005 reinforced neoliberal conditionalities of macroeconomic austerity and privatization of services, despite acknowledgment by the Bank that the objectives of financial liberalization were not met, as billions of dollars a year flow offshore into private accounts.[99]

The New Partnership for Africa's Development (NEPAD), an African initiative agreed to by the G-8 (anticipating the formation of the African Union in 2002), continues this policy, urging African leaders to promote "democracy and human rights in their respective countries . . . [while simultaneously] instituting transparent legal and regulatory frameworks for financial markets."[100] Capital flight from every African country to open up its financial markets is endemic: "Africa's continued poverty ('marginalization') is a direct outcome of excess globalization, not of insufficient globalization, because of the drain from ever declining prices of raw materials (Africa's main exports), crippling debt repayments and profit repatriation to transnational corporations."[101]

An optimistic report in 2010 by consultants McKinsey and Company, titled "Lions on the Move," portrayed a continent with growing national economies, an expanding middle class of consumers (who accounted for 316 million cell phone purchases since 2000) and the prospect of the highest rates of return in the global South for foreign investors. It noted the changing economic landscape with China providing more financing of roads, power, railways, and other infrastructure than the World Bank.[102] Under the neoliberal mantle, it appears Africa is designated as an "extractive resource."

CASE STUDY   **Ethnic Politics, Resources, and the Recolonization of Nigeria**

Nigeria, with more than 250 ethnic groups, has three dominant groups: the Hausa-Fulani, the Yoruba, and the Ibo, with quite distinct political practices. The Hausa-Fulani in the north have roots in autocratic, bureaucratic, and hierarchical precolonial states; the Yoruba in the west have a tradition of loose confederation among centralized kingdoms where monarchs were elected by, and shared power with, a council of chiefs; and the Ibo in the south practiced decentralized and egalitarian forms of social organization. National unity is routinely compromised by ethnically driven politics, with interethnic competition heightened by resource scarcities.

Related to these fracture lines is an elemental division of Nigeria into a Muslim north and a Christian south, exacerbated by the exploitation of the south's oil resources by the north, where oil rents have financed a string of corrupt generals since Nigeria's independence in 1960. Per capita income is now one-quarter of what it was in the 1980s. The generals have not reinvested profits in the Niger Delta (population of 7 million) to preempt secession of the south, like the Biafran secession in 1967. In an internationally condemned incident in 1995, Nigerian writer Ken Saro-Wiwa was executed by the regime for protesting southern underdevelopment, linking it to exploitation by the northern-dominated government and foreign oil interests, and demanding compensation for the region and his Ogoni people.

Mobil, Shell, Texaco, Chevron, and other Western oil companies extract oil from the Delta—for example, Chevron's worldwide revenues of $30.6 billion in 1998 matched Nigeria's GNP of $30.7 billion in 1997 (one of Africa's biggest). Meanwhile, between 1970 and 2000, extreme poverty among Nigerians grew from 19 million (36 percent) to 90 million (70 percent). Mobil, Shell, and Chevron now play a *de facto* government role in the absence of state investment. Local movements demanding compensation have managed to involve these firms in financing basic community development needs such as running water, electricity, hospitals, and roads. But the oil companies' social "license to operate" enables an industry to extract profits from price rises justified by political instability, and the representation of Africa as the new frontier of terrorism.

All modern states embody historic tensions between formal secularism and historical layering of race and ethnic political relations, which are exacerbated by the impact of globalization. Why should African states be any different?

Sources: Cohen (1998: A1); Onishi (1998: A1, A6; 1999: 20–29); Sandbrook (1995: 93–94); Zalik (2004); Zalik and Watts (2006).

Governance reforms enable the "resource grab" in Africa, where natural resource exports accounted for almost 80 percent of exports in 2000, compared with 31 percent for the global South and 16 percent for the North. UNCTAD noted in 2003 that 12 African countries depended on a single export commodity: crude petroleum (Angola, 92 percent; Congo, 57; Gabon, 70; Nigeria, 96; and Equatorial Guinea, 91), copper (Zambia, 52 percent), diamonds (Botswana, 91 percent), coffee (Burundi, 76 percent;

Ethiopia, 62; Uganda 83), tobacco (Malawi, 59 percent), and uranium (Niger, 59 percent).[103] In 2004, foreign direct investment in Africa was $15 billion ($2 billion in 1986), with most new investment concentrated in mineral extraction, especially in Angola, Equatorial Guinea, Nigeria, and Sudan, and in deepwater oilfields off the West African coast—from which 25 percent of North American oil imports will come by 2015.[104]

In an era of Chinese ascendancy, the resource grab intensifies. Once self-sufficient in oil (1990), China was the second largest importer of oil after the United States by 2003, accounting for 40 percent of rising demand for oil in 2001–2005.[105] One-third of its oil is African. The Chinese National Petroleum Corporation (which overtook Shell in 2006 as the world's sixth largest oil company) and two other large Chinese oil firms operate in 17 African countries, including Sudan (Darfur notwithstanding), where a Chinese state-owned company owns 40 percent of the oil concession in the south (with 4,000 Chinese troops protecting Beijing's oil interests).[106] In 2006, China made a $1.4 billion deal to develop new oilfields in Angola, which became the largest supplier to China, ahead of Saudi Arabia. The deal includes China rebuilding Angola's railway and bridges, inland roads, irrigation systems, hospitals, and schools.[107]

For controversial anti-foreign aid economist Dambisa Moyo, the "explosive development of infrastructure" is a "transformational moment for Africa" leading to a maturing civil society as the middle class expands. But such "resource for infrastructure" development, while boosting economic growth statistics (and a middle class linked to state patronage) raises questions about the infrastructure of dependency and long-term incapacity. A Congolese lawyer remarked, "Six billion dollars in infrastructure is not development. . . . China is taking the place of the West . . . our cobalt goes off to China in the form of dusty ore and returns here in the form of expensive batteries." And a Congolese law-school dean commented, "the Chinese are not even making use of Congolese talent. They hire laborers, and that's it. When they pack up and go, the Congo will be left with nothing, not even an upgrade in our human resources. Our earth will be dug up, emptied, and left that way."[108]

China's relation to Africa resembles colonization, but with a twenty-first century twist. Between 2001 and 2006, China's trade with Africa rose five-fold, to $50 billion, exceeding its trade with the EU, and positioning it as Africa's third largest trading partner. It has almost 700 state companies with investments in 800 joint projects in Africa.[109] The Council on Foreign Relations reported in 2006, "China is acquiring control of natural resource assets, outbidding Western contractors on major infrastructural projects and providing soft loans and other incentives to bolster its competitive advantage."[110] That same year, exploiting a "South-South" rhetoric, China claimed its growing interests as a "strategic partnership with Africa, featuring political equality and mutual trust, economic win-win cooperation"—implying that China does not require governance reforms and anti-corruption initiatives as a condition for aid and trade, as do the IFIs, "which some see as a way to justify links with abusive regimes, such as those in Zimbabwe and Sudan."[111] Sociologist Ching Kwan Lee cautions that these relations are not monolithic and the Chinese impact depends on local political conditions and the learning curve of Chinese firms. Thus she finds Zambian copper miners, with an organizing tradition, able to leverage concessions from the new Chinese owner of the Chambishi mine in the name of resource nationalism, and in the context of rising world copper prices, compared with the unchecked casualization of textile workers in the Tanzania-China Friendship Mills in Dar es Salaam. She remarks, "China has become a compelling and effective conduit of capitalism in Africa. Its unparalleled rise . . . achieved largely independent of international financial institutions, have lent it enormous credential as a model of development for many African countries."[112]

In the wake of debilitating neoliberal reforms and endless debt servicing, and NEPAD, African countries now have access to a super-wealthy state not from the global North, and lacking its colonial baggage. Yet neo-colonial relations obtain. South Africa, where 86 percent of clothing imports are Chinese, has lost 300,000 textile jobs since 2002. Since 2000, Nigeria lost 350,000 jobs directly and 1.5 million indirectly due to Chinese competition.[113] Cheap imports of Chinese manufactured goods are matched by Chinese investment in the sectors such as commercial aviation, agricultural machinery, urban transportation, and telecommunications.[114] Human Rights Watch claims Chinese policies in Africa (following the historic lead of the West) have "propped up some of the continent's worst human-rights abusers."[115] Exploitation of natural resources reproduces the colonial pattern of "export of sustainability"—concerns have been raised over "the environmental impact of various Chinese-run mining operations in Africa, including copper mines in Zambia and Congo, and titanium sands projects in ecologically sensitive parts of Mozambique, Kenya, Tanzania, and Madagascar."[116]

Loss of resource sovereignty accompanies compromised political authority: "particularly in Sub-Saharan Africa, government forces are in decay and private security organizations are on the rise, including forces loyal to regional warlords, citizens' self-defense groups, corporate-sponsored forces, foreign mercenaries, and criminal gangs. In fact, it is becoming more difficult to make clear-cut distinctions between legitimate and illegitimate, and between public and private, security forces."[117] One dramatic manifestation of the loss of political cohesion of some African states is an exploding refugee population, consisting of "international refugees" and "internally displaced persons," underlining the civilian casualty in the militarization of the continent, which has deep roots linking the colonial era to an era of recolonization. The nineteenth century scramble for Africa, symbolized by the Berlin Conference of 1884, is on again—with the United States, France, Britain, India, and China competing for oil, gas, timber, bauxite, copper, diamonds, gold, and coltan.

SUMMARY

The globalization project has had many social and political dimensions. We have examined just five of its vectors: poverty governance, outsourcing, displacement, informalization, and recolonization. None of these is unique to the global project. They have all appeared in previous eras in different forms, and not on the scale found today. They are linked—indeed, they are mutually conditioning processes, being dimensions of a single process of global restructuring affecting all countries, although with local variation.

Poverty governance shifts responsibility by embedding impoverishing policies in states themselves. These are supplemented by the technological shedding of labor and the downsizing and stagnation produced by structural adjustment programs, in turn expanding the informal sector, as wage labor is casualized. Corporate strategies of flexibility contribute to this informalization as much as the displacement of populations from their land and livelihood. Some observers see informalization as a countermovement to the official economy and to state regulation—asserting a culture of the "new commons." Informalization is a by-product of neglect, exclusion, and resource dispossession—processes endemic in Africa today, where the resource race is being played out via a recolonization process. The globalization project may have a universal vision, but it is often unequal in its outcomes.

FURTHER READING

Caraway, Teri L. *Assembling Women: The Feminization of Global Manufacturing.* Ithaca, NY: Cornell University Press, 2007.

Davis, Mike. *Planet of Slums.* London: Verso, 2006.

Elyachar, Julia. *Markets of Dispossession: NGOs, Economic Development, and the State in Cairo.* Durham, NC: Duke University Press, 2005.

Ferguson, James. *Global Shadows: Africa in the Neoliberal World Order.* Durham, NC: Duke University Press, 2006.

Guerrero, Dorothy-Grace, and Firoze Manji, eds. *China's New Role in Africa and the South.* Capetown: Fahamu & Bangkok: Focus on the Global South, 2008.

SELECT WEBSITES

China Labor Watch: www.chinalaborwatch.org

FoodFirst Information and Action Network: www.fian.org

Grameen Bank: www.grameen-info.org

International Labor Rights Forum: www.laborrights.org

International Labour Organization (ILO): www.ilo.org

Maquila Solidarity Network (Canada): www.maquilasolidarity.org

Migrant Rights International (Switzerland): www.migrantwatch.org

TransAfrica Forum (USA): www.transafricaforum.org

Transparency International: www.transparency.org

Union Network International: www.union-network.org

United Nations High Commissioner for Refugees (UNHCR): www.unhcr.ch

7

Global Countermovements

The globalization project has been a relatively coherent perspective and has had a powerful set of states, agencies, and corporations working on its behalf. Nevertheless, its discourse and rules are always in contention *because* this project is realized through various inequalities. Like the development project, the globalization project attempts to fashion the world around a central principle (the free market) through powerful political and financial institutions. Framed as a discourse of rights and freedom, the power of the organizing principle ultimately depends on the interpretation and effect of these ideals. Diane Perrons puts it this way: "Neoliberalism is a powerful ideology and appeals to people's self-interest. It implies that free markets are somehow a natural and inevitable state of affairs in which individual endeavor will be rewarded, and perhaps because of this the poor accept growing inequalities because they think they have a chance of becoming rich themselves as society appears to be freer and more open."[1]

Countermovements resist aspects of globalization. Most governments feel the pressure to play by the new and emerging global rules, but their citizens do not always share their outlook. This chapter surveys some of these countermovements, exploring their origins and goals. Examining each movement offers a particular angle on the reformulation of development in the globalization project. Most countermovements converge as "global justice movements" (environmentalism, feminism, cosmopolitan activism, and food sovereignty), but there are conservative countermovements, notably religious fundamentalism of all kinds.

Environmentalism

Environmentalism as a countermovement questions modern assumptions that nature and its bounty are infinite. It has two main and non-mutually exclusive strands. One derives from growing environmental awareness among Northern citizens, inspired by the 1962 publication of Rachel Carson's *Silent Spring*. This path-breaking work documented the disruption in the earth's ecosystems caused by agricultural chemicals. Its title refers to the absence of birdsong in the spring. Carson's metaphor dramatized the dependence of life on sustainable ecological systems. It also emphasized the West's rationalized perception of nature as "external" to society, a perception that encourages the belief that nature is an infinitely exploitable domain.[2]

A range of "green" movements has mushroomed throughout the North as the simple truths revealed by Carson's study have gained an audience. "Greens" typically challenge the assumptions and practices of unbridled economic growth, arguing for scaling back to a renewable economic system of resource use. One focus is agricultural sustainability—that is, reversing the environmental stress associated with capital- and chemical-intensive agriculture, linked to a fast-growing movement for organic food. A key goal is maintaining a natural aesthetic to complement the consumer lifestyle, the emphasis being on preserving human health and enhancing leisure activities.

The second strand of environmentalism involves Southern movements (known as the "environmentalism of the poor") to protect particular bioregions from environmentally damaging practices. Across the world, where rural populations produce 60 percent of their food, human communities depend greatly on the viability of regional ecologies for their livelihood. Such movements are therefore often distinguished by their attempts to protect existing cultural habitats. In contrast to Northern environmentalism, seeking to regulate the environmental implications of the market, Southern environmentalism questions market forces. This is especially true where states and firms seek to "monetize" and harvest natural resources on which human communities depend.

Local communities have always challenged environmentally damaging practices where natural conservation is integral to local culture. In the late twentieth century, forest dwellers across the tropics grabbed the world's attention as they attempted to preserve tropical rainforests from extensive timber cutting. Logging and beef cattle pasturing in degraded forest areas intensified with the agro-export boom of the 1980s, amplifying Southern environmentalism. Demands for Northern-style environmental regulation gathered momentum to address environmental stresses from resource mining and river damming to the overuse of natural resources, resulting in desertification, excessive water salinity, and chemical contamination associated with the green revolution.

The common denominator of most environmental movements is a belief that natural resources are not infinitely renewable. The finiteness of nature has been a global preoccupation, from the neo-Malthusian specter of population growth overwhelming land and the food grown on it to anxiety about the dwindling supplies of raw materials, such as the fossil fuels and timber that sustain modern economies.

Lately, however, this rather linear perspective has yielded to a more dynamic one that sees a serious threat to natural processes such as the atmosphere, climates, and biodiversity. Trees may be renewable through replanting schemes, but the atmospheric conditions that nurture them may not so easily be replenished. The world has moved to a new threshold of risk to its sustainability:

> It used to be feared that we would run out of non-renewable resources—things like oil, or gold. Yet these, it seems, are the ones we need worry least about. It is the renewables—the ones we thought would last forever—that are being destroyed at an accelerating rate. They are all living things, or dynamic parts of living ecosystems.[3]

Furthermore, the very survival of the human species is increasingly at risk as pollution and environmental degradation lead to public health epidemics. These include lead poisoning, new strains of cancer, cataracts from ozone destruction, immune suppression by ultraviolet radiation, and loss of genetic and biological resources for producing food and medicines.[4]

Producing "renewable" resources undermines ecological sustainability. While a monocultural tree plantation may provide timber products, it cannot perform the regenerative function that natural systems perform: "The result can be illusory gains in income and permanent losses in wealth."[5]

As a consequence of the appreciation of "nature's services," a form of **ecological accounting** is emerging—for example, the economic value of the world's ecosystem services is currently estimated at around $33 trillion a year, exceeding the global gross national product (GNP) of $25 trillion. However appropriate it is to value nature thus, this trend is an antidote to traditional economics reasoning, which renders environmental impact invisible.[6]

The change in thinking has been stimulated from several quarters. In the first place, there are the new social movements (conceptualized in the following box), some of which are the subject of this chapter. Their appearance on the historical stage reflects a critique of capitalist developmentalism and a search for new forms of social and political action, and subjectivity.[7]

WHAT ARE THE NEW SOCIAL MOVEMENTS?

"New social movements,"—the greens, feminism, shack dwellers, food sovereignty, worker-owned cooperatives, participatory budgeting, food policy councils, self-housing associations, neighborhood assemblies, landless workers, and so on—share a criticism of the economism, centralism, and hierarchies of the development project. Gaining formal rights as abstract citizens in the state (the "old social movement" goal) is secondary to developing particular practices that question dominant values and power relations. As J. K. Gibson-Graham suggests, when unemployed workers in Argentina occupied abandoned factories during the 2001 financial crisis, they had to learn to transcend their individualist and wage-oriented worker mentalities to construct "an economy and sociality of 'solidarity' as members of the unemployed workers' movement." Similarly, slumdwellers in the Alliance, in Mumbai, India—in dialogue with the Homeless People's Federation in South Africa—build community-managed savings schemes, and use self-surveying and resident enumeration as a politics of visibility to affirm their presence.

Sources: Gibson-Graham (2006: xxv, xxxv); Menon (2010).

The second indication of a change in thinking is a growing awareness of the limits of "spaceship earth." From the late 1960s, space photographs of planet earth dramatized the biophysical finiteness of our world. The dangerous synergies arising from global economic intercourse and ecology were driven home by the Brundtland Commission's declaration in 1987: "The Earth is one but the world is not. We all depend on one biosphere for sustaining our lives."[8]

Third, various grassroots movements focus attention on the growing conflict on the margins between local cultures and the global market. For example, the Kayapo Indians of the Amazon strengthened their demands by appealing to the global community regarding defense of their forest habitat from logging, cattle pasturing, and extraction of genetic resources. One response by the Brazilian government to this kind of demand was the creation of self-managing **extractive reserves** for native tribes and rubber tappers to protect them from encroaching ranchers and colonists. These reserves are relatively large areas of forestland set aside, with government protection, for extractive activities by forest dwellers.[9]

Finally, during the era of neoliberalism, the pressure on natural resources from the rural poor has intensified. This pressure stems from the long-term impoverishment of rural populations forced to overwork their land and fuel sources to eke out a subsistence living. As land and forests were increasingly devoted to export production in the 1980s, millions of rural poor were pushed into occupying marginal tropical forest ecosystems. Environmental degradation, including deforestation, resulted.

Environmental movements pursue "sustainable development"—emphasizing self-organizing rather than centralizing development. Resistance to the Narmada Dam is a case in point. Since the 1980s, the Indian government has been implementing a huge dam project in the Narmada River valley, with assistance from the World Bank. This massive project expected to displace more than 2 million people. In 1992, at the time of the Earth Summit, there was an embarrassing release of an independent review (the first ever) of the World Bank's Sardar Sarovar dam project in India. Commissioned by the World Bank president at that time, the review claimed "gross delinquency" on the part of the World Bank and the Indian government in both the engineering and the forcible resettlement of indigenous peoples. These revelations and the growing resistance movement, the Narmada Bachao Andolan (Movement to Save the Narmada), forced the World Bank to withdraw its support for this project. Grassroots opponents to the dam argue that the resistance

articulates . . . the critical legacy of Mahatma Gandhi . . . of the struggles all over the country that continue to challenge both the growing centralization and authoritarianism of the state and the extractive character of the dominant economic process—a process which not only erodes and destroys the subsistence economies of these areas, but also the diversity of their systems. . . . The movement is therefore representative of growing assertions of marginal populations for greater economic and political control over their lives.[10]

Sustainable Development

The concept of sustainable development gained currency as a result of the 1987 Brundtland report, titled *Our Common Future*. The report defined sustainable development as "meet[ing] the needs of the present without compromising the ability of future generations to meet their own needs."[11] How to achieve this remains a puzzle. The Brundtland Commission suggested steps such as conserving and enhancing natural resources, encouraging grassroots involvement in development, and adopting appropriate technologies (smaller scale, energy conserving). While acknowledging that "an additional person in an industrial country consumes far more and places far greater pressure on natural resources than an additional person in the Third World," the Commission nevertheless recommended economic growth to reduce the pressure of the poor on the environment.[12]

The report did not resolve the interpretive debate over the root cause of environmental deterioration—whether the threat to our common future stems from poverty or from affluence:

- Those who argue that poverty is the cause consider the gravest stress on the environment to be impoverished masses pressing on resources. Population control and economic growth are the suggested solutions.
- Those who identify affluence as the problem believe that the gravest stress on the environment comes from global inequality and the consumption of resources to support affluent lifestyles.

Measures of this latter effect abound, one of the more provocative being the claim that each U.S. citizen contributes 60 times more to global warming than each Mexican and that a Canadian's contribution equals that of 190 Indonesians. This perspective has generated former World Bank economist Herman E. Daly's "impossibility theorem": that "a U.S. style high-resource consumption standard" is no longer appropriate for planetary sustainability.[13]

Earth Summits

The terms of this debate infused the 1992 United Nations Conference on Environment and Development (UNCED). Popularized as the Rio de Janeiro "Earth Summit," it was the largest diplomatic gathering ever held. The United Nations Environment Program (UNEP) organized the conference to review progress on the Brundtland report. Conference preparations resulted in a document, known as Agenda 21, addressing all sides of the debate, which continued through the decade, to the rather low-key and ineffectual follow-up 2002 World Summit on Sustainability in Johannesburg.

The South, for instance, recognizes that the North has an interest in reducing carbon dioxide emissions and preserving biodiversity and the tropical rainforests for planetary survival. It agreed to participate in a global program in return for financial assistance, and called for massive investment by the North in sustainable development measures in the South, including health, sanitation, education, technical assistance, and conservation.[14]

However, UNCED detoured from the question of global inequities, stressing environmental protection to be a priority, but "without distorting international trade and investment."[15] The outcome was a shift in emphasis from the Brundtland report: privileging *global* management of the environment over local/national concerns, and maintaining the viability of the global economy rather than addressing deteriorating economic conditions in the South. The globalization project was alive and well. Thus the WTO has a national treatment code allowing foreign investors to claim the same rights as domestic ones, which threatens to institutionalize "cut-and-run" logging around the world.[16]

Managing the Global Commons

Environmental management is as old as the need for human communities to ensure material and cultural survival. Global environmental management seeks to preserve planetary resources, but there is not yet any resolution as to what end, nor as to the terms on which states will participate. Within the globalization project, it is not difficult to see that states, strapped for foreign exchange and sometimes required to undergo reform to earn foreign exchange, are beholden to corporations that want to exploit natural resources and/or secure control over their supply in the future. In many cases, local inhabitants—with NGO support—have led the charge to question the commercialization and degradation of environments to which they are historically and spiritually attached.

Southern grassroots movements, in particular, regard global environmental managers and their powerful state allies as focused on managing the global environment to ensure the profitability of global economic activity. This includes regulating the use of planetary resources and global waste sinks such as forests, wetlands, and bodies of water. Instead of linking environmental concerns to issues of social justice and resource distribution, the new Northern-centered **"global ecology"** has converged on four priorities:

- reducing greenhouse gas emissions, mainly from automobiles and burning forests;
- protecting biodiversity, mainly in tropical forests;
- reducing pollution in international waters; and
- curbing ozone-layer depletion.

The institutional fallout from UNCED strengthened global economic management. A **Global Environmental Facility (GEF)** was installed, geared to funding global ecology initiatives. The World Bank initiated the establishment of the GEF to channel monies into global environmental projects, especially in the four areas identified above; 50 percent of the projects approved in the GEF's first tranche were for biodiversity protection.

In addition, UNCED, via the Food and Agricultural Organization (FAO), planned to zone Southern land for cash cropping with the assistance of national governments. Under this facility, subsistence farming would be allowed only where "natural resource limitations" or "environmental or socioeconomic constraints" prevent intensification. And where governments deem marginal land to be overpopulated, the inhabitants would be forced into transmigration or resettlement programs.[17]

This scenario means managing the "global commons" and viewing surplus populations and their relation to scarce natural resources as the immediate problem, rather than situating the problem of "surplus population" in a broader framework that recognizes extreme inequality of access to resources. In Brazil, for example, less than 1 percent of the population owns about 44 percent of the fertile agricultural land, and 32 million people are officially considered destitute. Structural adjustment policies, grain imports, and expansion of soy export production have dispossessed small peasants. Under conditions where Brazilian social ministries have lost power, landless peasants who do not join the *Sem Terra* (see below) or the mass migration to the towns or the frontier are incorporated into NGO-organized "poverty management" programs, constituting a cheap labor force for wealthy landowners.[18]

Global ecology, geared to environmental management on a large scale, has priorities for sustainability that often differ from those of the remaining local environmental managers. It is estimated that there are 200 to 300 million forest-dwellers in South and South-East Asia, distinct from lowland communities dependent on irrigated agriculture. Some of these people have been given official group names assigning them a special—and usually second-class—status in their national society: India's "scheduled tribes" (*adivasis*), Thailand's "hill tribes," China's "minority nationalities," the Philippines' "cultural minorities," Indonesia's "isolated and alien peoples," Taiwan's "aboriginal tribes," and Malaysia's "aborigines." Challenging their national status and elevating their internationally common bonds, these groups have redefined themselves as "indigenous."[19]

Indigenous and tribal people around the world have had their rights to land and self-determination enshrined in the International Labor Organization Convention. Nevertheless, they are routinely viewed from afar as marginal. The World Bank, in adopting the term "indigenous" in its documents, stated in 1990, "The term indigenous covers indigenous, tribal, low caste, and ethnic minority groups. Despite their historical and cultural differences, they often have a limited capacity to participate in the national development process because of cultural barriers or low social and political status."[20]

Viewed through the development lens, this perspective carries a significant implication. On the one hand, it perpetuates the unexamined assumption that these cultural minorities need guidance. On the other hand, it often subordinates minorities to national development initiatives, such as commercial logging or government forestry projects involving tree plantations. Often indigenous peoples are the object of large-scale resettlement programs justified by the belief that forest destruction results from their poverty and subsistence lifestyle.

Environmental Resistance Movements

In all these cases, there is a discernible pattern of collaboration between the multilateral financiers and governments concerned with securing territory and foreign exchange. Indigenous cultures, on the other hand, are typically marginalized. Indonesia's Forestry Department controls 74 percent of the national territory, and the minister for forestry claimed in 1989, "In Indonesia, the forest belongs to the state and not to the people. . . . They have no right of compensation" when their habitats fall to logging concessions.[21]

Under these conditions, "environmentalism of the poor" proliferates. It takes two forms: active resistance, which seeks to curb invasion of habitats by states and markets; and adaptation, which exemplifies the centuries-old practice of renewing habitats in the face of environmental deterioration. In the latter practice lie some answers to current problems.

One dramatic form of resistance was undertaken by the Chipko movement in the central Himalaya region of India. Renewing an ancient tradition of peasant resistance in 1973, the Chipko adopted a Gandhian strategy of nonviolence, symbolized in the primarily women-led tree-hugging protests against commercial logging. Similar protests spread across northern India in a move to protect forest habitats for tribal peoples. Emulating the Chipko practice of tree planting to restore forests and soils, the movement developed a "pluck-and-plant" tactic. Its members uprooted eucalyptus seedlings—the tree of choice in official social forestry, even though it does not provide shade and ravishes aquifers—and replaced them with indigenous species of trees that yield products useful to the locals.[22] Environmental activism proliferates across the South. In Thailand, where the state promotes eucalyptus plantations that displace forest dwellers, there has been sustained rural activism in the name of community rights to local forests versus eucalyptus monoculture.[23]

CASE STUDY   Las Gaviotas—Tropical Sustainability

In the early 1970s, Paulo Lugari and collaborators (engineers, artists, students, Indians, and even street children) built a sustainable village in the remote plains of Colombia, 500 kilometers from the capital, Bogotá. Despite continuous violence within the country around the coca economy, Las Gaviotas has survived, supported by ingenious renewable energy technology (water systems, distillers, solar-powered cookers, windmills, and pumps), hydroponic farming, and a project of regenerating surrounding rainforest from the barren savannah soil. Knowing the savannah was once part of the Amazon forest, Lugari managed to introduce Caribbean pine seedlings to provide shade, increase soil moisture, and promote biodiversity. The regenerated forest yields drinking water, with valuable resins, oils, and fragrances from the forest supporting this experiment in self-sufficiency. The village supports 200 workers with piece rate wages and room, board, and medical care; 50 resident families, and approximately 500 children from the region, have accessed its school. Adults rotate among jobs in the village (construction, planting, gardening, and cooking). Aside from providing a haven from civil strife, social collaboration involves all in the project of sustainability. "The success of Las Gaviotas in sustainably supporting the community from the products of the regenerated rainforest has prompted new dreams of expanding the forest across the savannah, with both environmental and social benefits. . . . Plans to achieve this extraordinary environmental and social transformation, beginning with a tenfold expansion of the forest around Las Gaviotas," won government endorsement in 2004. Further plans for developing the carbon sequestration system, production of potable water, and ecotourism have obtained financial support from a Belgian socially responsible corporation, Zero Emissions Research and Initiatives (ZERI).

Can the marriage of grassroots environmentalism with "green capitalism" be sustainable, in both senses of the term?

Source: White and Marino (2007: 22).

As grassroots environmentalism mushrooms across the South, community control gains credibility by example. At the same time, the institutional aspects of technology transfer associated with the development project come under question. An ex-director of forestry at the Food and Agricultural Organization commented,

Only very much later did it dawn on the development establishment that the very act of establishing new institutions often meant the weakening, even the destruction of existing indigenous institutions which ought to have served as the basis for sane and durable development: the family, the clans, the tribe, the village, sundry mutual aid organizations, peasant associations, rural trade unions, marketing and distribution systems and so on.[24]

Forest dwellers have *always* managed their environment. From the perspective of colonial rule and developers, these communities did not appear to be involved in management because their practices were alien to the specialized pursuit of commercial wealth characterizing Western ways beginning under colonialism. Local practices were therefore either suppressed or ignored.

Now, where colonial forestry practices erased local knowledge and eroded natural resources, recent grassroots mobilization, such as the Green Belt Movement in Kenya organized by women, has reestablished intercropping to replenish soils and tree planting to sustain forests. Where development agencies and planners have attempted to impose irrigated cash cropping, such as in eastern Senegal, movements such as the Senegalese Federation of Sarakolle Villages have collectively resisted in the interests of sustainable peasant farming.[25]

The challenge for environmental movements in the South is twofold: to create alternatives to the capital- and energy-intensive forms of specialized agriculture and agro-forestry appropriate to the goal of restoring and sustaining local ecologies; and to build alternative models to the bureaucratic, top-down development plans that have typically subordinated natural resource use to commercial, rather than sustainable, social ends. Perhaps the fundamental challenge to Southern environmentalism is the perspective that has defined World Bank programming: "Promoting development is the best way to protect the environment."[26] The question is whether development, understood from the World Bank's perspective, is a source of sustainability.

Feminism

The term *féminisme* first appeared in France in the 1880s, referring to a movement for women's rights. It reappeared in the 1970s as "second-wave feminism," in the midst of the women's liberation movement for gender equality, taking on multiple meanings for women in the Third World, women of color, lesbians, and working women.[27] With respect to development, feminism has served to transform our understanding of the meaning, and implications of development, as well as to institutionalize policy agendas committed to broad gender equality in a transformed concept of human development: "supporting the development of peoples' potential to lead creative, useful, and fulfilling lives."[28] Thus, in 1999, the Women's International Coalition for Economic Justice issued a Declaration for Economic Justice and Women's Empowerment, which demanded "macro-policies designed to defend the rights of women and poor people and protect the environment, rather than expand growth, trade, and corporate profits exclusively. . . . Redefining economic efficiency to include measuring and valuing women's unpaid as well as paid work. Economic efficiency needs to be reoriented towards the effective realization of human development and human rights rather than growth, trade, and corporate profits."[29]

Embedded within this statement are three feminist threads that weave an alternative development agenda: valuing equality in productive work; valuing the work of social reproduction; and reorienting social values from economism to humanism. These threads have informed successive phases of feminist influence on development thinking—in particular, issues concerning economic justice in the workplace, social policy supporting unpaid labor, and identification of the threat to human sustainability embodied in the mutual reinforcement of patriarchy and the market system. Thus the "Advocacy Guide to Women's World Demands," arising from the 2000 World March of Women, declared,

> We live in a world whose dominant economic system, neoliberal capitalism, is fundamentally inhuman. It is a system governed by unbridled competition that strives for privatization, liberalization, and deregulation. It is a system entirely driven by the dictates of the market and where full enjoyment of basic human rights ranks below the laws of the marketplace. The result: the crushing social exclusion of large segments of the population, threatening world peace and the future of the planet. . . .
>
> Neoliberalism and patriarchy feed off each other and reinforce each other in order to maintain the vast majority of women in a situation of cultural inferiority, social devaluation, economic marginalization, "invisibility" of their existence and labor, and the marketing and commercialization of their bodies. All these situations closely resemble apartheid.[30]

The trajectory of feminist influence on development began with the first UN World Conference on Women, held in Mexico City in 1975, focused on extending existing development programs to include women—especially regarding equality in employment and education, political participation, and health services. This movement was known as Women in Development (WID), and framed the UN Decade for Women (1976–1985). Since then, the movement has changed gears, shifting from remedies to alternatives,[31] or what Rounaq Jahan terms an "integrationist" approach to an "agenda-setting" approach, which challenges conventional development thinking with a feminist perspective.[32] The goal includes involving women as decision makers concerned with empowering all women in their various life situations, and championing opposition to all forms of gender discrimination (e.g., gendered divisions of labor). This has come to be known as Gender and Development (GAD), which refocuses on the different development priorities and needs of women and men without segregating gender issues into separate projects. The WID/GAD initiatives have focused on influencing development discourse and practice, especially through policy making in the development agencies.

An important resource in this project has been the Convention on the Elimination of All Forms of Discrimination against Women (CEDAW), adopted by the United Nations Assembly in 1979, Article 5 of which imposes the responsibility on states to transform customs, attitudes, and practices that discriminate against women. This convention was the culmination of 30 years' work by the UN Commission on the Status of Women, instrumental in documenting discrimination against women.

Feminist Formulations

The WID position redresses the absence of gender issues in development theory and practice, in particular "women's inequality of access to and participation in the definition of economic structures and policies and the productive process itself."[33] In the development debate, WID feminists identified problems and formulated remedies in the following ways:

- Women have always been *de facto* producers, but technological and vocational supports have been minimal because development focuses on male cash-earning activity. Planners should therefore recognize women's contributions, especially as food producers for rural households and even urban markets, where males labor when not migrating to the agro-export or cash crop sector.
- Women bear children, and a more robust understanding of development would include education, health care, family planning, and nutrition as social supports.
- Finally, since women perform unpaid household/farm labor in addition to any paid labor, development planners should pursue ameliorative measures. Findings reveal that where women can be incorporated into income-earning activities, a net benefit accrues to community welfare since male income is often dissipated in consumer/urban markets. Thus, in addition to claiming what women need from development, WID advocates what development needs from women.[34]

In contrast, GAD feminism has offered development remedies as follows:

- Since gender is socially constructed, it is important to address gender inequality not simply on the basis of who is doing what, and whether it is valued, but also by asking how activities come to be valued, by whom, and in whose interest. The goal is to not simply identify women's discrimination, but also to understand the structuring of gender discrimination.
- Households are differentiated social units, with conflictive and/or cooperative gendered divisions of labor. Therefore it is important to understand the nature of relations between productive and reproductive work, to understand the impact of development on household relations and vice versa.
- By shifting the focus to gender relations, or roles, and making visible the work of social reproduction, GAD enables policy makers to see where it "pays" (in development/efficiency, rather than equity, terms) to deliver resources to women.

The WID/GAD project has served as a platform for reforming development initiatives, with the World Bank initiating WID projects in 1987, and shifting toward the GAD approach in the mid-1990s. WID projects were largely supplemental, and left unchallenged questions of differential access to services, resources, and opportunities between women and men, and the social and development consequences. Since the 1995 Beijing Conference on Women, the World Bank has attempted to "mainstream" gender issues, with variable results.[35]

Outside of what might be called "policy-feminism," feminist movements have proliferated into a matrix of "transnational feminist networks" or TFNs (see the list of websites at the end of this chapter), working in national organizations, multilateral, and intergovernmental organizations, and with local organizations to advocate for particular questions such as human rights, demilitarization, labor standards, and so on. Valentine Moghadam notes that global communication technology allows these TFNs a fluid constituency and flexibility, which combines with non-hierarchical feminist principles and both formal and informal ways of operating. Some TFNs include[36]

- DAWN (Development Alternatives with Women for a New Era): gender and economic justice, IFI policy, reproductive rights, and health—especially for poor Southern women, redistribution of global wealth;
- WIDE (Women in Development Europe): enhanced European aid to ACP (African, Caribbean, and Pacific) countries, feminist alternatives to economic theory and development policies of the North, the IFIs, and the WTO;

- WEDO (Women's Environment and Development Organization): equal participation of women in policymaking, formulation of alternative and sustainable solutions to global problems, democratization of the WTO;
- WLUML (Women Living Under Muslim Laws): promotes human rights of women in Muslim states, exposes fundamentalist and state collusion, implementation of CEDAW in all Muslim states; and
- SIGI (Sisterhood Is Global Institute): human rights advocacy for women.

In keeping with the "new social movement" designation, DAWN, for example, argues that "women should not depend on government but develop autonomously through self-organization," and its manifesto spells out its humanistic vision:

> Each person will have the opportunity to develop her or his full potential and creativity, and values of nurturance and solidarity will characterize human relationships. In such a world women's reproductive role will be redefined: men will be responsible for their sexual behavior, fertility and the well-being of both partners. Child care will be shared by men, women, and society as a whole.[37]

The humanism evolved from an initial identification of "male bias" in social attitudes and thought, and in public policy, as laid out in Diane Elson's *Male Bias in the Development Process* (1991). Elson notes that structural adjustment policies assume an infinite capacity of women to perform the work of social reproduction, given austerity cutbacks in social services: "the hidden 'equilibrating factor' is the household's, and particularly women's ability to absorb the shocks of stabilization programs, through more work and 'making do' on limited incomes."[38] Male bias that ignores unpaid labor uses terms like "efficiency" so that streamlining costs for a public hospital, for example, achieves efficiency by "transferring costs from the productive to the reproductive economy," where women's additional and unpaid work in caring for convalescing patients at home compensates for the shortfall in hospital care."[39] And WIDE, for example, extended this to a general critique of the "free market" thesis, arguing that women must "reclaim the market in a global system where every part of life—even a person's kidney—is increasingly peddled as a commodity, and which sees people as consumers rather than citizens."[40]

Thus a feminist paradigm has emerged which is not simply about adding women to the equation. Rather, from the standpoint of women's experience, feminists have gained a unique perspective on the limits, silences, and violence of an economic model that accounts only for certain definitions of what constitutes "productive" work, via an unsustainable system of accounting that has no debit side (for what economists term "externalities"). It stems from the UN System of National Accounts, which records additions to Gross National Product, but not "costs" such as discrimination (in schooling, nutrition, employment), environmental degradation, the invisible work of social reproduction in the home, and so forth. As Marilyn Waring notes in *If Women Counted: A New Feminist Economics* (1988), economics serves as a "tool of people in power," insofar as value is imputed to a narrow band of cash-generating activity: women, assigned to the household, are discounted, and informals—indigenous peasants, nomads, and forest dwellers—are marginalized or displaced as "unproductive," along with disregard for "nature's economy." Thus economic theory conditions the possibility of a predatory relationship toward women and nature through development practices. The conventional development paradigm, in positing a rationalist (Eurocentric) approach, discounts diverse non-European knowledges governed by ecological and cultural practices, where stewardship of nature is cultural, rather than a program.[41]

Broadly, the feminist paradigm stresses that development is a relational, not a universal, process, and we should be aware of how our ideals shape assumptions about other societies and their needs. Concerns for the empowerment of women in Third World settings should refer to those circumstances, not to abstract ideals of individual emancipation. Consider the "feminization of global labor." As Jeffrey Sachs argues, regarding the garment factory expansion in Bangladesh, "sweatshops are the first rung on the ladder out of extreme poverty" for the female workers who have "grown up in the countryside, extraordinarily poor, illiterate and unschooled, and vulnerable to chronic hunger and hardship in a domineering patriarchal society."[42] Far from an unproblematic gain for women, sweatshop jobs are constructed for women as repetitive, dead-end, and often debilitating, so that their introduction to the global economy is on unequal terms. Cynthia Enloe's research, guided by the question of what makes labor cheap, argues that women are not simply acted on by globalization; rather, corporate strategies depend on local constructions of femininity.[43] And, while Asian women have experienced wage gains (until "defeminization" through industrial upgrading in the Asian regional division of labor), research on Mexican *maquiladoras* reveals a different experience, where wages stagnate.[44] As Lourdes Benería argues, for contextualization, "evaluation of the effects of employment for women needs to take into consideration what happens at the level of gender socialization and power relations."[45] As it happens, women's organizations in the *maquiladoras* have gone beyond traditional male concerns with wages—considering health, reproduction freedom, and environmental concerns, and challenging "the idea that what happens in the factory is separate from what happens in the community and that the company's responsibility does not extend beyond the factory gate."[46]

Women and the Environment

Where Southern grassroots movements entail protection of local resources and community, women typically play a defining role. This has always been so, but one consequence of colonialism is that this activity has become almost exclusively a women's preserve. As private property in land emerged, women's work tended to specialize in use of the commons for livestock grazing, firewood collection, game hunting, and seed gathering for medicinal purposes. These activities allowed women to supplement the incomes earned by men in the commercial sector. Women assumed a role as environmental managers, often forced to adapt to deteriorating conditions as commercial extractions increased over time.

The establishment of individual rights to property under colonialism typically privileged men. The result was to fragment social systems built on the complementarity of male and female work. Men's work became specialized: In national statistics, it is routinely counted as contributing to the commercial sector. Conversely, the specialization of women's labor as "non-income earning" work means that women's work remains outside the commercial sector, leaving much of it invisible. The domain of invisible work includes maintaining the commons. It is not, however, sufficient to assume—as some eco-feminists do—that women constitute a "natural" constituency for environmental stewardship. Rather, women's relationship to nature is part of their labor of social reproduction: "Women relate to natural resources as part of their livelihood strategies, which reflect multiple objectives, powerful wider political forces and, crucially, gender relations, i.e., social relations which systematically differentiate men and women in processes of production and reproduction."[47]

At the practical level, women engage in multifaceted activity. Across the world, women's organizations have mobilized to manage local resources, empower poor women and communities, and pressure governments and international agencies on behalf of women's rights. Countless activities of resource management undertaken by women form the basis of these practices. Perhaps most basic is the preservation of biodiversity in market and kitchen gardens. In Peru, the Aguarun Jivaro women nurture more than 100 varieties of manioc, the local staple root crop. Women have devised ingenious ways of household provisioning beside and within the cash-cropping systems managed by men.[48] Forest products (game, medicinal plants, condiments) are cultivated and harvested routinely by women.

In Kenya, the Kikuyu women in Laikipia have formed 354 women's groups to help them coordinate community decisions about access to and use of resources. Groups vary in size from 20 to 100 neighbors, both squatters and peasants; members contribute cash, products, and/or labor to the group, which in turn distributes resources equally among them. The groups have been able to pool funds to purchase land and establish small enterprises for the members. One such group, the Mwenda-Niire, was formed among landless squatters. Through saving funds, by growing maize and potatoes among the owner's crops, and through political negotiation, the group purchased the 567 hectare farm, allowing 130 landless families to become farmers. Group dynamics continue through labor-sharing schemes, collective infrastructure projects, and collective marketing. Collective movements such as this go beyond remedying development failures. They restore women's access to resources removed from them under colonial and postcolonial developments.[49]

Women, Poverty, and Fertility

Women's resource management can be ingenious, but often poverty subverts their ingenuity. For example, where women have no secure rights to land, they are less able to engage in sustainable resource extraction. Environmental deterioration may follow. When we see women stripping forests and overworking fragile land, we see just the tip of the iceberg. Many of these women have been displaced from lands converted for export cropping, or they have lost common land on which to subsist.

Environmental damage stemming from poverty has fueled the debate surrounding population growth in the former Third World. Population control has typically been directed at women—ranging from female infanticide to forced sterilization (as in India) to family planning interventions by development agencies.[50] Feminists entered this debate to protect women from such manipulation of their social and biological contributions.

Feminists advocate enabling women to take control of their fertility without targeting women as the source of the population problem. On a global scale, the current world population of about 7 billion could possibly double by 2050, according to UN projections, unless more aggressive intervention occurs. Studies suggest that female education and health services reduce birthrates. The 1992 World Bank report noted that women without secondary education, on average, have seven children; if almost half these women receive secondary education, the average declines to three children per woman.[51]

In addition, evidence based on the results of contraceptive use in Bangladesh has been cited as superseding conventional theories of "demographic transition."

Demographic theory extrapolates from the Western experience a pattern of demographic transition whereby birthrates decline significantly as economic growth proceeds. The threshold is the shift from preindustrial to industrial society, in which education and health technologies spread. Children are viewed increasingly as an economic liability rather than as necessary hands in the household economy or as a response to high childhood mortality rates. Evidence from Bangladesh showed a 21 percent decline in fertility rates during the decade and a half (1975–1991) in which a national family planning program was in effect. The study's authors claimed that these findings "dispute the notion that 'development is the best contraceptive,'" adding, "contraceptives are the best contraceptive."[52]

Feminist groups argue that family planning and contraception need to be rooted in the broader context of women's rights. Almost twice as many women as men are illiterate, and that difference is growing. Poor women with no education often do not understand their rights or contraceptive choices. The International Women's Health Coalition identified the Bangladesh Women's Health Coalition, serving 110,000 women at 10 clinics around the country, as a model for future UN planning. This group began in 1980 to offer abortions. With suggestions from the women it served, the coalition has expanded into family planning, basic health care services, child immunizations, legal aid, and training in literacy and employment skills.[53]

The correlation between women's rights and low fertility rates has ample confirmation. In Tunisia, the 1956 Code of Individual Rights guaranteed women political equality, backed with family planning and other social programs that included free, legal abortions. Tunisia is a leader in Africa, with a population growth rate of only 1.9 percent. The director-general of Tunisia's National Office of Family and Population, Nebiha Gueddana, claims that successful family planning can occur in a Muslim society: "We have 30 years of experience with the equality of women and . . . none of it has come at the expense of family values."[54] And in Kerala, where the literacy rate for women is two and a half times the average for India and where the status of women has long been high relative to the rest of the country, land reforms and comprehensive social welfare programs were instrumental in achieving a 40 percent reduction in the fertility rate between 1960 and 1985, reducing the population growth rate to 1.8 percent in the 1980s.[55]

With supportive social conditions, fertility decisions by women can have both individual and social benefits. Fertility decisions by individual women usually occur within patriarchal settings—households or societies. Recent population debates incorporate elements of the feminist perspective, emphasizing women's reproductive rights and health in the context of their need for secure livelihoods and political participation.[56] This view was embedded in the document from the 1994 UN Conference on Population and Development. Although contested by the Vatican and some Muslim nations (particularly Iran), the document states that women have the right to reproductive and sexual health, defined as "a state of complete physical, mental, and social well-being" in all matters relating to reproduction.[57]

Women's Rights

Feminism has clearly made an impact on the development agenda since the days of WID's inception. However, the improvement of women's material condition and social status across the world has not followed in step, even if the statistical reporting of women's work in subsistence production has improved.[58]

In 1989, at the end of a decade of structural adjustment, the United Nations made the following report in its World Survey on the Role of Women in Development:

> The bottom line shows that, despite economic progress measured in growth rates, at least for the majority of developing countries, economic progress for women has virtually stopped, social progress has slowed, and social well-being in many cases has deteriorated, and because of the importance of women's social and economic roles, the aspirations for them in current development strategies will not be met.[59]

In 2005, UNESCO sponsored a 10-year anniversary "stock-taking" of the condition of women, including proposals for measuring women's empowerment—a timely complement to CEDAW. The core of this report was twofold: first, that the Millennium Development Goals, in producing gender-neutral development indicators (other than primary education), remained silent regarding women's unpaid care work, reproductive and sexual rights, subjection to violence, and empowerment needs (for example, emphasizing secondary school opportunities which in turn would increase marriage age, reduce fertility, improve employment prospects, and reduce child malnutrition); and second, that in developing empowerment measures, "it is as important to determine women's participation and rights *across* social groups as it is to understand women's access and rights in relation to men's access and rights."[60] And in 2011, the first report of the new agency UN Women claimed more than half of working women in the world, 600 million, have insecure jobs without legal protection, and justice remains out of reach for many: "In Cambodia, for example, the forensic test necessary to lay a rape charge costs two weeks' wages. In Kenya, a land claim in an inheritance case can cost $800."[61]

The question of women's rights also concerns how different cultures regulate women's private lifestyles. In Muslim cultures, with considerable variation, women's rights remain subordinated to Islamic law or, as Muslim feminists claim, to a male interpretation of the Koran. In Morocco, for example, women require the permission of male relatives to marry, name their children, or work. Sisters inherit half as much as brothers, and male coercion in marriage is customary. Islamic women's groups across the Muslim world are mobilizing against what they term *Muslim apartheid,* in addition to working to eliminate "honor killings" of daughters/sisters who have sex outside of marriage. In the Mediterranean region, rapid urbanization has produced more educated and professional women who focus on changing secular laws to make an end run around Islamic law.[62] Different methodologies have emerged to assist the balancing of women's international rights with the question of cultural relativism (respecting cultural differences). They include the "principled approach," in which human rights trump state religious laws; a "balanced approach," which juxtaposes gender rights and religious freedoms to clarify boundary claims; and the "world-traveler approach," emphasizing cultural sensitivity.[63]

Finally, in an evaluation of the Beijing Conference, the Women's Environment and Development Organization reported that 70 percent of 187 national governments had laid plans to improve women's rights, 66 countries have offices for women's affairs, and 34 of these have legislative input. Pressure from local and international women's organizations since the Beijing conference—in countries as different as Mexico, Germany, New Zealand, and China—has made some gains, such as instituting laws against domestic violence.[64] But the 2005 UNESCO report noted that much is yet to be accomplished across the world—for example, just 15.6 percent of elected parliamentarians are women; women account for two-thirds of illiteracy; nowhere do women earn the same as men—the wage gap (on average 50–80 percent) is especially wide in the private sector; only 2 of the 49 presidents of the UN General Assembly have been women; and violence against women continues.[65]

Cosmopolitan Activism

Perhaps the litmus test of the globalization project is that, as global integration intensifies, the currents of cosmopolitan activism deepen. This is simply local activism that "thinks globally," meaning that movements situate their conditions and possibilities within a world-historical context. Wolfgang Sachs formulated the notion of **"cosmopolitan localism,"** based in the valuing of diversity as a universal right:

> Today, more than ever, universalism is under siege. To be sure, the victorious march of science, state, and market has not come to a stop, but the enthusiasm of the onlookers is flagging. . . . The globe is not any longer imagined as a homogeneous space where contrasts ought to be leveled out, but as a discontinuous space where differences flourish in a multiplicity of places.[66]

Cosmopolitan activism questions the assumption of uniformity in the global development project and asserts the need to respect alternative cultural traditions as a matter of respect and global survival. It embodies different initiatives to preserve or assert human and democratic rights within broader settings, generating the companion concept of "cosmopolitan democracy."[67]

CASE STUDY   **Andean Counterdevelopment or "Cultural Affirmation"**

Cosmopolitan localism takes a variety of forms. One form is a dialogical method of privileging the local worldview, including an evaluation of modern Western knowledge from the local standpoint. This means learning to value local culture and developing a contextualized understanding of foreign knowledges so that they do not assume some universal truth and inevitability, as claimed by Western knowledge and its officialdom. In this sense, modernity is understood as a peculiarly Western cosmology arising from European culture and history, which includes universalist claims legitimizing imperial expansion across the world. In the Peruvian Andes, indigenous writers and activists formed an NGO in 1987 called PRATEC (*Proyecto Andino de Tecnologías Campesinas*), which is concerned with recovering and implementing traditional Andean peasant culture and technologies via education of would-be rural developers. PRATEC links the Andean cosmology to its particular history and local ecology. It does not see itself as a political movement, but rather as a form of cultural politics dedicated to revaluing Andean culture and affirming local diversity over abstract homogenizing knowledge associated with modernity. One PRATEC peasant explained, "We have great faith in what nature transmits

(Continued)

(Continued)

to us. These indicators are neither the result of the science of humans, nor the invention of people with great experience. Rather, it is the voice of nature itself which announces to us the manner in which we must plant our crops." Andean peasants grow and know some 1,500 varieties of quinoa, 330 of kaniwa, 228 of tarwi, 3,500 of potatoes, 610 of oca (another tuber), and so on. A core founding member of PRATEC explained that "to decolonize ourselves is to break with the global enterprise of development." In the context of the collapse of Peru's formal economy, the delegitimization of government development initiatives, and environmental deterioration, PRATEC is one alternative, rooted in indigenous ecology and a participatory culture that puts the particularity of the Western project in perspective.

Is it possible to question development as a particularization of Western power, and yet incorporate some "universals" (reason, rights, etc.), as Anna Tsing suggests—as "engaged universals [which] travel across difference and are charged and changed by their travels"?

Sources: Apffel-Marglin (1997); Tsing (2005: 8).

A potent example of cosmopolitan activism was the peasant revolt in Mexico's southern state of Chiapas, a region in which huge cattle ranches and coffee plantations surround small peasant farms. About a third of the unresolved land reforms in the Mexican agrarian reform department, going back more than half a century, are in Chiapas. The government's solution over the years was to allow landless *campesinos* to colonize the Lacandon jungle and produce subsistence crops, coffee, and cattle. During the 1980s, coffee, cattle, and corn prices all fell, and *campesinos* were prohibited from logging—even though timber companies continued the practice.[68] The revolt had these deepening class inequalities as its foundation. But the source of the inequalities transcended the region.

On New Year's Day, 1994, hundreds of impoverished peasants rose up against what they perceived to be the Mexican state's continued violation of local rights. Not coincidentally, the revolt fell on the day NAFTA was implemented. To the Chiapas rebels, NAFTA symbolized the undermining of the revolutionary heritage in the Mexican Constitution of 1917, by which communal lands were protected from alienation. In 1992, under the pretext of structural adjustment policies and the promise of NAFTA, the Mexican government opened these lands for sale to Mexican and foreign agribusinesses. In addition, NAFTA included a provision to deregulate commodity markets—especially the market for corn, the staple peasant food.

The Chiapas revolt illustrates cosmopolitan localism well because it linked the struggle for local rights to a broader political and historical context. That is, the *Zapatistas* (as the rebels call themselves, after Mexican revolutionary Emilio Zapata) perceive the Mexican state as the chief agent of exploitation of the region's cultural and natural wealth. In one of many communiqués aimed at the global community, Subcomandante Marcos, the *Zapatista* spokesperson, characterized the Chiapas condition as follows:

> Oil, electric energy, cattle, money, coffee, bananas, honey, corn, cocoa, tobacco, sugar, soy, melons, sorghum, mamey, mangos, tamarind, avocados, and Chiapan blood flow out through a thousand and one fangs sunk into the neck of Southeastern Mexico. Billions of tons of natural resources go through Mexican ports, railway stations, airports, and road systems to various destinations: the United States, Canada, Holland, Germany, Italy, Japan—but all with the same destiny: to feed the empire. . . . The jungle is opened with machetes, wielded by the same campesinos whose land has been taken away by the insatiable beast. . . . Poor people cannot cut down trees, but the oil company, more and more in the hands of foreigners, can. . . . Why does the federal government take the question of national politics off the proposed agenda of the dialogue for peace? Are the indigenous Chiapan people only Mexican enough to be exploited, but not Mexican enough to be allowed an opinion on national politics? . . . What kind of citizens are the indigenous people of Chiapas? "Citizens in formation?"[69]

The Ejército Zapatista de Liberación Nacional (EZLN) movement inspired disadvantaged communities throughout Mexico and the world who have mobilized around similar demands. Timed to coincide with the implementation of NAFTA, the Chiapas rebellion wove together a powerful and symbolic critique of the politics of globalization—in that sense its "local" demands for regional self-determination within the Mexican state struck a cosmopolitan chord.

CASE STUDY **The New Labor Cosmopolitanism and Social Movement Unionism**

The concept of "cosmopolitan activism" applies equally to labor movements as they adapt to their transnational context. For labor, the globalization project has been double-edged. On the one hand, global sourcing has weakened traditional blue-collar industries (textiles, automobiles, household appliances)

(Continued)

(Continued)

in the North, but on the other, it has relocated those industries to the South, where they have reconstituted core labor forces. At the same time, the microelectronics revolution, in particular, is the new industrial core (including transforming all other production systems with the semiconductor)—its labor force centered in a new (and distinctly feminized) labor force in the South. Beverley Silver notes, "As a result of these combined processes, the mass-production industrial proletariat has continued to grow rapidly in size and centrality in many lower-wage countries." Silver argues that the geographical relocation of production "has not created a simple race to the bottom" as labor movements (particularly in the NICs) have nonetheless played a key role in politicizing working conditions and in political democracy movements. However, while globalization has generalized manufacturing, the key role of transnational corporate organization and the international division of labor has limited the relocation of wealth in the south.

Nevertheless, a new labor internationalism is emerging to present a combined front to global and/or footloose firms that divide labor forces across national borders, and to states that sign anti-labor free trade agreements (FTAs). A key example comes from the politics of NAFTA. Initially, led by the rank and file, organized labor joined a national political coalition of consumers, environmentalists, and others in opposing NAFTA, arguing that since Mexican unions were organs of the state, which maintained a low minimum wage, NAFTA could not protect U.S. labor from unfair competition. Subsequently, cross-border unionism to protect labor on either side took off. The stranglehold of the Mexican government on union organization frayed, evidenced by the formation of an independent union, the Authentic Labor Front, which formed an alliance with the U.S. United Electrical Workers, Teamsters, Steel Workers, and four other U.S. and Canadian unions in the early 1990s. The American Federation of Labor and Congress of Industrial Organizations (AFL-CIO) has since sought alliances with independent Mexican (and Central American) unions, including supporting independent labor organizing in the *maquiladoras*. In December, 1997, following a long struggle, the Korean-owned Han Young plant in Tijuana agreed to the formation of an independent union among its *maquila* factory workers, a 30-percent pay raise, and reinstatement of fired activists. This exemplifies what Peter Evans calls "reverse whipsawing," whereby solidarity networks allow stronger labor organizations to champion the rights of weaker ones.

This development mirrors movements elsewhere in the global South, where independent unions respond to global integration. For instance, the Transnationals Information Exchange (TIE) forged networks of labor organization across the world, targeting the production of the "world car," and formed the Cocoa-Chocolate Network, based on the global commodity chain, whereby TIE linked European industrial workers with Asian and Latin American plantation workers and peasants, linking chocolate factories to the cacao bean fields. Communication technologies enable such organizing, not simply via information exchange, but, as Evans argues, by reshaping cultural possibilities for solidarity. In addition, there has been a substantial alliance building via NGOs joining with labor organizations to mobilize consumers around fair trade/production norms. TIE practiced **social movement unionism**, centered on community-based organizing (often because low-wage labor works under decentralized subcontracting arrangements). Such unionism extends to connecting casualized labor across national boundaries, and addressing issues of racism and immigrant workers. Social movement unionism is spreading in middle-income states such as Brazil, South Africa, Taiwan, and South Korea, where unions spearhead broad coalitions demanding democratization of political systems, linking economic rights (working conditions) with political rights (independent organization) and social rights (restoration of the social contract and responsiveness to social justice concerns). Their employment in globally competitive industries often lends them a strategic power through the strike.

If labor organizes transnationally, what institutional mechanisms beyond the nation-state does it need to protect and sustain its rights to secure employment, fair wages, and just working conditions?

Sources: Beneria (1995: 48); Brecher and Costello (1994: 153–154); Calvo (1997); Dillon (1997, 1998); Moody (1999: 255–262); Ross and Trachte (1990); Rowling (2001: 24); Seidman (1994); Silver (2003: 105, 168, 172); Evans (2010).

Food Sovereignty Movements

In the early twenty-first century, about 1 billion people (mostly in the global South) are food insecure—that is, unable to meet their daily energy requirements. Meanwhile, six corporations handle 85 percent of the world grain trade, and integrated, centralized control of the food chain—from gene to supermarket shelf—intensifies. In the name of globalization, this northern model (including risks associated with factory farming and food scares) is exported as the solution to food insecurity, displacing Northern and Southern farmers. Canadian farmer Nettie Wiebe remarks, "The difficulty for us, as farming people, is that we are rooted in the places where we live and grow our food. The other side, the corporate world, is globally mobile."[70]

Resistances to the global conception of food security are mushrooming—framed by the alternative conception of **food sovereignty**. This means not just protecting local farming but revitalizing democratic, cultural, and ecological processes at the subnational level. The 200 million-strong farmers' transnational movement, *Vía Campesina*, asserts that "farmers' rights are eminently collective" and "should therefore be considered as a different legal framework from those of private property." Vía Campesina, formed in 1992, unites 150 local and regional chapters of landless peasants, family farmers, agricultural workers, rural women, and indigenous communities in 70 countries across Africa, Europe, Asia, and North, Central, and South America.[71] It claims that "biodiversity has as a fundamental base the recognition of human diversity, the acceptance that we are different and that every people and each individual has the freedom to think and to be. Seen in this way, biodiversity is not only flora, fauna, earth, water, and ecosystems; it is also cultures, systems of production, human and economic relations, forms of government; in essence it is freedom."[72] In addition to defending biodiversity, and development agro-ecology, Vía Campesina claims to be the principle agent to "feed the world and cool the planet," insofar as the stability of diverse smallholding farm systems addresses the global concentration of undernutrition in the countryside and practices a low-input agriculture.

Food sovereignty, in this vision, is "the right of peoples, communities, and countries to define their own agricultural, labor, fishing, food and land policies which are ecologically, socially, economically, and culturally appropriate to their unique circumstances."[73] Vía Campesina argues that food should not come under the WTO regime: Food production plays a unique social role and should not be subordinated to market dictates. Food self-reliance comes first, followed by trade. The movement would subordinate trade relations to the question of access to land, credit, and fair prices, set politically via the rules of fair trade to be negotiated in the United Nations Conference on Trade and Development (UNCTAD), with active participation of farmers in building democratic definitions of agricultural and food policies. A key to the food sovereignty movement is the farmer-to-farmer (*campesino a campesino*) networks, through which farmers exchange seeds, knowledge, and labor as essential to the development of self-reliance and resilience.[74]

While the consumer movement (e.g., the 60,000 towns and villages of the European slow food movement) has discovered that "eating has become a political act," Vía Campesina adds, "Producing quality products for our own people has also become a political act . . . this touches our very identities as citizens of this world."[75] Access to land is a first step, and Vía Campesina declares,

> Access to the land by peasants has to be understood as a guarantee for survival and the valorization of their culture, the autonomy of their communities and a new vision of the preservation of natural resources for humanity and future generations. Land is a good of nature that needs to be used for the welfare of all. Land is not, and cannot be, a marketable good that can be obtained in whatever quantity by those that have the financial means.[76]

Perhaps the most significant chapter of Vía Campesina is the Brazilian landless-workers' movement, the *Movimento dos Trabalhadores Rurais Sem Terra* (MST). Over two decades, the MST has settled almost half a million families on millions of acres of land seized by takeovers of unworked land. The stimulus has been a Brazilian development model of structural adjustment, in a context where 1 percent of landowners own (but do not necessarily cultivate) 50 percent of the land, leaving 4.8 million families landless. While Brazil's extensive system of agricultural subsidies was withdrawn, the Organisation for Economic Co-operation and Development (OECD) member states' agricultural subsidies continued at over US$300 billion a year. As the MST website notes, "From 1985 to 1996, according to the agrarian census, 942,000 farms disappeared, 96% of which were smaller than one hundred hectares. From that total, 400 thousand establishments went bankrupt in the first two years of the Cardoso government, 1995–96." Between 1985 and 1996, rural unemployment rose by 5.5 million, and between 1995 and 1999, a rural exodus of 4 million Brazilians occurred. While in the 1980s, Brazil imported roughly US$1 million worth of wheat, apples, and products not produced in Brazil, from "1995 to 1999, this annual average leapt to 6.8 billion dollars, with the importation of many products cultivable . . . in Brazil."[77]

The landless workers' movement draws legitimacy for its land occupations from the Brazilian constitution, which sanctions confiscation of uncultivated private property: "It is incumbent upon the Republic to expropriate for social interest, for purposes of agrarian reform, rural property, which is not performing its social function."[78] The MST is organized in 23 of 26 states of Brazil, and while dispossessed farmers comprise 60 percent of its membership, it also includes unemployed workers and disillusioned civil servants.

Land seizures—under the slogan of "Occupy! Resist! Produce!"—lead to the formation of cooperatives, which involve social mobilization "transforming the economic struggle into a political and ideological struggle."[79] Democratic decision making develops cooperative relations among workers and alternative patterns of land use, financed by socializing a portion of settlement income. Participatory budgeting allocates funds for repairs, soil improvement, cattle feeding, computers, housing, teachers' salaries, child care, mobilization, and so on. Fundamental to this social project is Paulo Freire's dictum that "a settlement, precisely because it is a production unit, should also be a whole pedagogic unit."[80] Education starts from children's daily perspective, building on the learner's direct experience and communicating the inherent value of rural life. This differs from the productivism of the corporate economic model, including its disregard for rural well-being, farmer knowledge, and farmer rights.[81] João Pedro Stedile, president of the MST, observes,

> Under the objective economic conditions, our proposal for land reform has to avoid the oversimplification of classical capitalist land reform, which merely divides up large landholdings and encourages their productive use. We are convinced that nowadays it is necessary to reorganize agriculture on a different social base, democratize access to capital, democratize the agro-industrial process (something just as important as landownership), and democratize access to know-how, that is, to formal education.[82]

The MST's 1,600 government-recognized settlements include medical clinics and training centers for health care workers and 1,200 public schools employing an estimated 3,800 teachers serving about 150,000 children at any one time. A UNESCO grant enables adult literacy classes for 25,000, and the MST sponsors technical classes and teacher training. MST cooperative enterprises generate $50 million annually, producing jobs for thousands of members and (increasingly organic) foodstuffs and clothing for local, national, and global consumption. The priority given to producing staple foods for low-income consumers (rather than foods for affluent consumers in cities and abroad) led to a 2003 agreement with the Lula government for the direct purchase of settlement produce for the national Zero Hunger campaign.

As one commentator notes,

> These collective enterprises show why the MST is considered a leader in the international fair trade movement. The movement is supplying a real, workable alternative to corporate globalization, putting community values and environmental stewardship before profit-making. MST co-ops offer a glimpse of what environmentally sustainable and socially just commerce would look like.[83]

CASE STUDY	The Case for Fair Trade

The idea of fair trade paralleled the intensification of global integration, with aid agencies sponsoring links between craftspeople from the global South and Northern consumers with a taste for "ethnic" products. Fair trade has now blossomed as a method of transcending abuses in the free trade system and rendering more visible the conditions of production of globally traded commodities to establish just prices, environmentally sound practices, healthy consumption, and direct understanding between producers and consumers of their respective needs.

Fair trade exchanges have an annual market value of $400 million, and the market for fair trade products (organic products such as coffee, bananas, cocoa, honey, tea, and orange juice—representing about 60 percent of the fair trade market, alongside organic cotton jeans and an array of handicrafts) expands at between 10 and 25 percent a year. Three fair trade labels—Transfair, Max Havelaar, and Fairtrade Mark—broke into European markets in the late 1980s and are now united under the Fairtrade Labelling Organizations International (FLO), an umbrella NGO that harmonizes different standards and organizes a single fair trade market (in the absence of national regulations). FLO aims to "raise awareness among consumers of the negative effects on producers of international trade so that they exercise their purchasing power positively." Laura Raynolds notes that certification of fair trade practices requires "democratically organized associations of small growers or plantations where workers are fully represented by independent democratic unions or other groups... [and] labor conditions... uphold basic ILO conventions (including rights to association, freedom from discrimination, prohibition of child and forced labor, minimum social conditions, and rights to safe and healthy work conditions)." Above-world market prices are guaranteed. In Costa Rica, for instance, a cooperative, Coopetrabasur, achieved Fairtrade registration to supply bananas, and in so doing eliminated herbicide use, reduced chemical fertilizers, built democratic union procedures, raised wages, and established a "social premium" set aside for community projects such as housing improvement, electrification, and environmental monitoring.

Daniel Jaffee notes that fair trade embodies a "fundamental paradox" in utilizing the "mechanisms of the very markets that have generated... injustices." Thus TNCs such as Starbucks offer a fair trade variety, in the new phase of "green capitalism." Will fair trade remain a parallel movement only, encouraging at the most and primarily offering a fair outlet for dependent tropical producers, or can it mobilize public education and consumer purchasing power to democratize the global market?

Sources: Jaffee (2007: 1) Ransom (2001b); Raynolds (2000: 298, 301, 306); J. Smith (2002: 40–41).

SUMMARY

We have toured a few of the world's hot spots in this chapter, noting the particular forms social movements take in responding to the failures of developmentalism and the further disorganizing impact of corporate globalization. Responses range from withdrawal into alternative projects (e.g., women's cooperatives, recovery of noncapitalist practices) to attempts to reframe development as a question of rights and social protections (such as the feminist movement, social environmentalism, local autonomy rebellions). All of these responses express the uncertainties of social arrangements under globalizing tendencies. Many express a fundamental desire to break out of the homogenizing and disempowering dynamics of the globalization project and to establish a sustainable form of social life based on new forms of associative politics.

Other forms of resistance to the globalization project include mushrooming consumer advocacy. One broad consumer movement has been the United Students Against Sweatshops (USAS), formed in 1998 after several years of campus organizing against the link between U.S. universities and offshore sweatshops producing logo-emblazoned clothing. In related human rights areas, consumer movements have successfully focused attention on child labor stitching soccer balls in Pakistan, although monitoring remains incomplete.

In sum, the road to the political future has several forks. Across the world, countermovements are forming in regional cereal banks in Zimbabwe, ecological campaigns by women's groups in West Bengal, *campesino* credit unions in Mexico, the emergence of solidarity networks among labor forces, slow food networks in Europe, and the defense of forest dwellers throughout the tropics. How effectively these movements will interconnect politically—at the national, regional, and global levels (through proliferating social forums)—is an open question. Another question concerns how these movements will negotiate with existing states over the terms of local and/or cultural sustenance. Potentially, the new movements breathe new life into politics. They transcend the centralizing thrust of the development states of the postwar era and present models for the recovery of democratic forms of social organization at different scales, as well as the extension of the meaning of civil society. Many communities left behind by the development and globalization projects look to NGOs, rather than to states or international agencies, to represent and assist them. At a time of official legitimacy deficit, when NGOs take the initiative in guiding grassroots development activities, there are questions about the representativeness and accountability of NGOs themselves.

As the new century unfolds, it is clear that the assumptions and content of the global development project are in question from global justice movements, and even from the boardrooms of TNCs and development agencies, and the corridors of state power. Indeed the crisis of the globalization project is the subject of the following chapter.

FURTHER READING

Baviskar, Amita. *In the Belly of the River: Tribal Conflicts over the Development in the Narmada Valley.* New York: Oxford University Press, 2005.

Desmarais, Annette Aurélie. *La Vía Campesina: Globalization and the Power of Peasants.* Halifax, NS: Fernwood, 2007.

George, Susan. *Another World Is Possible If. . . .* London: Verso, 2004.

Harcourt, Wendy. 2009. *Body Politics in Development: Critical Debates in Gender and Development.* London and New York: Zed Books.

Hawken, Paul. *Blessed Unrest.* New York: Penguin, 2008.

Martinez-Alier, Joan. *The Environmentalism of the Poor: A Study of Ecological Conflicts and Valuation.* London: Edward Elgar, 2002.

Raynolds, Laura T., Douglas Murray, and John Wilkinson, eds. *Fair Trade: The Challenges of Transforming Globalization.* Abingdon, UK: Routledge, 2007.

Starr, Amory. *Naming the Enemy: Anti-Corporate Movements Confront Globalization.* London: Zed Books, 2000.

Wolford, Wendy. *This Land Is Ours Now: Social Mobilization and the Meanings of Land in Brazil.* Durham and London: Duke University Press, 2010.

SELECT WEBSITES

Amnesty International: www.amnesty.org

Behind the Label (USA): www.behindthelabel.org

Corporate Watch (USA): www.corpwatch.org

Development Alternatives with Women for a New Era (DAWN): www.dawnnet.org

Equal Exchange: www.equalexchange.com

Erosion, Technology, and Concentration: www.etcgroup.org

Fairtrade Labelling Organizations International (FLO, Germany): www.fairtrade.net

Focus on the Global South (Thailand): www.focusweb.org

Food First (USA): www.foodfirst.org

Friends of the Earth International (Netherlands): www.foei.org

Genetic Resources Action International (GRAIN): www.grain.org

Global Environment Facility (USA): www.gefweb.org

Global Exchange (USA): www.globalexchange.org

Greenpeace International (Netherlands): www.greenpeace.org/international/

International Forum on Globalization (USA): www.ifg.org
Jubilee South: www.jubileesouth.org
Médecins Sans Frontières: www.msf.org
Oxfam International (UK): www.oxfam.org
Public Citizen Global Trade Watch (USA): www.citizen.org/trade
Rainforest Action Network (USA): www.ran.org
Survival International (UK: tribal peoples' rights): www.survival-international.org
Sweatshop Watch (USA): www.sweatshopwatch.org
Third World Network (Malaysia): www.twnside.org.sg
Transnational Institute (Netherlands): www.tni.org
United Nations Development Fund for Women (UNIFEM): www.unifem.org
United Students Against Sweatshops (USA): www.studentsagainstsweatshops.org
Via Campesina (Honduras): www.viacampesina.org

PART III

Millennial Reckonings (2000s to Present)

8

The Globalization
Project in Crisis

While the globalization project still shapes development initiatives and policies, there are signs that its claim (and ability) to represent the most rational development path is eroding. Having fashioned a development agenda via structural adjustment policies, the arrival of such policies in the global North in the twenty-first century raises some key questions. First, what does structural adjustment mean for northern "development"? Does this undo the conventional distinction between "developed" and "developing" countries? Is this signal crisis of the globalization project the beginning of a transition toward a new project? Finally, is peak oil a threshold for development—as we exit the age of fossil fuels and enter an era of energy constraint and conservation—upending development as we have known it and ushering in a new regime based on militarized security, or democratic resilience, or something in between?

To answer these questions it is important to *situate* the economic crisis facing the global North. Its debt crisis recalls the 1980s debt regime, in which Southern governments were enjoined by the international financial institutions (IFIs) to privatize their public assets to stabilize the financial sector. This was the end of the so-called "development state," as the discipline of debt imposed a neoliberal model of privatization on the global South. The anti-state syndrome spread to the North, where during the 1990s corporate tax reduction in the name of promoting productive investment eroded public finance without growth—leaving states (other than in Scandinavia) living beyond their means.[1] When the debt crisis hit the global North in the first decade of the twenty-first century, privatization and new financial disciplinary strictures rolled back Northern public services. Spending cuts exacerbated already weakened economies following two decades of offshoring of industry. The decline in stable employment has reduced tax bases and means of livelihood for significant numbers of Northerners.

Unemployment has become the great leveler across the North/South divide. By the end of the twenty-first century's first decade, global unemployment was running at around 200 million, in addition to 1.4 billion working poor. About half of the world's workforce holds casual jobs—which means that around 90 percent of the global workforce is poor, vulnerable, or unemployed. The

Figure 8.1   Total Employment: Percentage Change From Same Period in Previous Year

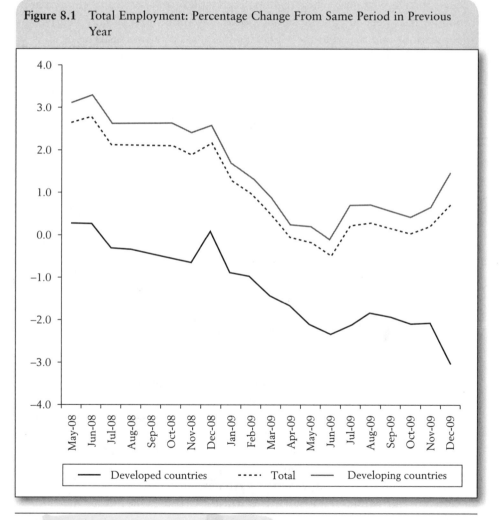

Source: International Labor Organization (ILO) 2010. http://www.ilo.org/pls/apex/f?p=109:11: 1760200573224936, accessed July 28, 2010.

European Union has about 50 million "vulnerable" workers, and 72 million working poor. Most dramatic of all was the approximately 9 percent unemployment rate at the end of 2009 in the so-called "Developed Economies and the EU"—higher than any other global region, including Central and Southeastern Europe, and Latin America and the Caribbean.[2]

Two related processes are at work: first, a slow-down or hollowing-out of Northern economies; and second, the relocation of goods and services production to parts of the global South. The consequence is a distinctive bifurcation between a global consumer class and a large casual and unemployed labor force across both world regions. The viability and security of the global middle class depends on the simultaneous containment of socially deprived populations and access to their labor and habitats as resources. The result is an unstable world—with widespread state incapacity—as the wealthy withdraw allegiance to their nation and social rebellions simmer with growing shortages of jobs, food, and public resources. From this tension emerges a multiplicity of creative social and ecological experiments out of necessity and enlightened planning. This chapter will focus mainly on the contours of crisis, followed by descriptions of responses in Chapter 9.

Legitimacy Crisis

If the development project started with the aim of poverty alleviation, then by the end of the twentieth ("development") century, it became clear that development was not working. It was facing a legitimacy crisis. In 2000 World Bank president James Wolfensohn said, "We have yet to solve old problems—above all, that of the yawning gulf between the haves and the have-nots of the world."[3] The United Nations coordinated a response in the form of the **Millennium Development Goals** (2000), with the key goal of halving world hunger by 2015, as well as halting the spread of HIV/AIDS, addressing gender inequality, and providing universal primary education. A decade later, the 2010 MDGs Report stated that despite gains in reducing malnutrition in the 1990s, since 2000 such progress stalled. The 817 million undernourished in 1990–1992 were predicted to exceed 1 billion in 2010, following the food and financial crises of 2008.[4]

The "gulf" was "yawning" wider. Despite a general reduction in the proportion of the world's population living in absolute poverty (the "China effect"), there has been a widely observed expansion of global inequalities between and within countries: "The world's rich benefited disproportionately from global growth over the 1990s and the per capita consumption of the poor increased at only half the average global rate."[5]

The legitimacy crisis is doubly expressed in the refusal, or inability, of the development agencies (as in the MDGs) to address global *inequality*, to

Figure 8.2   Number of Hungry People, 1969–2010

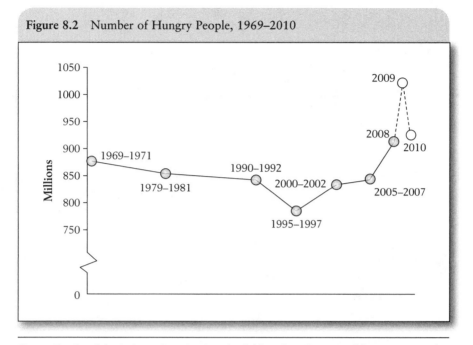

Source: Food and Agriculture Organization. Available at http://www.worldhunger.org/articles/
Learn/world%20hunger%20facts%202002.htm#Number_of_hungry_people_in_the_world

refocus on how neoliberal development aids the rich more than—or at the expense of—the poor. Thus, "the object of concern is not global inequality but global poverty, the instrument of analysis is economic data processing, and the bottom-line remedy is freeing up market forces, now with a human face."[6] Hence, the fixation on the so-called "bottom billion"—reproducing a conception of development as a (staged) "ladder" rather than as an unequal relationship. The current focus is on the global poor rather than poor nations as the development target. This is how microcredit gained currency, targeting the poor with the instruments of the rich.

CASE STUDY   Relative Deprivations?

While the media focuses on the impact of the crisis in the global North, Jan Breman cautions, "The global downturn has taken a disproportionately higher toll on the most vulnerable sectors: the huge armies of the poorly paid, under-educated, resourceless workers that constitute the overcrowded lower depths of the world economy." In 2008, the ILO estimated informal workers comprise over 50 percent of the Latin American workforce, over 70 percent in Sub-Saharan

(Continued)

(Continued)

Africa, and over 80 percent in India. There, (female) garbage pickers "are now paid half what they used to get for the harvest of paper, rags. and plastic gleaned from the waste dumps on their daily rounds. To make up the loss, they now begin their work at 3 a.m. instead of at 5 a.m., bringing along their children to provide more hands. The Self-Employed Women's Association, which organizes informal-sector workers in [Ahmedabad], reports that 'incomes have declined, days of work decreased, prices have fallen, and livelihoods disappeared.'" Meanwhile, the *Wall Street Journal* reported in 2009 that the informal sector is "one of the last safe havens in a darkening financial climate . . . and a critical safety net as the economic crisis spreads"—rephrased by Breman as, "These streetwise operators are able to get by without expensive social provisions or unemployment benefit," meaning "informals" absorb the casualties of neoliberal policies.

With fraying social safety nets everywhere, do southern scenarios portend northern futures?

Source: Breman (2009).

Microfinance, or Poverty Capital

Microfinance performs three tasks at once: providing credit to the poor as an entrepreneurial "leg up," deepening market relations, and enlarging financial opportunity in the form of legitimacy repair. Originating in non-profit organizations such as the Grameen Bank, microfinance has, in Ananya Roy's terms, evolved as "poverty capital," with commercial banks, investment vehicles, and money markets now embracing it.[7] In the words of the governor of Israel's central bank, Stanley Fischer (formerly IMF Deputy Managing Director): microfinance provides "bankers with a profitable business opportunity" and "poor people a stake in the economic future of their countries."[8] These poor are the so-called "bottom billion."

As Nobel Prize–winner Muhammad Yunus of Bangladesh, wrote, "In 1983, I founded Grameen Bank to provide small loans that people, especially poor women, could use to bring themselves out of poverty. At that time, I never imagined that one day microcredit would give rise to its own breed of loan sharks."[9] There are now about 650 million clients at over 3,000 institutions spreading across the world (with India claiming about 180 million clients), the average loan is $250, and interest rates often exceed 20 percent.[10]

Microfinance embodies the neoliberal philosophy of devolving responsibility for development to the individual, as self-maximizer. In echoing the "bad state/good market" axiom, it reproduces the ideology of the globalization project. Working through the NGO community in dispensing and monitoring credit and its repayment, microfinance simultaneously empowers and disciplines its recipients—an ideal form of development as rule (financial opportunity by financial dependency). Where it valorizes the poor as consumers of credit, consolidating the notion of development as consumption, it also realizes Yunus's questionable claim that "credit is a fundamental human right."

Microfinance has various criteria of success—empowerment of marginalized women, stabilization of the poor, extension of frontiers of bank profits, reduction of the informal economy, expansion of microenterprise, enhancement of World Bank legitimacy, the NGO-ization of development, or new development "rents." But perhaps its fundamental significance is the renewal of the legitimacy of neoliberal development via "bankrolling the poor." Anthropologist Julia Elyachar's research in Cairo suggests microcredit appropriates alternative values and visions of social life: "Indigenous forms of production, markets, and sociability are transformed into resources for reproducing dominant forms of power."[11] Replacing social networks of survival with "empowerment debt" has proven to be a double-edged sword, incorporating "informal" workers and craftspeople into credit relations that may create both new microenterprises and/or new individual dependencies (infused with class/gender inequalities), with the loans often being used to meet daily consumption needs.[12] Sometimes debt has intergenerational effects, such as taking children—especially girls—out of school in order to make loan payments.[13] A report by the World Bank–based Consultative Group to Assist the Poor on the microfinance portfolios of the UN and the Bank concluded, "Less than a quarter of the projects that funded microlending were judged successful."[14]

Where classifying informal practices as "poverty"—and thus targeting the practices for reduction via "empowerment debt"—disempowers informal cultural networks, the development establishment seeks to renew its legitimacy through performing development on a "human scale." But it is one thing to bring credit to the grassroots, and another for people at the grassroots to self-organize. For example, there are many examples of community-managed microfinance, via local cooperative banks and financial institutions with accountability to local savers and the wider community—the principle being that enabling savings within poor communities is more effective than credit provision that is followed by debt.[15]

Post-Washington Consensus?

The legitimacy crisis of neoliberal development, under the leadership of the so-called Washington Consensus, has simmered across the last two decades. By 2006, ex–World Bank chief economist Joseph Stiglitz warned of a new era of protectionism because of deepening inequalities.[16] Public opposition to neoliberalism has been continuous, ranging from IMF riots through opposition to free trade deals to the global justice movements, culminating in the formation of the World Social Forum (WSF), as a counterpart to the World Economic Forum.

The WSF was inaugurated in 2001 to channel the politics of hundreds of global civil societies. While the WSF slogan is "another world is possible," it views itself as a process, not an organization. Its Charter of Principles declares that it is a body "representing world civil society." The WSF is a broad movement dedicated to socially re-embedding markets. A spokesperson for the Living Democracy Movement, Vandana Shiva, claims,

> The philosophical and ethical bankruptcy of globalization was based on reducing every aspect of our lives to commodities and reducing our identities to [those] of mere consumers in the global marketplace. Our capacities as producers, our identity as members of communities, our role as custodians of our natural and cultural heritage were all to disappear or be destroyed. Markets and consumerism expanded. Our capacity to give and share was to shrink. But the human spirit refuses to be subjugated by a world-view based on the dispensability of our humanity.[17]

The crisis of confidence in the globalization project permeated the new century, starting with the 1997 Asian financial crisis, that is now infecting the North. Malaysia's defiance of liberalization policy, protecting it from the crisis, symbolized the general retreat from the IMF, by heightening its "arrears crisis."[18] From 2005 to 2008, Latin American states dramatically reduced their dependence on IMF funding, with outstanding loans falling from 80 percent to 1 percent of the IMF's loan portfolio.[19] As we shall see, the migration of financial crisis to the global North by 2008 has turned a smoldering legitimacy crisis into a unfolding catastrophe.

The Latin Rebellion

The legitimacy crisis of neoliberal development has been most pronounced in Latin America. At the start of the twenty-first century a democratic revolution swept the continent, with the pendulum swinging back from market rule to the restoration of social rights and the role of the development state. New social-democratic presidents were elected in eleven countries—Venezuela, Brazil, Argentina, Uruguay, Bolivia, Chile, Ecuador, Nicaragua, Guatemala, Paraguay, and El Salvador—alongside Cuban socialism. More pragmatic and populist than ideological, these governments espouse a social egalitarianism, drawing on the deepening frustration of poor and indigenous citizens with the deprivations of the globalization project.

Latin America has the highest levels of inequality in the world.[20] After three decades of neoliberalism, three-quarters of Latin Americans remain poor, and social movements have mobilized against privatization, low-wage labor, alienation of habitat, crippling foreign debt inherited from previous dictatorships, and the erosion of national sovereignty. But only in the three countries (Venezuela, Bolivia, and Ecuador) has "postneoliberalism" gained real traction in regulating capital—in particular substituting productive for speculative investment, supporting labor rights, and encouraging fair rather than "free" trade.[21] Nevertheless, candidates from Mexico to Paraguay positioned themselves electorally against the Washington Consensus, blocking a proposal for a Free Trade Area of the Americas (FTAA) in the mid-2000s.

In addition to the electoral shift, distinctive political initiatives emerged in the crucible of the Latin American rebellion. In Argentina, for example, workers occupied almost 200 empty factories, and workplaces, organizing production themselves via cooperative models.[22] And Bolivian indigenous peoples institutionalized their new-found voice in the Movement for Socialism (MAS) party, powering the electoral victory of the first indigenous president, Evo Morales.[23] Venezuela adopted a new constitution (1999) centered on the theme of human development, with a vision of citizens empowering themselves through the political (participation in communal councils) and economic (establishment of cooperatives) spheres.[24]

Controversial Venezuelan president, Hugo Chávez, blessed—or cursed, as resource economists might say—with oil wealth, has poured billions of dollars into his "Bolivarian Revolution," expanding health care and education (Venezuela is now an "illiteracy-free territory" by UN criteria), subsidizing food and fuel, providing cash benefits for single mothers and low-interest loans for small businesses, and encouraging farm worker–owned cooperatives on ranches and sugar plantations seized by the state.[25] Venezuela's new constitution "guarantees all citizens the right to health care and forbids the privatization of health services," representing the government's goal of remaking health care via social and participatory medicine. Venezuela invites Cuban doctors to treat, train, and dwell in working-class communities, which organize neighborhood local health committees to oversee clinic operations with government funds.[26] Integral to Chávez's "petro-populism" (which is not anti-capitalist) is its social mobilization strategy—celebrated as "participatory democracy" by rank-and-file Chavistas, and denigrated as client politics by critics of the Chávez regime.[27]

To finance this revolution, Chávez instigated a new wave of **resource nationalism** in Latin America in 2002, demanding that foreign oil companies enter into joint ventures, with the Venezuelan state holding at least 60 percent of the capital. Ecuador (expropriating Occidental Petroleum), Peru, and Bolivia followed, "where foreign companies, in particular the Brazilian Petrobras, accepted the nationalization of gas fields without a fight."[28] The drawback, at least in Venezuela, is that oil money has corrupted the state bureaucracy, where a parallel national development fund operates as an unaccountable source of patronage (Transparency International has ranked Venezuela among the region's worst performers).[29] Nevertheless, the resource nationalism taps into a historic antipathy toward foreign control, with the populist dimension rooted deeply in indigenous suspicion of the "[European] white-settler elite that has dominated the continent for so many centuries."[30]

Drawing on the anti-colonial heritage of Simón Bolívar (leader of nineteenth century Latin independence movements), contemporary movements demand a second independence—from foreign corporations, banks, and U.S. military involvement across the continent—forming the South American Community of Nations. This community evolved into the **Union of South American Nations (UNASUR)** in 2007, moving the region closer to greater independence from the United States via economic integration around a single currency (the *sucre*), destined to be an international reserve currency. By 2009, the Bank of the South (*Banc del Sur*) was established as an alternative to the IMF (a move endorsed by Joseph Stiglitz).

A radical offshoot of the integration initiative, begun by Chávez and Cuban president Fidel Castro, is an alternative regional economic bloc named the **Bolivarian Alternative for the Americas (ALBA)**, based on the concept of "cooperative advantage"—fostering mutual cultural and economic exchanges, such as cheap oil from Venezuela for Cuban doctors and teachers, and building a form of cooperative development to encourage collective interest in sharing material goods and social services.[31]

How these various initiatives evolve depends on the viability of the new governments, and on the durability of the continental alliances.

Arab Spring?

In 2011, the African Development Bank (AfDB) claimed that the revolution in Tunisia reinserted "social inclusion" into the center of the development debate. Ironically, Tunisia (a north African country of 10 million) had been regarded by the development agencies as a macroeconomic success, with record growth of 6.7 percent in 2007—despite the persistence of long-standing social and spatial inequalities that characterized the North African region at large. In June 2011, the AfDB's regional director said "eight months ago, government officials were not interested in talking about such problems. It was not an option—but Tunisia has blown it all away." As President Zine al-Abidine Ben Ali stepped down after 23 years in power, the **Arab spring** stepped up, spreading to Egypt, Libya, Bahrain, Yemen, Syria, and even Palestine. With regard to Tunisia, the AfDB noted in its loan proposal,

> The revolution and the ensuing social protest demonstrate the urgency of addressing the issues of unemployment, especially among the youth in the country's interior, regional disparities, and the lack of transparency and individual freedoms. The social demands that were at the heart of the revolution will grow with heightened expectations from the Tunisian population.

The AfDB responded by awarding soft loans to the Tunisian government to implement a labor-intensive jobs program through the public sector, with transfers of public services to impoverished rural areas. Public services such as education and healthcare were required to submit to citizen evaluation.[32]

Much has been made of the youth component of the Arab spring—in Tunisia, for example, 72 percent of the unemployed were under 30 in 2008, and the unemployment of university graduates grew tenfold between 1990–2010.[33] The revolt began among working class youth, spreading to the middle classes as police brutality came in full view. Social networking among youth enabled new spaces of hope and initiative. Variation in the use of violence across the region (less so in Egypt, much more so in Bahrain, Libya. and Syria) depended on the balance of forces in each society—Egypt, despite its horrendous police state behind the scenes, was more open institutionally via the media and the electoral system, and its people drew on a democratic tradition which flowered during the late decolonization period (1919–1967).

Over half of the 350 million Arabs are under 30, with dim job prospects, and youth unemployment as high as 80 percent in some areas. Such conditions nurtured a simmering crisis of the globalization project across the region, coming to a head in the Arab spring of the 2010s.[34] As Nigel Gibson wrote in 2011,

> The date of the Egyptian revolution is 25 January but its prehistory includes years of labour struggle. The sit-ins, strikes, and demonstrations of 2006, the almost daily workers' actions of early 2007, and the massive strike of textile workers in Muhalla al-Kubra in 2008 initiated by working women. These

struggles led to beatings and imprisonments as well as some wage increases and bread subsidies as the regime tried to cheaply buy its way out of crisis. The mixture of economic hardship, political repression and social control indicate how deep the uprooting of the old regime had to be.[35]

Contrary to earlier patterns, labor protests in the 2000s were subject to less repression by a government anxious to attract foreign capital—opening the possibility to the Egyptian populace of open/mass struggle against an autocratic regime.[36] Bread protests recurred in Egypt during the era of the globalization project, as the government encouraged export crops instead of wheat, and diverted subsidies toward feed crops and the production of animal protein to provision wealthy consumers—pushing food prices up by 50 percent by the end of the 2000s.[37] The retaking of public space (via sophisticated self-organization in Tahrir Square) laid bare the deprivations of the majority, the savagery of the state apparatus, and the profiteering of the ruling and military elite, who controlled most large Egyptian businesses and contracts.[38]

Social inclusion via employment was the central demand. But unemployment is symptomatic of a deeper failing—the disregard of Arab governments for their responsibilities to the social contract, and the complicity of the western powers, particularly the United States, in the long-term security of these regimes, given their proximity to oil and Israel. These regimes have been termed the "Arab exception" insofar as they "remained immune to the great wave of democratization which has swept through Eastern Europe, Latin American, and Africa."[39] The exception perhaps proves the regional rule insofar as persistent authoritarianism within an imperial shell has resulted in predatory states, with continuing emergency laws and persistent human rights violations to control deeply unequal societies.

The Egyptian uprising forced some concessions from the state—the political ouster and arrest of President Mubarak, reduced (but not ended) military presence, freezing of accounts of regime cronies, promise of new elections, and constitutional changes. Revolutionary currents followed the uprising, encouraging reform movements in the Islamist religious organizations and in the military (as regular officers challenged the economic privileges of the military hierarchy), formation of the Egyptian National Congress (to Defend the Revolution), and empowerment of various civil society and professional organizations.[40] Egypt's interim government received a $3 billion loan package from the IMF in June 2011, complemented with a U.S. loan and G8 aid. As in Tunisia, a "social inclusion" sentiment shaped the package, "which include(d) raising of the national minimum wage from the near three-decades old level of $6 a month to around $120, and the establishment of a fund to pay for unemployment benefits."[41]

Meanwhile, alongside rhetoric hailing the democratic upheaval, the security of the region remains paramount for the United States and its allies. The swift crushing of protest in Bahrain with Saudi Arabian forces in March, 2011, was little reported in the media, but telling nonetheless, as Nelida Fuccaro noted: "This small island is a microcosm of the Middle East—you have sectarianism, class issues, poverty, repression, and a young generation coming up. [Even more important] Bahrain sits in the region that provides the most oil to the global economy—and it's the most volatile country there."[42]

CASE STUDY   Oiling the Wheels of Change

Oil makes the difference for the Middle East. And long-standing western support for repressive regimes in the Gulf region appears to be the rule that proves the exception, namely, development prospects are governed by geopolitical considerations and do not follow a path-dependent destiny of growth stages, country by country. In the years preceding the Arab spring, more than half of World Bank aid targeted financial and private sector development, with education, health, and other social services averaging only 6.5 percent. Egyptian scholar Noha El Shoky remarked, "IMF and Bank loans promoting neoliberalism allowed for the concentration of both political and economic power in the hands of a few, who systematically marginalized, oppressed, and tortured Egyptians until they revolted." Georges Corm summed it up:

The new Arab businessmen—billionaires created by squandered oil profits, the products of the innermost circles of government—were the best sign of the "modernisation" of Arab economies.

Everything else was swept under the carpet: unemployment figures well above the world average, especially among the young; a brain drain, growing migration figures; illiteracy, huge shantytowns, low disposable income among the many people who also lack any social cover; widespread corruption and demoralization; the disgust of the middle

(Continued)

(Continued)

class; the anarchic management of the private sector, which is highly corrupt and often, as in Tunisia, subject to the depredations of the leaders. Behind the relatively high growth figures and reforms designed to get good ratings from international financial institutions and the EU, the social and economic reality was very different.

Is it not ironic that the Arab rebellion over development failures is a product of the resource upon which development—as we know it—depends, and by which development is possibly digging its own grave?

Sources: Shoky (2011); Corm (2011).

In the terms of conventional development theory, the oil regimes in particular exhibit the extremes of the "resource curse,"—a one-sided specialization in extractive production of a resource with "magical" powers in short-circuiting productive economic diversification—by their reliance on oil revenues.[43] The UN *Arab Human Development Report* (2009) noted that Arab states overall were less industrialized in 2007 than they were in 1970, with governments maintaining large public workforces and cheap imports with oil, gas, and other outside receipts. Contrary to the Venezuelan case, such revenues have not been redistributed to contain and/or mobilize popular classes, rather they have supported *rentier* economies that will be that much more difficult to transform, especially given the strategic significance of this region. While Egypt is not a significant oil producer, it is *the* strategic state, and has relied on revenues from the Suez Canal, tourism, and foreign aid tied to its peace treaty with Israel.[44] The unfolding of the Arab spring, then, as an expression of the crisis of neoliberal austerity, must also contend with its location in the vortex of geopolitical strategic security for the global political economy.

Geopolitical Transitions

The institutional crisis of the globalization project was imminent through the 1990s. Austerity pushes stalked the global South, the revenues of the international financial institutions declined, the Asian financial crisis destabilized the world economy, and discontent grew in the South with the asymmetry of the WTO regime. As fall-out from the Asian financial crisis of 1997, the **Group of 20 (G-20)** formed, combining the original members of the G-8 with significant states from the global South, including Argentina, Brazil, China, India, Indonesia, Mexico, Saudi Arabia, South

Africa, South Korea, and Turkey (accounting for about 90 percent of the global economy). The G-20 as a bloc assumed significance as its key southern states, Brazil, India, and China, led an effective opposition to Northern attempts to retain their unequal economic power through WTO protocols in the Doha "Development Round," which first met in 2001, and then moved on to Cancun in 2003. The straw that broke the camel's back consisted of the undemocratic procedures of the North, its aggressive attempts to dominate Southern markets, and the hypocrisy of continuing farm subsidies in the North while the WTO outlawed them in the South.

The G-20's appearance signaled a *turning point in the balance of global forces*. Not only did the politics of the WTO precipitate a solidarity group from the global South but that solidarity group imprinted their economic rise and recognition in the G-20. Their leading edge, the so-called **BRIC** countries (Brazil, Russia, India, China) contribute more than 50 percent to world-economic growth, and account for about 15 percent of the world's economy.[45] In 2010, China surpassed Japan as the world's second-largest economic power (although the United States produces two-and-a-half times more). These shifts are portrayed in Figure 8.3. Commenting on the significance of the 2008 financial crisis, *Financial Times* columnist Martin Wolf declared in 2010,

> We already know that the earthquake of the past few years has damaged western economies, while leaving those of emerging countries, particularly Asia, standing. It has also destroyed western prestige. The west has dominated the world economically and intellectually for at least two centuries. That epoch is over. Hitherto, the rulers of emerging countries disliked the west's pretensions, but respected its competence. This is true no longer. Never again will the west have the sole word. The rise of the Group of 20 leading economies reflects new realities of power and authority.[46]

These new realities of power are emerging as increasingly polycentric. Cross-sectional comparison shows the economic dynamism of segments of these rising "middle-income countries" (MICs). As Susan George notes, "a third of all Brazilians are richer than the bottom 5 per cent of Germans; so, more surprisingly, are 200 million Chinese."[47] The center of world economic gravity may be shifting to the MICs, but their interests do not necessarily converge. For example, rising commodity prices benefit Russia (oil, wheat, minerals) and Brazil (soy, oil, sugar, orange juice), but not India and China. Nevertheless, the first BRIC summit, held in Russia in 2009, raised the question of replacing the U.S. dollar as the world's principal trading currency, as well as reforming international financial institutions to reflect the new balance of economic forces.

In April 2011, South Africa joined the club, rounding out the acronym appropriately: **BRICS**, and bringing to the table its influence in Africa

Figure 8.3 Changing of the World-Economic Guard?

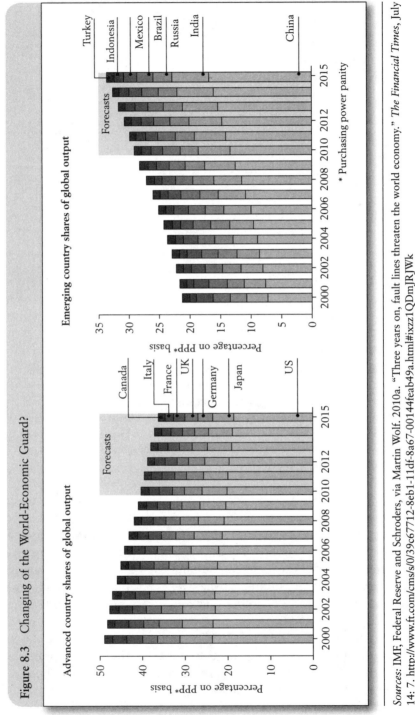

Sources: IMF, Federal Reserve and Schroders, *via* Martin Wolf. 2010a. "Three years on, fault lines threaten the world economy." *The Financial Times*, July 14: 7. http://www.ft.com/cms/s/0/39c67712-8eb1-11df-8a67-00144feab49a.html#ixzz1QDmJRJWk

and in the race to corner mineral and land resources, despite its smaller economy.[48] South Africa also brings its own strategic interests—and official foreign aid agency for conflict resolution—in the African continent. South-South aid programs (notably Chinese and Brazilian) already account for about 10 percent of total aid.[49] South-South aid is matched by South-South alliances, especially among the BRICS. In 2003, India, Brazil, and South Africa established their own forum, IBSA. Their goal is to amplify their presence and influence in the UN, the WTO, and the IMF, in addition to developing "minilateral" commercial relations, including technological collaboration in malaria and AIDS research, nanotechnology, biofuels, wind energy, and oceanography. By 2010, another grouping known as BASIC, which focuses on climate negotiations, included China.[50]

The new bloc of rising MICs expresses a geopolitical shift of growing significance. While U.S. corporations still dominate, the *Financial Times* charts a decline from 57 percent of its top 500 corporations in the late 1990s to 36 percent in 2008: "US corporations have somewhat larger share of the value than of the number, but the second place of China is underlined."[51] Further, the two leading finance and business services centers "are still on the two shores of the North Atlantic, but in the second tier, six of the seven nodes are on the western side of the Pacific."[52] Göran Therborn remarks, "looking backwards from 2010, globalization does not look so much an extension of U.S. capitalism as a delimitation of it, by the rise of China and India."[53]

CASE STUDY   Trans-local Developments

Development theory has lost its hierarchical national moorings in a global age. The conventional image of national societies arranged vertically is being overtaken by horizontal (and selective) markets responsive to shareholder responsibility rather than by states responsive to social contracts. This is a recipe for deepening inequality. India's super-rich—about 50 billionaires in 2010 compared with 10 in France and 35 in Britain—preside over an economic boom stimulated by liberalization. They account for 25 percent of India's GDP, but represent just 0.00001 percent of the population. In China—where Lamborghini sales tripled in 2010, and Rolls Royce rose 146 percent to 678 cars, overtaking the UK, and where in 2030 predictions are for more cars than in the whole world in 2000—Jonathan Watts notes a similar segmentation:

> In recent years, the planet's largest corporations have become dependent on the Wangs catching up with the Joneses. The U.S. had shopped until

(Continued)

(Continued)

its economy dropped. Sinking in debt, plagued by obesity and increasingly dependent on military might to protect its lifestyle, the world's superconsumer was groaning with indigestion. Europe was too decrepit and conservative to take up the slack, so global manufacturers, retailers and restaurant chains were desperate to stimulate the Chinese appetite. Shanghai was their beachhead.

The Chinese frontier was opened up in the early 1990s by companies like Mattel, the world's biggest toy company—now with the planet's largest Barbie emporium in Shanghai. More recently, international brands, Louis Vuitton, Gucci, Chanel, and Starbucks complement retailing giants: America's Walmart, France's Carrefour, Britain's Tesco, and Japan's Ito Yokado. The first KFC opened near Tiananmen Square in 1987, and now the firm has 2,000 outlets in 400 cities as the largest restaurant chain in China, and McDonalds has 800 outlets. Unsurprisingly 15 percent of the population is now overweight, with rising incidences of diabetes and heart disease.

Political scientist Sandra Halperin has for some time argued that "development" was originally about extending and integrating trans-local trade and investment circuits among European aristocracies, understood as a "single trans-regional elite." The national consequence was a distinctive economic "dualism," expressed as wealthy elites and impoverished nineteenth-century European working classes. Challenging twentieth-century assumptions of *national* development, Halperin argues that post-colonial elites exploited this nationalist myth as "part of a broad vision that they shared with retreating colonial administrators and with a wide set of transnational elites concerned with maintaining and reproducing the circuit." Given the selectivity of Chinese prosperity (10 percent of the population), Halperin's "dualism" reappears in the Chinese model, albeit via a band of affluence beyond elites to middle-class consumers hitching their fortunes to the global market.

Ultimately, what does this mean for the concept of "development"? Is the Rostovian stage of "high-mass consumption" both uniquely a post–World War II phenomenon in some First World states, and now a phenomenon of no country in particular, but a global class of affluent consumers?

Sources: Watts (2010); Halperin (2005: 42); Chang (2008); Ramesh (2009: 17); Wilson (2010: 17); Watts (2011b).

Alluding to a historical pendulum, Antoine van Agtmael in *The Emerging Markets Century* (2007) predicted that the Third World "will overtake the developed world by around 2030–2035." He extrapolates that prediction from the powerhouse companies: Samsung of South Korea, Infosys of India, Haier of China, and Cemex of Mexico.[54] Whatever "overtaking" means, there is no doubt that the phenomenon of "Chindia" has the attention of the business community—whether as an investment opportunity or a threat to northern businesses or jobs. Goldman Sachs' 2003 *Dreaming with BRICs: The Path to 2050*, predicted that by 2050 China would be the world's largest economy, followed by the United States and then India. It also predicted China would overtake Japan as the world's second largest economy by 2015, a feat which happened in 2011.[55]

In China, despite—and perhaps because of—its authoritarian socialist government, an economic revolution with global economic and ecological implications is underway. The average citizen now earns two and a half times as much a year than the average Indian.[56] Trade deficit data indicate that the majority of investment is regional, coming from Japan and the "East Asian tigers" (or NICs), as they have disaggregated manufacturing and shifted labor-intensive production to China.[57] China has been the final assembly station in transnational corporation (TNC) commodity chains, which account for 60 percent of products manufactured in China.[58] In this respect, China's transformation has been a part of the globalization project, as its economic opening coincided with late-1980s deregulation of capital flows, targeting export-processing zones consolidated by China's entry into the WTO in 2000.

While China is responsible for 70 percent of the world's toys, 60 percent of its bicycles, 50 percent of its shoes, and 33 percent of its luggage, it also manufactures over 55 percent of the world's laptop computers, 50 percent of its microwave ovens, 33 percent of its televisions sets, 25 percent of its dishwashers, and 20 percent of its refrigerators and microprocessors.[59] China has upgraded from low-value to high-value products, led by electronics and information technology goods, however it still assembles components designed and made elsewhere, or uses copied designs.[60] But this model is in transition, as China faces a labor shortage, and wages are rising. The reasons are complex, and include escalating labor disputes (170,000 alone in the first half of 2009) enabled by a new Labor Contract Law (2008); new lower-cost production sites in Vietnam, Bangladesh, and India; Chinese government investment in its hinterland as a policy shift in redistributing wealth regionally; and the legacy of China's historic "one child" policy.[61]

Such competition has encouraged China to outsource low-value manufacturing to Africa, via industrial parks jointly funded by the World Bank—over 100 of Ghana's 340 Chinese investment projects are in manufacturing, reflecting a Chinese desire to improve its image beyond that of resource grabbing.[62]

Meanwhile, in India there is a palpable shift from producing global services to manufacturing domestic products—an interesting twist (or reversal) of the globalization project. In a commentary on Americans' anxiety about globalization, Steven Pearlstein of the *Washington Post* offered an image of "dozens of ambitious 20-somethings . . . crammed in like commuters in a subway car, sitting at long banquet tables in front of well-worn computer screens creating websites for companies in the U.S. and around the world." Most of these workers in Pune make about $270 a month, "enough to pay for a small apartment, a scooter and weekend outings to the food courts at local shopping malls. And they are sufficiently in demand that 40 percent of them move on every year to bigger companies such as Wipro and Infosys, which offer . . . the glamour of working in one of the gleaming new hi-tech parks that have sprung around this Indian industrial center." In a gesture perhaps to Thomas Friedman, he suggested that this was

> emblematic of the Indian economic boom, one built on low wages, entrepreneurial energy and internet technology that has created the kind of perfectly competitive markets that once existed only in the imagination of neoclassical economists.[63]

However, Indian education is unable to meet the demand for skilled software operatives, a shortage that is inflating wages by 30–40 percent a year and eroding Indian high-tech cost advantages. Accordingly, policymakers have shifted gears, focusing more on the domestic market of middle-class consumers, requiring expanding employment of lower-skilled labor. Coinciding with this, "global manufacturers are already looking ahead to a serious demographic squeeze facing China. . . . India will have 116 million workers [aged 20 to 24 by 2020] to China's 94 million." While Indian infrastructure is still undeveloped (China invests seven times as much on roads, ports, electricity, and so on), the central government is pursuing an aggressive industrial park program in the "global/satellite cities" of Delhi, Mumbai, Kolkata, Hyderabad, and Chennai.[64]

TNCs like Renault-Nissan (joining forces with Mahindra & Mahindra of India), Ford, GM, Motorola, Hyundai, and Posco of South Korea, and Mittal Steel of the Netherlands are transforming India from a service to a manufacturing center: manufactured exports to the United States are rising faster in percentage terms than those from China, and over two-thirds of foreign investment in the mid-2000s entered manufacturing.[65] India itself has emerged as the eleventh largest auto market in the world (China is the most dynamic), and local manufacturers such as Tata and Rajav compete with Renault to build low-cost models for the domestic market.[66] *The Wall Street Journal* reported in 2009 that Chennai's production of 1.5 million cars would surpass auto production by any U.S. state, claiming that "the kind of manufacturing being done in Chennai is what India needs to bridge the gap between its agricultural workforce, which makes up 60 percent of its population, and high-end services industries, such as outsourcing, that employ relatively few." Hyundai, which made a $2 billion investment in Chennai, was attracted to the cheap factory floor labor as well as the abundance of Indian engineers (to manage robotic technology), supplied by the state's technical institutes as they shift their training from computer programmers and engineers to auto production skills—a decisive shift away from its recent IT/software profile.[67]

While two-thirds of Indians are still agrarian, India's rising middle class of some 300 million constitutes a sizable consumer market. And this is symbolized by the supermarket revolution emerging in India. Hypercity, a Western-style supermarket that opened in 2005 in the western suburbs of Mumbai, was India's first inroad into a global retailing culture, where before 97 percent of India's retail had been located in small family-run shops. India held the global supermarkets at bay for a few years longer than China, which opened its doors to the behemoths in 2000 and now has half of the top 70 global retailers operating in its prosperous urban markets.[68] In late 2006, India's Reliance Industries Limited opened its first wholly owned supermarket in Hyderabad, with the intention of beating Walmart to the punch. But for many Indians, this was not a cause for nationalist celebration: "At stake is the livelihood security of 12 million small shopkeepers, 40 million hawkers and at least 200 million (of the 600 million) small farmers."[69] Such tension symbolizes the distinct worlds in play—that of small-scale Indian family enterprises versus the reach of the global market as its agents attempt to recoup profits by creating new high-growth markets to compensate for the global capitalist downturn. Japanese companies like Toyota and Canon are redesigning products to capture lower class rupees in Indian slums and rural villages. A Canon senior vice president remarked, "Even the poorest person has to have photos of the wedding of his daughter."[70] And the Korean CEO of LG Electronics' Indian subsidiary claimed India as the last frontier—for electronic goods.

As a regional duo, *China and India represent a countertrend to the globalization project.* While they have certainly positioned their labor forces in the global marketplace, they have not fully embraced neoliberal principles. They retain capital and investment controls. China's currency is not freely convertible; the government still controls at least half of its industrial assets, and invests heavily in infrastructure, setting the pace for India.[71] The Chinese government responded to the 2008 economic meltdown by pumping over 4 trillion yuan ($586 billion) into infrastructural and industrial projects to manage the crisis.[72]

In the mid-2000s the newly-elected Indian Congress Party government refocused on an inclusive nationalism, rendered through a populist lens usually targeting small farmers displaced by highways, factories, mining, logging, and agro-industrial estates. Unlike China, Indian democracy promotes such appeals, concretized for example in a national experiment to facilitate channeling of public largesse to the poor via "social audits." These enable villagers to perform watchdog functions online, to reduce corruption, and to safeguard government plans to spend a quarter of a trillion dollars over the period 2010–2015 to stimulate employment and circulate purchasing power. Much of that money funds a Congress Party program to provide rural people with 100 days work at minimum wages on local village infrastructure projects.[73]

The nationalist turn in China and India is a social and ecological imperative. Agrarian populations predominate in both countries, and rural unrest is endemic. In 2007, the Indian central government suspended all land acquisition for establishing new Special Economic Zones (SEZs) and industrial parks pursuant to establishing a policy on rehabilitating displaced people. This followed pitched battles between the (communist) West Bengal government and peasants over plans to acquire 140,000 acres of land for SEZs to be developed by the Tata business group and Indonesia's Salim Group on the outskirts of Kolkata.[74] And in 2010, the Indian Supreme Court expressed concern about development (via land acquisition) and its politically destabilizing effects, given the long-standing Naxalite Maoist insurgency centered in mineral-rich forests in 200 of India's 588 districts. The Court observed, "The whole issue of development appears to be so simple, logical and commonsensical. And yet, to millions of Indians, development is a dreadful and hateful word that is aimed at denying them even the source of their sustenance."[75]

In China, land seizures by the government, in the name of development, generate a rising tide of rural resistance. This is exacerbated by fiscal decentralization, which incentivizes local government collusion with developers as opposed to villagers' lawful rights.[76] In 2007, the government sought to head off rural unrest by repealing agricultural taxation and local fees, providing minimal rural health insurance, and increasing compensation for loss of land.[77] Meanwhile, intensive agriculture has accelerated. Chinese soils are deteriorating from reduced crop rotation, erosion, overfertilization, and the loss of organic content of soils once nourished by manure-based farming. More than 2,000 square kilometers of land turn to desert annually.[78] Millions of Chinese farmers have abandoned farming to circulate as a highly exploited reserve army of cheap labor, and analysts predict a global grain crisis, as China's food dependency grows.[79] The authors of *Will the Boat Sink the Water? The Life of China's Peasants*, which is banned in China, remark,

> In the last analysis the Triple Agri [San-Nong: the problem of agriculture, the problem of the rural areas, and the problem of the peasant] is nothing less than the problem of China. Not exclusively an agricultural issue or an economic one, it is the greatest problem facing the ruling party of China today. The problem is staring us in the face.[80]

In the face of these fundamental questions of stabilizing socioeconomic transformation on such a large scale, Chinese and Indian forms of development echo Latin American initiatives to bring markets under social control, distinguished by the scale of depeasantization. Given a stagnant global economy and mounting socioecological crisis, we might anticipate the revival of forms of the development state, as a departure from the universal claims of neoliberalism. In some quarters this is referred to as a growing "Beijing Consensus."[81]

While the West views the rise of China as a threat—in the short run to jobs, and in the long run to geopolitical power—it is unclear what the future holds. Domestically, China faces growing unrest as class inequalities deepen, the peasant question is exacerbated, and an emergent middle class takes the lead in demanding political rights and democratization of the state. Internationally the Chinese government enunciated a New Security Concept that rejected hegemonism in 2004. At present, China is focused on securing resources from various world regions. And within Asia, as India's second-largest trading partner,[82] it is constructing a Chinese-centered regional political economy. Despite projections of India's superior economic growth rates over the next decades, the U.S. government and its European allies are more focused on India's potential role as a counterpoise to China in Asia.[83]

Financial Crisis

The severe financial downturn (near meltdown) in 2008 was a signal crisis of the era of "financialization." Financialization means investment shifts into financial transactions (mergers, acquisitions, derivatives) and away from goods or services production. During the 2000s, financial profits in the United States routinely outdid manufacturing profits by two or three times, and the British financial sector's annual profits reached new heights of 20 percent.[84] Contributing to this structural shift was financial deregulation in the late 1990s, by which commercial lending banks were allowed to develop financial and investment instruments. Economic power shifted to financiers, justified in turn by neoliberal claims for the greater allocative efficiency of the unrestrained market. Citicorp (banking) and the Travelers Group (insurance and securities) conducted the largest merger in corporate history, as Citigroup. Henceforth such firms "concentrated banking, investment, securities and insurance under a single roof" and changed their name to "financial services corporations."[85]

The most common, derivative financial instrument created was a security anchored in mortgage debt, then packaged and repackaged as the debt was sold and resold by financiers, thus recycling risk. Mortgage debt ballooned, enabled by loosening credit—in other words, "high mass consumption" was untethered from its material underpinnings. Supply soon outstripped demand, housing prices fell, and collapsing subprime loans led to rising mortgage rates and a foreclosure crisis in the United States. The consequent drop in mortgage-backed securities exposed financial institutions to huge debt/equity ratios and a general market crisis, cascading across the global North. Government oversight of the financial sector had all but disappeared, and only returned to bail out some of the deeply troubled banks to avoid a complete economic collapse.

Northern governments did not have the funds on hand, having already surrendered revenue to tax cuts for corporations and the wealthy. In the United States, corporate tax rates steadily declined over the last quarter of the twentieth century, and high personal income tax rates were slashed in the 2000s. When the 2008 financial crisis hit, public funds were short and taxpayers were expected to foot the bill. Taxpayer anger has taken the form of rolling strikes and prolonged demonstrations against cutbacks in social-democratic Europe, while anger has been directed at the state itself in the United States, where the political culture favors private initiative.

The northern debt crisis crystallizes several trends, both short- and long-term. The globalization project represented a long-term countermobilization by business interests against the restraints of the welfare state (complementing corporate tax breaks). As northern manufacturing was outsourced to lower-wage world regions, organized labor's real wages fell behind rising labor productivity, redistributing wealth upwards. The G-7 countries, for example, experienced a 6 percent drop in the wage share of national income between 1982 and 2005 (parallel to global trends).[86]

Offshoring of jobs reduced the tax base in the North at the same time as cheaper imports matched with easy credit seduced consumers into rising debt levels. Neoliberal development theory maintains that flexible labor markets (via the *dis*-organization of labor) are more attractive to investors in a competitive global economy. But the more flexible labor markets have been the site of the greatest unemployment, exposing the mismatch between economic orthodoxy and the reality of financialization (capital's preference for unproductive investments). The greatest increase in unemployment has been in countries like the United States and Spain, with institutionalized flexible labor markets. By contrast, in "Germany and Norway, with strong trade unions and long traditions of collective bargaining, the unemployment rate barely budged."[87]

While the IMF initially recommended government deficits to cure unemployment in 2010, policies instituted since (and embraced) under austerity plans in Europe, and in the United States, have favored the "market." That is, policy responses have uniformly focused on reducing government spending in the name of debt reduction. The argument for public austerity is market based, with neoliberals claiming that a retreat of the state will bring in the private sector to fill the gap, which has not happened significantly—a consequence of financialization. As a result, a growing proportion of the working population, "whose jobs are insecure, who have limited access to secure housing, and who juggle jobs and child-rearing in a frantic effort to keep up," represent, in Guy Standing's terms, a new "precariat." He estimates 40 percent of the UK population now belongs to the precariat, a more significant designation than the "middle class," and increasingly evident in a politics of frustration, expressed in the Tea Party movement in the United States—and elsewhere in rising ethnic tensions.[88]

CASE STUDY Limiting Assumptions of the Shock Doctrine

Naomi Klein's idea of the "shock doctrine" is that a wholesale implementation of neoliberal policies requires an exceptional moment of social destabilization, following a war, military coup, natural disaster, or financial crisis. In a state of emergency, far-reaching transformation, like shrinking the public sector can be accomplished under the guise of reconfiguring an economy in order to save it. . . . When governments downsize, citizens, and especially women, bear the cost.

In Britain, where women account for 40 percent of public-sector jobs, and 85 percent of part-time jobs in the civil service, research found women would

(Continued)

(Continued)

suffer 72 percent of the tax and benefit cuts. For example, cutbacks in the Sure Start maternity grant (affecting over 250,000 women), a freeze on child benefits, housing benefits reform, and removal of income support for single parents (90 percent women) exacerbates the unequal status of working women, who already collect lower wages. One minister described the budget as "the biggest attack on women in generations."

But citizens are fighting back with alternatives and reclaiming the public sector. British trade unions compete for tenders—for example, in Newcastle, the public-sector union Unison (in a Public Services Alliance) beat multinational telecom company BT for a 10-year, $250 million contract to deliver the city council's information technology services. Similarly in Trondheim, Norway, a coalition of unions and civil society organizations forced the Labor party to renounce support of privatization, thus reclaiming transport, cinemas, elderly care, schooling, and social assistance for single mothers as municipal services.

Just as crises, often naturalized as financial necessity, provide opportunity for corporate power plays, why not politicize them and open up possibility for citizens to reclaim development?

Sources: Klein (2007); Asthana (2010); TNI (2007).

Unlike the profile of the Third World debt crisis of the 1980s, the northern debt crisis morphed from unsustainable private debt, encouraged by deregulation, into "an alleged sovereign debt crisis."[89] This crisis is represented as a crisis of the state, rather than as a consequence of unregulated capitalism. In Europe the so-called **sovereign debt crisis** is exacerbated by membership in the European Union (EU). States are required to use the euro, a currency they do not issue, which forces them to borrow to cover their deficits. The financial crisis exposed the vulnerability of the weaker states (Portugal, Ireland, Greece, and Spain), subjecting them to austere loan conditions imposed by the European Central Bank and the IMF to preserve the union and the value of the euro, and the viability of the eurozone. For example, in 2010 (and again in 2011) German and French governments agreed to bail Greece out, but in return demanded massive public-sector cuts such as layoffs, salaries, pensions, and other benefits for which the Greeks had just voted.

The Greek bail-out exposed the limitations of the EU, which lacks European-wide institutions "with sufficient powers to coordinate the economic policies of the member states effectively," thereby amplifying taxpayer "liability for the budgetary risks of each of the other member states."[90] Taxpayer resentment in the stronger states (Germany, France) at having to pay for the (perceived) profligacy of the (citizens of the) weaker states expresses the dilemma of a union of states with different levels of economic development. But this hardly matches taxpayer vulnerability and resentment in the weaker states subject to draconian cutbacks. The Bretton Woods Project reported (on June 13, 2011) that conditionalities imposed on Portugal "mirror those the IMF typically imposed in Africa during the structural adjustment era," such as privatization, wage cuts, layoffs, increased health service user fees—in addition to "reducing: incentives for renewable energy; the number of municipalities; social security contributions paid by employers," and private bank bailouts. Portugal's largest trade union confederation, the CGTP, described the package as "an attack against democracy and national sovereignty, a clear capitulation to foreign interference, a denial of the country's development, and a genuine assault on workers and the people."[91]

The unsuccessful 2010 bailout of Greece, requiring savage cuts, contracted the Greek economy by 5.5 percent over the year, increasing unemployment by 40 percent, and with youth unemployment at a devastating 42 percent. By June 2011 Greece faced a solvency crisis (not just short-term debt), with new conditions requiring four years of retrenchment. Austerity policies were viewed as a result of excessive eurozone bank lending. Huge citizen protests in Greece in May and June 2011—turning Athens' main square into a semi-permanent encampment—produced comparisons with the Arab spring.[92] But political regimes were not the target so much as the politics of the debt regime itself, and its privileging of the banks: "Aided by the rating agencies, the announcements of the insolvency or financial fragility of the Eurozone's deficit members—Greece, Portugal, Ireland, Spain, and Italy—enabled [the big European banks] to amass enormous profits based on (highly inflated) debt-bond interest rates."[93]

Interpretations differ regarding the meaning and significance of the Northern crisis. A conventional American view is that Europe, with low birth rates and longer life expectancy, can no longer afford its social model, with national health care, extensive welfare benefits, generous vacations, and early retirements.[94]

An alternative view is that the *refocus* on sovereign debt represents a final attempt by neoliberal or corporate interests to completely dismantle the welfare state in its various forms. In the United States broad recognition of the recklessness of the financial institutions in exposing the nation to economic collapse did not result in convictions and reinstituting regulatory oversight, but rather in bailouts and subsequent bipartisan agreement to engage in massive deficit cutting, affecting social services of all kinds. The bailout of the financial sector is a prime source of sovereign debt.

A third, more radical interpretation is that this is now a permanent state of crisis, and is evidence that capitalism thrives on deregulation and risk, that destined to be borne by citizens. This view focuses on the separation of economics and politics implicit in the institution of private property. Here liberal democracy is the arena for struggle over regulatory powers and austerity choices, but corporate and financial interests remain insulated from ultimate political sanction (by constitutional law, lobbying, or simply system maintenance pressures on politicians).

From another angle, the depth, and terms, of the financial crisis suggest a double edge. The legitimacy claims of the globalization project for universal prosperity are contradicted by the universal reach of austerity politics. Now in question is whether this version of "globalization" is sustainable. Not only does austerity bring social unrest—as we have seen—but also rising food prices, energy shortages, and climate change all conspire to compound the crisis of global development.

Food Crises

Food riots cascading across the world in 2007–2008 (from Italy through Indonesia to Mexico and beyond) bore witness to rising basic food prices. As prices rose again, even further during 2010–2011, riots reappeared in Mozambique, India, Serbia, Pakistan, and the Middle East North African (MENA) states. Food riots protest neoliberal policies, insofar as they dismantle public capacity (specifically food reserves), and deepen food dependency across the global South through liberalization of trade in foodstuffs.

Northerners do not feel the price rises as keenly as southerners. While food accounts for only 16 percent of the budget of the poorest 20 percent of U.S. households, Nigerians spend 73 percent of their budgets on food, Vietnamese 65 percent, and Indonesians 50 percent (for Indians 70 percent and Chinese 50 percent).[95] Rising hunger rates across the global South concentrate in Sub-Saharan Africa. As of 2011, roughly 14 percent of humanity—about 1 billion people—was considered hungry or malnourished, especially women. The majority of the hungry (65 percent) are in India, China, the Democratic Republic of Congo, Bangladesh, Indonesia, Pakistan, and Ethiopia (see Figure 8.4).

Rising prices signal the intensification of energy and food demand under conditions of peak oil by a class of 1 billion new consumers in 20

Figure 8.4 Global Distribution of Undernourished People in 2009

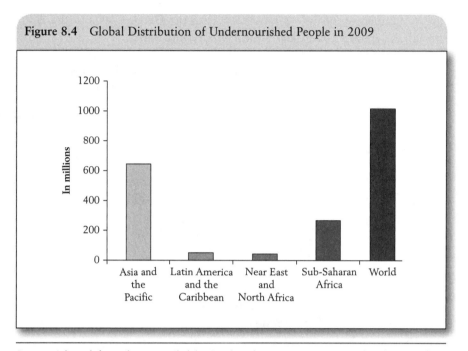

Source: Adapted from data compiled by Earth Policy Institute (www.earth-policy.org) from "Table I.6. Population of Urban Agglomerations with 10 Million Inhabitants or More, 1950, 1975, 2007 and 2025," and "Table A.11. The 30 Largest Urban Agglomerations Ranked by Population Size, 1950-2025," in U.N. Population Division (UNPop), World Urbanization Prospects: The 2007 Revision (New York: February 2008), pp. 10, 164–167; UNPop, World Urbanization Prospects: The 2007 Revision Population Database, electronic database, at http://esa.un.org/unup, updated 2008.

MICs "with an aggregate spending capacity, in purchasing power parity terms, to match that of the U.S."[96] The symbols of their affluence are car ownership and meat consumption. These commodities combine, via rising demand for biofuels and feed crops (corn and soy), to exacerbate food price inflation—the mutual competition for land has the perverse effect of rendering each crop more lucrative, and displacing land used for food crops. Financial speculation compounds the problem. The financial crisis contributed to speculation in commodity futures, encouraging investors to shift their funds into agricultural commodities and oil, thus driving up the price of food and farm inputs.[97]

The age of cheap food is widely regarded as over, with "agflation" bringing the world to a "post-food-surplus era."[98] Further, the Inter-Governmental Panel on Climate Change (IPCC) predicts that climate changes will increase hunger by between 40 and 170 million.[99] The food crisis intensifies pressures on social reproduction to such an extent that urban rebellions threaten public order (as we have seen with the Greek riots and the Arab spring). A January 2008 *New York Times* report noted,

> Governments in many poor countries have tried to respond by stepping up food subsidies, imposing or tightening price controls, restricting exports, and cutting food import duties. . . . No category of food prices has risen as quickly this winter as so-called edible oils. . . . Cooking oil may seem a trifling expense in the West. But in the developing world, cooking oil is an important source of calories and represents one of the biggest cash outlays for poor families, which grow much of their own food but have to buy oil in which to cook it.

The irony here is that palm oil, the principal cooking oil produced in Southeast Asia, also serves as biodiesel to supply rising (mandated) European demand for alternative energy. Not only do the poorest on the planet find their food necessities priced out of their range, but also their own countries export this particular food as fuel for their wealthy counterparts across the world—putting northern and southern living standards in competition with one another.

Central to the neoliberal food system is a relationship whereby the South exports high-value foods at the expense of its own local food supplies, requiring imports of cheap staple foods, which destabilize local food producers of the South, and reduce their ability to produce more when prices rise. Structural adjustment removed support for smallholders (credit, subsidies, government-administered food marketing systems) in the name of market efficiency, and privatized/sold grain reserves, traditionally maintained for emergencies.[100]

In January 2011, the BBC reported that "world leaders have warned that rising food prices could lead to social unrest and even 'economic war.' . . . But business leaders at the World Economic Forum rejected calls for curbs on commodity speculation."[101] This apparent disconnect reveals how profound the crisis of the globalization project is. Inequalities of access to food deepen when the global market captures agricultural output—either as livestock feed (70 percent agricultural land) for relatively affluent consumers of meat, or fuel, or simply an attractive object of financial speculation.

Ecological Crisis

The first thing to note about ecological crisis is that, according to a 2008 assessment of the environmental impact of economic globalization since 1961, the richest countries have generated 42 percent of global environmental degradation while paying only 3 percent of the resulting costs.[102] The second thing to note is that much of the degradation is the consequence of a fatal separation over the last two centuries of the natural from the social sciences. Development theory is a prime example—it has been fashioned as if human societies had no ecological basis. And yet it has informed agricultural and industrial practices that fully depend on extractions from nature. And the theory has ignored the environmental impact of development. Until now. This is the crisis—humanity faces depletion of its ecosystems.

While it would be easy to say that the environmental crisis is because of population growth and colonization of the earth, with rapidly diminishing wild spaces (wetlands, forests, grasslands, etc.) to sustain biodiversity, the problem is deeper than this. In a critical evaluation of conservation efforts Columbia University ecology professor Shahid Naeem observes,

> The more we relegate wild species to parks, zoos, gardens, and seed banks, and the more we place domestic species [e.g., cattle, commercial plants] in their stead, the more homogenized the world becomes. . . . As the average number of species found in each square of Earth's surface declines, so too will its biomass, its biogeochemistry, and its contribution to a stable, life-supporting biosphere.

His point is that "almost all aspects of human well-being and prosperity trace back to biodiversity for their foundation."[103]

We know, for example, that 40 percent of the world's oceans now have been damaged, especially the coral reefs, which constitute the bedrock of oceanic biodiversity, upon which the world's fishing stocks depend.[104] About one-third of the world's fisheries are severely depleted, with complete collapse, for example, of the once plentiful cod stocks on the Grand Banks off eastern Canada. It is now estimated that given current trends, within half a century there will be no commercially viable marine fisheries.[105]

While the oceans are the last resource frontier, and aquaculture is evolving into the next factory farm complex as wild fish stocks decline, freshwater supplies cannot be taken for granted. Only 3 percent of the world's water supply is freshwater, and two-thirds of that is frozen—so far. The Water Resources Group (WRG), a private sector consortium, predicts a global gap between demand and supply of 40 percent by 2030. The World Business Council for Sustainable Development estimates agriculture uses almost 70 percent of the world's freshwater supplies. China and India, with one-third of the world's population, have less than 10 percent of global water supply. Glacial melting in the Himalaya Mountains poses huge problems for them in the coming decades, as well as for Tibet, Pakistan, and Bangladesh. Agriculture is the flashpoint, since it uses 90 percent of India's and 70 percent of China's water. Currently India uses about 740 billion cubic meters, but by 2030 demand is predicted to reach 53 trillion cubic meters. Rising middle-class diets of meat and sugar are water-intensive.[106]

In this scenario, water is predicted to play a similar role to that of oil in geopolitical resource conflict. While agricultural scientists are under pressure to improve cropping and irrigation techniques, there will be rising tension around luxury crop production via water-intensive agriculture. For example, there is the "water footprint" of asparagus grown in Peru, its largest exporter. World Bank investments in reclaiming the Ica Valley desert have created 10,000 jobs and grown export revenues, but undermine local aquifers at the expense of local farmers.[107] In addition to a looming crisis in water access, conservation of healthy water supplies and wetlands to clean water is threatened by human activity.

The "world" was shocked to learn of America's largest oil spill—205 million gallons—in the Gulf of Mexico in April 2010, when British Petroleum's (BP) *Deepwater Horizon* rig exploded. Largely ignored by the global media have been oil spills by Shell and Exxon-Mobil over the last half century—spewing 546 million gallons of oil in the Niger Delta (at a rate of 11 million gallons a year): "This ecologically sensitive wetlands region, the source of 10 percent of American oil imports, has most of Africa's mangroves and, like the Louisiana coast, has fed the interior for generations with its abundance of fish, shellfish, wildlife, and crops."[108] Eco-system depletion of course includes climatic stress resulting from greenhouse gas emissions. A *Guardian* editorial in 2010 offered a dismal outlook:

> If all nations stopped burning fossil fuels immediately, the planet's oceans would still go on warming, sea levels would continue to rise, windstorms and floods would kill tens of thousands in the tropics. To have prevented the very modest levels of warming the world has seen so far, governments should have taken decisive action 30 years ago. But in 1980 nobody appreciated how swiftly climate might change.[109]

Perhaps the key issue of our era is the possibility of *irreversible global climate change*, which *The Economist* has called "a potential time bomb capable of wreaking global havoc."[110] The world has a short timespan within which it must learn to transform its energy-use patterns to reduce greenhouse gas emissions by up to 90 percent. Current levels of consumption of goods and services are unsustainable. In addition, they are quite inequitable; not only do Ethiopians emit on average about one-300th of the carbon dioxide generated by the average American, but also low-carbon users are more vulnerable to the impact of climate change: "The effort to tackle climate suffers from the problem of split incentives: those who are least responsible for it are the most likely to suffer its effects." The race against time involves preventing a 2 percent rise in global average temperature above preindustrial levels. The international scientific community regards this as the threshold for "critical positive feedbacks" wherein climate change would self-accelerate.[111]

The prospect of rendering the planet uninhabitable should—and will—be a call to action for the global community. So far the response is under-whelming, as nations commit to reducing emissions voluntarily but have difficulty with legally binding targets. Three significant obstacles spotlight tensions within the current global development model.

First is the objective obstacle of *inequality* between and within nations. Wealthy nations located in temperate regions are less vulnerable to ecological changes and have resources to protect citizens from natural disasters (flooding, drought, temperature extremes). Their wealthiest citizens have the resources to ensure that they are the last affected.[112] In the 1990s, while 90 percent of natural disaster fatalities resulted from hydro-meteorological events (such as droughts, floods, hurricanes, and windstorms), 97 percent of natural disaster-related deaths occurred in the global South.[113] About 20 percent of the world's population inhabit coastal zones that are vulnerable to rising sea levels, especially in the Caribbean, Central America, the Nile Delta, Bangladesh, and eastern India and China. Millions of environmental refugees are expected to result from climate change. At the ineffectual 2010 Cancun Climate Summit, Bolivian President Evo Morales observed, "It's easy for people in an air-conditioned room to continue with the policies of destruction of Mother Earth. We need instead to put ourselves in the shoes of families in Bolivia and worldwide that lack water and food and suffer misery and hunger."[114] Bolivians are on the front line—according to a World Bank report, global warming could eliminate Andean glaciers within 20 years, threatening dire water scarcity for almost 100 million people.[115] In the Arctic, the Ground Zero of global warming, temperatures are rising at a rate of double the earth's average—in part due to the declining albedo effect (heat reflection) as ice melts and the land absorbs more solar radiation in a vicious cycle that melts the permafrost.[116]

The second obstacle is the subjective consequence of *uneven development*. For example, while University College London researchers and the British Meteorological Office have reported that "the Amazonian forest is currently near its critical resiliency threshold,"[117] Brazil's president claimed the right to exploit the forest for Brazilian development, reminding the global North of its own path of development: "The wealthy countries are

Figure 8.5   Relative Proportion of Global Greenhouse Gas Emissions by Continent

Source: http://www.google.com/search?q=humanity%27s+ecological+footprint&hl=en&client=firefox-a&hs=TCr&rls=org.mozilla:en-US:official&channel=np&prmd=ivns&tbm=isch&tbo=u&source=univ&sa=X&ei=aPv_TYmjEOqy0AHx7LGvDg&ved=0CDMQsAQ&biw=1125&bih=821.   ©Copyright SASI Group (University of Sheffield) and Mark Newman (University of Michigan).

very smart, approving protocols, holding big speeches on the need to avoid deforestation, but they already deforested everything."[118] Such statements combine sovereignty with a strategy of leverage, Brazil having received a global fund to contain rainforest destruction, which remains ineffectual in the face of pressure from Amazonian farmers. Meanwhile, the Chinese Foreign Ministry claimed wealthier countries should take the lead in reducing greenhouse gas emissions. Following the U.S. president's declaration in Rio (1992) that the American lifestyle was not negotiable, the Chinese refused mandatory emissions limits to preserve their economic growth.[119] China and the United States together produce 30 percent of global output and 40 percent of greenhouse gasses from fossil fuels. While China is now the largest emitter of annual flows of greenhouse gasses, its *per capita* emissions are considerably less than those of the United States, the world's largest emitter of cumulative stocks of greenhouse gasses. Thus, China, distinguishing between luxury and sustenance emissions, claims Article 3.1 of the UN Framework Convention on Climate Change (UNFCCC) charter, which states, "The developed country Parties should take the lead in combating climate change and the adverse effects thereof." China insists that the United States adopt a national emissions reduction plan, such as cap and trade. Additionally, the Chinese point out that 25 percent of their emissions are from consumer products for the West, arguing for quantification of emissions based on consumption, rather than production, data.[120] Measurement disputes, however, are proxies for avoidance of responsibility.

The third obstacle is the *economism* that frames solutions to social and ecological crises. The discourse of development was founded in economic language, institutions, and rules. Activity that commands a price, or generates cash, counts overwhelmingly as the measure of development, despite a range of other valued cultural practices that reproduce societies and ecologies, for which money is meaningless. The international community only began to take the global warming threat seriously when the British government released the Stern Review in November 2006, containing financial calculation which showed that the cost of not addressing this threat would dwarf the cost of investing now in preventing catastrophic climate change. But, as some argue, the choice before us is not economic, but rather moral: "We must make that decision on the grounds of how much we value people and places as people and places, rather than as figures in a ledger."[121]

CONCLUSION

Is the globalization project over? Not yet. But it appears to be in transition to another project of ordering the world: the sustainability project. The series of crises outlined here are not uniformly coordinated so much as expressing the uneven and combined development of global political-economy. The political distance between the Latin rebellions (over economic sovereignty) and the Arab uprising (over popular sovereignty) is as striking as is their combined revolt against neoliberalism's impact (however distinctive to their region). While some crises are specific to the globalization project (the financial crisis, political rebellions, and institutional paralysis), other crises are long-term structural crises, such as the food crisis and of course the climate crisis—registering an era of fossil fuel dependence.

In the meantime, the general crisis is exposing a tectonic shift underway as the West loses ground to non-Western forces. While this shift is decades in the making, it is already perceptible. In *Losing Control: The Emerging Threats to Western Prosperity*, Stephen King, chief economist at HSBC, argues that Western policy makers suffer from the illusion that they are in control of events. For him, the BRICS challenge the monopolies of the West. This challenge is enabled by the rise of "state capitalism," where non-Western governments manage their own capital outflows as well as bilateral investment and trade deals—effectively eroding the authority and efficacy of the WTO as an instrument of Western superiority.[122] It is worth noting here the extraordinary fact that China holds most of the U.S. national debt, and that non-Western sovereign wealth funds propped up Western banks during the financial crisis. Ibrahim Warde noted, "In the age of globalization, just as the triumph of markets was being widely celebrated, governmental funds—almost always from so-called emerging countries—undertook to rescue the West's largest financial institutions."[123]

FURTHER READING

Arrighi, Giovanni. *Adam Smith in Beijing. Lineages of the Twenty-First Century.* London: Verso, 2007.

Bello, Walden. *The Food Wars.* London: Verso, 2009.

Calhoun, Craig and Georgi Derluguian, eds., *Aftermath: A New Global Economic Order?* New York: NYU Press, 2011.

Jha, Prem Shankar. *Crouching Dragon, Hidden Tiger: Can China and India Dominate the West?* New York: Soft Skull Press, 2010.

King, Stephen. *Losing Control: The Emerging Threats to Western Prosperity.* New Haven and London: Yale University Press, 2010.

Roberts, Timmons, and Bradley Parks. *A Climate of Injustice: Global Inequality, North-South Politics, and Climate Policy.* Cambridge, MA: MIT Press, 2007.

Roy, Ananya. *Poverty Capital:. Microfinance and the Making of Development.* New York and London: Routledge, 2010.

Shiva, Vandana. *Soil Not Oil.* Cambridge, MA: South End Press, 2008.

9

The Sustainability Project

The world faces a series of development challenges in an age of rising inequalities, diminishing industrial resources, and significantly compromised environments. The United Nations Human Development Report of 2011, *Sustainability and Equity: A Better Future for All,* centers on the so-called "**environmentalist's paradox**," declaring,

> Past Reports have shown that living standards in most countries have been rising—and converging—for several decades now. Yet the 2011 Report projects a disturbing reversal of those trends if environmental deterioration and social inequalities continue to intensify, with the least developed countries diverging downwards from global patterns of progress by 2050.[1]

Under these conditions, development possibilities unfold in various ways, depending on the social interests at stake. These scenarios group by three criteria: (1) attempts to consolidate material gains of the globalization project, in the name of sustainability; (2) attempts to recapture the social contract associated with Keynesian political-economy and reinvigorate public initiative with a democratic, green agenda; and (3) attempts to build social and ecological resilience within and across locales. Such criteria are not independent of one another, and many new initiatives today combine one or more of these strands. Even so, each strand represents the three development paradigms that have ordered social change since the mid-twentieth century—the social contract as the foundation of the development project, followed by the globalization project, and now an emergent sustainability project. How the latter will unfold is unclear, but it is no less governed by ideological and material tensions than the former two.

The ecological threshold we face today is a stark challenge to development thinking and its promise of expanding prosperity from an unbridled world market. More than ever before, the world's survival depends on developing a different set of international protocols, ones driven by principles of sufficiency rather than accelerating development along the path of insatiable consumption of dwindling resources. Rostow's *terminal* stage of "high mass consumption" is now perhaps a double *entendre*. This is the development challenge faced by the global community, and at base it means giving greater priority—and value—to resources that do not need to be priced—such as biodiversity, habitat, and the global commons (air, water, forests, wetlands, local knowledges, etc.). A reason for not subordinating the value of ecosystems to market values (prices) is that their processes and elements are not independent units. Their value instead lies in their interdependent complexity. James Lovelock describes this as the **Gaia hypothesis,** whereby the Earth is a "physiological system" that "behaves as if it were alive," maintaining the surface temperature of the planet and recycling nutrients (in soil, water, and forests) with the "unconscious goal of regulating the climate and the chemistry at a comfortable state for life."[2] Disrupting natural cycles and reducing them to market metrics discounts nature's enduring value, enabling risky substitutions (e.g., eucalyptus monocultures for biodiverse forests).

Nevertheless, continuing market conventions encourage "pricing of environmental services"—the latest being the United Nations Framework Convention on Climate Change's (UNFCCC) emergent protocol, Reducing Emissions from Deforestation and Forest Degradation (REDD) by paying farmers and forest-dwellers, as well as governments to protect forest capacity. The development paradigm has privileged monetary relations and measures often at the cost of nonmonetary resources. Thus we have seen the conversion of resources like water (in bottles), air (tradable pollution permits), survival networks of the poor (microcredit), and even maternal love (the global care industry) into commodities.[3] However, nature is now reminding us that to survive we need to revalue what we share as humans, rather than what we consume. Across the world there are a multitude of social experiments in reducing the human impact on the environment, involving re-embedding markets in more secure/durable cultural values and advocating for the so-called life economy at various scales of social and political organization.[4] At the same time the "development infrastructure" continues, but is forced to incorporate "sustainability" into its institutions and practices. This chapter looks at the variety of formal and informal responses to the ecological crisis.

The Problem of Climate Change

Undoubtedly climate change has the potential to swamp all other development challenges in the coming decades. Since "development" has always taken the climate (and environment) for granted, adverse climatic impacts are forcing us all (citizens, development agencies, firms, states) to recognize that the game is changing. The Stratigraphy Commission of the Geological Society of London, the world's oldest association of earth scientists, warned in 2008,

> The combination of extinctions, global species migrations and the widespread replacement of natural vegetation with agricultural monocultures is producing a distinctive contemporary biostratigraphic signal. These effects are permanent, as future evolution will take place from surviving (and frequently anthropogenically relocated) stocks.[5]

Bill McKibben, U.S. environmentalist, author of *Eaarth* (2010) and creator of 350.org, echoes, "Global warming is no longer a philosophical threat, no longer a future threat, *no longer a threat at all*. It's our reality. We've changed the planet, changed it in large and fundamental ways."[6] This is a thread spun by Barbara Ward, who wrote in *Only One Earth* (1972), "The relentless pursuit of separate national interests by rich and poor alike can, in a totally interdependent biosphere, produce global disasters of irreversible damage."[7]

The Pentagon

Even if development has assumed a global dimension, policies and responsibilities regarding climate change still devolve to individual states. Key responses reveal a reflexive nationalism born of *security* concerns. The U.S. Pentagon, for instance, produced a chilling report in 2004, considering the possibility of mega-droughts and mass starvation by 2020, as well as nuclear war resulting from conflict between China, India, and Pakistan over access to water and food. Further, it suggested a tipping point could be reached, where abrupt change in a span of five years or less could result in another ice age, freezing northern Europe, converting the American Midwest to a dustbowl, and undermining California's water supply.[8] Five years later the Pentagon and intelligence agencies were conducting exercises and war games in the event that vulnerable regions such as Sub-Saharan Africa, the Middle East, and South and Southeast Asia "face the prospect of food shortages, water crises, and catastrophic flooding driven by climate change that could demand an American humanitarian relief or military response."National defense and intelligence agencies are already creating strategic plans for likely outcomes such as hundreds of thousands of refugees, religious conflict, the spread of contagious diseases, and vast infrastructure damage.[9] Climate change security concerns by individual states will not only form the basis of geopolitical power relations, but will be woven into development policy.

The United Nations Framework Convention on Climate Change (UNFCCC)

While states gear up for dealing with political destabilization (already resulting in the division of the Sudan, following the Darfur conflict that has been linked to drought and climate change), the development industry is attempting to recalibrate its *modus operandi*. The first step is acknowledging the problem, as in the 2007/2008 UN *Human Development Report* declaration: "Climate change is the defining human development issue of our generation." At the Eighth Conference of Parties (COP8) of the UNFCCC in New Delhi (2002), a threshold report on *Poverty and Climate Change* declared, "climate change is a serious risk to poverty reduction and threatens to undo decades of development efforts."[10] Within the development policy and practitioner community the response is to incorporate "**climate proofing**" into development programs, as key to adaptation measures.

The COP7, which met in 2001, established adaptation as a development stabilizer. This action set the goal for Less Developed Countries to prepare priority adaptation measures, the **National Adaptation Programme of Action (NAPA)**, guided by a set of locally driven criteria, including degree of climate change impact, poverty reduction to enhance adaptive capacity, synergy with other multilateral environmental agreements, and cost-effectiveness. Adaptation measures focus on human and environmental concerns, such as health, food security, water availability and accessibility, biological diversity, land-use, and coastal zones.[11]

At the same meeting, northern states agreed to establish the **Clean Development Mechanism (CDM)**, which allows "countries who cannot meet their promised carbon emissions reductions under Kyoto [1997] to buy carbon from developing countries by paying for projects like reforestation, power plant energy efficiency, and capturing methane from landfills."[12] In 2007, the COP in Bali established an adaptation fund to be financed (among other sources) through taxing CDM transactions. By 2008, the World Bank was partnering with the COP, via a Less Developed Countries Fund (LDCF), for adaptation administered through its Global Environmental Facility (GEF).

The Commission on Climate Change and Development notes that the adaptation fund is "the first example of the use of market-based options to generate substantial financial resources to address climate change. The carbon market . . . has the potential to move huge financial flows to developing countries for mitigation and adaptation."[13] Unsurprisingly, "initial flows suggest that the money is narrowly targeting emission reductions in big countries like China and Brazil, . . . where there is a strong enabling environment for private sector investment."[14] Even so, a Stanford University study found that the UN's offset fund has been "routinely abused by chemical, wind, gas and hydro companies who are claiming emission reduction credits for [clean energy] projects that should not qualify," because they were scheduled for construction anyway, resulting in no change in emissions.[15]

UN-HABITAT: CITIES AND CLIMATE CHANGE

Following its alarming report of 2003, *The Challenge of Slums* that predicted that 2 billion would be slumdwellers by 2030 in the absence of concrete action (2003:xxv), UN-HABITAT released a new report in 2011, titled *Cities and Climate Change*, warning that cities were the "real battle-ground in the fight against climate change." The Executive Director of UN-HABITAT, Joan Clos, remarked, "Cities are responsible for the majority of our harmful greenhouse gases. But they are also places where the greatest efficiencies can be made." The UN-HABITAT assessment is that the world's cities occupy just 2 percent of the planet's land cover, but are responsible for about 70 percent of emissions. The report notes that some urban areas will have difficulty providing basic services—aside from the physical risks of climate change, such as droughts, landslides, cyclones, and flooding: "These changes will affect water supply, physical infrastructure, transport, ecosystem goods and services, energy provision, and industrial production. Local economies will be disrupted and populations will be stripped of their assets and livelihoods."

Cities at risk are in Sub-Saharan Africa, South and Southeast Asia, southern Europe, the east coast of South America and the west coast of the United States. The report advocates revisioning of urban development by local planners, combining adaptation (e.g., improving flood defenses) with mitigation measures (reducing energy demand and emissions), and including local community input (from residents and businesses) in addition to national and international policies to support urban areas and reduce emissions.

Sources: UN-HABITAT (2003); Kinver (2011).

The Stern Review and Grassroots Initiatives

The U.K.'s 2006 *Stern Review* stated that "adaptation is so broad and cross-cutting—affecting economic, social and environmental conditions, and vice versa—that it is difficult to attribute costs clearly." Oxfam estimates the cost of adaption in the global South at $50–80 billion a year.[16] Camilla Toulmin (of IIED) observes "investment in disaster preparedness produces high returns, with US$1 in costs invested in preparation yielding $7 in reduced damage," thereby underlining the importance of taking action now, including establishing early warning systems to reduce vulnerability—as Mozambique did, reducing casualties from massive floods in 2007.[17] The dilemma for the development community (and its subjects) is that adaptation measures via funding packages may repeat the large-scale approach of World Bank–financed projects, focusing on maximum yield rather than resilience, a key to managing a climate-challenged future.

While multilateral-driven climate proofing is important to address vulnerabilities (water access, disease patterns, natural disasters) it runs the risk of overriding local knowledge and solutions. To this end, the NGO ActionAid has produced reports advocating measures used by farmers adapting to climate change—documenting the wealth of grassroots experience of adaptation via resilience. In a report titled *We Know What We Need: South Asian Women Speak Out on Climate Change Adaption*, ActionAid and the Institute for Development Studies (IDS) situate adaptation in the more encompassing framework of grounded democratic development practices: "Adaptation funding alone will not be able to reduce the vulnerability of poor women to climate change. A broader enabling environment must exist that enables women equal access to decision making, rights, resources and services."[18] A second report, titled *The Time is NOW: Lessons from Farmers Adapting to Climate Change*, concludes,

> Many poor communities have been adapting to climate change for decades now, and already have ideas for adaptation strategies appropriate to their specific context . . . representatives of affected communities must be meaningfully involved in the governance of multilateral adaptation funds to enhance their effectiveness through transparency, accountability and stakeholder participation.[19]

Implicit in the details of how people on the front line of climate change are managing is the recognition that low-carbon lifestyles, appropriately valued, represent alternatives to the dominant paradigm. Nevertheless, the policy community has an inertial bias for recycling conventional wisdom, in which the poor, rather than the rich, remain the objects of development initiatives. Thus, a recent policy brief for the International Commission on

Climate Change and Development notes that supporting adaptation, deemed a necessary and "moral responsibility" by the North toward the South, is "often similar to, and sometimes indistinguishable from, development." Accordingly, "development agencies and NGOs can use their decades of experience in poverty alleviation and sustainable development to assist the poorest countries to meet the adaptation challenge."[20]

The emphasis is on adapting adaptation to development conventions rather than reconfiguring development itself. Thus mainstreaming adaptation "includes 'climate proofing,' i.e., the protection of existing ODA [Overseas Development Assistance] projects and programs" and ensuring "that future development plans and programs are actively designed to reduce the vulnerability to climate change."[21] Here "climate proofing" is understood as less about making communities resilient, and more about preserving infrastructures of "assistance."

Thus climate proofing has become a new profit frontier. Agrochemical and biotechnology firms like BASF, Monsanto, Bayer, Syngenta, and Dupont have filed over 500 patent documents on so-called climate ready genes. At a time when flexible seed selection by West African farming women, for example, has managed recurring drought, at least 55 gene patents threaten to shift resources away from farmer-based strategies for climate change survival and adaptation. In a reference to states' likely premium on *security*, the ETC Group notes that "[a]fter decades of seed industry mergers and acquisitions, accompanied by a steady decline in public sector plant breeding, the top 10 seed companies control 57% of the global seed market. As climate crisis deepens, there is a danger that governments will require farmers to adopt prescribed biotech traits that are deemed essential adaptation measures,"[22] rather than support documented local initiatives based on adaptive practices, largely by women. These practices are discounted by development corporations. Thus a spokesperson for Monsanto dismissed peasant knowledge as nonadaptive: "I think everyone recognizes that the old traditional ways just aren't able to address these new challenges. The problems in Africa are pretty severe."[23]

The problems in Africa are quite complex, starting with land access for small farmers. With more land converted to high-value export crops, less is available to accommodate rising farming populations. The International Centre for Soil Fertility and Agricultural Development reports land is overworked as small farmers reduce crop rotation and fallow methods to reproduce crops on the same land—a practice that depletes soil fertility—or encroach on fragile ecosystems, a common, global pattern.[24] Nevertheless, recent research questions the assumptions that desertification and land degradation necessarily results from local mismanagement and misuse of land.

Nature is always in flux, due to both climatic variation and human impact. And farmers not only have reversed desertification in southern Niger and Kenya; but also, along the edge of the Sahara, in Nigeria, Niger, Senegal, Burkina Faso, and Kenya, they have employed integrated farming, mixed cropping, and traditional soil and water conservation methods that have increased food production substantially ahead of population growth. Population density has proved essential for farming labor needs, especially with cooperative farming practices and developing sustaining social networks to exchange labor, seed, cattle, technology, and cash.[25]

Niger features a success story in the Tahoua region, which has "reclaimed hundreds of hectares of degraded land" and where the president of a women's group remarked on hearing reports claiming degradation of the Sahel, "these experts have never visited us." Following environmental and political crises in the 1980s and 1990s respectively, 250,000 hectares of strongly degraded land have been rehabilitated since the mid-1980s: "Dry season cultivation has been expanded considerably and according to FAO statistics Niger produced in 1980 100,000 tons of dry onions, but 270,000 tons in 2004, which was a drought year."[26] Further, in those areas where farmers have rehabilitated degraded land, household food security has improved. Overall, farmers in high population parts of Niger have succeeded on at least 3 million hectares in managing natural regeneration, which is unique for the Sahel.

Such resilient practices are discounted by labeling small farmers as "traditional," thereby denying their adaptive skills. Conventional development wisdom has focused on plant yields at the expense of recognizing the multifunctional role of biodiversity. In the drylands of India's Deccan Plateau—where there grows a variety of rainfed crops such as sorghum, millets, pulses, and oilseeds—the "symbiotic relationship between these crops provides solutions to a wide range of problems faced in today's Indian agriculture such as management of soils and their fertility, pest control as well as minimizing risk and uncertainty." While biodiversity may allow communities to manage climatic conditions in tenuous environments:

> The many values of uncultivated biodiversity used by people for food, fodder and medicine have generally been unseen and neglected by the official discourse. . . .
>
> The number of uncultivated foods that are harvested in Medak district (Andhra Pradesh) greatly exceeds the number of cultivated species. Some 80 species of uncultivated leafy greens are locally used as foods and many dozens more species of uncultivated plants including roots, tubers and fruits. This vast array of "wild" leafy greens, berries and fruits are sources of many nutrients. . . . Most of

them are rich sources of calcium, iron, carotene, vitamin C, riboflavin, and folic acid. Therefore they are a boon to pregnant and nursing women as well as to young children. Since they come at no monetary cost at all, they are a blessing for the poor. Dalits know it and have woven these uncultivated foods into their food system.[27]

Stabilizing Ecosystems

The Millennium Ecosystem Assessment (MA)

Nonmonetized resources such as wild plants and exchange networks do not appear through a conventional development lens, and are thereby easily marginalized. And yet these environmental and social resources are central to human resilience. The landmark 2005 UN **Millennium Ecosystem Assessment (MA)**, which addresses threats to the Millennium Development Goals by environmental degradation, states that "existing national and global institutions are not well designed to deal with the management of common pool resources, a characteristic of many ecosystem services." More than a thousand biological scientists proposed the integration of ecosystem management goals within development planning frameworks at large, noting that "the most important public policy decisions affecting ecosystems are often made by agencies and in policy arenas other than those charged with protecting ecosystems." The MA points to instances of Poverty Reduction Strategies that shape development priorities, noting that "in general these have not taken into account the importance of ecosystems to improving the basic human capabilities of the poorest."[28] Two important lessons of this report were that development has not understood the social and environmental significance of its ecological base (sources and sinks); and the interdependence of common pool resources (ecosystems) are understood and managed by precisely those populations often deemed "poor" by development agencies, that then discount these forms of local resilience.

The central paradox identified by the MA is the "environmentalist's paradox":

> Over the past 50 years, humans have changed ecosystems more rapidly and extensively than in any comparable period of time in human history, largely to meet rapidly growing demands for food, fresh water, timber, fiber, and fuel. This has resulted in a substantial and largely irreversible loss in the diversity of life on Earth. . . . . These problems, unless addressed, will substantially diminish the benefits that future generations obtain from ecosystems.[29]

This paradox has not gone unnoticed in the business community, which is sensitive to future profits if not to the environment as such. In 2010, the World Economic Forum (WEF) published a report on *Biodiversity and Business Risk*, with the following leading quotation from the World Resources Institute: "Global warming may dominate headlines today. Ecosystem degradation will do so tomorrow." The coincidence is telling, as in the same year, a UN report anticipated (and warned of) rising pressure on firms' profit margins should policy makers adopt the "polluter pays" principle. The report found that the estimated combined damage to the natural environment was in the order of $2.2 trillion in 2008, equating to an average of one-third of the profits of the 3,000 largest public companies in the world; the team leader reported, "What we're talking about is a completely new paradigm. Externalities of this scale and nature pose a major risk to the global economy and markets are not fully aware of these risks, nor do they know how to deal with them."[30]

Given their focus on the "bottom line," and their primary loyalty to the shareholder, corporations are not organized to synchronize business with environment cycles. While bio- and geochemical time follows natural rhythms, business is concerned with short-term horizons governed by the velocity of product circulation.[31] It is not in a position to manage ecological crisis adequately. Accordingly, the MA's goal is to orchestrate multilateral environmental agreements, and coordination between environmental agreements and other international social and economic institutions:

> International agreements are indispensable for addressing ecosystem-related concerns that span national boundaries, but numerous obstacles weaken their current effectiveness. Steps are now being taken to increase the coordination among these mechanisms, and this could help to broaden the focus of the array of instruments. However, coordination is also needed between the multilateral environmental agreements and more politically powerful international institutions, such as economic and trade agreements, to ensure that they are not acting at cross-purposes.[32]

Again, the intent is clear: to champion new development policy frameworks geared to acknowledging and reintegrating human activity with its ecological foundations. Ecological accounting by economists is one thing, but the broader goal is to build environmental impact assessment and restoration into economic activity. The key obstacle for a (minority) world addicted to economic growth is incorporating values other than price into the development equation. Price is convenient in standardizing what is measured and valued as economic activity. But the majority of human activity is local, nonmonetized, and diverse, despite the reach of the universalizing market. Hence the sensibility expressed in the MA, in advocating "use of all relevant forms of knowledge and information in assessments and decision-making," women's included. The report suggests that effective ecosystem management requires "place-based" knowledge about the specific dynamics of an ecosystem: "Traditional knowledge or practitioners' knowledge held by local resource managers can often be of considerable value in resource management, but it is too rarely incorporated into decision-making processes and indeed is often inappropriately dismissed."[33]

The Centrality of Agriculture

Ultimately, the Millennium Ecosystem Assessment underlines the centrality of agriculture to ecosystem management:

> Agricultural expansion will continue to be one of the major drivers of biodiversity loss well into the twenty-first century. Development, assessment, and diffusion of technologies that could increase the production of food per unit area sustainably without harmful trade-offs related to excessive consumption of water or use of nutrients or pesticides would significantly lessen pressure on other ecosystem services.[34]

And, given that healthy ecosystems are essential to human life it is clear that agriculture itself is the foundation of civilization—in both senses of the term. Unfortunately we have forgotten both senses, as evident in social theory and particularly development theory, which views agriculture as a method and source of resource extraction to power urban-industrial complexes.

Not only does the modernity narrative view farm labor, along with its ecological knowledge, as replaceable, but also agriculture, once an energy converter/provider, is now a heavy energy consumer—the industrial food system expends ten or more energy calories to produce one calorie of food. Instead of embracing live/biotic carbon, it burns dead carbon.[35] The reality is, that to preserve human civilization and its ecological base, farming the land sustainably means expanding carbon sinks via agro-forestry, based on the biodiversity principle, or agro-ecology, as a method of rebuilding soil carbon; both methods reduce carbon in the atmosphere and regenerate nature in the process.

International Assessment of Agricultural Science and Technology for Development (IAASTD)

Sustainable farming is the approach recommended in the 2008 UN and World Bank–sponsored **International Assessment of Agricultural Science**

and Technology for Development (IAASTD). This report, prepared by over 400 social and natural scientists and development practitioners, advocates a *multifunctional* role for agriculture in reducing poverty and social/gender inequality, stabilizing rural cultures, reversing environmental degradation, and global warming. Stating that "business as usual is not an option," in the face of multiple crises, the IAASTD questions industrial agriculture and transgenic food as solutions since markets fail to adequately value environmental and social harm.[36] With respect to the current food regime, the IAASTD documents its unfavorable impacts on small farmers, recommends ending subsidies for Northern surpluses and developing subsidies for environmental stewardship, and national policy flexibility to balance the needs of poor consumers and small farmers (vs. WTO liberalization).[37] Echoing the MA, the report recommends an integrative view of food, resource, and nutritional security, emphasizing that reinventing agriculture as farming requires scientists (natural, social, and health) to work with local farmers, governments, and civil society organizations.[38]

Complementing the substantial literature now on the greater overall productivity—and sustainability—of small-scale farming, an IAASTD contributor noted that a "half-hectare plot in Thailand can grow 70 species of vegetables, fruits, and herbs, providing far better nutrition and feeding more people than a half-hectare plot of high-yielding rice."[39] Similarly, studies in Mexico found that "a 1.73 [hectare] plot of land has to be planted with maize monoculture to produce as much food as one hectare planted with a mixture of maize, squash and beans. In addition, the maize-squash-bean polyculture produces up to 4 t per ha of dry matter for plowing into the soil, compared with 2 t in a maize monoculture."[40]

To strengthen and secure small farming, IAASTD recommends altering institutional arrangements to ensure **agricultural multifunctionality**, suggesting that the "shift to nonhierarchical development models," must be accompanied by building trust and valuing farmer knowledge and natural and agricultural biodiversity, as well as seed exchange and common resource management systems.[41] IAASTD maps out a general strategy to strengthen food system *resilience* in the face of environmental crises—including promoting agro-ecological practices with "triple-bottom-line" goals, such as full-cost accounting to incorporate energy, health, and environmental costs, and, as important, a rights-based framework rather than a market-centric organization of the agricultural and food production and delivery system. This approach was advocated by Olivier de Schutter, the UN special rapporteur on the Right to Food, addressing the UN Commission on Human Rights in March, 2011: "Agriculture should be fundamentally redirected toward modes of production that are more environmentally sustainable and socially just. . . . [agro-ecology] helps "small farmers who must be able to farm in ways that are less expensive and more productive. But it benefits all of us, because it decelerates global warming and ecological destruction."[42]

The IAASTD report has been largely ignored by the development establishment (likely due to opposition from those who advocate "business as usual," including relying on biotechnology), but its prescriptions are nevertheless practiced across the world. This disconnect is reflected in the controversy over whether organic/agro-ecological farming can feed the world.

Feeding the World

Several recent studies have concluded that the relative yields of organic/agro-ecological versus nonorganic farming are sufficient to provision the current daily average consumption of calories across the world.[43] Most notably, Catherine Badgley and colleagues examined 293 cases in a global dataset, finding that on average, organic farming in the global North produces 92 percent of conventional agricultural yields, but in the global South organic farming produces 80 percent *more* than conventional agriculture.[44] Further, the researchers found that sufficient food could be produced organically to feed the world, even without expanding farmland, and that leguminous cover crops could provide sufficient nitrogen to replace current applications of synthetic fertilizers (which, with overuse, undermine soil health). Organic fertilizer is cheap as it is produced on farm (as compared to chemical fertilizer, which has risen in cost by 300 percent over the last few years). And, since most inputs take place directly on farm and replenish soil and watersheds, organic/agro-ecological farming uses much less energy than industrial agriculture.

CASE STUDY **The Real Cuban Revolution in a Peak-Oil Age**

As a consequence of the collapse of the Soviet Union in 1990, and the end of imports of oil, agrochemicals, and farm machinery from the Soviet bloc, Cuba was forced by a U.S. trade embargo to transform its energy and food system. Cuban agriculture developed around organic farming, urban gardens, animal traction, and biological pest control. This was the "Special Period" when Cuba

(Continued)

survived a substantial crisis in a hostile international environment, managing to convert its industrial and agricultural economy to increasingly sustainable practices.

A recent study revealed that in less than a decade, depending on the region, 46–72 percent of peasant farms use agro-ecological practices, producing about 60 percent of the vegetables, maize, beans, fruits, and pork meat consumed on the island. Following Hurricane Ike in 2008 it was found that agro-ecological farms suffered a damage level of 50 percent compared to that of monocultures with levels of 90–100 percent. Agro-ecological farms recovered faster and about 80 percent of the farms were producing 40 days after the hurricane. Agro-ecology has proven to be the most efficient, inexpensive, and stable form of food production per unit of land, input, and labor, attracting more small farmers and government land subsidies.

Cuba's urban agricultural achievements are well known: 383,000 urban farms are producing more than 1.5 million tons of vegetables with no synthetic chemicals—enough to supply 40–60 percent or more of all the fresh vegetables in Havana, Villa Clara, and other cities. No other country in the world has achieved such success with a form of agriculture that reduces food miles, energy and input use, and integrates production and consumption cycles so effectively.

Given the extraordinary conditions driving this agro-ecological revolution, is it possible to imagine a similar conversion in other countries under future (possibly catastrophic) pressure of climate, food, and energy crises?

Source: Altieri and Toledo (2011).

Criticism that agro-ecological organics are too expensive compared with conventional farming forgets the huge—energy as well as farming—subsidies to industrial agriculture. Ecologist Ivette Perfecto contests the idea that conventional agriculture is cheap, pointing out that its real costs include the substantial health and environmental costs borne by consumers and further public subsidies.[45] Badgley and Perfecto recognize their research is controversial, but they stress that their study is a claim of sufficiency, and that the actuality of a global organic food secure system "depends on policies and prices as much as on yields." Further, "achievements would multiply with additional research on locally suitable cropping systems, fertility methods, and pest management for different agricultural regions."[46] A standard criticism of organic agriculture is its greater labor requirement, but this stems from the modernist assumption that farm work is inferior to other work. For example, economist Carl Pray suggests "the likelihood of all farms reverting to 'small farmerdom' is a big question in an age in which labor is becoming more and more expensive. Take China and India, for instance: the demand for labor is such that people are continually being pulled out of the countryside."[47]

The disconnect is the assumption that the rural exodus is an inevitable and sustainable process at a time when a different paradigm for human and environmental sustainability is emerging, one that revalues farming and farm labor. The depopulation of the countryside is as much push as pull within a global system of urban bias/predation, but even more problematic is the attempt to sustain the world with high-input agriculture. High inputs not only displace farm labor and vital knowledge of local ecosystems, they also have high economic and environmental costs.

The Agro-Ecology Project

As suggested above, agro-ecological methods (including permaculture) are proliferating, under the radar, as they do not represent the conventional—and increasingly unrealistic—understandings of modernity. Ecologist Miguel Altieri defines **agro-ecology** as a science and a set of place-specific practices. As science, it consists of the "application of ecological science to the study, design, and management of sustainable agro-ecosystems," requiring diversification of farms to promote biological interactions to regenerate soil fertility, maintain productivity, and protect crops.[48] Altieri and Toledo summarize:

> The core principles of agro-ecology include recycling nutrients and energy on the farm, rather than introducing external inputs; enhancing soil organic matter and soil biological activity; diversifying plant species and genetic resources in agro-ecosystems over time and space; integrating crops and livestock, and optimizing interactions and productivity of the total farming system, rather than the yields of individual species.[49]

Further, despite the convention of theorizing the disappearance of the peasantry, Latin American peasants have increased their regional presence. Peasants currently account for two-thirds of the world's food producers, and the majority of staple crops.[50] "**Re-peasantization**" has occurred over the last quarter century in Latin America (involving 220 million people in the 1990s) and Europe, where farmers are regrouping under neoliberal pressures of rising input costs, and delinking from input suppliers to refocus on building "ecological capital" for their farms."[51] *State of the World 2011* reports that agro-ecological methods are

> especially important in regions facing high food insecurity and high pressure for agricultural intensification. These methods can not only help farmers in areas with soil degradation and poor water quality, but also provide a sustainable alternative when industrial inputs are unaffordable, unavailable, or economically risky. Slowly but surely, commercial demand is creating attractive market opportunities for eco-certified cropping systems.[52]

The World Bank World Development Report (2008)

High food insecurity became abundantly obvious during the first phase of the food crisis, beginning in 2007. Much of the official discourse viewed the crisis as an opportunity to reverse a long period of declining investment in agriculture and to secure world food supplies,[53] and for smallholders to take advantage of high food prices by bringing them into, or deepening their connection to, national and global markets. The World Bank's *World Development Report*, 2008, the theme of which was "Agriculture for Development," declared, "It is time to place agriculture afresh at the center of the development agenda."[54] After ignoring agriculture for a quarter of a century, the World Bank, among many others, was recognizing its centrality, as food prices, according to *The Economist,* hit their highest level since 1845.[55]

At the time of the Rome Food Summit of 2008, FAO Secretary General Jacques Diouf stated, "World leaders looking for ways to save the global economy from disaster and to create jobs and income for millions of people in rural areas would be well advised to invest heavily in agriculture."[56] The goal of "saving the global economy" was thus linked to a call for rural development associated with new export agriculture initiatives. This goal raises two related issues: (1) whether "feeding the world" (that is, saving the global economy) can be accomplished via agro-exporting, and (2) how to develop export agriculture. The dilemma is, as the above quotes suggest, the improvement of African farming, and its links to urban areas and local markets (a clear need), is only attractive to foreign investors if there is a *quid pro quo*, namely, new markets for inputs (seed, fertilizer, pesticides) and/or new opportunities for transnational **value-chain agriculture**.

For the World Bank, having acknowledged that its structural adjustment policies of the 1980s "dismantled the elaborate system of public agencies that provided farmers with access to land, credit, insurance, inputs, and cooperative organization," its new approach is now governed by market intensification via agribusiness in partnership with the state: "The private sector drives the organization of value chains that bring the market to smallholders and commercial farms."[57]

In these plans there are distinct consequences for food, as well as development, policy. While economic theory postulates that high-value exports can finance staple food imports, the food crisis revealed the limits of this scenario, as grain-exporting nations (Kazakhstan, Indonesia, Vietnam, Egypt, China, Cambodia, and India) halted exports. High-value (not grain) export agriculture may increase rural income, but it also may reduce the availability of local food for local markets or even self-consumption—one of the key determinants of hunger in the food crisis. Thus, actually "feeding the world" may not be synonymous with intensifying export agriculture.

CASE STUDY   The "Meatification" Controversy

The World Bank modeling for "feeding the world" extrapolates present trends, which include unsustainable and inequitable impacts of dietary "meatification." The *World Development Report* observes, "To meet projected demand, cereal production will have to increase by nearly 50 percent and meat production 85 percent from 2000 to 2030." Geographer Tony Weis claims "meatification" is "normalized in taking the current demand for food as the basis for assessing the overall land-space needed for agriculture, when the current demand for food is not an immutable function of humanity's dietary needs."

For Weis, meat production creates a substantial "ecological hoofprint"—agriculture produces 22–30 percent of global greenhouse gas emissions (GHG), of which livestock (including its feed and transport) accounts for nearly 80 percent. The intensive-livestock complex links specialized feed crop regions with proliferating factory farms, with feed crops using 70 percent of agricultural land.

Per capita demand for beef, poultry, and pigmeat in China will double by 2020. Since Chinese intensive meat production is sourced by Brazilian soybeans, and U.S. corn in particular, this single complex produces GHG emissions in multiple ways, from deforestation of the Amazon, fossil fuel-based transport, fertilizer use on intensive grain production, and animal methane.

Meanwhile, climate scientists urge a reversal of livestock production to reduce GHGs, as methane and N2O contribute more than CO^2 to agriculture's warming effect. Contrarily, conservation scientist Tim Flannery argues for a "sustainabilitarian diet"—cautioning that meat can be produced more sustainably (but not feedlots). His point is this: "plant-animal interactions are at the heart of Gaia's self-regulation. Plants capture the sun's energy, and animals, by feeding upon plants, create and swiftly recycle nutrients that plants need in order to grow."

What is it about meat that represents modernity? And why does modernity eschew mixed farming?

Sources: World Bank (2007: 8, 17); Weis (2007: 17, 20, 168, 171); McMichael, et al. (2007); Kumar (2011); Flannery (2009: 86–7, 90, 93).

A key technology proposed for "feeding the world" is genetically modified organisms (GMOs). In 2008, at the FAO World Food Security summit in Rome, the FAO, the International Fund for Agricultural Development (IFAD), and the World Food Programme (WFP) signed a Memorandum of Understanding with the Rockefeller/Gates Foundation jointly funded **Alliance for a Green Revolution in Africa (AGRA)** to convert Africa's breadbasket regions into a source of emergency food aid for the continent. While the Rockefeller Foundation sponsored the earlier Green Revolution, using hybrid seeds, the difference here is that the Gates Foundation is allied with Monsanto, a global biotech corporation, and AGRA is committed to introducing imported fertilizers and purchased (some fortified through biotech initiatives) seeds.[58]

Analogous to the controversy over Vitamin A rice, designed to supplement Asian diets to prevent blindness, the growing interest of the biotech industry in the fortification of food represents a profitable ("nutritionalization") fix to the problem created by the elimination of dietary diversity (e.g., green leafy vegetables) by green revolution monocultures.[59] Micronutrient deficiency affects about 1 billion people worldwide, but is being addressed ecologically via the smaller-scale "revolution of greens" underway in Africa, whereby farmers are rediscovering traditional diets through improving indigenous vegetables. Native vegetables have greater tolerance to drought and resistance to pests, have shorter growing cycles than cereal crops, and use less space. They also strengthen resilience to price shocks and enable farmers to protect biodiversity and mitigate climate change impacts. Accordingly, researchers with AVRDC/The World Vegetable Center have developed improved varieties of African eggplant, amaranth, African nightshade, and cowpea. Project DISC (Developing Innovations in School Cultivation) in Uganda partners with Slow Food International to teach students how to grow and cook indigenous vegetables.[60]

The difference between these approaches exemplifies the distinct interests and outcomes of a grass-roots strategy to empower farming communities and boost their ecological resilience versus a top-down market-driven strategy organized by global interests associated with dependency and displacement of African farmers (incorporated into the debt relations of input-driven commercial agriculture). This is exemplified in a confidential Agricultural Development Strategy of the Gates Foundation:

> Smallholders with the potential to produce a surplus can create a market-oriented agricultural system serving the health and welfare needs of rural populations to exit poverty. . . . The vision of success involves market-oriented farmers operating profitable farms that generate enough income to sustain their rise out of poverty. Over time, this *will require some degree of land mobility and a lower percentage of total employment involved in direct agricultural production.*[61]

While the conventional development model presumes the expulsion of (some) small farmers in the name of productivity, there is no accounting here for where the displaced would go, particularly in an era of jobless growth. In consequence, there are rising claims for a rethinking of the current development paradigm—particularly given the evidence regarding organic/agro-ecological farming. Nobel laureate Wangari Maathai of Kenya's Green Belt Movement writes, "Africa needn't intensify its farming sector so that it takes on the character of the industrial-style agriculture that dominates the West. . . . As we are learning, industrial farming may be efficient, but it has enormous downsides for the environment."[62]

A 2008 study by the UN Conference on Trade and Development (UNCTAD) and the UN Environment Program (UNEP), *Organic Agriculture and Food Security in Africa,* found that "organic agriculture outperformed conventional production systems based on chemical-intensive farming and is thus more conducive to food security in Africa."[63] Analyzing 114 projects across 24 African countries, the study showed doubling of yields where organic (or near-organic) practices were used—confirming the findings in the research of Badgley et al. cited above. The study also found "strong environmental benefits such as improved soil fertility, better retention of water, and resistance to drought in these areas."[64]

The World Bank's goal in its *World Development Report* of "capturing the benefits of GMOs for the poor" is questionable, given that transgenics have focused on feed crops and traits suited to the extension of chemical agriculture. The deepening of peasant and farmer dependency on commercial inputs is foreshadowed in the World Bank's *World Development Report,* where the World Bank advocates "'market-smart' subsidies to stimulate input markets."[65] For rain-fed areas, the World Bank proposes that one of "agriculture's major success stories in the past two decades is conservation (or zero) tillage"[66]—a less soil-disruptive technology that nevertheless delivers genetically modified seeds along with networks of fertilizer dealers, thereby deepening the control of the chemical and seed companies.

CASE STUDY   Seeding the World?

Rural communities have always saved and exchanged their seeds. In research on the dry Deccan Plateau of South India, Carine Pionetti documents the value of women's seed work in forming a "localized seed economy" through seed exchanges with ecological, economic, and socio-cultural significance. In contrast

(Continued)

(Continued)

to seed commercialization (monopolization under patents, the method favored by the development industry for feeding the world) she notes,

> The continuous exchange of seeds for local crop varieties circulates genetic resources from one field to another within a village territory and beyond. The dynamic management of genetic resources enhances the stability of traditional agrosystems, increases the adaptation potential of local crops to evolving environmental conditions and limits the risk of genetic erosion. Seed transactions also help ensure that land is not left fallow for lack of seeds, thus avoiding soil erosion and increasing the soil's organic matter content and water retention capacity.

Seed saving minimizes risk, increases crop diversity and nutrition, and provides "self-reliance and bargaining power within the household" for women. It also allows women to select seeds to meet specific individual, environmental, and climatic needs; allows planting at appropriate times, and provides assets—seeds constitute a currency, particularly among women with few resources. It constitutes the security of a "knowledge commons."

Once farmers buy or receive agro-industrial seeds, they are "locked into a production chain where the choices of inputs and the use of the harvest are predetermined by agro-chemical and food-processing firms" and depend increasingly on "a network of technical information generated by specialists (agricultural scientists, chemists, genetic engineers, nutritionists . . .)." In short, control over farming practices relocates from the farm to agribusiness complexes: Farming the landscape is converted into an economic sector (agriculture) that is disconnected from ecosystems.

Can we imagine low-input farming (ecosystem reproduction), rather than high-input agriculture (plant production), as the more *modern* way to manage our future?

Sources: Pionetti (2005: xv, 154, 166); Holt-Giménez (2006: 97).

The Global Land Grab

The so-called "**global land grab**" continues the historic process of land enclosures described by Sir Thomas More in *Utopia* (1516) as "sheep eating men," when English peasants were evicted from the commons to make way for private estates. Colonialism extended the enclosure movement as lands and habitats were commandeered for export monocultures and/or settled by colonists at the expense of indigenous peoples—a practice continued during the development project as new states sought export revenues. The globalization project intensified the process of market-driven enclosure for mineral and agro-exporting to defray debt. Now in the twenty-first century, enclosure by "land grabbing" is driven by a combination of the food/energy/climate crisis and the financial crisis. With rising energy and food prices, land has become the object of speculative investment and a hedge against food and fuel supply shortfalls.

In its 2009 report, *Rising Global Interest in Farmland: Can It Yield Sustainable and Equitable Benefits?* the World Bank notes that global investors acquired 111 million hectares of agricultural lands over four years, 75 percent of which were in Africa.[67] In 2011, the Bank reported a 12-fold increase in the amount of agricultural land acquired by foreign investors.[68] China and the Middle Eastern countries were the first players in the land rush. Since 2008, China, Saudi Arabia, Egypt, Bahrain, the Gulf countries, Jordan, Kuwait, Libya, Qatar, United Arab Emirates, India, Malaysia, Japan, and South Korea have been on a land rush to Africa, South and Southeast Asia, South America, and Central Asia.

Aside from these food-insecure countries, other investors include agribusiness firms, investment houses, private equity funds, and fund managers. They work either through local private partners, host governments, or through their own governments in joint ventures with target countries. The Japanese firm Mitsui, for example, purchased 100,000 hectares of land in Brazil for soybean production. Host governments, with Bank assistance, alter national laws, policies, and land owning practices to facilitate foreign acquisition for food or biofuels (sugar cane, soya, eucalyptus, oil palm, maize, wheat, and jatropha). Thus, the Sudanese government, owning most of the country's land (typical of most African states) issues leases at very low prices.[69]

By the end of the first decade of the new century, there were 389 land deals in 80 countries, where the "bulk (37%) of the so-called investment projects are meant to produce food (crops and livestock), while biofuels come in second place (35%)."[70] Not only does the crisis of the globalization project propel and justify investment in land offshore in the name of addressing food shortages and alternative energy, but also investment in agriculture offers a new profit frontier for investors at a time of jobless growth, when investors prefer speculative versus real investments. Land grabbing pushes up prices—but over time and for large investment houses, it is a relatively safe investment haven for the relatively long-term.

Susan Payne, founder and CEO of the UK firm Emergent Asset Management (EAM), raising $450–750 million for investment to consolidate and industrialize farmland in Sub-Saharan Africa for food and biofuels (jatropha), stated, "We are getting strong response from institutional investors—pensions, insurance companies, endowments, some sovereign wealth funds." EAM selected Africa because "land values are very, very inexpensive, compared to other agriculture-based economies. Its microclimates are enticing, allowing a range of different crops. There's accessible labor. And there's good logistics—wide open roads, good truck transport, sea transport."[71] She added later, "Farmland in Sub-Saharan Africa is giving 25% returns a year and new technology can treble crop yields in short time frames. . . . Agricultural development is not only sustainable, it is our future. If we do not pay great care and attention now to increase food production by over 50% before 2050, we will face serious food shortages globally."[72]

The cost of land may be low for investors, but not to the locals. And governments are typically classifying lands, whether common lands or privately used, as "idle" or "unproductive." For example, in Ethiopia, an attractive investment site for biofuels, an agriculture ministry official identified over 7 million acres of "virgin land," to be leased at an annual rate of about 50 cents per acre.[73] And the minimum wage in Ethiopia is about 8 birr (39p) a day.[74] Ethiopia's "land lease project," intended to develop large-scale commercial farming (mainly for export of food and fuel), will involve allocation of three million hectares of "idle land" by 2013 (about 20 percent of currently cultivated land). An indigenous Anuak from the fertile Gambella region of Ethiopia observed, "All the land 'round my family village of Illia has been taken over and is being cleared. People now have to work for an Indian company. Their land has been compulsorily taken and they have been given no compensation."[75]

International Land Coalition policy specialist Michael Taylor has noted, "If land in Africa hasn't been planted, it's probably for a reason. Maybe it's used to graze livestock or deliberately left fallow to prevent nutrient depletion and erosion. Anybody who has seen these areas identified as unused understands that there is no land in Ethiopia that has no owners and users."[76] The FAO has highlighted the marginalizing impact of biofuels on women in rural areas: noting that marginal lands provide important subsistence functions to rural peoples and are often farmed by women, who are denied access to property.[77]

Inherent in the development narrative is the idea that subsistence or near-subsistence farmers are necessarily poor, and would benefit from jobs. Cash is viewed as the currency of modernity, identifying wealth with money, rather than intact habitat and common lands, and the security of landholding.

When farmers become laborers on private estates or plantations, two questions arise: (1) While they may ostensibly choose to do so, what are the conditions under which they choose (e.g., are alternative possibilities, including independent farming, deteriorating), and (2) what are they giving up in the long term?

Biofuels

When producing biofuels, not only are farmers surrendering possibility of a renewable livelihood, but also the community loses sovereignty over its food system, since most land grabbed is for export agriculture, if not speculative purposes. The World Bank's report *Rising Global Interest in Farmland* views large-scale land acquisition as a vehicle for poverty reduction via rural employment, contract farming, and selling or renting.[78] Anthropologist Tania Li critiques these claims with the World Bank's own data. For example, on employment, while the report claims oil-palm employs 1.7–3 million people on 6 million hectares, "field data indicates that an established plantation uses only one worker per four to ten hectares of land, depending on the efficiency and stage of production."[79] For fuel crops, other estimates are that in tropical regions "100 hectares dedicated to family farming generates 35 jobs. Oil-palm and sugarcane provide ten jobs, eucalyptus two, and soybeans a scant half-job per 100 hectares, all poorly paid. . . . Hundreds of thousands [of smallholders] have already been displaced by the soybean plantations in the "Republic of Soy," a 50-million hectare area in southern Brazil, northern Argentina, Paraguay, and eastern Bolivia."[80]

While fuel crops such as oil-palm deplete soil and compromise local food availability by displacing farmers and food crops,[81] the land grab in general is both a food and water grab insofar as the products are exported to feed the rich, or their vehicles. The Bank noted in its 2008 report that the "grain required to fill the tank of a sports utility vehicle with ethanol (240 kilograms of maize for 100 liters of ethanol) could feed one person for a year."[82]

Following the commodity chain the other way, when land grabbing is by foreign investors, and agriculture and its products are absorbed into financial chains, the mix of physical crops becomes increasingly irrelevant to the financial profit calculus. Production decisions conform to a boardroom financial calculus, often with little concern for allocations between crops for food or fuels and/or environmental integrity. Thus the UN Human Rights Rapporteur Jean Ziegler charged in 2007 that biofuels are a "crime against humanity."[83] Social movements have renamed biofuels *agrofuels* in recognition of this tradeoff between food and fuel crops. Subsequent attempts by the World Bank (and IFPRI) to elaborate "Principles for Responsible Agricultural Investment" (RAI) have been met with UN Right to Food Rapporteur Olivier de Schutter's charge of "responsibly destroying the world's peasantry,"[84] followed by an attempt to construct more democratic Voluntary Guidelines through the FAO and its Committee on Food Security.

Since peasants constitute the majority of the world's food producers and provide the majority of the world's staple foods, there is rising concern about the long-term impact of the land grab. Not only does it portend a deepening of the homogenization of landscapes with ecological implications, but also it redirects food resources away from local communities—whether as high-value foods for foreign consumers or as agrofuels. The popular slogan "feeding the world" (once claimed by the biotech industry) appears to have been sacrificed to sustaining the lifestyle of a minority of the global population.

Biofuels are heavily subsidized by governments—the European Union targets 2020 as a date by which to supply 10 percent of its fuel needs from biofuels. In 2007 the UN reported that biofuels were the fastest growing segment of the world agricultural market,[85] fueled by cross-sectoral (and infrastructural) alliances between energy, agribusiness, trading companies, hedge funds, sovereign funds, states, UN agencies and universities.[86] The International Energy Agency estimates that by 2030 biofuels will "barely offset the yearly increase in global oil demand,"[87] and all renewables, including biofuels, will amount to only 9 percent of global energy consumption.[88]

Recognition of the contribution of biofuels to the 2008 food crisis (conservatively estimated at approximately one-third), and the claim that one ton of palm oil produces 33 tons of CO^2—ten times more per ton of petroleum,[89] emphasizes the socioecological impact of biofuels. In this context, the UK Climate Change Minister claimed in 2007, "the global community must as a matter of urgency work towards the development of internationally recognized standards for biomass grown to produce biofuels."[90] The subject of *certification* of course raises questions about how to standardize a sustainable biofuel metric. A Biofuelwatch survey claims a "majority of biofuel industry responses . . . reject any mandatory safeguards. . . . Many responses suggest that not enough is known about life-cycle greenhouse gas emissions from biofuels, but nonetheless demand government support for rapid market expansion."[91]

Ignoring the precautionary principle in this way has drawbacks, in particular the longer-term effects of greenhouse gas emissions. Just as carbon emissions from transport have been omitted from the globalization ledger, enabling a false economy (with "externalities"), so do biofuels threaten to perpetuate a false economy. A study in *Science* claimed that the conversion of rainforests, peatlands, savannas, or grasslands to produce biofuels in Brazil, Southeast Asia, and the United States "creates a 'biofuel carbon debt' by releasing 17 to 420 times more CO^2 than the annual greenhouse gas (GHG) reductions these biofuels provide by displacing fossil fuel."[92] In 2007, Nobel Prize winner Paul Crutzen observes that biofuels raise rather than lower emissions, and from research with colleagues on nitrous oxide emissions from crop fertilizers, he concluded, "Depending on N content, the use of several agricultural crops for energy production can readily lead to N2O emissions large enough to cause climate warming instead of cooling by 'saved fossil CO^2.' "[93]

Such evidence invokes the issues in the *sustainability project*. The land grab parallels plans to incorporate southern peasants into the World Bank's "agriculture for development." Whether it is land or labor or both, the goal is to anticipate food and fuel shortages, and, in the case of biofuels, to develop a renewable alternative to fossil fuels. Sustaining food supplies for distant consumers is a form of sustainability for the few, similar to the biofuels initiative—a "green fuel" for northerners (who pay in cash and taxes) premised on the "export of sustainability" from southerners (who pay in loss of long-term livelihood and habitat). As reported in *Land Is Life*, published in 2007 by indigenous organizations,

> The people first found out about the oil-palm scheme when workers started work on their lands, clearing the lands which included rubber trees and fruit trees belonging to the indigenous communities. As the oil-palm land clearing work continued, the rivers that supplied water to the people and the fish stock were affected. In addition to the crops, and polluted rivers, the people's burial ground and farm lands were also destroyed. People were then unable to hunt for the game which is an important element in their diet. There was no more rattan to harvest either, the raw material for handicrafts which had provided extra cash income to the communities. Jungle food sources, like vegetables, were also destroyed.[94]

Green Technology

The sustainability project includes a wide range of green technology developments. When Sir Nicholas Stern presented his 2006 report, with the famous admonition that climate change was the "greatest market failure the world has ever seen," he identified the fundamental shortcoming of markets—the inability to address long-term social objectives. There is now a growing recognition that industrial policy "cannot be relevant, cannot be effective, and cannot be credible, unless it is explicitly framed in the context of natural resource scarcity"—according to Wilfried Lütkenhorst, a Managing Director of the United Nations Industrial Development Organization (UNIDO).[95]

Following the 2000 World Economic Forum meeting, which declared "climate change is the greatest threat facing the world," corporate leaders (from firms like Dupont, BP, Shell, Suncor, Alcan, Ontario Power, and French aluminum manufacturer Pechiney) joined with U.S. advocacy group Environmental Defense to form the Partnership for Climate Action, announcing, "The primary purpose of the Partnership is to champion market-based mechanisms as a means of achieving early and credible action on reducing greenhouse gas emissions that is efficient and cost-effective." In 2004, Goldman Sachs established its Center for Environmental Markets, announcing that it would "aggressively seek market-making and investment opportunities in environmental markets," and "that the management of risks and opportunities arising from climate change and its regulation will be particularly significant and will garner increasing attention from capital market participants."[96] When *Newsweek* noted in March 2007 that "Wall Street is experiencing a climate change," recognizing that "the way to get the green is to go green," it captured the legacy of the globalization project—namely, a double movement of posing market solutions to modern problems, responding to ethical/environmental movements with "green capitalism." It is this combination that constitutes part of the sustainability project.

The practice of marketing emissions has been institutionalized in the EU's Emissions Trading Scheme (2005), whereby carbon emission permits have been assigned, free of charge, to European corporations. Noting that "the polluter was paid," and that, for example, the British government then calculated power firms would earn a windfall profit of about £1 billion, George Monbiot concluded, "The Emissions Trading Scheme is a classic act of enclosure. It has seized something which should belong to all of us—the right, within the system, to produce a certain amount of carbon dioxide— and given it to the corporations."[97] Monbiot's solution is public management of the problem, including a carbon rationing system based on principles of fairness, recognizing existing (global) inequalities of responsibility for emissions. Whether public management will rise to the occasion will be determined by the severity of climatic feedback, and, as below, the challenge from a greening China.

Meanwhile, green technologies are sprouting everywhere, with the majority focused on energy efficiency and reduction. Energy is considered the one essential item missing in the *Millennium Development Goals*. What is called a "decoupling" between economic growth and energy growth began in the global North following the energy crisis of the 1970s. The EU has achieved a 50 percent reduction in energy consumption since then, and, more recently, since 1990; while China's GDP increased nine times, its carbon emissions are only two and half times greater.[98]

Industrial activity accounts for one-third of global energy demand and almost 40 percent of carbon emissions—centered in materials industries such as chemicals and petrochemicals, iron and steel, cement, pulp and paper, and aluminum. Given current trends, by 2050 the South will account for 80 percent of industrial carbon emissions. The Clean Development Mechanism has slowed green technologies in the North since firms offset their pollution by investing in conservation (reforestation) or pollution-abatement (coal scrubbing, carbon capture) initiatives in the South. Greening is nevertheless under way—especially via fuel substitutes, carbon capture and storage (CCS), heat loss reduction, and energy recovery from waste capture.[99] In the transport sector, mass transit is the obvious choice, although it is also likely that as energy resources decline, communities, towns, and cities will be redesigned to reduce travel and promote bicycle and pedestrian traffic. Cities across the world are moving in this latter direction, and reducing automobile access to inner urban areas.

Alternative power sources are a key target of green technology. About 10 percent of Europe's electricity demand is to be powered by offshore wind projects.[100] Denmark has the largest offshore wind farm, accounting for 20 percent of its electricity. The Danes built a grassroots movement given that wind is "everyone's business," encouraging a national policy of subsidizing wind farms and guaranteeing community participation in the planning process.[101] Wind power machinery prices are declining as a result of these developments, subsidized by governments.

Europe is planning a renewable power "supergrid" to "connect turbines off the wind-lashed north coast of Scotland with Germany's vast arrays of solar panels, and join the power of waves crashing on to the Belgian and Danish coasts with the hydroelectric dams located in Norway's fjords." The goal is to solve the ultimate criticism of renewable power, namely, that weather is unpredictable and so power delivery is unpredictable. The supergrid combines several different forms of natural energy across a variety of regions, including Germany, France, Belgium, the Netherlands, Luxembourg, Denmark, Sweden, Ireland, and the UK—targeting the EU's pledge to convert 20 percent of its energy to renewable sources by 2020. EU scientists are looking ahead to link solar farms in southern Europe with wind, geothermal, and marine projects elsewhere on the continent, and even stray further south to capture just 0.3 percent of sunlight in the Sahara and Middle Eastern deserts to power all of Europe's needs. Concentrated solar power technology would use mirrors to concentrate solar rays on a fluid container, heating the liquid to drive turbines.[102]

For the South, solar thermal energy has enormous potential once costs come down. In the meantime, at the household level, plastic solar collectors or cooking stoves are being developed, and in China and Brazil subsidized solar panels allow water heating and supplementary electricity generation.[103] In addition, the private sector is teaming up with NGOs to provide lighting products to the poor: India's Solar Electric Light Company stimulated the global Lighting a Billion Lives campaign geared to replacing kerosene and paraffin lanterns with solar lanterns.[104] Meanwhile, the Chinese firm Suntech Power, a global leader in solar energy in over 80 countries, has launched a product called the Solar Home System to serve small, off-grid markets. It is a complete entry-level package for solar electricity generation to power light bulbs and charge cell phones at the household level.[105]

In India, the Bright Green Energy Foundation, set up by a founding member of the Grameen Bank in Bangladesh, has evolved out of Grameen Shakti—a nonprofit organization established to promote and supply renewable energy to millions of rural people: beginning with solar home systems, and diversifying into biogas for cooking, electricity and organic fertilizer, and improved cooking stoves to reduce indoor air pollution. Grameen Shakti succeeded by recognizing that women needed to be involved in the adoption of renewable energy, and establishing over 40 technology centers to train women in assembly, installation, and maintenance of solar home systems. Founder Dipal Barua claimed, "Women are the main victims of the energy crisis. They are the ones who suffer most from indoor air pollution, drudgery, and a lack of time because of the onerous tasks of wood-gathering and cooking." The Bright Green Energy Foundation is poised to expand its operations so that every household and business in Bangladesh "will have access to environmentally-friendly and pollution-free energy at an affordable cost."[106]

CASE STUDY   **The Promise and Problems of the Eco-City: a New China Syndrome?**

Chinese central government policy has been coming to terms with its enormous pollution issues and its rising GHG emissions. State-driven clean energy investments have overshadowed those of other countries, including high-speed rail systems and developing low-carbon cities. The government is expecting another 300 million migrants from the land, requiring it to build some 400 cities by 2020.

In 1999, the Chinese government proposed the first eco-city in the world, Dongtan, on an island in the midst of a nature preserve at the mouth of the Yangtze River. It was designed to be compact, socially diverse, and energy self-sufficient (supplied with solar, wind, and biomass energy), with an ecological footprint three times less than neighboring Shanghai, or London, or Paris. Cars would be carbon-neutral, depending on hydrogen filling stations for fuel cells, and all housing would be within seven minutes walk from public transport. Up to 80 percent of the city's waste would be recycled, with some organic waste used for power generation. Rooftop gardens would insulate and filter rainwater, with natural ventilation depending on building positioning in the local microclimate. By 2030 it was intended to house half a million residents. The director of the consulting firm Arup claimed the Chinese government was "committed to developing a new paradigm of economic development."

However, by 2009 construction was halted because the project coordinator was jailed for corruption, a charge also leveled at the consultant. A problem was identified in that building low-tech housing is far too slow and deliberate for a society undergoing such rapid change, especially for local elites expecting financial gain. In addition, farm land is grabbed and farmers moved into apartment blocks, highlighting "the promise—as well as the limits—of China's efforts to reconcile breakneck economic development with environmental concerns." In sister eco-city Dezhou, municipal authorities erected posters in 2009 "promoting low-carbon living on billboards once devoted to political slogans [but] residents bought 60,000 new cars, an increase of 114 percent over 2008."

Beyond the problems of hybridity—the juxtaposition of ecological initiatives with consumption pressures—perhaps a more fundamental problem for eco-cities will be the question of farming, and whether it is viewed as obstacle or partner.

Sources: Eilperin (2010: 18); Langellier and Pedroletti (2006); Sustainable Cities (2010); Williams (2009).

Solar and wind technologies are likely to outlast biofuels, which, in their industrial form (versus traditional, local use of recycled biomass in farming communities) are controversial. This development is to China's advantage—in 2009 it surpassed the United States and other members of the G-20 as the clean energy investment leader.[107] Certainly one of the first acts of the Obama administration was to commit the United States to $40.75 billion to clear energy initiatives (energy efficiency, weatherizing houses, public transportation, a national electricity grid, and cleaner cars). But China has committed to almost double that investment per year.[108] China is now the world's leader in clean energy, including compact fluorescent light bulbs, solar water heaters, solar photovoltaic cells, and wind turbines. The executive director of the Environmental Defense Fund, David Yarnold, observed of the Chinese, "The government realizes green energy technology is the new Industrial Revolution. They say, We missed the first one, and we're not going to miss this one."[109] This does not mean China will mothball its coal industry and coal-fired plants, as it is at the same time committed to expand its citizen-consumer population. While it is investing in biomass, wind, and solar power at a record pace (to cover 8 percent of its electricity needs by 2020), it is also investing in energy sources offshore, such as hydroelectric power in Burma, oil-palm in the Democratic Republic of the Congo, natural gas fields in Texas, and oil fields in Sudan.[110]

The *Sustainability Project* involves a river of green experimentation with an endless number of tributaries of large and small-scale technologies dedicated to reducing, sequestering, and replacing carbon consumption/emission. But China is taking the lead—with massive government (five-year) planning and incentives, economies of scale to reduce the cost of solar and wind energy technologies, and more. China leads in carbon capture technology. A report in *The Wall Street Journal* in December 2009 noted, "The so-called China price—the combination of cheap labor and capital that rewrote the rulebook in manufacturing—is spreading to green technology, especially for energy that relies on capital-intensive projects."[111] The goal is to replicate the success of the Special Economic Zones, via low-carbon centers with preferential policies to promote low carbon manufacturing and associated exports.

Whereas in 2004 foreign firms owned 80 percent of China's wind-turbine market, five years later Chinese firms owned 75 percent of the market, with costs one-third cheaper than European producers. Competitors accuse China of subsidizing its own companies from state banks, and dumping the excess supply of solar panels and wind turbines overseas. With 30 percent of the global market for photovoltaic solar panels, availability of the whole supply chain now within its borders, and a low-cost regime, China challenges its competitors to relocate to China, for the "China price" (combining Chinese and foreign corporate exploitation of labor and environment).[112] Meanwhile Volkswagen, Nissan, GM, and Daimler expect to build electric vehicles in China, where consumers are subsidized to buy such cars.[113]

The International Energy Agency (IEA) predicts China will move from 17 percent of world demand for energy in 2010 to 22 percent by 2035, which will surely sustain the efforts to produce clean energy—even as China continues to pollute its citizens, fields, and waterways as well as the atmosphere. As the IEA noted, "One point is certain. The center of gravity of global energy demand growth now lies in the developing world, especially in China and India."[114] Arguably, if the world's future is founded in low-carbon technology—and humanity survives the climate warming challenge—China is poised to become the dominant power in a global climate regime.

WHAT ARE THE INGREDIENTS OF THE SUSTAINABILITY PROJECT?

The sustainability project is emergent, rather than institutionalized. Its properties include

- a growing consensus among global policy makers for mitigation and adaptation procedures to stem climate change and ecosystem deterioration;
- a global groundswell of communities and movements, numbering perhaps over 2 million organizations working for ecological sustainability and social justice—and often ahead of political-economic elites that are beholden first to electorates and shareholders;
- institutional forms of green environmentalism (payment for ecological services) and green capitalism (eco-certified products);
- green technologies to save energy, produce renewable energy, sequester carbon, recycle;
- rising recognition of the greater equity, productivity and sustainability of agro-ecology;
- political and economic offset mechanisms in the global North to shift pollution southwards (the "export of sustainability");
- methods of "greenwash," as corporate complexes rebrand (Beyond Petroleum) and invest in sustainability claims (shade-grown coffee, offshore organics); and
- an emerging institutional complex including the UN Global Compact (branding corporate social and environmental responsibility initiatives), the UNFCCC as climate science monitor, the UN Commission on Sustainable Development, the Convention on Biodiversity, and so on.

SUMMARY

As above, the Sustainability Project is multifaceted and resembles a social tendency rather than a coordinated and/or coherent political-economic reality. It represents an emergent organizing principle in the complex world of development, whereby agencies, policies, and movements are struggling to establish interrelated institutional frameworks and a multitude of practices that reduce or eliminate the so-called "externalities" of the market economy. The two principal strands are the *extant* low-carbon activities and techniques of the *majority world*'s lifestyles and which inspire environmental movements and alternative practices in progress, and the *minority world*'s attempts to curb its disproportionate global emissions—whether by "downshifting" or offsetting or greening business. Of course the boundary between these two broad strands is porous, and there is much mutual appropriation of knowledge, technique, and posture.

The point is, however, whether all this activity will be enough to stem the rising climatic tide, so to speak. Chairman of the Copenhagen Climate Council, Tim Flannery, has stated, "I think that there is now a better than even risk that, despite our best efforts, in the coming two or three decades Earth's climate system will pass the point of no return."[115] He assigns responsibility for the potential for a "new dark age following the break-down of our global civilization" entirely with us. His understanding of "sustainability" is about expanding the Eighth Commandment, namely, "to forbid stealing from future generations." His conclusion—which may be a blueprint for a form of "development" based in a principle of sustainability that is socially universal—is that

> Societies which treat their members fairly in law, which seek to eliminate poverty and great inequalities of circumstances and wealth, and in which care—perhaps one could use the word love—for one another is manifest in day-to-day life, are surely best equipped to grant to future generations their just consideration, and so deal with the great challenges of this century.[116]

U.S. environmentalist Bill McKibben's response concerns implementation of sustainable practices and technologies. McKibben's solution is this: "There's only one lever even possibly big enough to make our system move as fast as it needs to, and that's the force of markets."[117] In other words, use the market to raise the price of fossil fuel to radically change ingrained habits of high mass consumption—which has, up to now, been enabled "because fossil fuel doesn't bear the cost of the damage it does to the environment."

And the way to "rewrite the economics of carbon in time to prevent the worst catastrophes" is to move governments, and the way to move governments "is to build a real citizen's movement that demands change."[118] This would be a radical, and therefore energetically contested, use of a market instrument to transcend the current carbon credit-swapping market (largely "business as usual") and return "economics" toward its ecological foundations. Of course it is directed at the "fast world" and would need to be complemented with recognition and support of widespread existing alternative economies based in ecological principles.

FURTHER READING

Borras, Saturnino, Jr., Philip McMichael, and Ian Scoones, eds. *Biofuels, Land and Agrarian Change*. London and New York: Routledge, 2011.

Flannery, Tim. *Now or Never: Why We Must Act Now to End Climate Change and Create a Sustainable Future*. New York: Atlantic Monthly Press, 2009.

Holt-Giménez, Eric, and Raj Patel, with Annie Shattuck. *Food Rebellions! Crisis and the Hunger for Justice*. Oakland: FoodFirst Books, 2009

Houtart, Francois. *Agrofuels: Big Profits, Ruined Lives and Ecological Destruction*. London: Pluto Press, 2010.

Mol, Arthur, David Sonnenfeld, and Gert Spaargaren, eds. *The Ecological Modernisation Reader: Environmental Reform in Theory and Practice*. London and New York, 2010.

Perfecto, Ivette, John Vandermeer, and Angus Wright, *Nature's Matrix: Linking Agriculture, Conservation and Food Sovereignty*. London: Earthscan, 2009.

Wittman, Hannah, Annette A. Desmarais, and Nettie Wiebe, eds. *Food Sovereignty: Reconnecting Food, Nature and Community*. Halifax and Winnipeg: Fernwood, 2010.

SELECT WEBSITES

IAASTD Report: http://www.agassessment.org/

UN Human Settlements Program: http://ww2.unhabitat.org/mdg/

UN Millennium Ecosystem Assessment: http://www.maweb.org/en/index.aspx

Women Organizing for Change in Agriculture and Natural Resource Management: http://www.wocan.org/documents/category/agriculture-and-rural-development.html

World Bank, *World Development Report (2008)*: http://wdronline.worldbank.org/

WorldWatch Institute: http://blogs.worldwatch.org/nourishingtheplanet/

10

Rethinking Development

How the globalization project will evolve, or unravel, toward a new project to order the world is not yet clear. Of course its internal tensions will condition future possibilities. But this time around, the increasingly evident resource and environmental limits will have a disproportionate effect on the shape of things to come, governed by an emerging climate change regime. Development is already about how to manage the future, rather than simply improving on the past. The reason for this shift in perspective has much to do with the conjunction of energy, food, climate, and financial crises.

Managing the future means rethinking development in an age of crisis. There is no single understanding of what the necessary steps are. Different social interests envision different development futures, especially when institutions, such as the market, that have been taken for granted, falter. One of the key debates is over whether and to what extent the future can be managed through "business as usual." At a crisis moment, the forces of the *status quo* are most likely to argue for reinvigorating business, whereas those social forces seeking change will view crisis as a signal to shift course. We saw, in the previous chapter, how an emergent "sustainability project" includes a variety of responses reflecting the diversity of social forces across the world. To simplify, we might say that the Polanyian cycle of market versus nonmarket values overlays these responses—both because modernity self-defines through the market institution and because that institution is now facing its greatest material challenge as ecosystems deteriorate. In large part the struggle for the future concerns this central contradiction. In this closing chapter, we focus on the growing recognition of the limits of conventional development thinking, and of the need to imprint sustainable practices in development futures.

Development in the Gear of Social Change

To say development is in crisis has perhaps a double meaning. On the one hand, the pain of financial adjustment registers in the widespread rollback of public goods (education, welfare, health care, infrastructure, affordable housing), shrinking employment, and degraded environments. On the other hand, how we understand, and measure, development (and what we value) is in disarray. To illustrate from officialdom, consider the 2009 findings of the Commission on the Measurement of Economic Performance and Social Progress, whose mandate was to produce "more relevant indicators of social progress."

Commenting on the sudden shock of the 2008 financial crisis, the Commission noted "our measurement system failed us," failing to alert officials that the world-economic boom of 2004–2007 "may have been achieved at the expense of future growth" and that "metrics which incorporated assessments of sustainability (e.g., measures for increased indebtedness) would have provided a more cautious view of economic performance." In a moment of clarity, the Commission also observed "the time is ripe for our measurement system to shift emphasis from measuring economic production to measuring people's well-being. And measures of well-being should be put in a context of sustainability." This observation signals a turning point in public discourse about development—away from the conventional focus on economic growth and consumption targets, and toward institutional appreciation for human development, such as health, education, and possibility for enhancement of life experiences.[1]

Nonmarket Values

The Commission's declaration opens the door to taking seriously non-market services (e.g., intergenerational care and community service, health, environmental and economic security), and even disaggregating averages to document, as the Commission noted, "the diversity of peoples' experiences." Aside from the difficulty of measuring subjective experiences, the report signals a growing recognition that market-driven metrics (such as national income data) are no longer adequate to assess the well-being of citizenries. In 1990 the United Nations *Human Development Report* complemented income measures with a composite of life expectancy and literacy in the

Human Development Index, leading with the premise that "(p)eople are the real wealth of a nation." Identifying human resources (including public health measures) was an important step toward recognition that the well-being of citizens was a holistic conception linked to the 1948 **UN Declaration of Human Rights,** and its promotion of a government/citizen **social contract** entitling all to freedom and dignity.

To now suggest citizen "well-being" extends to the diversity of subjective experience is an astounding advance in an age where development has been equated with rising levels of consumption. And diversity extends to development policy insofar as conditions differ across countries and regions. Thus, the 2010 UN Development Report states, "The new strands in development thinking recognize that one size does not fit all, that the payoffs to policy reform differ with circumstances and that appropriate strategies need to be identified and developed locally."[2] For some—such as economist Jean-Paul Fitoussi, a Commission Coordinator—a measurement system needs to be standardized "otherwise it has no validity."[3] However, the emerging **Capabilities Approach** privileges a diversified commitment to, and attainment for, the equal dignity of all people.[4] Drawing on Nobel Laureate Amartya Sen's original formulation of "substantive freedoms—the capabilities to choose a life one has reason to value," Martha Nussbaum argues the new paradigm of capabilities does not assume such choice is equally distributed, rather it "takes into account that people may need different quantities of resources if they are to come up to the same level of ability to choose and act, particularly if they begin from different social positions."[5]

Politicizing Inequality

In this sense, addressing inequality is a *precondition* for promoting human development. It is one thing to temper the fixation on economic growth, it is another to acknowledge that this fixation has allowed and legitimized the deepening of material inequalities, experienced the most by those subject to gender, race, ethnic, age, and disability discrimination. Indices of global wealth distribution reveal deepening inequalities, which, themselves, call into question assumptions that development is about improvement on the past. In a recent publication, *Other Worlds Are Possible: Human Progress in an Age of Climate Change,* Oxfam notes recent research demonstrates "global economic growth is an extremely inefficient way of achieving poverty reduction," especially given that humanity uses more resources and generates more waste than ecosystems around the world can replace and absorb:

A system has emerged in which the already wealthy become both relatively and absolutely wealthier, receiving the bulk of the benefits of growth. This happens as ownership of everything from property to company shares increases their earning potential. At the same time, the poorest slip further behind, and have their well-being and prospects further undermined by environmental degradation and the fall-out from inequality.[6]

This "system" is now transnational, upending the "stages of growth" scenario. For instance, there has been a divergence between the United States, as standard-bearer of development, and one of its neighbors to the South. In the 1940s the top 1 percent of the U.S. population controlled about 10 percent of income, compared to 20 percent in Argentina. Since then, these ratios have reversed: The "share controlled by the top 1 percent in Argentina has fallen to a bit more than 15 percent. Meanwhile, inequality in the United States has soared to levels comparable to those in Argentina six decades ago—with 1 percent controlling 24 percent of American income in 2007."[7] Between 2000–2007, the top 1 percent received over 70 percent of the total income increase.[8]

Aside from observing the United States' experience of what has been termed "Latin Americanization," such trends dramatize the hollowing out of social democracy. In Polanyi's terms, this means the disembedding of the market from society—where privatization and individual market relations trump the kind of social cohesion associated with the mid-twentieth century development project. That is, class polarization in the United States clearly evidences the reversal of the social model of development, following three decades of neoliberalism. Ironically, while there is much discussion of the decline of the middle class in the United States, a new (global) middle class consolidates across the global South.

New Geography of Inequality

While a global middle class, has emerged, centered in the **BRICS** (Brazil, Russia, India, China, and South Africa), there is nevertheless a rising trend in global inequality (if we remove China from consideration). But this inequality is distributed differently now. Whereas twenty years ago 93 percent of poor people lived in low-income countries, now three-quarters of the world's poorest live in middle-income countries, such as the BRICS, Nigeria, Pakistan, and Indonesia.[9] Put another way, over "80% of the world's population lives in countries where income differentials are widening."[10] The World Bank's prediction that there will still be around 1 billion poor in 2015, but these will be concentrated in the middle-income countries and the most difficult to reach, has inspired a new perspective from the University of Sussex's Institute of Development Studies (IDS). Since "poverty may be increasingly turning from an international to a national distribution problem," IDS proposes a new approach to poverty, arguing that "development policy needs to be about poor *people*, not just about poor *countries*."[11]

Such a condition and policy intervention departs from the Rostovian assumption that development means moving countries up a hierarchy of wealth. What has changed? There are two (related) processes in play here. There is *first* a progressive incorporation of all ("traditional") sub-cultures into market networks via the institutions and price relations imposed by the globalization project. In World Bank terms, development is about participation in the world market, suggesting that subnational regions and resource complexes, rather than countries, develop. And this occurs through the *second* process: the deepening of global circuits of affluence that reinforce inequality of access and/or actively exclude populations within nations from a horizontal (transnational) dynamic integrating a global consumer class.[12] Here, global inequalities no longer appear as geographical divisions, rather they reappear as social divisions everywhere—with a universal distribution of elites and middle classes across the nation-state system. By 2010, the African Development Bank was claiming an African middle class represented about 34 percent of that continent's population (about 313 million people, up from 111 million in 1980).[13]

This rising middle class identifies increasingly with access to what the United Nations Department of Economic and Social Affairs (UNDESA) refers to as "largely unregulated global value chains dominated by international companies."[14] The redistribution of the "new bottom billion" to middle-income countries means, for the IDS, a "new focus on relative poverty and supporting the expansion of the tax-paying middle classes . . . to help build the domestic tax system and improve governance and accountability." This generates a new development paradox where such middle classes, given their horizontal affiliation, may be less inclined to redistribute new-found wealth to their lagging fellow citizens, socially excluded via neoliberal norms. Over the past 25 years of privatization, public assistance has dwindled as social policies have been divorced from development strategy, with the poor excluded from the global marketplace.[15] Angus Cameron and Ronen Palan suggest that "social exclusion" has become a discursive strategy of pathologizing the poor as embodying deficiencies that assign personal and individual—rather than social—responsibility for their condition.[16] Microcredit initiatives acknowledge this, and have sought to fill the void left by shrinking states. But given the recent globalization of austerity, the burden of cutbacks and economic stagnation is borne disproportionately by the poor and unemployed.

CASE STUDY   **The Debt Crisis in the North and the Detroit Revival (Motown Becomes Growtown)**

Public debt in the global North is huge: U.S. cities and states are indebted to the tune of $2 trillion, while local and regional government debt was $1.7 trillion in 2010. From Detroit to Madrid, through Barcelona to Florence, Naples, Budapest, and Istanbul, city administrators struggle to pay creditors at the expense of providing basic services such as street cleaning. U.S. states are $1 trillion short in pension funds; California raised state university tuition fees by 32 percent; and Arizona sold its State Capitol and Supreme Court buildings to investors, leasing them back. High unemployment rates do not help, as one in seven Americans are destitute—the highest level in half a century, with millions more hovering just above the official poverty line of $22,000 for a family of four, and 6.1 million officially long-term unemployed—almost half of the nation's jobless workers. From 2007–2010 the percentage of two-earner families in which one partner lost a job in a given year doubled.

Detroit, home of the U.S. auto industry, much of which has moved offshore, has cut police, lighting, road repairs, and cleaning services, affecting 20 percent of its citizens—25 percent of whom left the city in the first decade of the twenty-first century (the largest percentage drop in history for a U.S. city), leaving 33,000 empty lots and vacant houses. White flight and some black flight to suburbs reduced the tax base of the city, exacerbating an unemployment rate of around 50 percent.

However . . . drastic urban decay has given way to a revitalization of the inner city, as urban farming has taken over, with about 40 square miles available (acreage the size of San Francisco). Individuals and nonprofit community groups (such as Urban Farming) farm alongside Hantz Farms, the world's largest urban corporate farm (seen by activists as engaging in an urban "land grab"). For the thousands of people developing urban farming, they are returning Detroit to its preindustrial roots, finding new cooperative ways to make ends meet, and pioneering a template for other declining inner cities in the global North. Urban Farming's founder Taja Sevelle says, "Detroit will be number one in showing people how to pull a city out of a situation like this." Her cooperative serves food banks in Detroit and 25 other cities, as part of a general philosophy of food justice. The food these organizations grow is available free to residents, and farms are unfenced, open to all (vandalism is almost unknown), and run by volunteers or charity workers. Patrick Crouch, a farmer for Earthworks (a soup kitchen provider), is skilled in agricultural activism and manages a "model plot"

(Continued)

(Continued)

complete with vegetables and beehive, with the potential for replication as a source for a living wage. Urban farms adapt agro-ecological methods developed in Havana, Cuba, and other Latin American sites. 800 million people worldwide engage in urban agriculture, producing 15–20 percent of the world's food.

If the northern development model is in decline, or moving offshore, what else is there but the possibility of communities rediscovering how to feed themselves—rather than the "world"? Is this the new "stage of growth"?

Sources: Harris (2010); Fletcher (2010); Seelye (2011); Uchitelle, 2011; Nourishing the Planet (2010).

The Analytical and Political "Purchase" of Development

The occurrence of social exclusion on a world scale raises a *key question about the development condition* at large. As suggested, a rising global middle class with weakening ties to national civic purpose indicates transformation of the development frame. Recent development literature represents this as the end of "methodological nationalism," that is, conceiving of development as a national process. Further, transnational relations unsettle "statecentric" theories that would prioritize the role of the "development state." Drawing on global commodity chain analysis, Anthony Payne and Nicola Phillips argue the focus is "thus on firms rather than states, as the primary drivers of the emerging 'global' (as opposed to international) division of labour."[17] So the recent "rise" of China, for example, is not adequately understood via methodological nationalism. Rather China's emergence is situated in a specific process of the transnationalization of capital, via the globalization project. That is, for Payne and Phillips, transnational capital

> has "landed" in parts of coastal China as a result of particular sets of factor endowments, facilitated by the internal economic reforms undertaken by the Chinese government from the late 1970s onwards. Equally, the growth pattern has been fuelled primarily by the production and investment strategies of companies in the advanced industrialized economies, which in turn are premised largely on demand in these markets. It is consequently misleading to talk about the development of "China" as a national unit—rather, we are seeing the consolidation of a contemporary phase in the evolution of global production networks and value chains, which is manifested in certain spatial sites within the territorial boundaries of the Chinese state.[18]

Sociologist William Robinson puts it this way: "Development connotes a social rather than a geographic, spatial, or territorial process: we need to reconceive of development not in terms of nations but in terms of social groups in a transnational setting."[19]

Of course, "development" was never a national process. Rather it informed an ideological representation of the post-colonial world order, comprising a hierarchy of political and economic relations. The development project, under U.S. leadership, involved a political ordering of the world via a set of rules and institutions providing the architecture of the mid-twentieth century world, a world constituted by decolonization and Cold War rivalry. "Development" was a powerful ideology combining themes of political emancipation, material assistance, and military security—appealing to a proliferating and unequal system of states, which were designated as enablers and/or sites of development. States provided the scaffolding for the development project. A development narrative, exemplified in Rostow's "stages of growth," provided a rationale for national development as a serial process across a state system within which a free enterprise model could be institutionalized.

The project of national development was always a partial (ideological) representation of social reality, in the sense that development unfolded within definite international relations. Accordingly, various social patterns (from wage food provisioning to labor skill distributions) could only be explained within a global political-economic framework (food regime, international division of labor, respectively). Deepening of this framework laid the foundations of the globalization project, through which new rules and institutions opened markets and deepened transnational enterprise. As we have seen, northern manufacturing migrated to strategic regions of the global South, spawning world factories and a global labor force supplied by peasant dispossession as industrial agriculture displaced smallholders across the world.

The information revolution in turn has enabled the service sector (e.g., transport, telecommunication and computer services, construction, financial services, wholesale and retail distribution, hotel and catering, insurance, real estate, health and education, professional, marketing, and other business support) to overtake manufacturing and agriculture, contributing two-thirds of world GDP by 2003.[20] Information-based services, as we all know too well, have been transformed by digitization, allowing office functions to be fragmented and relocated to computers or offshore call centers, fashioning a new form of global economy that, for sociologist Manuel Castells, develops "the capacity to work *as a unit in real time* on a planetary scale."[21] As sociologist Ankie Hoogvelt points out, the existence and dynamic of this kind of economic networking in real time allows instantaneous adjustment to competitive relations, such that this twenty-first century "global economy is highly dynamic, highly exclusionary, and highly unstable in its boundaries." In consequence, "globalization has rearranged the architecture of world order. Economic, social, and power relations have been recast to resemble *not* a pyramid of rich nations (at the top) and poor nations (at the bottom) but instead a three-tier structure of circles."[22]

The layered structuring of the global population by access to the world economy is represented in Figure 10.1. Hoogvelt's following characterization of such layering preceded the 2008 crisis, which only solidified this hierarchical and centrifugal force:

Figure 10.1 Transnational Distribution of Global Population by Relative Inclusion/Exclusion

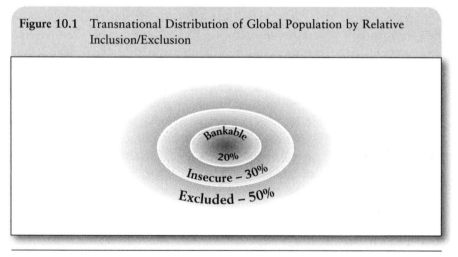

Source: Hoogvelt, 2006: 164.

All three circles cut across national and regional boundaries. In the core circle, we find the elites of all continents and nations, albeit in different proportions in relation to their respective geographic hinterlands. Very roughly, the figures are 40-30-30 in the rich countries, and 20-30-50 in the poor countries. In Sub-Saharan Africa, where the middle layer is largely missing, the respective proportions are more like 10-20-70 or even 10-10-80. We may count in the core some 20% of the world population who are deemed "bankable" and therefore able to borrow funds. They are encircled by a fluid, larger social layer of between 20% and 30% of the world population (workers and their families) who labour in insecure forms of employment. . . . The third, and largest, circle comprises those who are already effectively excluded from the global system. This does not mean that they are not affected by the global system; on the contrary, they carry more than their fair share of its burdens, of environmental degradation and resource depletion, of war and conflict, of forcible dispossession. But what it means is that they are *expendable*. On a very rough count they comprise the 2.8 billion people who are estimated to be surviving on US$2 per day.[23]

Paradigm Change

Once we reconfigure the framework of development, as above, the question becomes, how does this alter the meaning and practice, or paradigm, of development? The key point here is that generally development agencies and practitioners are professionally bound to treat the symptoms. This means focusing, for example, on the so-called "bottom billion" (e.g., with direct cash transfers to the poor, such as the Brazilian *Bolsa Familia* program), worrying about the appropriate mix of economic and social remedies, and modifying the scope and scale of development interventions. During the period of the neoliberal globalization project, there has been a discernible shift away from targeting states toward targeting subject populations for development, in pendulum fashion between economic and social foci, and toward participation as the litmus test of "development subject responsibility" (whether of states authoring poverty reduction, individuals embracing microcredit, or NGO-led social mobilizations).

Participation may be double-edged, conferring legitimacy on a policy/ development initiative, despite filtering it through existing unequal relations of access to resources, rights, and power.[24] It is here that the **development paradox** reappears, insofar as participatory methods still reproduce inequalities, which in turn renew development's legitimacy as poverty adversary. One way out of this paradox is through self-organizing democratic participation in determining social need and ecological possibility. There is currently a vast range of social experimentation underway across the world, often under the radar, driven by the shortcomings of development writ large, and in anticipation of deteriorating environments. Naturally the antennae of the development agencies are picking up on these movements, with the goal of appropriation, partnership, or even recognition of a shifting paradigm.

CASE STUDY **Slow Food: An International Movement of Good Taste**

The Slow Food movement, originating in Italy in the 1980s but now a global movement, builds on principles of localizing food-sheds, retaining local cuisines, and protecting "local" farming in particular, and food heritage in general. It seeks to restore direct links between producers and consumers and thereby encourage healthy growing and eating. It proceeds from the premise that progressive social change can be sparked by transformation of attitudes about food and practices of eating. Founder of Slow Food, Carlo Petrini, claims, "The real remedies for the gastronomic ills of the twenty-first century are the assumption of responsibility for the future; the salvation of a heritage of memory, biodiversity, and creative capacity; and the affirmation of a pleasure principle."

The Slow Food Foundation for Biodiversity formed in Italy, 2003, to "know, catalogue and safeguard small quality productions and to guarantee them and economic and commercial future." In relation to this, COOP-Italia, a consortium with over 200 consumer cooperatives, coordinates production and sale of quality food products traceable to their socio-spatial origins, within a broader ethical engagement that includes supporting fair trade initiatives, water provisioning in Africa, and contesting diffusion of genetically modified organisms. Alternative Food Networks also contribute to the proliferation of new rural development practices, such as agro-tourism, energy production, and landscape management. These developments, known as "multi-functionality," have potential as a new Northern agricultural policy paradigm.

The Official Slow Food Manifesto proclaims, "In the name of productivity, Fast Life has changed our way of being and threatens our environment and our landscapes. So Slow Food is now the only truly progressive answer."

What is the difference between Fast and Slow Food paradigms in development terms?

Sources: Petrini (2001: xix, xxiv); Fonte (2006); Pretty (2002).

Within the mainstream development community, Oxfam contests the persistent received wisdom that "you can't have development without all that global economic growth entails in terms of its human and environmental costs." Noting that 1987 was the last year when humanity's level of resource use "fell within the means of our life-supporting natural assets," Oxfam calls for a new form of "ecological solidarity" where managing climate change requires a "new development paradigm—a paradigm that has broken free from its carbon chains and its addiction to growth." This would involve "rethinking how to share a finite planet, meeting our collective needs whilst living within environmental limits could not only rescue civilization . . . but be a way to tackle deeply entrenched problems of social injustice, and greatly improve overall human well-being."[25]

Paradigm change thinking is a product of the contradictions of economic growth: from the King of Thailand's articulation of the idea of scaling back to the "sufficiency economy," through the King of Bhutan's notion of *Gross National Happiness* (GNH) as a qualitative benchmark combining material and spiritual development (emphasizing equality, cultural values, environmental sustainability, and good governance), to the Index of Sustainable Economic Welfare, or the *Genuine Progress Indicator*. The GPI offers a quantifiable national balance sheet that includes the benefits *and costs* of economic growth—for example, where "GDP counts the value of timber from native forests as a benefit and stops there, the GPI also counts the environmental costs of logging."[26]

Degrowth Economics

Then there is the concept of "**degrowth economics.**" This is a provocative term designed to counter the prevailing economic orthodoxy of unbridled "growth" that translates into "development" today, and to create "integrated, self-sufficient and materially responsible societies in both the North and the South." Using a dramatic metaphor to make the point, economist Serge Latouche suggests, "Growth economics, like HIV, destroys societies' immune systems against social ills. And growth needs a constant supply of new markets to survive, so, like a drug dealer, it deliberately creates new needs and dependencies that did not exist before."[27]

Latouche claims the French term *décroissance* (translated as degrowth) actually means "a-growth," and proposes "we have to change our values. We need to replace egoism with altruism, competition with cooperation and obsessive performance with leisure. But values are systemic . . . Without a radical questioning of the system, the value change will remain limited."[28] It is in this context that the phenomenon of "downshifting" has taken hold in the North, as people take leave of the consumer treadmill and pursue a more balanced and rewarding life. In her book *The Overspent American*, Juliet Schor reports that 19 percent of the adult U.S. population has downshifted, "voluntarily switching to lower paid jobs, choosing to reduce their hours of work, and deciding to stay at home and look after their children."[29] The proliferation of alternative conceptions and practices reflects our times, as people rediscover values other than market values in individual and collective attempts to redefine the meaning of development. As we will see, such redefinition preoccupies proliferating social justice and sovereignty movements.

According to ecological economist Joan Martinez-Alier, degrowth springs from social movement experiences of cohousing, squatting, neoruralism, reclaiming the streets, alternative energies, waste prevention and recycling, in addition to activist-led science.[30] Degrowth economics has spawned an originating Paris Conference (2008), and an allied *decrescita* movement in Italy, spreading to Spain, Canada, the UK, Mexico, and South America.

At the Paris Conference, delegates concluded business as usual would result in a "process of involuntary and uncontrolled economic decline or collapse," and called for a "paradigm shift from the general and unlimited pursuit of economic growth to a concept of 'right-sizing' the global and national economies," involving "degrowth in wealthy parts of the world" to preserve environmental space for poorer nations. Practical steps include mainstreaming the concept into public debate and economic institutions, and development of policy tools and nonmonetary indicators (including subjective indicators) to assess progress toward economic "right-sizing" (i.e., sustainable ecological footprint)—although it is unclear how capitalist property relations would lose their economic and political sway.[31] The Second International Conference on Degrowth (2010), in Barcelona, deepened the critique, arguing that "an international elite and a 'global middle class' are causing havoc to the environment through conspicuous consumption and the excessive appropriation of human and natural resources," and that the "illusion of debt-fuelled growth" will end in social disaster. The conference advanced a series of practical proposals (e.g., local currencies, ecological taxes, establishment of new jurisdictions for a global commons, universal basic income, decommercialization of politics), concluding that degrowth must originate in the rich countries. Note that these are all parts of a general attempt to restore a version of the "development state," a growing movement in the North especially, but, as we have seen, definitive of the challenge from China and India.

At the Barcelona conference, Patricia Perkins put forward a feminist critique of the degrowth movement, centered on the interface between paid and unpaid inputs into the measured economy. She notes much of women's work and nature's services are undervalued, and unpaid, generally dwarfing the measured economy in value, yet discounted in policy:

> To the extent that Degrowth is just about—or includes—pushing the frontier between the paid and the unpaid further towards "unpaid," it fails to address

these concerns about relative values, undervaluation, and justice—and in fact Degrowth might even exacerbate the exploitation of underpaid workers, and of nature. This is because, as economies become more local and more service-oriented in order to generate less material throughput, there will be shifts in how much work is done and who does it, how much trade takes place and who is put out of work as a result, and whose economic needs are met and unmet.[32]

Two other important practical points raised by Perkins are first, how does Degrowth address the point that growth is central to (the possibility of) reducing material inequality? Without growth "someone must give up resources if others are to gain them"—a question partially answered by the notion of a paradigm shift toward revaluing local resources (especially non-monetized ones such as care work, barter, cooperatives, and resource-sharing) in such a way as to redefine what we mean by resources.[33] Second, Perkins introduces a critical point about voice/participation:

> Without growth as the engine, what drives progressive redistribution? . . . It is fundamentally important for Degrowth theoreticians and activists to seek out assistance from those who already—and generally by default rather than choice—have a great deal of experience with unpaid and low-paid work, with recycling and reusing materials, with living very simply, doing without cars, eating no meat, letting others eat first, using animal or human traction rather than fossil-fuels to accomplish their daily work, fabricating shelter and the other necessities of life from non-industrial materials. These people are all around in this diverse world we inhabit; they are not just in other countries, or in the global South. But are they here at this conference? Why is this? The disenfranchised must be invited to share their views on Degrowth and how to build more equitable societies while living lightly on the earth. They are the experts![34]

From another angle, claiming that degrowth is unpalatable under present circumstances—because of global economic stagnation and high unemployment rates—"zero growth" advocate Tim Jackson, Economics Commissioner for the British Sustainable Development Commission, articulates a profound dilemma: "To resist growth is to risk economic and social collapse. To pursue it relentlessly is to endanger the ecosystems on which we depend for long-term survival." He continues: "In a world of 9 billion people all aspiring to western lifestyles, the carbon intensity of every dollar of output must be at least 130 times lower in 2050 than it is today. By the end of the century, economic activity will need to be taking carbon out of the atmosphere, not adding to it."[35]

The Jackson study concludes that relying on capitalist efficiency is delusional, given the combination of a profit motive and the grip of consumerism.

The principle of decoupling, to reduce material throughput in the economy, *would allow governments to dispense with short-term growth imperatives and refocus on protecting the long-term by delivering on social and ecological goals.* A new vision is necessary, based on "rebuilding prosperity from the bottom up," to invest in public/shared goals, assets, and infrastructures. A new, "flourishing"—rather than profit–based—economy should gravitate to service-based activities, ecological/green investment, and a work-time policy to reduce working hours and improve work-life balance. Such a policy suggestion reappears in the literature—for example, a zero growth model depends on a shorter work year, to spread employment around, coupled with the redistribution of productivity gains toward leisure time rather than profits and GDP: for Canada "a reduction in the average work year of around 15% by 2035, to 1,500 hours a year, would secure full employment. This work year would still be longer than in some European countries. In Germany, for example, the average paid employee worked 1,430 hours in 2008."[36]

Ultimately, Jackson argues for a well-regulated form of capitalism, where a responsive public sector combines with a reframing of productivity and wealth distribution. Opposition by propertied and financial interests would be likely. However, touching a current nerve he notes, "Interestingly, the fairness argument for a larger public stake in ownership was already rehearsed explicitly during the recent financial crisis. Why should the taxpayer bear all the risk and reap none of the benefits of underwriting the financial sector?"[37]

Such emergent visions draw strength from the perceived injustices of a global economy and environment in crisis. In this sense, it is not so much whether they are immediately practical or popular, but that they anticipate future needs for inhabiting, collectively, a diminishing material world. The practical sensibility underlying much of this new visioning process recognizes that the most effective way forward is to acknowledge and learn from mistakes.

Transition Towns

The **Transition Town** movement is a prime example of this kind of future visioning, emphasizing relocalization. Emerging in the 2000s, it is a movement, or network, by and across communities anticipating peak oil and climate change. As of 2010, there were over 300 official towns, from the UK and Ireland to Canada, the United States, Australia, New Zealand, Chile, and Italy, engaged in processes to manage "energy descent."[38]

The goal is to build social and ecological resilience into local towns and communities (and their governance) by reducing and eliminating fossil-fuel dependence and rebuilding local resources via principles of **permaculture**. Sustainable land use design reintegrates humans with their environment, localizing food systems, and restoring and emulating natural cycles to replenish ecological relations and reduce waste. The expectation is that work is reduced by its greater productivity in reproducing community—rather than profits—and biodiversity—rather than products. Local currencies enhance local business and new green jobs, and recycle wealth through the community—versus repatriating profits to a corporate offshore brass-plate bank. Local markets encourage environmental stewardship and social connection. Education includes adults and children, geared to reestablishing generational and bioregional connection, developing grounded skills, local knowledge, and emotional resilience. As the people of the borough of Southend on Sea in the UK claim,

> Climate Change and Peak Oil can cause us to feel confronted by something overwhelmingly huge that we cannot do anything about. The central message of the Transition Movement is that this state of mind is not the place to start from if we want to achieve something, do something, or create something. Indeed, by shifting our mind-set we can actually recognize the coming post-cheap oil era as an opportunity rather than a threat, and design the future low-carbon age to be thriving, resilient, and abundant—somewhere much better to live than our current alienated consumer culture based on greed, war, and the myth of perpetual growth.[39]

Ultimately, the Transition Town movement is a proactive approach to managing the energy- and climate-challenged future—involving mobilization of community resources in such a way as to rediscover local capacity, reduce ecological footprints, and increase resilience. And as a movement, it is about alliances across communities, as opposed to a conventional development model that encourages communities and regions to compete with one another.

The Commons

The proliferation of alternative conceptions and practices reflects our times, as people rediscover values other than market values in individual and collective attempts to redefine the meaning of development. One key value concept is the "**commons**," the source of shared popular livelihoods and cultural meaning enclosed by private property relations during the rise of capitalism, and currently the target of much of the global land grab primarily in the global South. J. K. Gibson-Graham claims there is today "a revival of interest in reclaiming and enlarging the commons in the industrialized countries, and protecting the yet-to-be completely destroyed or expropriated commons in the 'developing' world." Such a revival is at the same time a rejection of the modern ontology of development, and the rediscovery of local possibility—exemplified in the Transition Town movement and its variants. Gibson-Graham notes,

> The practice of economic development has been dominated by the naturalized universal of the capitalist economy (as the model of economy, as the only true, viable economy, as something that effaces its particularistic origins in the West, in certain forms of market, in certain types of enterprise). Development discourse centers on the problematic of bringing capitalist economic development to those spaces that are "lacking" its dynamic presence and allure of beneficence. Countless strategies are advocated that will engender (or more proactively "kick start") capitalist industrialization. . . . All strategies are pursued with the promise that increased well-being will trickle down from the capitalist sector and its employees to the wider community. And all are beholden to the conviction that economic growth . . . is unquestionably desirable.[40]

The quest for a new paradigm echoes across the world. For instance, in South Korea, a new desire for a culture of "fairness" confronts its ruthless, ultra-competitive, and increasingly corrupt social system.[41] In West Africa the concept *Bamtaare* means "harmonious development," integrating community and environment. Ecuador and Bolivia captured the world's imagination in 2008 when their national constitutions reinvented development as "living well" (in Spanish: *buen vivir*, or Quechua: *sumak kawsay*). **Buen vivir**—the fruit of decades of political struggles and alliances between indigenous peoples, peasants, Afro-descendants, women, environmentalists, and youth—subordinates economy to ecology, human dignity and social justice. *Buen vivir* is not dissimilar to Polanyi's reembedding of the market. It complements legal passage in each state of the rights of nature alongside human rights.[42]

Andean cosmology, placing *Pachamama* (planet earth) at the center of all life, "represents an unprecendented 'biocentric turn,' away from the anthropocentrism of modernity."[43] The Bolivian vice president, Alvaro Gardia Linera, claimed, "It makes world history. Earth is the mother of all. It establishes a new relationship between man and nature, the harmony of which must be preserved as a guarantee of its regeneration." Of course making world history and actually implementing such a relationship are not the same. The Bolivian Law of Mother Earth also redefines the country's mineral deposits as "blessings," that is, as targets of new conservation measures.[44] As Nicola Bullard, of NGO Focus on the Global South, observes, "The obstacles to be overcome are tremendous. Bolivia is still deeply embedded in an international division of labor dating back to sixteenth century colonialism, consigned to providing cheap labor, land, and resources to the rest of the world," despite the mobilization of the Bolivian populace for social and environmental justice.[45]

Nevertheless, for Arturo Escobar, this "biocentric turn" exemplifies the civilizational transformation imagined by emerging **"transition discourses."** Such discourses stem from a variety of social movements, and traverse the fields of culture, ecology, religion and spirituality, and alternative science (such as living systems and complexity). They invoke a transition, in Thomas Berry's words: "from the period when humans were a disruptive force on the planet Earth to the period when humans become present to the planet in a manner that is mutually enhancing."[46] Further, the essence of transition discourses is the rejection of the one-world view that informs modern ontology, and is reproduced in the currency of "globalization." Arturo Escobar observes,

> Globalization discourses of all kinds assume that the world is some sort of "global space" that will progressively and inevitably be fully occupied by capitalist modernity. . . . This view of globalization as universal, fully econo-mized, and de-localized is made possible by the immense power of corporations and maintained within manageable levels of dis/order by military might. From its very global conditions are emerging, however, responses and forms of creativity and resistance that make increasingly visible the poverty, pernicious-ness, and destructiveness of this imaginary.[47]

His point is that the world contains multiple ontologies or worldviews, forming a "pluriverse"—as the Zapatistas claimed, "a world where many worlds fit."

CONCLUSION

So—how should we rethink development? In the first place it is necessary to underline that "development" has been normalized in modern discourse as such a comforting "buzz" word[48] that it is difficult to understand it as anything but natural. We inhabit a world in which our experience of social change pivots on a belief in "development." That is, despite modern catastrophes of one kind or another (chemical contamination, displacements, gender violence, labor exploitation, climate change, forms of malnutrition, and so on), "development" itself commands positive association. Today it is symbolized in modern advertising, and experienced through consumption— for the planetary minority with the purchasing power to consume.

And here is the rub: Development is thought of and measured only in terms of the positive side of the material ledger. This offers an unrealistic image of development because wealth accumulation has always depended on access to resources to exploit. And so modern accounting depends on, even if it doesn't measure, a negative side of the ledger, whether it is the exploitation of labor or of nature. Just as economic growth measures include clear-cutting forests and oil spill cleanups, so they are also enhanced by labor cost reduction. In this sense "development" is of capitalism, rather than of humans and their relationship with their natural conditions. This does not mean modern capitalism has not brought advances, rather it means its enumerators and evaluators render only a partial account of its development processes.

While there have always been counterviews, and counterpractices, these are bubbling to the surface irrepressibly as humans face their greatest challenge in attempting to sustain their earthly and atmospheric environment equitably; hence an emerging Sustainability Project, which registers a growing recognition of our material and temporal limits—from myriad localization movements all the way up to the United Nations.

Thus, in accounting for a shifting development paradigm, the UN Department of Economic and Social Affairs claims that the Millennium Development Goals "rediscovered the insight that market-based growth strategies were insufficient by themselves to solve the problem of widespread poverty," and that the triple crisis of 2008 exposed the flaws of market deregulation, requiring government intervention, which "dealt a blow to the conventional wisdom underpinning the Washington Consensus" (the globalization project). Related to the market-based neoliberal development paradigm, the "aid architecture fragmented, as aid focused on poverty alleviation and social welfare at the expense of promoting broader, transformative development processes." In consequence of what it terms "systemic failures" exposed by the global economic crisis of 2008–2009, the UN Department of Economic and Social Affairs observes, "While the strong desire for quick economic recovery is understandable, getting 'back on track' would mean returning to an unsustainable path of global development. . . . A central concern of the new thinking will be the need for a focus on sustainable development."[49]

Of course the question is, what does sustainable development look like? How should we think about it? Nicola Bullard has a provocative angle:

> Perhaps the greatest challenge we face is not so much how we understand sustainability, but rather how we understand development. . . . Confronted with collapsing ecosystems, toxic environments, soil depletion, climate chaos, disappearing species, and finite fossil fuels, does sustainability even make sense when

there is so little left to sustain? Instead, we should be talking about regenerating and restoring what has been destroyed . . . too much human imagination is channeled into "solving" problems the wrong way. What we lack is the imagination to think about how to live differently, how to unravel the power structures that obstruct change, and how to rethink "development."[50]

Rethinking development is already underway, as we have seen, but not in any coordinated fashion. Rethinking may well require a first step of unthinking "development," as we know it, recognizing values routinely discounted in conventional development metrics—from reproductive activity in households and communities to ecological balance—values that are far more resilient and sustaining than monetary relations. As above, there are international bodies and myriad social movements already adopting this perspective.

In sum, development futures will be governed by the tensions between the "one world" ontology, symbolized by the descriptor concept "globalization," and the "pluriverse" world view, symbolized by an alternative descriptor, "localization," and its appeal to "cosmopolitan localism." This is not to reproduce a global/local binary, rather it is to juxtapose two distinctive organizing principles in which development is either a homogenizing, or a diversifying, force—with all the democratic and ecological implications. This is the axis around which humans will manage or mismanage the future.

FURTHER READING

Borras, Saturnino M., Jr., Marc Edelman, and Cristóbal Kay, eds. *Transnational Agrarian Movements Confronting Globalization*. Oxford: Wiley-Blackwell, 2008.

Da Costa, Dia. *Development Dramas: Reimagining Rural Political Action in Eastern India*. London, New York, and Delhi, 2010.

Escobar, Arturo. *Territories of Difference: Place, Movements, Life, Redes*. Durham and London: Duke University Press, 2008.

Flannery, Tim. *Now or Never: Why We Must Act Now to End Climate Change and Create a Sustainable Future*. New York: Atlantic Monthly Press, 2009.

Gibson-Graham, J. K. A *Post-Capitalist Politics*. Minneapolis and London: University of Minnesota Press, 2006.

Latouche, Serge. *Farewell to Growth*. Cambridge: Polity, 2009.

Patel, Raj. *The Value of Nothing: How to Reshape Market Society and Redefine Democracy*. London: Portobello Books, 2009.

Santos, Boaventura de Sousa, ed. 2007. *Another Knowledge Is Possible*. London: Verso, 2007.

Turney, Jon. *The Rough Guide to the Future*. London: Rough Guides, 2010.

Notes

Chapter 1. Development: Theory and Reality

1. Watts (2011a:10).
2. Cowan and Shenton (1996).
3. Mitchell (1991: 68–75, 96).
4. Smith (1776/1904).
5. Polanyi (1944/2001).
6. Rostow (1960).
7. Singer (1950), Prebisch (1950), Lenin (1916/1997).
8. Frank (1970: 5, 7).
9. Wallerstein (1974).
10. Friedman (2005:383). (Nonetheless this sector provides only 0.2 percent of India's jobs.)
11. Wallerstein (1988).
12. Huntington (2000: 146).
13. Sachs (2005).
14. Amin (2003:2).
15. Badgeley et al. (2007).
16. McMichael (2010).
17. UNDP 2011a.
18. UNDP 2011b.
19. Millennium Ecosystem Assessment (2005).
20. Raudsepp-Hearne et al. (2010: 579, 576).
21. Cooper (1997: 66–67); Davis (2001); Wolf (1969).
22. Marx (1965).
23. Polanyi (1944/2001).
24. Brecher, Costello, and Smith (2000).
25. Held and Kaya (2007: 1, 13).
26. The Economist (2010); Sengupta (2009).
27. Barnet and Cavanagh (1994: 383); Crossette (1997).
28. Galeano (2000: 25).
29. http://wikipedia.org/wiki/Coltan.
30. Chan (2011: 19).
31. Lang and Heasman (2004: 240).
32. Lang and Heasman (2004: 240–241).
33. Lang and Heasman (2004: 241).
34. Lawrence (2011).
35. World Institute for Development Economics Research (2006).
36. Hamilton (2003: 28–30).

Chapter 2. Instituting the Development Project

1. Davidson (1992: 83, 99–101).
2. Quoted in Rist (1997: 58).
3. Bunker (1985).
4. Gupta (1998: 309).

5. Friedmann (1999: 39).
6. Bujra (1992: 146).
7. Quoted in Stavrianos (1981: 247).
8. Day (2010: 25).
9. McMichael (1985).
10. Ali (2002: 168).
11. Chirot (1977: 124).
12. Davis (2001: 26, 299, 315).
13. Davis (2001: 327).
14. Davis (2001: 328–329).
15. Davis (2001: 332–335).
16. Wolf (1982: 369, 377).
17. Mitchell (1991: 175).
18. Cooper and Stoler (1997).
19. James (1963).
20. Memmi (1967: 74).
21. Fanon (1967: 254–255).
22. F. Cooper (1997: 66–67).
23. Stavrianos (1981: 624).
24. Quoted in Clarke and Barlow (1997: 9).

25. Duncan (1996: 120).
26. Adams (1993: 2–3, 6–7).
27. Quoted in Esteva (1992: 6).
28. Quoted in Davidson (1992: 167).
29. Esteva (1992: 7).
30. Rist (1997: 79).
31. Ake (1996: 36).
32. Cited in F. Cooper (1997: 79).
33. Rostow (1960).
34. Sachs (1999: 9).
35. Quoted in Hettne (1990: 3).
36. Quoted in Dube (1988: 16).
37. Bose (1997: 153).
38. Lehman (1990: 5–6).
39. Lehman (1990: 5–6).
40. Kemp (1989: 162–165).
41. Cardoso and Faletto (1979: 129–131).

Chapter 3. The Development Project: International Framework

1. Block (1977: 76–77).
2. Quoted in Brett (1985: 106–107).
3. Quoted in Kolko (1988: 17).
4. Wood (1986: 38–61).
5. Magdoff (1969: 124).
6. Rich (1994: 72).
7. Woods (2006: 207).
8. Rich (1994: 58); George and Sabelli (1994: 15).
9. Rich (1994: 73).
10. Rich (1994: 75).
11. Adams (1993: 68–69).
12. Quoted in Magdoff (1969: 54).
13. Magdoff (1969: 124); Chirot (1977: 164–165).
14. Quoted in Williams (1981: 6–57).

15. Brett (1985: 209); Wood (1986: 73); Rist (1997: 88).
16. Brett (1985: 209); Wood (1986: 73).
17. Adams (1993: 73).
18. Rich (1994: 84).
19. Harris (1987: 28).
20. The term *newly industrializing countries* (NICs) was coined by the Organisation for Economic Co-operation and Development in 1979, and it included four southern European countries: Spain, Portugal, Yugoslavia, and Greece. The common attributes of NICs were rapid penetration of the world market with manufactured exports; a rising share of industrial employment; and an increase in real gross domestic product per

capita relative to the First World. See Hoogvelt (1987: 25).

21. Brett (1985: 185–186).

22. Brett (1985: 188).

23. Knox and Agnew (1994: 347).

24. Hoogvelt (1987: 64).

25. Knox and Agnew (1994: 331). (Between 1975 and 1989, this group enlarged to include China, South Africa, Thailand, and Taiwan; Argentina dropped out.)

26. Martin and Schumann (1997: 100–101).

27. Quoted in Brett (1985: 188).

28. Harris (1987: 102).

29. Grigg (1993: 251).

30. Revel and Riboud (1986: 43–44).

31. Grigg (1993: 243–244); Bradley and Carter (1989: 104). Self-sufficiency measures do not necessarily reveal the state of nutrition in a country or region, as a country—for example, Japan—may have a low self-sufficiency because its population eats an affluent diet, which depends on imports.

32. Friedmann (1982).

33. Quoted in Magdoff (1969: 135).

34. Dudley and Sandilands (1975).

35. Friedmann (1990: 20).

36. Perkins (1997).

37. Quoted in George (1977: 170).

38. Friedmann (1990: 20); H. Friedmann (1992: 373).

39. McMichael and Raynolds (1994: 322). The terms *peasant foods* and *wage foods* are from de Janvry (1981).

40. Segelken (1995: 5).

41. Quoted in Briscoe (2002: 182–183).

42. Rifkin (1992: 229–230).

43. Wessel (1983: 158).

44. Berlan (1991: 126–127); see also Dixon (2002).

45. Kimbrell (2002: 16).

46. Burbach and Flynn (1980: 66); George (1977: 171).

47. Quoted in George (1977: 171–172).

48. H. Friedmann (1992: 377).

49. Gupta (1998: 53, 58–59).

50. Kloppenburg (1988: xiv).

51. Gupta (1998: 54); Busch and Lacy (1983).

52. Gupta (1998: 54–56).

53. Patnaik (2003: 13).

54. Gupta (1998: 50).

55. Patel (2007: 146–147).

56. Cleaver (1977: 17); Walker (2004: 185).

57. Cleaver (1977: 28).

58. Vandana Shiva, quoted in Newman (2006: 2).

59. Quoted in Gupta (1998: 4).

60. Shiva (1997: 50–51); Barndt (2002: 38–39).

61. Newman (2006: 1).

62. Dalrymple (1985: 1069); Andrae and Beckman (1985); Raikes (1988).

63. George (1977: 174–175).

64. Griffin (1974); Pearse (1980); Byres (1981); Sanderson (1986a); Dhanagare (1988); Raikes (1988); Llambi (1990).

65. Lipton (1977).

66. McMichael and Kim (1994); Araghi (1995).

67. Grigg (1993: 103–104, 185); Araghi (1995).

68. Deere and León (2001: 332).

69. Rich (1994: 95, 155).

70. Rich (1994: 91, 97); Feder (1983: 222).

71. Davis (2006).

Chapter 4. Globalizing Developments

1. Arrighi (1994: 68).
2. Gereffi (1989).
3. Cf. Evans (1995).
4. Cf. Barndt (2002).
5. Hoogvelt (1987: 26–31). At the same time, as a consequence of import-substitution industrialization and the buoyancy of the export-oriented industrialization strategy in the 1970s, the composition of imports mainly from the First World moved from manufactured consumer goods to capital goods.
6. Landsberg (1979: 52, 54).
7. See Gereffi (1994).
8. Quoted in Baird and McCaughan (1979: 130).
9. Baird and McCaughan (1979: 130–132); Bernard (1996). For an excellent and detailed study of the *maquiladora* industry, see Sklair (1989).
10. French (2000: 83–85).
11. Henderson (1991: 3).
12. Barnet and Cavanagh (1994: 300); Dicken (1998: 131); Ellwood (2001: 68): Boyenge (2007: 1).
13. Fuentes and Ehrenreich (1983).
14. Ibid.
15. Elson and Pearson (1981:91).
16. On the gendered restructuring of the world labor force, see Mies (1991); Benería and Feldman (1992).
17. Perrons (2005: 100); Baird and McCaughan (1979); *Instituto Nacional de Estadística Geografía e informática* (2004).
18. Perrons (2005: 100).
19. Baird and McCaughan (1979: 135–36).
20. Grossman (1979).
21. Baird and McCaughan (1979: 135).
22. Hobsbawm (1992: 56); Araghi (1999).
23. Davis (2006).
24. *Pacific Basin Reports* (August 1973), quoted in NACLA (1977: 171).
25. Fröbel, Heinrichs, and Kreye (1979: 34–36).
26. Henderson (1991: 54).
27. Korzeniewicz (1994: 261).
28. Henderson (1991).
29. *The Economist* (June 3, 1995: 59); "Slavery in the 21st Century" (2001: 8).
30. Moody (1999: 183, 188).
31. Lang and Hines (1993: 24); Holusha (1996).
32. Woodall (1994: 24); Martin and Schumann (1997: 100–101).
33. Milbank (1994: A1, A6).
34. Cited in Lewin (1995: A5).
35. *The Nation* (November 8, 1993: 3).
36. Schoenberger (1994: 59).
37. Daly and Logan (1989: 13); Schoenberger (1994: 59–61); Chossudovsky (1997: 87–88); Herbert (1996).
38. Hayden (2003).
39. Sanderson (1986b); Raynolds et al. (1993); Raynolds (1994).
40. Friedland (1994).
41. http://web.unfpa.org/intercenter/food/womenas.htm.
42. Friedmann (1991).
43. P. McMichael (1993a).
44. Watts (1994: 52–53).
45. Goss et al. (2000).
46. *The Economist* (June 3, 1995: 59).
47. Reardon and Timmer (2005: 35–37).

48. Collins (1995).
49. Strange (1994: 112).
50. Crook (1992: 10).
51. Helleiner (1996: 111–119).
52. Strange (1994: 107).
53. *The New Internationalist* (August 1993: 18); Kolko (1988: 24).
54. *Debt Crisis Network* (1986: 25).
55. Kolko (1988: 26).
56. Roodman (2001: 21); George (1988: 33).
57. Lissakers (1993: 66).
58. Roodman (2001: 26).
59. Lissakers (1993: 59).

Chapter 5. Instituting the Globalization Project

1. Hoogvelt (1987: 58).
2. Pilger (2002: 28).
3. Pilger (2002: 26–39).
4. Quoted in Magdoff (1969: 53).
5. Quoted in Wood (1986: 197).
6. Quoted in Adams (1993: 123).
7. Rist (1997: 152–153).
8. See Hoogvelt (1987: 87–95).
9. Quoted in Saul (2005: 209).
10. Ruggiero (2000: xiii, xv).
11. Roodman (2001: 21).
12. Lissakers (1993: 67).
13. A. Singh (1992: 141).
14. A. Singh (1992: 144).
15. Quoted in Roodman (2001: 30).
16. Barkin (1990:104–105).
17. Quoted in Helleiner (1996: 177).
18. George (1988: 41, 49).
19. Quoted in Roodman (2001: 35).
20. Kohl and Farthing (2006: 62, 72); Graham (1994); Beneria (2003: 55).
21. de la Rocha (1994: 270–271).
22. Barkin (1990: 101, 103).
23. George (1988: 139, 143).
24. Cheru (1989: 24, 27–28, 41–42).
25. Cheru (1989: 24, 27–28, 41–42); Redding (2000).
26. Rich (1994: 186–187).
27. A. Singh (1992: 138–139, 147–148).
28. Bello et al. (1994).
29. George (1992: 97).
30. Cox (1987: 301).
31. Calculated from Crook (1993: 16); Avery (1994: 95); Hoogvelt (1997: 138).
32. Crook (1992: 9).
33. Crook (1993: 16).
34. Canak (1989).
35. Beckman (1992: 99).
36. Sachs (1998: 17).
37. Kagarlitsky (1995); Klein (2007); Kolko (1988: 278–296).
38. Quoted in Saul (2005: 209).
39. Ruggiero (2000: xiii, xv).
40. The South Centre (1993: 13). Emphasis added.
41. Cahn (1993: 161, 163); Rich (1994); Corbridge (1993: 127).
42. Ricardo (1951).
43. Noreena Hertz, quoted in Collins (2007: 179).
44. Barnet and Cavanagh (1994: 236).
45. Klare (2002: 14–17).
46. George (1992: 11).
47. Nash (1994: C4): Bello et al. (1994: 59).
48. Rich (1994: 188).
49. Quoted in Bello et al. (1994: 63).

50. Rich (1994: 188).

51. Denny (2002: 6).

52. Black (2002: 62).

53. McMichael (1993b).

54. Adams (1993: 196–197).

55. Middleton et al. (1993: 127–129).

56. Quoted in Watkins (1991: 44).

57. Quoted in Ritchie (1993: n. 25).

58. Quoted in Wallach and Sforza (1999: x).

59. Quoted in Ransom (2001a: 27).

60. Quoted in Wallach and Woodall (2004: 219).

61. Quoted in Wallach and Sforza (1999: x).

62. Ritchie (1999).

63. Lehman and Krebs (1996); Gorelick (2000: 28–30); Madeley (2000: 75); Carlsen (2003).

64. McMichael (2005).

65. LeQuesne (1997).

66. Quoted in Bailey (2000); Murphy (1999: 3).

67. Quoted in Madeley (2000: 79).

68. Salmon (2001: 22).

69. Clarke and Barlow (1997: 21).

70. Quoted in Schott (2000: 237).

71. Moran (2000: 235).

72. Moran (2000: 224–226).

73. Dawkins (2000).

74. Tuxill (1999).

75. ActionAid (2000: 2).

76. Madden and Madeley (1993: 17).

77. Quoted in Weissman (1991: 337).

78. Greenfield (1999).

79. Clarke (2001).

80. Clarke (2001).

81. Wallach (2003).

82. Watkins (2002: 21).

Chapter 6. The Globalization Project in Practice

1. United Nations Development Programme (1997).

2. Quoted in Saul (2005: 157).

3. Woods (2006: 164).

4. Woods (2006: 168).

5. Wolfensohn (2000).

6. Narayan et al. (2002); Rademacher and Patel (2002).

7. Woods (2006: 168).

8. Fraser (2005: 317).

9. Fraser (2005: 318).

10. Quoted in Weber (2004: 197).

11. Harrison (2004).

12. Weber (2004: 197).

13. Ferguson (2006: 102–103).

14. Quoted in Fraser (2005: 336).

15. Goldman (2005: 229–230).

16. Abrahamsen (2004: 186).

17. Fraser (2005: 332).

18. Elyachar (2005).

19. See www.uncdf.org.

20. Bond (2006: 82–83).

21. Diokno-Pascual (2003).

22. Iriart and Waitzkin (2004).

23. Perrons (2005: 169).

24. Robinson (2004: 18).

25. Woodall (1994: 24); Martin and Schumann (1997: 100–01); Thompson (2005).

26. Friedman (2000: 52); Greenlees (2006).

27. Giridharadas (2007b).

28. Caulkin (2007).

29. Harding (2001: 23).

30. Tripathi (2004); Leader (2004); Müller and Patel (2004).

31. Davis (2006: 172).

32. Watkins (2006).

33. Bunsha (2006).

34. Chan (1996).

35. Barboza (2004: C3).

36. Eyferth et al. (2003).

37. Gereffi (1994).

38. Dugger (2004).

39. Busch and Bain (2004).

40. Dolan and Humphrey (2000: 167).

41. Dolan (2004).

42. Marsden (2003: 30, 56–57).

43. Bauman (2004).

44. Saul (2005: 146).

45. Kennedy (2001).

46. Davis (2006: 169, 199).

47. Quoted in ActionAid (2004: 11).

48. Parrott and Marsden (2002: 5, 62).

49. *Vía Campesina* (2000).

50. Quoted in Paringaux (2001: 4).

51. Patel and Delwiche (2002a: 2).

52. Attali (1991: 5, 14).

53. Richburg (2002:29).

54. Hochschild (2003).

55. Enzenburger (1994: 112); www.unfpa.org/modules/factsheets/emergencies_overview .htm.

56. Montalbano (1991: H7); Ride (1998: 9).

57. World Bank Press Release No: 2003/266/S.

58. World Bank (2011).

59. Thompson (2002b: A3); Perlez (2002: 10); *The Economist* (February 23, 2002: 42); DeParle (2007).

60. DeParle (2007).

61. Tan (1991a).

62. Ball (1990).

63. Tan (1991b).

64. MacShane (1991).

65. Quoted in Perrons (2005: 220).

66. Dawson (2006: 135); Uchitelle (2007). Mize and Swords (2010).

67. Sadasivam (1997: 636).

68. McDougall (2007).

69. Davis (2006: 23); Vidal (2004: 18).

70. Davis (2006: 1–2).

71. Reich (1991: 42).

72. Boyd (2006: 491, 495, 497).

73. Harvey (2005: 127). Boyd (2006: 493–494).

74. Chen and Wu (2006: 205).

75. ActionAid (2004: 35–36, 40).

76. de Soto (1990: 11).

77. Sharma (2000: 78–79).

78. Menon (2010: 152).

79. Cheru (1989: 8, 19).

80. LaTouche (1993: 130).

81. de la Rocha (1994).

82. Esteva (1992: 21).

83. Rankin (2001: 32).

84. Quoted in Davis (2006: 184).

85. Davis (2006: 190).

86. Giridharadas (2007a: 3).

87. Davis (2006: 200–201).

88. Harvey (2003).

89. Mamdani (2003).

90. Davidson (1992: 206, 257).

91. Bond (2001: 53); Mamdani (2003).

92. Mamdani (1996: 17–20).

93. Maathai (2010: 184).

94. Ferguson (2006: 41, 12, 101).

95. Ferguson (2006: 198–199).

96. Ferguson (2006: 204).

97. Berthelot (2005: 10).

98. Arrighi (2002: 5).

99. Hawkins (1998: I); *The Economist* (June 26, 1999: 23–25); Bond (2006: 39, 42, 51, 106).

100. Patel (2002b).

101. Bond (2002).

102. Dugger (2010).

103. Bond (2006: 58).

104. Ferguson (2006: 194).

105. Harvey (2005: 139); Watts (2005–2006: 36).

106. Elliott (2007: 23).

107. McGreal (2006–2007: 6); Brautigam (2009).

108. All quoted in French (2010).

109. McGreal (2006–07:6); Muchena (2006: 23).

110. Quoted in Muchena (2006: 23).

111. McGreal (2006–07: 6).

112. Lee (2009: 652).

113. Bond (2006: 60).

114. Muchena (2006: 24–25).

115. Quoted in Elliott (2007: 23).

116. Bond (2006: 74); Turner (2007).

117. Renner (2002: 18).

Chapter 7. Global Countermovements

1. Perrons (2005: 276).

2. A. J. McMichael (1993: 51); Carson (1962).

3. Harrison (1993: 54).

4. See A. J. McMichael (1993).

5. Quoted in Abramovitz (1999: 12).

6. Abramovitz (1999: 18–19).

7. Amin et al. (1990).

8. http://www.un-documents.net/wced-ocf.htm.

9. Stewart (1994: 108–109).

10. Kothari and Parajuli (1993: 233).

11. Quoted in Rich (1994: 197).

12. Quoted in Middleton et al. (1993: 19).

13. Quoted in J. Friedmann (1992: 123).

14. Rich (1994: 244–245).

15. Middleton et al. (1993: 25).

16. Tautz (1997); Menotti (1998: 352–362; 1999: 181).

17. Hildyard (1993: 32–34).

18. Chossudovsky (1997: 187–188).

19. Colchester (1994: 71–72).

20. Quoted in Colchester (1994: 72).

21. Quoted in Colchester (1994: 78).

22. Colchester (1994: 83, 88).

23. Lohmann (1993: 10).

24. Quoted in Colchester (1994: 89).

25. Rau (1991: 156–157, 160).

26. Quoted in George and Sabelli (1994: 170).

27. Van der Gaag (2004: 15).

28. Gita Sen, quoted in Moghadam (2005a: 103).

29. Quoted Moghadam (2005a: 73).

30. Quoted in Moghadam (2005a: 75–76).

31. Harcourt (1994: 4).

32. Jahan (1995: 13).

33. Razavi and Miller (1995: 3).

34. Razavi and Miller (1995).

35. Sadasivam (1997: 647–648).

36. Moghadam (2005a: 14–17, 95).

37. Quoted in Moghadam (2005a: 108).

38. Elson (1993: 241).

39. Sadasivam (1997: 636).

40. Quoted in Moghadam (2005a: 112).

41. Harcourt (1994).
42. Sachs (2005: 11–12).
43. Enloe (2004: 59–60).
44. Fussell (2000).
45. Benería (2003: 126).
46. Collins (2003: 164–165).
47. Jackson (1993: 1949).
48. Rocheleau (1991).
49. Wacker (1994: 135–139).
50. Boyd (1998).
51. "Battle of the Bulge" (1994: 25).
52. Robey et al., quoted in Stevens (1994: A8).
53. Chira (1994: A12).
54. Quoted in Crossette (1994: A8).
55. Bello (1992–1993: 5).
56. Sen (1994: 221).
57. Quoted in Hedges (1994: A10).
58. Benería (1992).
59. Quoted in Jahan (1995: 77).
60. Moghadam et al. (2005b: 401), emphasis added.
61. Bunting (2011: 44).
62. Simons (1999: A1, A6); Moghadam (1993).
63. Coomaraswamy (2001).
64. Crossette (1998a: A14).
65. Moghadam (2005b: 203).
66. Sachs (1992a: 112).
67. Held (1995).
68. Fox (1994).
69. Communiqués No. 1, 22, quoted in AVA 42, 31 (1994: 1).
70. "Food and Farming" (2003: 20); Ainger (2003: 10–11).
71. http://www.viacampesina.org/en/index.php?Itemid=44; Desmarais (2007: 6–17).
72. http://ns.rds.org.hn/via/theme.bio diversity.htm.
73. Quoted in Ainger (2003: 11).
74. Holt-Giménez (2006).
75. http://ns.rds.org.hn/via (Seattle Declaration, December 3, 1999).
76. http://ns.rds.org.hn/via/themeagrarian.htm.
77. www.mstbrazil.org/Economic Model.html.
78. Article 184, quoted in Lappé and Lappé (2002: 70).
79. Flavio de Almeida and Sanchez (2000).
80. Quoted in Dias Martins (2000).
81. Lappé and Lappé (2002: 86–87).
82. Quoted in Orlanda Pinnasi et al. (2000).
83. Mark (2001).

Chapter 8. The Globalization Project in Crisis

1. Stancil (2010).
2. George (2010: 100–101).
3. Wolfensohn (2000).
4. UNDESA (2010b: 11).
5. Payne and Phillips (2010: 161).
6. Pieterse (2002: 1033).
7. Roy (2010).
8. Quoted in Roy (2010: 31).
9. Yunus (2011: A19).
10. Bunting (2010c).
11. Elyachar (2005: 29).
12. Menon (2001); Rankin (2001); Elyachar (2005).
13. Cons and Paprocki (2010: 647).
14. Quoted in Roy (2010: 27).
15. Bateman (2010).
16. *The Observer,* September 10, 2006.

17. Shiva (2003: 115).

18. Woods (2006: 165).

19. http://en.wikipedia.org/wiki/ Bank_of_the_South.

20. Sader (2008: 6).

21. Sader (2008).

22. Sekler (2009: 63–64).

23. Sader (2009: 178).

24. Harnecker (2010: 37, 58).

25. Eviatar (2006:5).

26. Maybarduk (2004).

27. Parenti (2005: 17).

28. Séréni (2007: 12).

29. Paranagua (2007: 27).

30. Gott (2006: 33).

31. Landsberg (2010).

32. Tran (2011).

33. Tran (2011); Piot (2011).

34. Abderrahim (2011); *Guardian* reporters (2011).

35. Gibson (2011).

36. Benin (2011: 8).

37. Mitchell (1991).

38. Gibson (2011).

39. Gresh (2011: 1).

40. Amar (2011).

41. Shenker (2011: 18).

42. Quoted in Morrow (2011: A10).

43. Coronil (1997).

44. Schneider (2011: 17).

45. Rozhnov (2010).

46. Wolf (2010a: 7).

47. George (2010: 84).

48. Hervieu (2011: 11).

49. Glennie (2011: 44).

50. Danglin (2011: 11).

51. Therborn (2011: 51)

52. Therborn (2011: 137).

53. Therborn (2011: 52–53).

54. Kotkin (2007: 4).

55. Jha (2010: 11).

56. Bradsher (2002: A1, A8); Jha (2010: 30).

57. Jha (2010: 33).

58. Bobin (2006: 17).

59. Jha (2010: 32).

60. Bulard (2006: 6).

61. Barboza (2006: 1); Rocca (2007: 10); Harvey (2005: 148–149); Wong (2010); Lee (2009).

62. Branigan (2009: 17).

63. Pearlstein (2011: 20).

64. Bradsher (2006).

65. Bradsher (2006).

66. Gow (2007).

67. Bellman (2010b: B1).

68. Ramesh (2006).

69. Sharma (2007).

70. Bellman (2010a: B1).

71. Saul (2005: 205).

72. Jha (2010: 357).

73. Polgreen (2010: A6, A9).

74. Bidwai (2007).

75. *The Economist* (2010: 77); J. Venkatesan (2010).

76. Lee (2008: 15).

77. Jha (2010: 54).

78. Brown (2001: 19).

79. Tyler (1994: D8); Brown (1994: 19).

80. Chen and Wu (2006: ix, xi).

81. Huang (2011); Arrighi (2007).

82. Saul (2005: 205).

83. Jha (2010: 17).

84. George (2010: 34).

85. George (2010: 41–42).

86. Mitchell (2011: 12).

87. Elliott (2010: 18).

88. Bunting (2010b: 21).

89. Mitchell (2011: 11).

90. Habermas (2010: 18).

91. Bretton Woods Project (2011).

92. Bretton Woods Project (2011).

93. López and Rodríguez (2011: 24).

94. Erlanger (2010).

95. *New York Times* editorial, April 10, 2008.

96. Myers and Kent (2003).

97. Shattuck (2008); McMichael (2009b).

98. Vidal (2007b).

99. Evans (2009: 96).

100. Patnaik (2008); McMichael (2009b).

101. RajPatel.org, January 31, 2011.

102. Davis (2010: 39).

103. Naeem (2009: 64–67).

104. Jha (2008: 3).

105. Black (2008).

106. Wheatley (2010: 24).

107. Lawrence (2010: 29).

108. Nossiter (2010: A18).

109. Guardian editorial (2010).

110. Roberts and Park (2007: 9).

111. Monbiot (2006: 15, 21).

112. Monbiot (2006: 21).

113. Roberts and Parks (2007: 9–10).

114. Quoted in Bond (2010).

115. Rosenthal (2009: A1).

116. Pilkington (2009: 27).

117. Monbiot (2006: 9).

118. Quoted in Yardley (2007: A9).

119. Yardley (2007:A9).

120. Green-Weiskel (2011).

121. Monbiot (2006: 51).

122. Quoted in Wolf (2010b).

123. Warde (2008: 1–2).

Chapter 9. The Sustainability Project

1. United Nations Development Report (2011b).

2. Lovelock (2007: 15, 17).

3. Barlow (1999); Clarke (2001); Elyachar (2005); Hochschild (2003).

4. McMurtry (2002).

5. Quoted in Davis (2010: 31).

6. McKibben (2010:xiii).

7. Quoted in Toulmin (2009: 2).

8. Hertsgard (2004).

9. Broder (2009).

10. Quoted in McMichael (2009a: 248).

11. UNFCCC (2001: 12).

12. Hicks et al. (2008: 53).

13. Klein et al. (2008: 4).

14. Hicks et al. (2009: 259).

15. Vidal (2008:1).

16. Toulmin (2009: 27).

17. Toulmin (2009: 29–30).

18. ActionAid (2007: 21).

19. ActionAid (2008: 28).

20. Klein et al. (2008: 2).

21. Schaar (2008: 1).

22. ETC Group (2008: 3).

23. Weiss (2008: 4).

24. Palmer (2006).

25. Lim (2008).

26. Reij (2006).

27. DDS Community Media Trust et al. (2008: 35).

28. UNMA (2005: 20).

29. UNMA (2005: 1).

30. Jowit (2010: 17).

31. Martinez-Alier (2002).

32. UNMA (2005: 20). Emphasis added.

33. UNMA (2005: 24).

34. UNMA (2005: 22).

35. Shiva (2008: 19).

36. IAASTD (2008: 20).

37. IAASTD (2008: 19).

38. IAASTD (2008: 17–18).

39. Quoted in Leahy (2008).

40. Altieri and Toledo (2011: 596).

41. IAASTD (2008: 5, 7).

42. http://www.ohchr.org/en/
NewsEvents/Pages/DisplayNews
.aspx?NewsID=10819&LangID=E

43. Stanhill (1990); Pretty and
Hine (2001); Pretty, Morison, and
Hine (2003): Halberg et al. (2005);
Badgley et al. (2007).

44. Badgley et al. (2007).

45. Brahic (2007).

46. Badgley and Perfecto (2007:
80, 82).

47. Quoted in Brahic (2007).

48. Altieri (2002).

49. Altieri and Toledo (2011:
588).

50. Altieri and Nicholls (2008).

51. Altieri and Toledo (2011:
606); Van der Ploeg (2009); Isakson
(2010).

52. Buck and Scherr (2011: 21).

53. FAO (2008).

54. World Bank (2007: 1).

55. Holt-Giménez and Kenfield
(2008: 3).

56. Quoted in IFAD (2009).

57. World Bank (2007: 138, 8).

58. Mittal (2009).

59. Shiva (1991).

60. Tenkouano (2011: 29, 36–37).

61. Quoted in Mittal (2009: 4).
Emphasis added.

62. Maathai (2010: 236).

63. UNCTAD and UNEP
(2008: 236).

64. Mittal (2009: 5).

65. McMichael (2009c: 239fn).

66. World Bank (2007: 16).

67. Bulatlat (2011).

68. GMA News (2011).

69. Bulatlat (2011).

70. GRAIN (2010).

71. Henriques (2008).

72. Quoted in Vidal (2010).

73. Rice (2009).

74. Rice (2010).

75. Quoted in Daniel (2009: 28).

76. Quoted in Daniel (2009: 20).

77. Gaia Foundation et al.
(2008: 4).

78. World Bank (2010).

79. Li (2011: 284).

80. Holt-Giménez (2007: 10).

81. Orth (2007: 51).

82. World Bank (2007), Policy
Brief, "Biofuels: The Promise and the
Risks."

83. Ferrett (2007).

84. de Schutter (2010).

85. ETC (2007: 2).

86. For details see ETC (2007),
GRAIN (2007), and McMichael
(2009d).

87. Holt-Giménez (2007).

88. GRAIN (2007: 6).

89. Rainforest Action Network
(2007).

90. Quoted in Rainforest Action
Network (2007).

91. Ibid.

92. Fargione et al. (2008).

93. Crutzen et al. (2007).

94. Colchester et al. (2007: 54).

95. Lütkenhorst (2010: 18).

96. Noble (2007).

97. Monbiot (2006: 46).

98. Goldemberg and Lucon
(2010: 18).

99. Tanaka (2010: 20–21).

100. Jha (2010: 28).

101. D'Armagnac (2010: 31)

102. Jha (2010: 28).

103. Goldemberg and Lucon
(2010: 18).

104. Yumkella and Srivastava
2010: 26.

105. Shi (2010: 35).

106. Arthur (2010: 31).

107. Eilperin (2010: 18).

108. Flannery (2009: 57); Eilperin
(2010: 18).

109. Dreyfuss (2010: 14).
110. Krauss (2010: D7).
111. Oster (2009).
112. Oster (2009); Harney (2009).
113. Krauss (2010).
114. Quoted in Krauss (2010).

115. Flannery (2009: 100).
116. Ibid., 103.
117. Quoted in Flannery (2009: 116).
118. Quoted in Flannery (2009: 117–118).

Chapter 10. Rethinking Development

1. The Commission is based in France and represents the United States, France, India, and the United Kingdom. Its principals were Joseph Stiglitz (Columbia University), Amartya Sen (Harvard University), and Jean-Paul Fitoussi (IEP). Quotes from 7–9, 12 of the Executive Summary. Available at www.stiglitz-sen-fitoussi.fr.
2. UNDP (2010: 19).
3. Quoted in Press (2011: 25).
4. See, e.g., Martha Nussbaum (2011a).
5. Nussbaum (2011b: 23).
6. Oxfam (2009).
7. Kristoff (2010).
8. Wade (2010).
9. Hale (2011); Sumner (2010).
10. Sundaram (2010).
11. Sumner (2010).
12. Halperin (2005).
13. Smith (2011: 6).
14. UNDESA (2010a: viii).
15. Sundaram (2010: 39).
16. Cameron and Palan (2004).
17. Payne and Phillips (2010: 165–167).
18. Ibid., 168.
19. Robinson (2002: 1062).
20. Hoogvelt (2006: 163).
21. Quoted in Hoogvelt (2006: 163). Emphasis added.
22. Ibid, 163.

23. Ibid., 164.
24. See, e.g., Mosse (2004: 649–650, 662); Baviskar (2005).
25. Oxfam (2009).
26. Hamilton (2003: 56–58).
27. LaTouche (2004: 15).
28. Godoy (2010: 19).
29. Hamilton (2003: 206).
30. Martinez-Alier (2010).
31. Foster (2011).
32. Perkins (2010).
33. Gibson-Graham (2006).
34. Perkins (2010).
35. Jackson (2009: 187).
36. Victor (2010: 370–371).
37. Jackson (2009: 200–201).
38. http://www.transitionnetwork.org/.
39. Southend in Transition (2007).
40. Gibson-Graham (2006: 188, 166).
41. Harlan (2011: 30).
42. Escobar (2011: 138).
43. Ibid.
44. Vidal (2011: 7).
45. Bullard (2011: 141–142).
46. Quoted in Escobar (2011: 138).
47. Escobar (2011: 139).
48. Rist (2007).
49. UNDESA (2010b: ix, xiii, v).
50. Bullard (2011: 141–142).

References

Abderrahim, Kader A. 2011. "Algeria: North African Perestroika Starts Here." *Le Monde Diplomatique*, February: 6.

Abrahamsen, Rita. 2004. "Review Essay: Poverty Reduction or Adjustment by Another Name?" *Review of African Political Economy* 99: 184–87.

Abramovitz, Janet N. 1999. "Nature's Hidden Economy." *World Watch* 11(1): 10–19.

ActionAid. 2000. "Crops and Robbers: Biopiracy and the Patenting of Staple Food Crops." Retrieved from www.actionaid.org.

———. 2004. *Power Hungry: Six Reasons to Regulate Global Food Corporations.* Johannesburg: ActionAid International.

———. 2007. *We Know What We Need: South Asian Women Speak Out on Climate Change.* Retrieved from www.actionaid.org.

———. 2008. *The Time Is NOW: Lessons From Farmers Adapting to Climate Change.* Retrieved from www.actionaid.org.

Adams, Nassau A. 1993. *Worlds Apart: The North–South Divide and the International System.* London: Zed.

Agarwal, Bina. 1988. "Patriarchy and the 'Modernising State': An Introduction." In *Structures of Patriarchy: The State, the Community and the Household,* edited by Bina Agarwal. London: Zed.

Ainger, Katherine. 2003. "The New Peasants' Revolt." *New Internationalist* 353 (January/February): 9–13.

Ake, Claude. 1996. *Democracy and Development in Africa.* Washington, DC: Brookings Institute.

Ali, Tariq. 2002. *The Clash of Fundamentalisms: Crusades, Jihads, and Modernity.* London: Verso.

Alperovitz, Gar. 2003. "Tax the Plutocrats!" *The Nation*, January 27: 15–18.

Altieri, Miguel. 2002. "Agroecology: The Science of Natural Resource Management for Poor Farmers In Marginal Environments." *Agriculture, Ecosystems and Environment*, 93: 1–24.

Altieri, Miguel A., and Clara I. Nicholls. 2008. "Scaling Up Agroecological Approaches for Food Sovereignty in Latin America." *Development*, 51(4): 472–480.

Altieri, Miguel A., and Victor Manuel Toledo. 2011. "The Agroecological Revolution in Latin America: Rescuing Nature, Ensuring Food Sovereignty and empowering

Peasants." *The Journal of Peasant Studies,* 38(3): 587–612.

Amar, Paul. 2011. "Egypt after Mubarak." *The Nation,* May 23: 11–15.

Amenga-Etego, Rudolf. 2003. "Stalling the Big Steal." *New Internationalist* 354: 20–21.

Amin, Samir. 1997. *Capitalism in the Age of Globalization.* London: Zed.

———. 2003. "World Poverty: Pauperization and Capital Accumulation." *Monthly Review,* 55(5): 1–9.

Amin, Samir, Giovanni Arrighi, Andre Gunder Frank, and Immanuel Wallerstein. 1990. *Transforming the Revolution: Social Movements and the World System.* New York: Monthly Review Press.

Apffel-Marglin, Frédérique. 1997. "Counter-Development in the Andes." *The Ecologist* 27(6): 221–224.

Araghi, Farshad. 1995. "Global Depeasantization, 1945–1990." *The Sociological Quarterly* 36(2): 337–368.

———. 1999. "The Great Global Enclosure of Our Times: Peasants and the Agrarian Question at the End of the Twentieth Century." In *Hungry for Profit: The Agribusiness Threat to Farmers, Food, and the Environment,* edited by Fred Magdoff, John Bellamy Foster, and Frederick H. Buttel. New York: Monthly Review Press.

Arrighi, Giovanni. 1994. *The Long Twentieth Century: Money, Power, and the Origins of Our Times.* London: Verso.

———. 2002. "The African Crisis," *New Left Review,* 15: 5–38.

———. 2007. *Adam Smith in Beijing. Lineages of the Twenty-First Century.* London and New York: Verso.

Arthur, Charles. 2010. "Women Entrepreneurs Transforming Bangladesh." *MakingIt,* 2, April: 30–31.

Asthana, Anushka. 2010. "Thousands of Women Fear Loss of Jobs as They Bear Brunt of Cuts." *The Guardian Weekly,* August 13: 13.

Attali, Jacques. 1991. *Millennium: Winners and Losers in the Coming World Order.* New York: Times Books.

Avery, Natalie. 1994. "Stealing from the State." In *50 Years Is Enough: The Case Against the World Bank and the IMF,* edited by Kevin Danaher and Muhammad Yunus. Boston: South End.

Ayittey, George. 2002. "AIDS Scourge Saps Africa's Vitality." *The Financial Gazette,* April 18. Available at www .fingaz.co.zw.

Badgley, Catherine, and Ivette Perfecto. 2007. "Can Organic Agriculture Feed the World?" *Renewable Agriculture and Food Systems,* 22(2): 80–85.

Badgley, C., J. Moghtader, E. Quintero, E. Zakem, M.J., Chappell, K., Aviles-Vazquez, A., Samulon, and I. Perfecto, 2007. "Organic Agriculture and the Global Food Supply," *Renewable Agriculture and Food Systems* 22(2): 86–108.

Bailey, Mark. 2000. "Agricultural Trade and the Livelihoods of Small Farmers." Oxfam GB Discussion Paper No. 3/00, Oxfam, GB Policy Department Oxford, UK. Retrieved from www.oxfam.org.uk/policy/ papers/agricultural_trade/agric.htm.

Baird, Peter, and Ed McCaughan. 1979. *Beyond the Border: Mexico & the*

U.S. Today. New York: North American Congress on Latin America.

Baird, Vanessa. 2002. "Fear Eats the Soul." *New Internationalist,* October: 9–12.

Ball, Rochelle. 1990. "The Process of International Contract Labor Migration from the Philippines: The Case of Filipino Nurses." PhD dissertation, Department of Geography, University of Sydney, Australia.

Barboza, David. 2004. "In Roaring China, Sweaters Are West of Socks City," *The New York Times,* December 24: C1, C3.

———. 2006. "Labor Shortage in China May Lead to Trade Shift," *The New York Times,* April 3: 1.

Barkin, David. 1990. *Distorted Development: Mexico in the World Economy.* Boulder, CO: Westview.

Barlow, Maude. 1999. *Blue Gold.* San Francisco: International Forum on Globalization.

Barndt, Deborah. 1997. "Bio/cultural Diversity and Equity in Post-NAFTA Mexico (or: Tomasita Comes North While Big Mac Goes South)." In *Global Justice, Global Democracy,* edited by Jay Drydyk and Peter Penz. Winnipeg/Halifax: Fernwood.

———. 2002. *Tangled Routes: Women, Work, and Globalization on the Tomato Trail.* New York: Rowman & Littlefield.

Barnet, Richard J., and John Cavanagh. 1994. *Global Dreams: Imperial Corporations and the New World Order.* New York: Touchstone.

Bateman, Milford. 2010. "The Power of the Community," *Making It,* No. 4. Venice: UNIDO.

"Battle of the Bulge." 1994. *The Economist,* September 3: 25.

Bauman, Zygmut. 2004. *Wasted Lives. Modernity and Its Outcasts.* Cambridge: Polity.

Baviskar, Amita. 2005. "The Dream Machine: The Model Development Project and the Remaking of the State." In *Waterscapes: The Cultural Politics of a Natural Resource,* edited by Amita Baviskar. New Delhi: Oxford University Press.

Beams, Nick. 1999. "UN Figures Show: International Production System Developing." Retrieved from www .wsws.org/articles/1999/Oct1999/ un-009.html.

Becker, Elizabeth. 2003. "U.S. Unilateralism Worries Trade Officials." *The New York Times,* March 17: 5.

Beckman, Björn. 1992. "Empowerment or Repression? The World Bank and the Politics of African Adjustment." In *Authoritarianism, Democracy and Adjustment: The Politics of Economic Reform in Africa,* edited by Peter Gibbon, Yusuf Bangura, and Arve Ofstad. Uppsala, Sweden: Nordiska Afrikainstitutet.

Bello, Walden. 1992–1993. "Population and the Environment." *Food First Action Alert,* Winter, 5.

Bello, Walden, with Shea Cunningham and Bill Rau. 1994. *Dark Victory: The United States, Structural Adjustment and Global Poverty.* London: Pluto Press, with Food First and Transnational Institute.

Bellman, Eric. 2010a. "Japan's Exporters Eye Every Rupee." *The Wall Street Journal,* July 7:B1.

———. 2010b. "A New Detroit Rises in India's South." *The Wall Street Journal,* July 9:B1.

Benería, Lourdes. 1992. "Accounting for Women's Work: The Progress of Two Decades." *World Development* 20(11): 1547–1560.

———. 1995. "Response: The Dynamics of Globalization" (Scholarly Controversy: Global Flows of Labor and Capital). *International Labor and Working-Class History* 47: 45–52.

———. 2003. *Gender, Development, and Globalization: Economics as if All People Mattered.* New York: Routledge.

Benería, Lourdes, and Shelley Feldman, eds. 1992. *Unequal Burden: Economic Crises, Persistent Poverty, and Women's Work.* Boulder, CO: Westview.

Benin, Joel. 2011. "Egypt's Workers Rise Up." *The Nation,* March 7/14: 8.

Berlan, Jean-Pierre. 1991. "The Historical Roots of the Present Agricultural Crisis." In *Towards a New Political Economy of Agriculture,* edited by W. Friedland, L. Busch, F. Buttel, and A. Rudy. Boulder, CO: Westview.

Bernard, Mitchell. 1996. "Beyond the Local–Global Divide in the Formation of the Eastern Asian Region." *New Political Economy* 1(3): 335–353.

Berthelot, Jacques. 2005. "The WTO: Food for Thought?" *Le Monde Diplomatique,* December: 10–11.

Bidwai, Praful. 2007. "India: Special Economic Zones on the Backburner." *Inter Press Service,* February 12. Available at www.ips.org.

Black, Maggie. 2002. *The No-Nonsense Guide to International Development.* London: Verso.

Black, Richard. 2008. "Fisheries Waste 'Costs Billions.' " Available at *BBC News,* October 8. http://news.bbc.co.uk/2/hi/science/nature/7660011.stm.

Block, Fred L. 1977. *The Origins of International Economic Disorder: A Study of United States International Monetary Policy from World War II to the Present.* Berkeley: University of California Press.

Bobin, Frédéric. 2006. "Mutually Assured Dependence," *Guardian Weekly,* July 14–20: 17.

Bond, Patrick. 2001. "Radical Rhetoric and the Working Class during Zimbabwean Nationalism's Dying Days." *Journal of World-Systems Research* 7(1): 52–89.

———. 2002. "NEPAD." Retrieved from www.ifg.org/analysis/un/wssd/bondZnet.htm.

———. 2006. *Looting Africa: The Economics of Exploitation.* Pietermaritzburg: University of Kwa-Zulu Natal Press.

———. 2010. "Climate Capitalism Won at Cancun—Everyone Else Loses.' *Transnational Institute,* December. Available at www.tni.org.

Booth, Karen. 1998. "National Mother, Global Whore, and Transnational Femocrats: The Politics of AIDS and the Construction of Women at the World Health Organization." *Feminist Studies* 24(1): 115–139.

Bose, Sugata. 1997. "Instruments and Idioms of Colonial and National Development: India's Historical Experience in Comparative Perspective." In *International*

Development and the Social Sciences, edited by Frederick Cooper and Randall Packard. Berkeley, CA: University of California Press.

Boseley, Sarah. 2007. "Scientists Find Way to Bring Cheap Drugs to Poor Nations." *Guardian Weekly,* January 5–11: 1.

Boyd, Rosalind. 2006. "Labour's Response to the Informalization of Work in the Current Restructuring of Global Capitalism: China, South Korea and South Africa." *Canadian Journal of Development Studies* 27(4): 487–502.

Boyd, Stephanie. 1998. "Secrets and Lies." *The New Internationalist* 303: 16–17.

Boyenge, Jean-Pierre Singa. 2007. *ILO Database on Export Processing Zones.* Geneva: International Labor Office.

Bradley, P. N., and S. E. Carter. 1989. "Food Production and Distribution—and Hunger." In *A World in Crisis? Geographical Perspectives,* edited by R. J. Johnston and P. J. Taylor. Oxford, UK: Blackwell.

Bradsher, Keith. 1995. "White House Moves to Increase Aid to Mexico." *The New York Times,* January 12: D6.

———. 2002. "India Slips Far Behind China, Once Its Closest Rival." *The New York Times,* November 29: A1, A8.

———. 2006. "A Younger India Is Flexing Its Industrial Brawn." *The New York Times,* September 1: 1, C4.

Brahic, Catherine. 2007. "Organic Farming Could Feed the World." *New Scientist,* July 12. Retrieved from http://www.newscientist.com/article/dn12245.

Branigan, Tania. 2009. "China 'Ready to Export Factories,'" *The Guardian Weekly,* December 11: 17.

Brautigam, Deborah. 2009. *The Dragon's Gift: The Real Story of China in Africa.* Oxford: Oxford University Press.

Brecher, Jeremy and Tim Costello. 1994. *Global Village or Global Pillage? Economic Reconstruction from the Bottom Up.* Boston: South End.

Brecher, Jeremy, Tim Costello, and Brendan Smith. 2000. *Globalization From Below: The Power of Solidarity.* Cambridge, MA: South End.

Breman, Jan. 2009. "Myth of the Global Safety Net." *New Left Review,* 59: 29–36.

Brett, E. A. 1985. *The World Economy Since the War: The Politics of Uneven Development.* London: Macmillan.

Bretton Woods Project. 2011. "IMF's Austerity Drive Goes On Despite Failures and Protests." News, June 13. Available at http://www.brettonwoodsproject.org/.

Briscoe, Mark. 2002. "Water: The Untapped Resource." In *The Fatal Harvest Reader: The Tragedy of Industrial Agriculture,* edited by Andrew Kimball. Washington: Island Press.

Broder, John M. 2009. "Climate Change Seen as Threat to U.S. Security." *The New York Times,* August 8.

Brown, Lester R. 1994. "Who Will Feed China?" *World Watch* 7(5): 10–19.

———. 2001. "Bad Tidings on the Wind for Chinese." *Guardian Weekly,* June 7–13: 19.

Brown, Michael Barratt. 1993. *Fair Trade*. London: Zed.

Buck, Louis E., and Sara J. Scherr. 2011. "Moving Ecoagriculture into the Mainstream." In *State of the World 2011: Innovations that Nourish the Planet*. New York and London: Norton.

Bujra, Janet. 1992. "Diversity in Pre-Capitalist Societies." In *Poverty and Development in the 1990s*, edited by Tim Allen and Allan Thomas. Oxford, UK: Oxford University Press.

Bulard, Martine. 2006. "China Breaks the Iron Rice Bowl." *Guardian Weekly*, January: 6.

Bulatlat. 2011. "Foreign Land Deals: Global Land Grabbing?" June 16. *Food Crisis and the Global Land Grab* Retrieved from http://farmlandgrab.org/post/view/18813.

Bullard, Nicola. 2011. "It's Too Late for Sustainability: What We Need Is System Change." *Development*, 54(2): 141–142.

Bunker, Stephen. 1985. *Underdeveloping the Amazon: Extraction, Unequal Exchange and the Failure of the Modern State*. Urbana, IL: University of Illinois Press.

Bunker, Stephen G., and Paul S. Ciccantell. 2005. *Globalization and the Race for Resources*. Baltimore: Johns Hopkins University Press.

Bunsha, D. 2006. "Rural Resistance." *Frontline* 23(20), October: 1.

Bunting, Madeleine. 2010a. "Promoting Happiness and Cutting Welfare: What a Devious Combination." *The Guardian*, November 28.

———. 2010b. "Cameron's Myth of Happiness." *The Guardian Weekly*, December 3: 21.

———. 2010c. "Microfinance: Development Panacea, or Exorbitant, Ineffective Poverty Trap?" *The Guardian*, December 22. Available at http://www.guardian.co.uk/global-development/poverty-matters/2010/dec/22/microfinance-india-sector-regulated.

———. 2011. "Justice for Women a Work in Progress." *The Guardian Weekly*, July 15: 44.

Burbach, Roger, and Patricia Flynn. 1980. *Agribusiness in the Americas*. New York: Monthly Review Press.

Busch, L., and C. Bain. 2004. "New! Improved? The Transformation of the Global Agrifood System." *Rural Sociology* 69(3): 321–346.

Busch, Lawrence, and William B. Lacy. 1983. *Science, Agriculture, and the Politics of Research*. Boulder, CO: Westview.

Byres, Terry J. 1981. "The New Technology, Class Formation and Class Action in the Indian Countryside." *Journal of Peasant Studies* 8(4): 405–454.

Cahn, Jonathan. 1993. "Challenging the New Imperial Authority: The World Bank and the Democratization of Development." *Harvard Human Rights Journal* 6: 159–194.

Calvo, Dana. 1997. "Tijuana Workers Win Labor Battle." Retrieved from tw-list@essential.org.

Cameron, Angus, and Ronen Palan. 2004. *The Imagined Economies of Globalization*. London: Sage.

Canak, William L. 1989. "Debt, Austerity, and Latin America in the New International Division of Labor." In *Lost Promises: Debt, Austerity, and Development in Latin America*, edited by William L. Canak. Boulder, CO: Westview.

Cardoso, Fernando H., and Enzo Faletto. 1979. *Dependency and Development in Latin America.* Berkeley: University of California Press.

Carlsen, Laura. 2003. "The Mexican Farmers' Movement: Exposing the Myths of Free Trade." *Americas Program Policy Report.* Silver City (NM): Interhemispheric Resource Center. Available at www.americaspolicy.org.

Carson, Rachel. 1962. *Silent Spring.* Boston: Houghton Mifflin.

Caulkin, Simon. 2007. "If Everything Can Be Outsourced, What Is Left?" *Observer,* April 1.

Central Intelligence Agency. 2000. "The Global Infectious Disease Threat and Its Implications for the United States." Retrieved from www.cia.gov/cia/publications/nie/report/nie99–17d .html.

Chan, Anita. 1996. "Boot Camp at the Shoe Factory." *Guardian Weekly,* November 17: 20–21.

Chan, Jenny. 2011. "iSlave." *New Internationalist,* 441. Available at http://www.newint.org/features/2011/04/01/islave-foxconn-suicides-workers/.

Chang, Leslie T. 2008. "Gilded Age, Gilded Cage." *National Geographic,* May.

Chatterjee, Partha. 2001. *Nationalist Thought and the Colonial World.* Minneapolis, MN: University of Minnesota Press.

Chen, Guidi, and Wu Chuntao. 2006. *Will the Boat Sink the Water? The Life of China's Peasants.* New York: Public Affairs.

Cheru, Fantu. 1989. *The Silent Revolution in Africa: Debt, Development and Democracy.* London: Zed.

Chira, Susan. 1994. "Women Campaign for New Plan to Curb the World's Population." *The New York Times,* April 13: A12.

Chirot, Daniel. 1977. *Social Change in the Twentieth Century.* New York: Harcourt Brace Jovanovich.

Chomsky, Noam. 1994. *World Orders Old and New.* New York: Columbia University Press.

Chossudovsky, Michel. 1997. *The Globalisation of Poverty: Impacts of IMF and World Bank Reforms.* Penang: Third World Network.

———. 2003. *The Globalisation of Poverty and the New World Order.* Shanty Bay, ON: Global Outlook.

Chung, Youg-Il. 1990. "The Agricultural Foundation for Korean Industrial Development." In *The Economic Development of Japan and Korea,* edited by Chung Lee and Ippei Yamazawa. New York: Praeger.

Clarke, T., and M. Barlow. 1997. *MAI: The Multilateral Agreement on Investment and the Threat to Canadian Sovereignty.* Toronto: Stoddart.

Clarke, Tony. 2001. "Serving Up the Commons." *Multinational Monitor* 22(4). Retrieved from www.essential.org/monitor/mm2001/01april/corp2.html.

Cleaver, Harry. 1977. "Food, Famine and the International Crisis." *Zerowork* 2: 7–70.

Cohen, Roger. 1998. "High Claims in Spill Betray Depth of Nigerian Poverty." *The New York Times,* September 20: A1, A6.

Colchester, Marcus. 1994. "Sustaining the Forests: The Community-Based Approach in South and Southeast Asia." In *Development & Environment: Sustaining People and Nature,* edited by Dharam Ghai. Oxford, UK: Blackwell.

Colchester, Marcus, et. al. 2007. *Land Is Life: Land Rights and Oil Palm Development in Sarawak.* Moreton-in-Marsh, UK: Forest Peoples' Programme and Perkumpulan Saxit Watch.

Collins, Elizabeth Fuller. 2007. *Indonesia Betrayed: How Development Fails.* Honolulu: University of Hawaii Press.

Collins, Jane. 1995. "Gender and Cheap Labor in Agriculture." In *Food and Agrarian Orders in the World-Economy,* edited by Philip McMichael. Westport, CT: Praeger.

———. 2003. *Threads: Gender, Labor, and Power in the Global Apparel Industry.* Chicago: University of Chicago Press.

Collins, Joseph, and John Lear. 1996. *Chile's Free Market Miracle: A Second Look.* Oakland, CA: Food First Books.

Cons, Jason, and Kasia Paprocki. 2010. "Contested Credit Landscapes: Microcredit, Self-Help and Self-Determination in Rural Bangladesh." *Third World Quarterly,* 31(4): 637–654.

Coomaraswamy, Radhika. 2001. "Different But Free: Cultural Relativism and Women's Rights as Human Rights." In *Religious Fundamentalisms and the Human Rights of Women,* edited by Courtney W. Howland. New York: Palgrave.

Cooper, Frederick. 1997. "Modernizing Bureaucrats, Backward Africans, and the Development Concept." In *International Development and the Social Sciences,* edited by Frederick Cooper and Randall Packard. Berkeley: University of California Press.

Cooper, Frederick and Ann Laura Stoler, eds. 1997. *Tensions of Empire: Colonial Cultures in a Bourgeois World.* Berkeley, CA: University of California Press.

Corbridge, Stuart. 1993. "Ethics in Development Studies: The Example of Debt." In *Beyond the Impasse: New Directions in Development Theory,* edited by Frans J. Schuurman. London: Zed.

Corm, Georges. 2011. "Is This an Arab Spring?" *Le Monde Diplomatique,* April:1, 6–7.

Coronil, Fernando. 1997. *The Magical State: Nature, Money and Modernity in Venezuela.* Chicago: University of Chicago Press.

Cowan, M. P., and R. W. Shenton. 1996. *Doctrines of Development.* London: Routledge Kegan Paul.

Cox, Robert W. 1987. *Production, Power, and World Order: Social Forces in the Making of History.* New York: Columbia University Press.

Crook, Clive. 1992. "Fear of Finance: A Survey of the World Economy." *The Economist,* Special Supplement, September 19: 5–48.

———. 1993. "New Ways to Grow: A Survey of World Finance." *The Economist,* Special Supplement, September 25: 3–22.

Crossette, Barbara. 1994. "A Third-World Effort on Family Planning." *The New York Times,* September 7, A8.

———. 1997. "Kofi Annan's Astonishing Facts!" In *Human Development Report 1997.* New York: United Nations Development Program.

———. 1998. "Women See Key Gains since Talks in Beijing." *The New York Times,* March 8: A14.

Crutzen, P. J., et al. 2007. "N20 Release from Agro-Biofuel Production Negates Global Warming Reduction by Replacing Fossil Fuels." *Atmospheric Chemical Physics Discussion,* 7: 11191–11205.

Dalrymple, D. 1985. "The Development and Adoption of High-Yielding Varieties of Wheat and Rice in Developing Countries." *American Journal of Agricultural Economics* 67: 1067–1073.

Daly, Herman. 1990. "Sustainable Growth: An Impossibility Theorem." *Development,* 3–4: 45–47.

Daly, M. T., and M. I. Logan. 1989. *The Brittle Rim: Finance, Business and the Pacific Region.* Ringwood, Australia: Penguin.

Danglin, François. 2011. "A Model for South-South Alliances." *Le Monde Diplomatique,* March: 11.

Daniel, Shepard. 2009. *The Great Land Grab: Rush for World's Farmland Threatens Food Security for the Poor.* The Oakland Institute.

D'Armagnac, Bertrand. 2010. "Lesson in Wind Power." *The Guardian Weekly,* August 13: 31.

Davidson, Basil. 1992. *The Black Man's Burden: Africa and the Curse of the Nation-State.* New York: Times Books.

Davis, Mike. 2001. *Late Victorian Holocausts: El Nino Famines and the Making of the Third World.* London: Verso.

———. 2005. *The Monster at Our Door: The Global Threat of Avian Flu.* New York and London: The New Press.

———. 2006. *Planet of Slums.* London: Verso.

———. 2010. "Who Will Build the Ark?" *New Left Review,* 61: 29–46.

Dawkins, Kristin. 2000. "Battle Royale of the 21st Century." *Seedling* 17(1): 2–8.

Dawson, Alexander S. 2006. *Third World Dreams: Mexico Since 1989.* Nova Scotia: Fernwood.

Day, Elizabeth. 2010. "Cotton-Pickin' Trade." *The Guardian Weekly,* December 10: 25–27.

DDS Community Media Trust, P. V. Satheesh, and Michel Pimbert. 2009. *Affirming Life and Diversity: Rural Images and Voices on Food Sovereignty in South India.* London: International Institute for Environment and Development, and the Deccan Development Society.

de Castro, Josué. 1969. " Introduction: Not One Latin America." In *Latin American Radicalism,* edited by Irving Louis Horowitz, Josué de Castro, and John Gerassi. New York: Vintage.

Deere, Carmen Diana, and Magdalena León. 2001. *Empowering Women: Land and Property Rights in Latin America.* Pittsburgh: University of Pittsburgh Press.

de Janvry, Alain. 1981. *The Agrarian Question and Reformism in Latin America.* Baltimore: Johns Hopkins University Press.

de la Rocha, Mercedes Gonzaléz. 1994. *The Resources of Poverty: Women and Survival in a Mexican City.* Cambridge, MA: Blackwell.

Denny, Charlotte. 2002. "Poor Always the Losers in Trade Game." *Guardian Weekly: Earth,* August: 6.

DeParle, Jason. 2007. "Jobs Abroad Underwriting 'Model State.'" *The New York Times,* September 7: A1, A16.

De Schutter, Olivier. 2010. "Responsibly Destroying the World's Peasantry." Project Syndicate. Available at http://www.project-syndicate.org/commentary/deschutter1/English.

de Soto, Hernando. 1990. *The Other Path: The Invisible Revolution in the Third World.* New York: Harper & Row.

Desmarais, Annette Aurélie. 2007. *La Vía Campesina: Globalization and the Power of Peasants.* Halifax, NS: Fernwood.

De Waal, Alex. 2002. "What AIDS Means in a Famine." *The New York Times,* November 19: 25.

Dhanagare, D. N. 1988. "The Green Revolution and Social Inequalities in Rural India." *Bulletin of Concerned Asian Scholars* 20(2): 2–13.

Dias Martins, Monica. 2000. "The MST Challenge to Neoliberalism." *Latin American Perspectives* 27(5): 33–45.

Dicken, Peter. 1998. *Global Shift: Transforming the World Economy.* New York: Guilford.

Dillon, Sam. 1997. "After 4 Years of NAFTA, Labor Is Forging Cross-Border Ties." *The New York Times,* December 20: A1, A7.

———. 1998. "U.S. Labor Leader Seeks Union Support in Mexico." *The New York Times,* January 23: A3.

Diokno-Pascual, Maitet. 2003. "Power Splurge." *New Internationalist* 355, April: 25.

Dixon, Jane. 2002. *The Changing Chicken: Chooks, Cooks, and Culinary Culture.* Sydney, Australia: UNSW Press.

Dolan, C. S. 2004. "On Farm and Packhouse: Employment at the Bottom of a Global Value Chain." *Rural Sociology* 69(1): 99–126.

Dolan, C. and J. Humphrey. 2000. "Governance and Trade in Fresh Vegetables: The Impact of UK Supermarkets on the African Horticulture Industry." *Journal of Development Studies* 37: 147–176.

Dreyfuss, Robert. 2010. "The greening of China." *The Nation,* September 20: 14.

Dube, S. C. 1988. *Modernization and Development—the Search for Alternative Paradigms.* London: Zed.

Dudley, Leonard and Roger Sandilands. 1975. "The Side Effects of Foreign Aid: The Case of Public Law 480, Wheat in Colombia." *Economic Development and Cultural Change* 23(2): 325–336.

Dugger, Celia W. 2004. "Supermarket Giants Crush Central American Farmers." *The New York Times,* December 28: A1, A10.

———. 2007. "Clinton Foundation Announces a Bargain on Generic AIDS Drugs." *The New York Times,* May 9: 6.

———. 2010. "Report Optimistic on African Economies." *The New York Times,* June 23.

Duncan, Colin. 1996. *The Centrality of Agriculture: Between Humankind and the Rest of Nature.* Montreal and Kingston: McGill-Queen's University Press.

Economist, The. 2010. "A Bumpier but Freer Road." *Briefing,* October 2: 75–77.

———. 2011. "India's Surprising Economic Miracle." *Leaders,* October 2: 11.

Eilperin, Juliet. 2010. "Wrapped in a Mantle of Green." *The Guardian Weekly,* 8 October: 18.

Elliott, Larry. 2001. "Evil Triumphs in a Disease-Ridden World." *Guardian Weekly,* February 14–21: 12.

———. 2010. "When Austerity Is Not Enough." *The Guardian Weekly,* September 10: 18.

Elliott, Michael. 2007. "The Chinese Century." *Time,* January 22: 19–27.

Ellwood, Wayne. 1993. "Multinationals and the Subversion of Sovereignty." *New Internationalist* 246: 4–7.

———. 2001. *The No-Nonsense Guide to Globalization.* Oxford, UK: New Internationalist.

Elson, Diane, ed. 1991. *Male Bias in the Development Process.* Manchester: Manchester University Press.

———. 1993. "Gender-Aware Analysis and Development Economics." *Journal of International Development* 5(2): 237–247.

Elson, Diane, and Ruth Pearson. 1981. "Nimble Fingers Make Cheap Workers: An Analysis of Women's Employment in Third World Export Manufacturing," *Feminist Review* 7: 87–101.

Elyachar, Julia. 2005. *Markets of Dispossession: NGOs, Economic Development, and the State in Cairo.* Durham, NC: Duke University Press.

Enloe, Cynthia. 2004. *The Curious Feminist: Searching for Women in a New Age of Empire.* Berkeley: University of California Press.

Enzenburger, Hans Magnus. 1994. *Civil Wars: From L.A. to Bosnia.* New York: New Press.

Erlanger, Steven. 2010. "Europeans Fear Crisis Threatens Liberal Benefits." *The New York Times,* May 23.

Escobar, Arturo. 1995. *Encountering Development: The Making and Unmaking of the Third World.* Princeton, NJ: Princeton University Press.

———. 2011. "Sustainability: Design for the Pluriverse." *Development,* 54(2): 137–140.

Esteva, Gustavo. 1992. "Development." In *The Development Dictionary,* edited by Wolfgang Sachs. London: Zed.

ETC Group. 2007. "Peak Soil + Peak Oil = Peak Spoils." *ETC Group Communique,* #96. November/December, 1–14.

———. 2008 . "Patenting the 'Climate Genes' . . . and Capturing the Climate Agenda." ETC Group Communiqué, Issue 99. Available at www.etcgroup.org.

Evans, Alex. 2009. *The Feeding of the Nine Billion: Global Food Security for the 21st Century.* Chatham House Report. Available at www.chathamhouse.org.uk/files/13179_r0109.

Evans, Peter. 1979. *Dependent Development.* Princeton, NJ: Princeton University Press.

———. 1995. *Embedded Autonomy: States and Industrial Transformation.* Princeton, NJ: Princeton University Press.

———. 2010. "Is It Labor's Turn To Globalize? Twenty-First Century Opportunities and Strategic Responses." *Global Labour,* 1(3): 352–379.

Eviatar, Daphne. 2006. "Latin Left Turn." *The Nation,* December 25: 5–6.

Eyferth, J., P. Ho, and E. B. Vermeer. 2003. "Introduction: The Opening Up of China's Countryside." *The Journal of Peasant Studies* 30(3–4): 1–17.

EZLN Communiques. 1994–2005. Available at http://www.struggle.ws/mexico/ezlnco.html.

Faison, Seth. 1997. "Detours Behind It: The Giant Follows Asian's Growth Path." *The New York Times,* March 4: A1, D4.

Fanon, Frantz. 1967. *The Wretched of the Earth.* Harmondsworth, UK: Penguin.

FAO. 2008. *The State of Food Insecurity in the World 2008: High Food Prices and Food Security—Threats and Opportunities.* Retrieved from http://www.fao.org/docrep/fao/011/i0291_e/i0291e00a.htm.

Fargione, J., J. Hill, D. Tilman, S. Polasky, and P. Hawthorne. 2008. "Land Clearing and the Biofuel Carbon Debt." *Science,* February 7.

Feder, Ernst. 1983. *Perverse Development.* Quezon City, Philippines: Foundation for Nationalist Studies.

Ferguson, James. 2006. *Global Shadows: Africa in the Neoliberal World Order.* Durham, NC: Duke University Press.

Fernandez Kelly, Patricia. 1983. *For We Are Sold, I and My People: Women and Industry in Mexico's Frontier.* Albany, NY: SUNY Press.

Ferrett. Grant. 2007. "Biofuels 'Crime against Humanity.'" *BBC News,* 27 October.

Flannery, Tim. 2009. *Now or Never: Why We Must Act Now to End Climate Change and Create a Sustainable Future.* New York: Atlantic Monthly Press.

Flavio de Almeida, Lucio and Felix Ruiz Sanchez. 2000. "The Landless Workers' Movement and Social Struggles against Neoliberalism." *Latin American Perspectives* 22(5): 11–32.

Fletcher, Michael A. 2010. "Politicians 'Look Away' as One in Seven Americans Fall into Poverty." *The Guardian Weekly,* 24 September: 3.

Flynn, Matthew. 2002. "Cocktails and Carnival." *New Internationalist* 346: 16–17.

Fonte, Maria. 2006. "Slow Foods Presidia: What Do Small Producers Do with Big Retailers?" In *Between the Local and the Global: Confronting Complexity in the Contemporary Agri-Food Sector,* edited by Terry Marsden and Jonathan Murdoch. Oxford: Elsevier.

"Food and Farming: The Facts." 2003. *New Internationalist* 353: 20–21.

Foster, John Bellamy. 2011. "Capitalism and Degrowth: An Impossibility." *Monthly Review,* 62(8): 26–33.

Fox, Jonathan. 1994. "The Challenge of Democracy: Rebellion as Catalyst." *Akwekon* 11(2): 13–19.

Frank, Andre Gunder. 1970. "The Development of Underdevelopment." In *Imperialism and Underdevelopment,* edited by Robert H. Rhodes. New York: Monthly Review Press.

Fraser, Alistair. 2005. "Poverty Reduction Strategy Papers: Now Who Calls the Shots?" *Review of African Political Economy,* 104/5: 317–340.

Freeman, Carla. 2000. *High Tech and High Heels in the Global Economy: Women, Work, and Pink-Collar Identities in the Caribbean.* Durham, NC: Duke University Press.

French, Hilary. 2000. *Vanishing Borders: Protecting the Planet in the Age of Globalization*. New York: Norton.

French, Howard W. 2010. "The Next Empire." *The Atlantic,* May. Retrieved from www.theatlantic.com/magazine.

Friedland, William H. 1994. "The Global Fresh Fruit and Vegetable System: An Industrial Organization Analysis." In *The Global Restructuring of Agro-Food Systems,* edited by Philip McMichael. Ithaca, NY: Cornell University Press.

Friedman, Thomas. 2000. *The Lexus and the Olive Tree: Understanding Globalization.* New York: Anchor.

———. 2005. *The World Is Flat: A Brief History of the Twentieth Century.* New York: Farrar, Straus & Giroux.

Friedmann, Harriet. 1982. "The Political Economy of Food: The Rise and Fall of the Postwar International Food Order." *American Journal of Sociology* 88S: 248–286.

———. 1990. "The Origins of Third World Food Dependence." In *The Food Question: Profits versus People?* edited by Henry Bernstein, Ben Crow, Maureen Mackintosh, and Charlotte Martin. New York: Monthly Review Press.

———. 1991. "Changes in the International Division of Labor: Agri-Food Complexes and Export Agriculture." In *Towards a New Political Economy of Agriculture,* edited by William Friedland, Lawrence Busch, Frederick H. Buttel, and Alan P. Rudy. Boulder, CO: Westview.

———. 1992. "Distance and Durability: Shaky Foundations of the World Food Economy." *Third World Quarterly* 13(2): 371–383.

———. 1999. "Remaking 'Traditions': How We Eat, What We Eat, and the Changing Political Economy of Food." In *Women Working the NAFTA Food Chain,* edited by Deborah Barndt. Toronto: Second Story.

Friedmann, John. 1992. *Empowerment: The Politics of Alternative Development.* Cambridge, UK: Blackwell.

Fröbel, Folker, Jürgen Heinrichs, and Otto Kreye. 1979. *The New International Division of Labor.* New York: Cambridge University Press.

Fuentes, Anna, and Barbara Ehrenreich. 1983. "The New Factory Girls." *Multinational Monitor* 4(8). Available at www.multinationalmonitor.org.

Fussell, M. E. 2000. "Making Labor Flexible: The Recomposition of Tijuana's *Maquiladora* Female Labor Force." *Feminist Economics* 6(3): 59–80.

Gaia Foundation et al. 2008. *Agrofuels and the Myth of the Marginal Land.* Briefing. Retrieved from www.gaiafoundation.org/documents/Agrofuels&MarginalMyth.pdf.

Galeano, Eduardo. 2000. *Upside Down: A Primer for the Looking Glass World.* New York: Picador.

Gardner, Gary, and Brian Halweil. 2000. "Underfed and Overfed: The Global Epidemic of Malnutrition." Worldwatch Paper No. 150, Washington, DC: Worldwatch Institute.

George, Susan. 1977. *How the Other Half Dies: The Real Reasons for World Hunger.* Montclair, NJ: Allenheld, Osmun and Co.

———. 1988. *A Fate Worse Than Debt: The World Financial Crisis and the Poor.* New York: Grove.

———. 1992. *The Debt Boomerang: How Third World Debt Harms Us All.* Boulder, CO: Westview.

———. 2010. *Whose Crisis? Whose Future? Towards a Greener, Fairer, Richer World.* Cambridge: Polity.

George, Susan, and Fabrizio Sabelli. 1994. *Faith and Credit: The World Bank's Secular Empire.* Boulder, CO: Westview.

Gereffi, Gary. 1989. "Rethinking Development Theory: Insights from East Asia and Latin America." *Sociological Forum* 4(4): 505–533.

———. 1994. "The Organization of Buyer-Driven Global Commodity Chains: How U.S. Retailers Shape Overseas Production Networks." In *Commodity Chains and Global Capitalism,* edited by Gary Gereffi and Miguel Korzeniewicz. Westport, CT: Praeger.

Gevisser, Mark. 2001. "AIDS: The New Apartheid." *The Nation,* May 14: 5–6.

Gibson, Nigel C. 2011. "Egypt and the Revolution in Our Minds." *Pambazuka News,* February 17. Available at http://pambazuka.org/en/category/features/70972.

Gibson-Graham, J. K. 2006. *A Postcapitalist Politics.* Minneapolis: University of Minnesota Press.

Giridharadas, Anand 2007a. "'Second Tier' City to Rise Fast under India's Urban Plan." *The New York Times,* May 13: 3.

———. 2007b. "Outsourcing Works, So India Is Exporting Jobs." *The New York Times,* September 25.

Glennie, Jonathan. 2011. "The Rise of the 'South-South' Aid Agencies." *The Guardian Weekly,* March 4: 44.

GMA News. 2011. "Women around the World Unite vs landgrabbing." *Food Crisis and the Global Land Grab,* July 7. Retrieved from http://farmlandgrab.org/post/view/18917.

Godoy, Julio. 2010. "Vive la décroissance." *New Internationalist,* 434:19.

Godrej, Dinyar. 2003. "Precious Fluid." *New Internationalist* 354: 9–12.

Goldemberg, J., and O. Lucon. 2010. "Renewable Energy Options in Developing Countries." *Making It—Industry for Development Magazine,* 2: 16–18. Available at http://www.makingitmagazine.net.

Goldman, Michael. 2005. *Imperial Nature: The World Bank and Struggles for Social Justice in the Age of Globalization.* New Haven: Yale University Press.

Goldsmith, James. 1994. *The Trap.* New York: Carroll & Graf.

Gorelick, Sherry. 2000. "Facing the Farm Crisis." *The Ecologist* 30(4): 28–32.

Goss, Jasper, David Burch, and Roy E. Rickson. 2000. "Agri-Food Restructuring and Third World Transnationals: Thailand, the CP Group and the Global Shrimp Industry." *World Development* 28(3): 513–530.

Gott, Richard. 2006. "Latin America Is Preparing to Settle Accounts with Its White Settler Elite." *The Guardian,* November 15: 33.

Gow, David. 2007. "India Gets a Brand New Carmaker—As It Runs Out of Roads to Drive On." *The Guardian,* March 30: 8.

Gowan, Peter. 2003. "The American Campaign for Global Sovereignty." In *Fighting Identities: Socialist Register,* edited by Leo Panitch and Colin Leys. London: Merlin.

Graham, Carol. 1994. *Safety Nets, Politics, and the Poor: Transitions to Market Economies.* Washington DC: Brookings Institution.

GRAIN. 2007. "Agrofuels." *Seedling,* July. Available at www.grain.org/seedling/?type=68&1=0.

———. 2010. "The World Bank in the Hot Seat." *Seedling,* May 8. Available at www.grain.org/articles/?id=64.

Greenfield, Gerard. 1999. "The WTO, the World Food System, and the Politics of Harmonised Destruction." Retrieved from www.labournet.org/discuss/global/wto/html.

Greenlees, Donald. 2006. "Outsourcing Drifts to the Philippines after India Matures." *International Herald Tribune,* November 11: 1.

Greenpeace. 2006. "Eating Up the Amazon." Available at www.greenpeace.org.

Green-Weiskel, Lucia. 2011. "Climate Clash in Cancun." *The Nation,* January 3: 18–23.

Greider, William. 2001. "A New Giant Sucking Sound." *The Nation,* December 31: 22–24.

———. 2007. "The Establishment Rethinks Globalization." *The Nation,* April 30: 11–14.

Gresh, Alain. 2011. "Freedom Makes You Giddy." *Le Monde Diplomatique,* February: 1.

Griffin, K. B. 1974. *The Political Economy of Agrarian Change: An Essay on the Green Revolution.* Cambridge, MA: Harvard University Press.

Grigg, David. 1993. *The World Food Problem.* Oxford, UK: Blackwell.

Grossman, Raquel. 1979. "Globalization, Commodity Chains and Fruit Exporting Regions in Chile." *Tijdschrift voor Economische en Sociale Geographie* 90(2): 211–225.

Guardian editorial. 2010. "Climate Change: The Facts of life." *The Guardian,* August 31.

Guardian reporters. 2011. "Arab Youth Anger in the Ascendancy." *The Guardian Weekly,* February 25: 28.

Gupta. Akhil. 1998. *Postcolonial Developments: Agriculture in the Making of Modern India.* Durham, NC: Duke University Press.

Habermas, Jürgen. 2010. "Germany and the Euro-Crisis." *The Nation,* June 28: 18–22.

Halberg, N., H. F. Alroe, M. T. Knudsen, and E. S. Kristensen, eds. 2005. *Global Development of Organic Agriculture: Challenges and Promises.* Wallingford, UK: CAB International.

Hale, Stephen. 2011. "Global campaigning to tackle poverty and Injustice Is No Longer North v South." *The Guardian,* February 14.

Halperin, Sandra. 2005. "Trans-local and Trans-Regional Socio-Economic Structures in Global Development: A 'Horizontal' Perspective." In *New Directions in the Sociology of Global Development,* edited by Frederick H. Buttel and Philip McMichael, 19–56. Oxford: Elsevier.

Hamilton, Clive. 2003. *Growth Fetish.* Sydney, Australia: Allen & Unwin.

Harcourt, Wendy. 1994. "Introduction." In *Feminist Perspectives on Sustainable Development,* edited by Wendy Harcourt. London: Zed.

———. 2009. *Body Politics in Development: Critical Debates in Gender and Development*. London & New York: Zed Books.

Harding, Luke. 2001. "Delhi Calling." *Guardian Weekly*, March 15–21: 23.

Harlan, Chico. 2011. "All Together Now." *The Guardian Weekly*, 15 July: 30.

Harnecker, Marta. 2010. "Latin America & Twenty-First Century Socialism." *Monthly Review*, 62(3): 3–83.

Harney, Alexandra. 2009. *The China Price: The True Cost of Chinese Competitive Advantage*. New York: Penguin Books.

Harris, Nigel. 1987. *The End of the Third World: Newly Industrializing Countries and the Decline of an Ideology*. Harmondsworth, UK: Penguin.

Harris, Paul. 2010. "Detroit gets Growing." *The Observer*, July 11.

Harrison, Graham. 2004. *The World Bank and Africa: The Construction of Governance States*. London: Routledge.

Harrison, Paul. 1993. *The Third Revolution: Population, Environment and a Sustainable World*. Harmondsworth, UK: Penguin.

Harvey, David. 2003. *The New Imperialism*. Oxford: Oxford University Press.

———. 2005. *A Brief History of Neoliberalism*. Oxford, UK: Oxford University Press.

Hawkins, Tony. 1998. "At the Heart of Further Progress." *Financial Times*, June 2: I–VI.

Hayden, Tom. 2003. "Seeking a New Globalism in Chiapas." *The Nation*, April 7: 18–23.

Hedges, Chris. 1994. "Key Panel at Cairo Talks Agrees on Population Plan." *The New York Times*, September 13: A10.

Held, David. 1995. *Democracy and the Global Order: From the Modern State to Cosmopolitan Governance*. Stanford, CA: Stanford University Press.

Held, David, and Aysa Kaya, editors. 2007. *Global Inequality*. New York: Polity Press.

Helleiner, Eric. 1996. *States and the Reemergence of Global Finance: From Bretton Woods to the 1990s*. Ithaca, NY: Cornell University Press.

Henderson, Jeffrey. 1991. *The Globalisation of High Technology Production*. London: Routledge & Kegan Paul.

Henriques, Diana. 2008. "Food Is Gold, So Billions Invested in Farming." *The New York Times*, June 5.

Herbert, Bob. 1996. "Nike's Pyramid Scheme." *The New York Times*, June 10: 33.

Hertsgard, Mark. 2004. "Who's Afraid of climate Change Now? The Pentagon." *The Nation*, July.

Hervieu, Sébastien. 2011. "South Africa Gains Entry to Bric Club." *The Guardian Weekly*, April 22: 11.

Hettne, Björn. 1990. *Development Theory and the Three Worlds*. White Plains, NY: Longman.

Hicks, R. L., B. C. Parks, J. T. Roberts, and M. J. Tierney. 2008. *Greening Aid? Understanding the Environmental Impact of Development Assistance*. Oxford: Oxford University Press.

Hightower, Jim. 2002. "How Wal-Mart Is Remaking Our World." Pamphlet #7, Ithaca, NY.

Hildyard, Nicholas. 1993. "Foxes in Charge of Chickens." In *Global Ecology: A New Arena of Political Conflict,* edited by Wolfgang Sachs. London: Zed.

Hobsbawm, Eric J. 1992. "The Crisis of Today's Ideologies." *New Left Review* 192: 55–64.

Hochschild, Arlie Russell. 2003. "Love and Gold." In *Global Woman: Nannies, Maids, and Sex Workers in the New Economy.* New York: Metropolitan Books.

Holt-Giménez, Eric. 2006. *Campesino a Campesino: Voices from Latin America's Farmer to Farmer Movement for Sustainable Agriculture.* Oakland: FoodFirst.

———. 2007. "Exploding the Biofuel Myths." *Le Monde Diplomatique,* July: 10–11.

Holt-Giménez, Eric, and Isabella Kenfield. 2008. "When 'Renewable Isn't Sustainable: Agrofuels and the Inconvenient Truths Behind the 2007 U.S. Energy Independence and Security Act." *Policy Brief No. 13.* Oakland: Institute for Food and Development Policy.

Holusha, John. 1996. "Squeezing the Textile Workers." *The New York Times,* February 21: D1, D20.

Hoogvelt, Ankie M. M. 1987. *The Third World in Global Development.* London: Macmillan.

———. 1997. *Globalization and the Postcolonial World: The New Political Economy of Development.* London: Macmillan.

———. 2006. "Globalization and Post-Modern Imperialism." *Globalizations,* 3(2): 159–174.

Huang, Yasheng. 2000. "Change to Change: Modernization, Development and Politics." In *From Modernization to Globalization: Perspectives on Development and Social Change,* edited by J. Timmons Roberts and Amy Hite. London: Blackwell.

Huntington, Samuel P. 2011. "Rethinking the Beijing Consensus." *Asia Policy,* 11: 1–26.

Instituto Nacional de Estadíscita, Geografía e Informática. 2004. Available at www.inegi.gob.mx/inegi/default.asp.

International Assessment of Agricultural Knowledge, Science and Technology for Development (IAASTD). 2008. "Executive Summary of the Synthesis Report." Available at www.agassessment.org/docs/SR_Exec_Sum_280508_English.pdf.

International Confederation of Free Trade Unions. 1995. www.cftu.org.

International Fund for Agriculture (IFAD). 2009. "As Threat of a Renewed Food Crisis Looms, UN food Agencies to Join G8 Agricultural Ministers in Treviso," *ReliefWeb,* April 19. Available at www.relief-web.int/rw/rwb.nsf/db900sid/MYAI-7R98NJ?OpenDocument.

International Labor Organization. 1995. www.ilo.org.

International Labor Organization. 2003. www.ilo.org.

Iriart, Celia, and Howard Waitzkin. 2004. "Managed Care Goes Global." *Multinational Monitor* 25(10): Available at www.multinationalmonitor.org.

Isakson, S. Ryan. 2010. "*No hay ganancia en la milpa:* The Agrarian Question, Food Sovereignty, and the On-Farm Conservation of Agrobiodiversity in the Guatemalan Highlands." *The Journal of Peasant Studies,* 36(4), 725–760.

Jackson, Cecile. 1993. "Doing What Comes Naturally? Women and Environment in Development." *World Development* 21(12): 1947–1963.

Jackson, Tim. 2009. *Prosperity Without Growth: Economics for a Finite Planet.* London: Earthscan.

Jaffee, Daniel. 2007. *Brewing Justice: Fair Trade Coffee, Sustainability, and Survival.* Berkeley, CA: University of California Press.

Jahan, Rounaq. 1995. *The Elusive Agenda: Mainstreaming Women in Development.* London: Zed.

James, C. L. R. 1963. *The Black Jacobins: Toussaint L'Ouverture and the San Domingo Revolution.* New York: Vintage.

Jha, Alok. 2008. "Huge study Gives Wake-Up Call on State of World's Oceans." *The Guardian Weekly,* 22 March: 3.

Jha, Prem Shankar. 2010. *Crouching Dragon, Hidden Tiger: Can China and India Dominate the West?* New York: Soft Skull Press.

Jordan, Mary, and Kevin Sullivan. 2003. "Trade Brings Riches, but Not to Mexico's Poor." *Guardian Weekly,* April 3–9: 33.

Jowit, Juliette. 2010. "Trillion-Dollar Cost of Global Pollution." *The Guardian Weekly,* 26 February: 17.

Kagarlitsky, Boris. 1995. *The Mirage of Modernization.* New York: Monthly Review Press.

Karliner, Joshua. 1997. *The Corporate Planet: Ecology and Politics in the Age of Globalization.* San Francisco: Sierra Club Books.

Kemp, Tom. 1989. *Industrialization in the Non-Western World.* London: Longman.

Kennedy, Bruce. 2001. "China's Three Gorges Dam." *CNN.* Retrieved from http://www.cnn.com/SPECIALS/1999/china.50/asian.superpower/three.gorges/.

Kernaghan, Charles. 1995. *Zoned for Slavery: The Child Behind the Label* [Videotape]. New York: National Labor Committee.

Kidron, Michael, and Ronald Segal. 1981. *The State of the World Atlas.* London: Pan.

Kimbrell, Andrew. 2002. *The Fatal Harvest Reader: The Tragedy of Industrial Agriculture.* Washington, DC: Island Press.

Kinver, Mark. 2011. "UN Report: Cities Ignore Climate Change at Their Peril." *BBC News,* March 29. Retrieved from http://www.bbc.co.uk/news/science-environment-12881779.

Klare, Michael T. 2002. *Resource Wars: The New Landscape of Global Conflict.* New York: Henry Holt & Company.

Klein, Naomi. 2007. *The Shock Doctrine. The Rise of Disaster Capitalism.* New York: Metropolitan Books.

Klein, R., T. Banuri, S. Kartha, and L. Schipper. 2008. "International Climate Policy." *Commission on Climate Change and Development,* March. Retrieved from www.ccdcommission.org.

Kloppenburg, Jack R., Jr. 1988. *First the Seed: The Political Economy of Plant Biotechnology, 1492–2000.* Cambridge, MA: Cambridge University Press.

Knox, Paul, and John Agnew. 1994. *The Geography of the World Economy.* London: Edward Arnold.

Kohl, Benjamin, and Linda Farthing. 2006. *Impasse in Bolivia:*

Neoliberal Hegemony & Popular Resistance. London: Zed.

Kolko, Joyce. 1988. *Restructuring the World Economy.* New York: Pantheon.

Korten, David. 1995. *When Corporations Rule the World.* New York: Kumarian.

Korzeniewicz, Miguel. 1994. "Commodity Chains and Marketing Strategies: Nike and the Global Athletic Footwear Industry." In *Commodity Chains and Global Capitalism,* edited by Gary Gereffi and Miguel Korzeniewicz. Westport, CT: Praeger.

Kothari, Smitu, and Pramod Parajuli. 1993. "No Nature without Social Justice: A Plea for Cultural and Ecological Pluralism in India." In *Global Ecology: A New Arena of Political Conflict,* edited by Wolfgang Sachs. London: Zed.

Kotkin, Stephen. 2007. "First World, Third World (Maybe Not in That Order)." *The New York Times,* May 6: 4.

Krauss, Clifford. 2010. "In Global Forecast, China Looms Large as Energy User and Maker of Green Power." *The New York Times,* November 10: D7.

Kristoff, Nicholas D. 2010. "A Hedge Fund Republic?" *The New York Times,* November 18.

Kumar, Karthick. 2011. "Organic Farming—Can It Feed the World?" *EcoWalk the Talk,* March 11. Retrieved from www.ecowalkthe talk.com.

Landsberg, Martin. 1979. "Export-Led Industrialization in the Third World: Manufacturing Imperialism." *Review of Radical Political Economics* 2(4): 50–63.

———. 2010. "ALBA and the Promise of Cooperative Development." *Monthly Review,* 62(7):1–17.

Lang, Tim and Michael Heasman. 2004. *Food Wars: The Global Battle for Mouths, Minds and Markets.* London: Earthscan.

Lang, Tim, and Colin Hines. 1993. *The New Protectionism: Protecting the Future against Free Trade.* New York: The New Press.

Langellier, Jean-Pierre, and Brice Pedroletti. 2006. "China to Build First Eco-City." *The Guardian Weekly,* May 5–11: 28.

Lappé, Frances Moore, and Anna Lappé. 2002. *Hope's Edge.* New York: Tarcher/Putnam.

LaTouche, Serge. 1993. *In the Wake of the Affluent Society: An Exploration of Post-Development.* London: Zed.

———. 2004. "Degrowth Economics." *Le Monde Diplomatique,* November: 15.

Lawrence, Felicity. 2010. "Sucked Dry by Asparagus." *The Guardian Weekly,* 24 October: 24.

———. 2011. "Guatemala Pays a High Price for Global Food System Failings." *The Guardian,* June 1.

Leader, 2004. "Shining Example." *The Guardian,* April 23: 3.

Leahy, Stephen (2008) "Reinventing Agriculture." *Inter Press Service,* April 15.

Le Carre, John. 2001. "In Place of Nations." *The Nation,* April 9: 11–13.

Lee, Ching Kwan. 2008. Rights Activism in China. *Contexts.* Available at contexts.org.

———. 2009. "Raw Encounters, Chinese Managers, African Workers and the Politics of

Casualization in Africa's Chinese Enclaves." *The China Quarterly,* 199: 647–699.

Lehman, David. 1990. *Democracy and Development in Latin America.* Philadelphia: Temple University Press.

Lehman, K., and A. Krebs. 1996. "Control of the World's Food Supply." In *The Case against the Global Economy, and for a Turn toward the Local,* edited by J. Mander and E. Goldsmith. San Francisco: Sierra Club Books.

Lenin, Vladimir Ilych. 1997. *Imperialism: The Highest Stage of Capitalism.* New York: International Publishers. (Original work published 1916)

LeQuesne, C. 1997. "The World Trade Organization and Food Security." Talk to UK Food Group, July 15, London.

Leslie, Jacques. 2008. "The Last Empire." *Mother Jones,* January/February: 28–39, 83.

Lewin, Tamar. 1995. "Family Decay Global, Study Says." *The New York Times,* May 30: A5.

Lewis, Paul. 1997. "IMF Seeks Argentine Deal Linking Credit to Governing." *The New York Times,* July 15: D1, D19.

Li, Tania Murray. 2011. "Centering Labor in the Land Grab Debate." *The Journal of Peasant Studies,* 38(2): 281–298.

Lim, L.C. 2008. "Sustainable Agriculture Pushing Back the Desert." Institute of Science in Society. Available at i-sis.org.uk/desertification.php.

Lipton, Michael. 1977. *Why Poor People Stay Poor: Urban Bias in World Development.* London: Temple Smith.

Lissakers, Karin. 1993. *Banks, Borrowers, and the Establishment: A Revisionist Account of the International Debt Crisis.* New York: Basic Books.

Llambi, Luis. 1990. "Transitions to and Within Capitalism: Agrarian Transitions in Latin America." *Sociologia Ruralis* 30(2): 174–196.

Lohmann, Larry. 1993. "Resisting Green Globalism." In *Global Ecology: A New Arena of Political Conflict,* edited by Wolfgang Sachs. London: Zed.

López, Isidro, and Emmanuel Rodríguez. 2011. "The Spanish Model." *New Left Review,* 69: 5–29.

Lovelock, James. 2007. *The Revenge of Gaia. Earth's Climate Crisis and the Fate of Humanity.* New York: Basic Books.

Lütkenhorst, Manfried. 2010. "A Changing Climate for Industrial Policy." *Making It,* 3, July: 16–19.

Maathai, Wangari. 2010. *The Challenge for Africa.* New York: Anchor Books.

MacShane, Denis. 1991. "Working in Virtual Slavery: Gulf Migrant Labor." *The Nation,* March 18: 325, 343–344.

Madden, Peter and John Madeley. 1993. "Winners and Losers: The Impact of the GATT Uruguay Round in Developing Countries." *Christian Aid,* December: 17.

Madeley, John. 2000. *Hungry for Trade.* London: Zed.

Magdoff, Harry. 1969. *The Age of Imperialism.* New York: Monthly Review Press.

Mamdani, Mahmood. 1996. *Citizen and Subject: Contemporary Africa and the Legacy of Late Colonialism.*

Princeton, NJ: Princeton University Press.

———. 2003. "Making Sense of Political Violence in Post-Colonial Africa." In *Fighting Identities: Race, Religion and Ethno-Nationalism: Socialist Register 2003,* edited by Leo Panitch and Colin Leys. London: Merlin.

Mark, Jason. 2001. "Brazil's MST: Taking Back the Land." *Multinational Monitor* 22: 10–12.

Marsden, Terry K. 2003. *The Condition of Rural Sustainability.* Wageningen: Van Gorcum.

Marsden, Terry and Jonathan Murdoch, eds, 2006. *Between the Local and the Global: Confronting Complexity in the Contemporary Agri-Food Sector.* Oxford: Elsevier.

Martin, Hans-Peter, and Harold Schumann. 1997. *The Global Trap: Globalisation and the Assault on Democracy and Prosperity.* London: Zed.

Martinez-Alier, Joan. 2002. *The Environmentalism of the Poor: A Study of Ecological Conflicts and Valuation.* Cheltenham, UK: Edward Elgar.

———. 2010. "Beyond GDP lies economic degrowth." *European Alternatives,* March. Available at http://www.euroalter.com/2010/beyond-gdp-lies-economic-degrowth/.

Marx, Karl. 1965. *Das Kapital.* Moscow: Progress Publishers.

Maybarduk, Peter. 2004. "A People's Health System." *Multinational Monitor* 25(10). Available at www.multinationalmonitor.org.

McBride, Stephen. 2006. "Reconfiguring Sovereignty: NAFTA Chapter 11 Dispute Settlement Procedures and the Issue of Public-Private Authority." *Canadian Journal of Political Science/Revue canadienne de science politique* 39(4): 1–21.

McDougall, Dan. 2007. "Success in a Slum." *Guardian Weekly,* March 16–22: 29.

McGreal, Chris. 2006–07. "Continent Waits to See Cost of Lavish Embrace." *Guardian Weekly,* December 22–January 4: 6.

McKay, Steven C. 2006. *Satanic Mills or Silicon Islands? The Politics of High-Tech Production in the Philippines.* Ithaca: Cornell University Press.

McKibben, Bill. 2010. *Eaarth: Making a Life on a Tough New Planet.* New York: Times Books.

McMichael, A. J. 1993. *Planetary Overload: Global Environmental Change and the Health of the Human Species.* Cambridge, UK: Cambridge University Press.

McMichael, A. J., J. W. Powles, C. D. Butler and R. Uauy. 2007. "Food, Livestock Production, Energy, Climate Change and Health." *Lancet,* September 13.

McMichael, Philip. 1985. *Settlers and the Agrarian Question: Foundations of Capitalism in Colonial Australia.* Cambridge: Cambridge University Press.

———. 1993a. "World Food System Restructuring under a GATT Regime." *Political Geography* 12(3): 198–214.

———. 1993b. "Agro-Food Restructuring in the Pacific Rim: A Comparative-International Perspective on Japan, South Korea, the United States, Australia, and Thailand." In *Pacific-Asia and the Future of the World-System,* edited by Ravi Palat. Westport, CT: Greenwood.

———. 2005. "Global Development and the Corporate Food Regime." In *New Directions in the Sociology of Global Development*, edited by Frederick H. Buttel and Philip McMichael. Amsterdam: Elsevier.

———. 2009a. "Contemporary Contradictions of the Global Development Project: Geopolitics, Global Ecology, and the 'Development Climate.'" *Third World Quarterly*, 30(1): 247–262.

———. 2009b. "A Food Regime Analysis of the 'World Food Crisis.'" *Agriculture and Human Values*, 4: 281–295.

———. 2009c. "Banking on Agriculture: A Review of the World Development Report 2008." *Journal of Agrarian Change*, 9(2): 235–246.

———. 2009d. "The Agrofuels Project at Large." *Critical Sociology*, 35(6): 825-839.

———. 2010. "Agrofuels in the Food Regime." *The Journal of Peasant Studies*, 37(4): 609-629.

McMichael, Philip, and Chul-Kyoo Kim. 1994. "Japanese and South Korean Agricultural Restructuring in Comparative and Global Perspective." In *The Global Restructuring of Agro-Food Systems,* edited by Philip McMichael. Ithaca, NY: Cornell University Press.

McMichael, Philip, and Laura T. Raynolds. 1994. "Capitalism, Agriculture, and World Economy." In *Capitalism and Development,* edited by Leslie Sklair. London: Routledge Kegan Paul.

McMurtry, John. 2002. *Value Wars: The Global Market Versus the Life Economy.* London: Pluto.

Memmi, Albert. 1967. *The Colonizer and the Colonized.* Boston: Beacon.

Menon, Gayatri A. 2001. *The Multivalency of Microcredit: The Cultural Politics of Credit and Citizenship in India.* Unpublished Master's thesis, Development Sociology, Cornell University, New York.

———. 2010. "Recoveries of Space and Subjectivity in the Shadow of Violence: The Clandestine Politics of Pavement Dwellers in Mumbai." In *Contesting Development: Critical Struggles for Social Change,* edited by Philip McMichael, pp. 151–164. New York and London: Routledge.

Menotti, Victor. 1998. "Globalization and the Acceleration of Forest Destruction Since Rio." *The Ecologist* 28(6): 354–362.

———. 1999. "Forest Destruction and Globalisation." *The Ecologist* 29(3): 180–181.

Middleton, Neil, Phil O'Keefe, and Sam Moyo. 1993. *Tears of the Crocodile: From Rio to Reality in the Developing World.* Boulder, CO: Pluto.

Mies, Maria. 1991. *Patriarchy and Accumulation on a World Scale: Women in the International Division of Labor.* London: Zed.

Milbank, Dana. 1994. "Unlike Rest of Europe, Britain Is Creating Jobs, but They Pay Poorly." *Wall Street Journal,* March 28: A1, A6.

Millennium Ecosystem Assessment. 2005. *Ecosystems and Human Well-Being.* Washington, DC: Island Press.

Mitchell, Timothy. 1991. *Colonizing Egypt.* Berkeley, CA: University of California Press.

Mitchell, William. 2011. "Deficit mania Is Built on a Series of Destructive Neoliberal Myths." *The Nation,* April 4: 12.

Mittal, Anuradha. 2009. "Introduction." In *Voices from Africa: African Farmers and Environmentalists Speak Out Against a New Green Revolution in Africa,* edited by Anuradha Mittal with Melissa Moore. The Oakland Institute.

Mize, Ronald L., and Alicia C. S. Swords. 2010. *Consuming Mexican Labor. From the Bracero Program to NAFTA.* Toronto: University of Toronto Press.

Moghadam, Valentine M. 1993. *Modernizing Women: Gender and Social Change in the Middle East.* Boulder, CO: Lynne Rienner.

———. 2005a. *Globalization Women: Transnational Feminist Networks.* Baltimore: Johns Hopkins University Press.

———. 2005b. "Editorial." *International Social Science Journal,* 184: 203–206.

Monbiot, George. 2006. *Heat: How to Stop the Planet Burning.* London: Allen Lane.

Montalbano, William D. 1991. "A Global Pursuit of Happiness." *Los Angeles Times,* October 1: F1.

Mooallem, Jon. 2008. "The Afterlife of Cellphones." *The New York Times,* January 13.

Moody, Kim. 1999. *Workers in a Lean World: Unions in the International Economy.* London: Verso.

Moran, Theodore H. 2000. "Investment Issues." In *The WTO After Seattle,* edited by Jeffrey J. Schott. Washington, DC: Institute for International Economics.

Morrow, Adrian. 2011. "Big Problems in Little Bahrain." *The Global and Mail,* March 18: A10.

Mosse, David. 2004. "Is Good Policy Unimplementable? Reflections on the Ethnography of Aid Policy and Practice." *Development and Change,* 35(4): 639–671.

Muchena, D. T. 2006. "The China Factor in Southern Africa." *Openspace,* 1(4): 22–26.

Müller, Anders Riel, and Raj Patel. 2004. "Shining India? Economic Liberalization and Rural Poverty in the 1990s." *Food First Policy Brief No. 10.*

Murphy, Sophia. 1999. "WTO, Agricultural Deregulation, and Food Security." Paper presented at the Globalization Challenge Initiative, December. Retrieved from www .foreignpolicy-infocus.org/briefs/ v0114n34wto_body.html.

Myers, N., and J. Kent. 2003. "New Consumers: The Influence of Affluence on the Environment." *Proceedings of the National Academy of Sciences of the USA,* 100(8): 4963–4968.

Myerson, Allen R. 1997. "In Principle, a Case for More 'Sweatshops.'" *The New York Times,* June 22: 5.

NACLA. 1977. "A Run for Their Money." *North American Congress on Latin America,* 11(4): 168–175.

Naeem, Shahid. 2009. "Lessons from the Reverse Engineering of Nature." *Miller-McCune,* 2(3): 56–71.

Narayan, Deepa, with Raj Patel, Kai Schaft, Anne Rademacher, and Sarah Koch-Schulte. 2002. *Can*

Anyone Hear Us? Voices of the Poor. New York: Oxford.

Nash, Nathaniel C. 1994. "Vast Areas of Rain Forest Are Being Destroyed in Chile." *The New York Times,* May 31: C4.

Newman, Bryan. 2006. "Indian Farmer Suicides: A Lesson for Africa's Farmers." *Food First Backgrounder* 12(4): 2.

Noble, David. 2007. "The Corporate Climate Coup." *ZNet/Science,* May 8. Available at www.zmag .org/content/print_article .cfm?itemID=12771&section.

Nossiter, Adam. 2010. "Half a World from the Gulf, a Spill Scourge 5 Decades Old." *The New York Times,* June 17: A1, A18.

Nourishing the Planet. 2010. "Farming the Cities, Feeding an Urban Future." *World Watch Institute.* Retrieved from http://blogs.world-watch.org/nourishingtheplanet/.

Nussbaum, Martha. 2011a. *Creating Capabilities: The Human Development Approach.* Cambridge: Harvard University Press.

———. 2011b. "What Makes Life Good?" *The Nation,* May 2: 23.

O'Meara, Molly. 1999. "Reinventing Cities for People and the Planet." Worldwatch Paper No. 147, Washington, DC: Worldwatch.

Ong, Aihwa. 1997. "The Gender and Labor Politics of Postmodernity." In *The Politics of Culture in the Shadow of Capital,* edited by Lisa Lowe and David Lloyd. Durham, NC: Duke University Press.

Onishi, Norimitsu. 1998. "Nigeria Combustible as South's Oil Enriches North." *The New York Times,* November 22: A1, A6.

———. 1999. "Deep in the Republic of Chevron." *The New York Times Magazine,* July 4: 26–31.

Orlanda Pinnasi, Maria, Fatima Cabral, and Mirian Claudia Lourencao. 2000. "An Interview with Joao Pedro Stedile." *Latin American Perspectives* 27(5): 46–62.

Orth, Sheri. 2007. *Subsistence Foods to Export Goods: The Impact of an Oil Palm Plantation on Local Food Sovereignty, North Bariot, Central Kalimantan, Indonesia.* Sawit Watch, Wagenigen: Van Hall Larenstein.

Oster, Shai. 2009. "World's Top Polluter Emerges as Green-Technology Leader." *The Wall Street Journal,* December 15.

Oxfam. 2009. *Other Worlds Are Possible: Human Progress in an Age of Climate Change.* Available at http://www.oxfam.org.uk/ resources/policy/climate_change/ other-worlds-are-possible.html.

Palmer, Karen. 2006. "Africa Faces Barren Future." *The Star,* March 31. Retrieved from www.foodnews.ca.

Paranagua, Paulo A. 2007. "Caracas Runs on Easy Money." *Guardian Weekly,* February 9–15: 27.

Parenti, Christian. 2005. "Hugo Chávez and Petro Populism." *The Nation,* April 11: 15–21.

Paringaux, R.-P. 2001. "The Deliberate Destruction of Agriculture: India: Free Markets, Empty Bellies." *Le Monde Diplomatique,* September: 1–9.

Parrott, Nicholas, and Terry Marsden. 2002. *The Real Green Revolution: Organic and Agroecological Farming in the South.* London: Greenpeace Environmental Trust.

Patel, Raj. 2007. *Stuffed and Starved: Markets, Power and the Hidden Battle for the World Food System.* London: Portobello Books.

Patel, Raj, with A. Delwiche. 2002a. "The Profits of Famine: Southern Africa's Long Decade of Hunger." *Backgrounder, Food First* 8(4). Retrieved from www.foodfirst.org/pubs/backgrdrs/ 2002/f02v8n4.html.

———. 2002b. "What Does NEPAD Stand For?" Retrieved from http://voiceoftheturtle.org/show_article.php?aid=97.

Patnaik, Probat. 2008. "The Accumulation Process in the Period of Globalization." *Economic & Political Weekly,* 28: 108–113.

Patnaik, Utsa. 2003. "Global Capitalism, Deflation and Agrarian Crisis in Developing Countries." *Social Policy and Development Programme Paper Number 15.* Geneva: UNRISD.

Payne, Anthony, and Nicola Phillips. 2010. *Development.* Cambridge: Polity.

Pearlstein, Steven. 2011. "What's Retarding India's Growth?" *The Guardian Weekly,* 22 April: 20.

Pearse, A. 1980. *Seeds of Plenty, Seeds of Want.* Oxford, UK: Clarendon.

Perkins, John H. 1997. *Geopolitics and the Green Revolution: Wheat, Genes and the Cold War.* New York: Oxford University Press.

Perkins, Patricia E. 2010. "Equitable, Ecological Degrowth: Feminist Contributions." Available at http://www.google.com/url?sa=t&source=web&cd=1&ved=0CB4QFjAA&url=http%3A%2F%2Fwww.degrowth.org%2Ffileadmin%2Fcontent%2F2Fdocuments%2FProceedings%2FPerkins.pdf&rct=j&q=de-growth%20movement%20feminist&ei=YrL7TeCxIY_3gAfN6JHeCw&usg=AFQjCNHNmTpbSG0BvMiAKD00Ej2XEb10GA.

Perlez, Jane. 2001. "U.N. Chief Calls on U.S. Companies to Donate to AIDS Fund." *The New York Times,* June 2: A1.

———. 2002. "For Some Indonesians, Echoes of 'Coolie' Nation." *The New York Times,* August 18: 10.

Perrons, Diane. 2005. *Globalization and Social Change: People and Places in a Divided World.* London: Routledge.

Petrini, Carlo. 2001. *Slow Food: The Case for Taste.* New York: Columbia University Press.

Pieterse, Jan Niederveen. 2002. "Global Inequality: Bringing Politics Back In." *Third World Quarterly,* 23(6):1023–1046.

Pilger, John. 2002. *The New Rulers of the World.* London: Verso.

Pilkington, Ed. 2009. "On the Edge of the Ice." *The Guardian Weekly,* 17 October: 25–27.

Pionetti, Carine. 2005. *Sowing Autonomy: Gender and Seed Politics in Semi-Arid India.* London: IIED.

Piot, Olivier. 2011. "Tunisia: Diary of a Revolution." *Le Monde Diplomatique,* February: 4.

Polanyi, Karl. 1944/2001. *The Great Transformation.* Boston: Beacon Press.

Polgreen, Lydia. 2007. "Africa's Storied Colleges, Jammed and Crumbling." *The New York Times,* May 20: A1, 4.

Prebisch, Raúl. 1950. "The Economic Development of Latin America and its Principal Problems." Reprinted in

Economic Bulletin for Latin America, Vol. 7, No. 1, 1962: 1–22.

Press, Eyal. 2011. "Beyond GDP." *The Nation*, May 2: 25.

Pretty, Jules. 2002. *Agri-Culture: Reconnecting People, Land and Nature*. London: Earthscan.

Pretty, J., and R. Hine. 2001. "Reducing Food Poverty with Sustainable Agriculture: A Summary of New Evidence." Final report from the "SAFE World" Research Project, University of Essex. Available at www2.essex.ac.uk/ces/Fresearch Programmes/SAFEWexecsumm finalreport.htm.

Pretty, J. N., J. J. L. Morison, and R. E. Hine. 2003. "Reducing Food Poverty by Increasing Agricultural Sustainability in Developing Countries." *Agriculture, Ecosystems and Environment*, 95: 217–234.

Public Citizen. 2001. "Down on the Farm: NAFTA's Seven-Year War on Farmers and Ranchers in the U.S., Canada and Mexico." Retrieved from www.citizen.org.

Pyle, Jean L. 2001. "Sex, Maids, and Export Processing: Risks and Reasons for Gendered Global Production Networks." *International Journal of Politics, Culture and Society* 15(1): 55–76.

Rademacher, Anne, and Raj Patel. 2002. "Retelling Worlds of Poverty: Reflections on Transforming Participatory Research for a Global Narrative." In *Knowing Poverty: Critical Reflections on Participatory Research and Policy*, edited by K. Brock and R. McGee. London: Earthscan.

Raikes, Philip. 1988. *Modernising Hunger: Famine, Food Surplus & Farm Policy in the EC and Africa*. London: Catholic Institute for International Affairs.

Rainforest Action Network. 2007. "Getting Real about Biofuels." Available at www.ran.org/ content/fact-sheet-getting-real-about-biofuels.

Ramesh, Randeep. 2006. "Indians Get First Taste of Supermarket Shopping, but Wal-Mart is Kept at Bay." *Guardian Weekly*, June 9–15: 16.

———. 2009. "India Grows Its Crop of Billionaires." *The Guardian Weekly*, November 27: 17.

Rankin, Kathy. 2001. "Governing Development: Neoliberalism, Microcredit, and Rational Economic Woman." *Economy and Society* 30(1): 18–37.

Ransom, David. 2001a. "A World Turned Upside Down." *New Internationalist* 334: 9–11.

———. 2001b. *The No-Nonsense Guide to Fair Trade*. London: Verso.

Rau, Bill. 1991. *From Feast to Famine: Official Cures and Grassroots Remedies to Africa's Food Crisis*. London: Zed.

Raudsepp-Hearne, Ciara, Garry D. Peterson, Maria Tengö, Elena M. Bennett, Tim Holland, Karina Benessaiah, Graham K. MacDonald, and Laura Pfeifer. 2010. "Untangling the Environmentalist's Paradox: Why Is Human Well-Being Increasing as Ecosystem Services Degrade?" *BioScience*, September.

Raynolds, Laura T. 1994. "The Restructuring of Export Agriculture in the Dominican Republic:

Changing Agrarian Relations and the State." In *The Global Restructuring of Agro-Food Systems,* edited by Philip McMichael. Ithaca, NY: Cornell University Press.

———. 2000. "Re-Embedding Global Agriculture: The International Organic and Fair Trade Movements." *Agriculture and Human Values* 17: 297–309.

———. 2001. "New Plantations, New Workers: Gender and Production Politics in the Dominican Republic." *Gender & Society* 15(1): 7–28.

Raynolds, Laura T., David Myhre, Philip McMichael, Viviana Carro-Figueroa, and Frederick H. Buttel. 1993. "The 'New' Internationalization of Agriculture: A Reformulation." *World Development* 21(7): 1101–1121.

Razavi, Shahrashoub, and Carol Miller. 1995. *From WID to GAD: Conceptual Shifts in the Women and Development Discourse.* Occasional Paper 1, Geneva: UN Research Institute for Social Development, UNDP.

Reardon, Tom. and C. P. Timmer. 2005. "Transformation of Markets for Agricultural Output in Developing Countries Since 1950: How Has Thinking Changed?" In *Handbook of Agricultural Economics,* edited by R. E. Evenson, P. Pingali, and T. P. Schultz. Oxford: Elsevier.

Redding, Sean. 2000. "Structural Adjustment and the Decline of Subsistence Agriculture in Africa." Retrieved from http://women crossing.org/redding.html.

Reich, Robert B. 1991. "Secession of the Successful." *The New York Times Magazine,* January 20: 42.

———. 1992. *The Work of Nations: Preparing Ourselves for 21st Century Capitalism.* New York: Vintage.

Reij, Chris. 2006. "More Success Stories in Africa's Drylands Than Often Assumed." *ROPPA* (The Network of Peasant Organizations and Producers in West Africa). Available at roppa. info?IMG/pdf/More_success_stories_ in_Africa-Reij_Chris.pdf.

Renner, Michael. 2002. *The Anatomy of Resource Wars.* Worldwatch Paper No. 162. Washington, DC: Worldwatch.

Revel, Alain, and Christophe Riboud. 1986. *American Green Power.* Baltimore: Johns Hopkins University Press.

Ricardo, David. 1951 [1821]. *On the Principles of Political Economy and Taxation.* 3rd ed. In *The Works and Correspondence of David Ricardo,* vol. 1, edited by P. Sraffe with the collaboration of M. M. Dobb. Cambridge, UK: Cambridge University Press.

Rice, A. 2009. "Is There Such a Thing as Agro-Imperialism?" *The New York Times,* November 22.

Rice, Xan. 2010. "Ethiopia—Country of the Silver Sickle—Offers Land Dirt Cheap to Farming Giants." *The Guardian,* January 15.

Rich, Bruce. 1994. *Mortgaging the Earth: The World Bank, Environmental Impoverishment, and the Crisis of Development.* Boston: Beacon.

Richburg, Keith B. 2002. "Illegal Workers Do Europe's Dirty Work." *Guardian Weekly,* August 15–21: 29.

Ride, Anouk. 1998. "Maps, Myths, and Migrants." *New Internationalist* 305: 9.

Rifkin, Jeremy. 1992. *Beyond Beef: The Rise and Fall of the Cattle Culture.* New York: Penguin.

———. 1998. *The Biotech Century: Harnessing the Gene and Remaking the World.* New York: Tarcher/Putnam.

Rist, Gilbert. 1997. *The History of Development: From Western Origins to Global Faith.* London: Zed.

———. 2007. "Development as Buzzword." *Development in Practice,* 17(4–5).

Ritchie, Mark. 1993. *Breaking the Deadlock: The United States and Agriculture Policy in the Uruguay Round.* Minneapolis: Institute for Agriculture and Trade Policy.

———. 1999. "The World Trade Organization and the Human Right to Food Security." Paper presented at the International Cooperative Agriculture Organization General Assembly, August 29, Quebec City, Canada. Available from www.agricoop.org/activities/mark_ritchie.htm.

Roberts, Timmons J., and Bradley C. Park. 2007. *A Climate of Injustice. Global Inequality, North–South Politics, and Climate Policy.* Cambridge, MA: MIT Press.

Robinson, William I. 2002. "Remapping Development in Light of Globalization: From a Territorial to a Social Cartography." *Third World Quarterly,* 23(6): 1047–1071.

———. 2004. *A Theory of Global Capitalism: Production, Class, and State in a Transnational World.* Baltimore: Johns Hopkins University Press.

Rocca, Jean-Louis. 2007. "The Flaws in the Chinese Economic Miracle." *Le Monde Diplomatique,* May: 10.

Rocheleau, Dianne E. 1991. "Gender, Ecology, and the Science of Survival: Stories and Lessons from Kenya." In *Feminist Perspectives on Sustainable Development,* edited by Wendy Harcourt. London: Zed.

Roodman, David Malin. 2001. "Still Waiting for the Jubilee: Pragmatic Solutions for the Third World Debt Crisis." Worldwatch Paper No. 155. Washington, DC: Worldwatch.

Rosenthal, Elisabeth. 2009. "In Bolivia, Water and Ice Tell a Story of a Changing Climate." *The New York Times,* December 14: A1, A7.

Ross, Robert J. S., and Kent C. Trachte. 1990. *Global Capitalism: The New Leviathan.* Albany, NY: SUNY Press.

Rostow, Walt W. 1960. *The Stages of Economic Growth: A Non-Communist Manifesto.* Cambridge, UK: Cambridge University Press.

Rowley, C. D. 1974. *The Destruction of Aboriginal Society.* Ringwood, Australia: Penguin.

Rowling, Megan. 2001. "Sea Change." *New Internationalist* 341: 23–24.

Roy, Ananya. 2010. *Poverty Capital. Microfinance and the Making of Development.* New York and London: Routledge.

Rozhnov, Konstantin. 2010. "Bric Tries to Shift Power Balance." *BBC News,* July 16.

Ruggiero, Renato. 2000. "Reflections from Seattle." In *The WTO After Seattle,* edited by Jeffrey Schott.

Washington, DC: Institute for International Economics.

Sachs, Jeffrey. 1998. "The IMF and the Asian Flu." *The American Prospect,* March–April: 16–21.

———. 2005. *The End of Poverty: Economic Possibilities for Our Time.* New York: Penguin.

Sachs, Wolfgang. 1992. "One World." In *The Development Dictionary,* edited by Wolfgang Sachs. London: Zed.

———. 1999. *Planet Dialectics: Explorations in Environment and Development.* London: Zed.

Sadasivam, Bharati. 1997. "The Impact of Structural Adjustment on Women: A Governance and Human Rights Agenda." *Human Rights Quarterly* 19(3): 630–665.

Sader, Emir. 2008. "The Weakest Link? Neoliberalism in Latin America." *New Left Review,* 52: 5–32.

———. 2009. "Postneoliberalism in Latin America." *Development Dialogue,* 51: 171–180.

Salehabadi, Djahane. 2011. "*Der Kampf um den Abfallstrom*: Conflict and Contestation in Re-valuing E-Waste in Germany." *Re/Cycling Histories* conference, Rachel Carson Center, Munich, Germany, May 27–29.

Salmon, Katy. 2001. "Where There Are No Subsidies." *New Internationalist* 334: 22.

Sandbrook, Richard. 1995. *The Politics of Africa's Economic Recovery.* Cambridge, UK: Cambridge University Press.

Sanderson, Steven. 1986a. *The Transformation of Mexican Agriculture: International Structure and the Politics of Rural Change.*

Princeton, NJ: Princeton University Press.

———. 1986b. "The Emergence of the 'World Steer': Internationalization and Foreign Domination in Latin American Cattle Production." In *Food, the State, and International Political Economy,* edited by F. L. Tullis and W. L. Hollist. Lincoln: University of Nebraska Press.

Sanger, David E. 1998. "Dissension Erupts at Talks on World Financial Crisis." *The New York Times,* October 7: A6.

Santos, B. de S. 2002. *Towards a New Legal Common Sense.* London: Butterworths.

Saul, John Ralston. 2005. *The Collapse of Globalism and the Reinvention of the World.* New York: Penguin.

Schaar, J. 2008. "Overview of Adaptation Mainstreaming Initiatives." *Commission on Climate Change and Development,* March. Available at www.ccdco mission.org.

Schneider, Cathy Lisa. 1995. *Shantytown Protest in Pinochet's Chile.* Philadelphia: Temple University Press.

Schneider, Howard. 2011. "Arab World Needs an Economic Revolution." *The Guardian Weekly,* March 4: 17.

Schoenberger, Erica. 1994. "Competition, Time, and Space in Industrial Change." In *Commodity Chains and Global Capitalism,* edited by Gary Gereffi and Miguel Korzeniewicz. Westport, CT: Praeger.

Schott, Jeffrey J. 2000. "The WTO After Seattle." In *The WTO After Seattle,* edited by Jeffrey J. Schott.

Washington, DC: Institute for International Economics.

Schwarzer, S., A. De Bono, G. Guiliani, S. Kluser, and P. Peduzzi. 2005. "E-Waste, the Hidden Side of IT Equipment's Manufacturing and Use." In *Environment Alert Bulletin,* edited by UNEP / GRID-Europe. United Nations Environment Programme DEWA / GRID-Europe.

Seelye, Katherine Q. 2011. "Detroit Census Figures Confirm a Grim Desertion Like No Other." *The New York Times,* March 23: A1, A20.

Segelken, Roger. 1995. "Fewer Foods Predicted for Crowded Future Meals." *Cornell Chronicle,* February 23: 5.

Seidman, Gay. 1994. *Manufacturing Militance: Workers' Movements in Brazil and South Africa, 1970–1985.* Berkeley, CA: University of California Press.

Sekler, Nicola. 2009. "Postneoliberalism from and as a Counter-Hegemonic Perspective." *Development Dialogue,* January: 59–71.

Sen, Gita. 1994. "Women, Poverty, and Population: Issues for the Concerned Environmentalist." In *Feminist Perspectives on Sustainable Development,* edited by Wendy Harcourt. London: Zed.

Sengupta, Somini. 2009. "As Indian Growth Soars, Child Hunger Persists." *The New York Times,* July 17.

Séréni, Jean-Pierre. 2007. "Hydrocarbon Nationalism." *Le Monde Diplomatique,* March: 12.

Sharma, Devinder. 2007. "Big Box Retail Will Boost Poverty." *India Together,* February 16.

Sharma, Kalpana. 2000. *Rediscovering Dharavi: Stories from Asia's Largest Slum.* New Delhi: Penguin.

Shattuck, Annie. 2008. "The Financial Crisis and the Food Crisis: Two Sides of the Same Coin." *FoodFirst,* September. Available at: www.foodfirst.org.

Sheller, Mimi. 2003: *Consuming the Caribbean.* New York: Routledge.

Shenker, Jack. 2011. "Cairo Strikes $3bn IMF Deal." *The Guardian Weekly,* June 10: 18.

Shi, Zhengrong. 2010. "Everywhere under the Sun." *Making It,* 2, April: 32–35.

Shiva, Vandana. 1991. *The Violence of the Green Revolution.* London: Zed Books.

———. 1997. *Biopiracy: The Plunder of Nature and Knowledge.* Boston: South End.

———. 2000. *The Violence of the Green Revolution.* London: Zed Books.

———. 2003. "The Living Democracy Movement: Alternatives to the Bankruptcy of Globalization." In *Another World Is Possible,* edited by William F. Fisher and Thomas Ponniah. London: Zed.

———. 2008. *Soil Not Oil: Environmental Justice in an Age of Climate Crisis.* Cambridge, Mass: South End Press.

Shoky, Noha El. 2011. Bretton Woods Project, *News,* June 13. Available at www.brettonwoodsproject.org.

Silver, Beverly. 2003. *Forces of Labor: Worker's Movements and Globalization Since 1870.* Cambridge, UK: Cambridge University Press.

Simons, Marlise. 1999. "Cry of Muslim Women for Equal Rights Is Rising." *The New York Times,* February 24: A1, A6.

Singer, Hans W. 1950. "U.S. Foreign Investment in Underdeveloped Areas: The Distribution of Gains Between Investing and Borrowing Countries." *American Economic Review, Papers and Proceedings,* 40: 473–485.

Singh, Ajit. 1992. "The Lost Decade: The Economic Crisis of the Third World in the 1980s: How the North Caused the South's Crisis." *Contention* 2: 58–80.

Sklair, Leslie. 1989. *Assembling for Development: The Maquila Industry in Mexico and the United States.* Boston: Unwin Hyman.

———. 2002. *Globalization. Capitalism & Its Alternatives.* Oxford, UK: Oxford University Press.

Skrobanek, Siripan, Nattaya Boonpakdi, and Chutina Janthakeero. 1997. *The Human Realities of Traffic in International Women.* London: Zed.

"Slavery in the 21st Century." 2001. *New Internationalist,* July–August: 18–19.

Smith, Adam. 1776/1904. *An Inquiry into the Nature and Causes of the Wealth of Nations,* 2 Vols. London: Dent & Sons.

Smith, David. 2011. "One in Three Africans 'Now Middle-Class.'" *The Guardian Weekly,* May 13: 6.

Smith, Jeremy. 2002. "An Unappealing Industry." *The Ecologist* 32(3): 40–41.

South Centre, The. 1993. *Facing the Challenge: Responses to the Report of the South Commission.* London: Zed.

Southend in Transition. 2007. Available at http://www.transitionwestcliff.org.uk/.

Stancil, Jordan. 2010. "Europe's Voodoo Economics." *The Nation,* June 28.

Stanhill, G. 1990. "The Comparative Productivity of Organic Agriculture." *Agriculture, Ecosystems and Environment,* 30: 1–26.

Starr, Amory. 2000. *Naming the Enemy: Anti-Corporate Movements Confront Globalization.* London: Zed.

Stavrianos, L. S. 1981. *Global Rift: The Third World Comes of Age.* New York: William Morrow.

Stern, Nicholas. 2006. *The Economics of Climate Change: The Stern Review.* Cambridge: Cambridge University Press.

Stevens, William K. 1994. "Poor Lands' Success in Cutting Birth Rate Upsets Old Theories." *The New York Times,* January 2: A8.

Stewart, Douglas Ian. 1994. *After the Trees: Living on the Amazon Highway.* Austin: University of Texas Press.

Strange, Susan. 1994. *States and Markets.* London: Pinter.

Stuart, Liz. 2003. "Journey's End for Trafficked Humans." *Guardian Weekly,* February 13–19: 21.

Subcomandante Marcos. 1994. "First Declaration of the Lacandon Jungle." *AVA,* 42 (31): 1.

Sumner, Andy. 2010. "The New Bottom Billion and the MDGs—A Plan of Action." *IDS in Focus Policy Briefing,* October. Retrieved from www.ids.ac.uk.

Sundaram, Jomo K. 2010. "Rethinking Poverty Reduction." *Making It,* 3: 38–39.

Sustainable Cities. 2010. "Dongtan: The World's First Large-Scale Eco-City?" Retrieved from http://sustainablecities .dk/en/city-projects/cases/dongtan-the-world-s-first-large-scale-eco-city.

Tan, Abby. 1991a. "Paychecks Sent Home May Not Cover Human Losses." *Los Angeles Times,* October 1: H2–H3.

———. 1991b. "The Labor Brokers: For a Price, There's a Job Abroad—Maybe." *Los Angeles Times,* October 1: H1.

Tanaka, Nobuo. 2010. "The Next Industrial Revolution." *Making It,* 2, April: 19–21.

Tautz, Carlos Sergio Figueiredo. 1997. "The Asian Invasion: Asian Multinationals Come to the Amazon." *Multinational Monitor* 18(9): 1–5.

Tenkouano, Abdou. 2011. "The Nutritional and Economic Potential of Vegetables." In *State of the World 2011: Innovations That Nourish the Planet.* New York and London: Norton.

Therborn, Göran. 2011. *The World: A Beginner's Guide.* Cambridge: Polity.

Thomas, Alan, and Ben Crow, eds. 1994. *Third World Atlas.* Washington, DC: Taylor and Francis (2nd Edition).

Thompson, Ginger. 2002. "Big Mexican Breadwinner: The Migrant Worker." *The New York Times,* March 25: A3.

Thompson, Tony. 2005. "All Work and No Play in 'Virtual Sweatshop.'" *Guardian Weekly,* March 25–31: 17.

TNI. 2007. "Look to Trondheim: Alternatives for Public Sector Reform in Europe." *Transnational Institute.* Available at http://www .tni.org/archives/eurotopia4_little_ alternatives.

Toulmin, Camilla. 2009. *Climate Change in Africa.* London: Zed Books.

Tran, Mark. 2011. "Tunisia Offers Wake-Up Call for Development." *Guardian,* June 9.

Tripathi, Salil. 2004. "Shine On." *Guardian Unlimited,* May 13. Available at www.guardian.co.uk.

Tripp, Aili Mari. 1997. *Changing the Rules: The Politics of Liberalization and the Urban Informal Economy in Tanzania.* Berkeley, CA: University of California Press.

Tsing, Anna Lowenhaupt. 2005. *Friction: An Ethnography of Global Connection.* Princeton: Princeton University Press.

Turner, Mandy. 2007. "Scramble for Africa." *The Guardian,* May 2. Available at www.guardian.co.uk.

Tuxill, John. 1999. "Nature's Cornucopia: Our Stake in Plant Diversity." Worldwatch Paper No. 148, Washington, DC: Worldwatch.

Tyler, Patrick E. 1994. "China Planning People's Car to Put Masses behind Wheel." *The New York Times,* September 22: A1, D8.

Uchitelle, Louis. 2007. "NAFTA Should Have Stopped Illegal Immigration, Right?" *The New York Times,* February 18: 4.

———. 2011. "From Two Breadwinners to One." *The Nation,* May 23: 17–19.

United Nations. 1997. *Human Development Report.* New York: Oxford University Press.

United Nations Development Programme (UNDP). 2010. *Human Development Report 2010.* New York: Oxford University Press.

———. 2011a. *Human Development Report.* New York: United Nations. Retrieved from http://hdr.undp.org/en/statistics/indices/.

———. 2011b. *Human Development Report.* New York: United Nations. Retrieved from http://hdr.undp.org/en/reports/global/hdr2011/.

UNCTAD. 1996. *Trade and Development Report 1996.* Geneva: UNCTAD.

UNCTAD and UNEP. 2008. *Organic Agriculture and Food Security in Africa.* New York and Geneva: United Nations.

UN Department of Economic and Social Affairs (UNDESA). 2010a. "Retooling Global Development." *World Economic and Social Survey.* New York: United Nations.

———. 2010b. The Millennium Development Goals Report. Available at http://www.unfpa.org/public/site/global/lang/en/pid/6090.

UN-HABITAT. 2003. *The Challenge of Slums.* Global Report on Human Settlements. London: Earthscan.

United Nations Development Programme (UNDP). 1997. *United Nations Development Report.* New York: Oxford University Press.

United Nations Framework Convention on Climate Change (UNFCCC). 2001. *Report of the 7th Conference of Parties.* New York. United Nations. Available at http://unfccc.int/national_reports/napa/items/2719.php.

UNMA. 2005. *Millennium Ecosystem Assessment.* Available at http://www.maweb.org/en/index.aspx.

Van der Gaag, Nikki. 2004. *The No-Nonsense Guide to Women's Rights.* London: Verso.

Van der Ploeg, J.D. 2009. *The New Peasantries: New Struggles for Autonomy and Sustainability in an Era of Empire and Globalization.* London: Earthscan.

Venkatesan, J. 2010. "Supreme Court Report." *The Hindu,* July 22. Available at www/thehindu.com/2010/07/22/stories/2010072261200300.htm.

Vía Campesina. 2000. "Bangalore Declaration. October 6. Available at http://viacampesina. org/main_en/index.php?option=com_content&task=view&id=53&Itemid=28.

Victor, Peter. 2010. "Questioning Economic Growth." *Nature,* 468: 370–371.

Vidal, John. 2003. "All Dried Up." *Guardian Weekly,* March 27–April 2: 24.

———. 2004. "Beyond the city limits." *The Guardian,* 8 September: 18.

———. 2007a. "Climate Change to Force Mass Migration." *The Guardian,* May 14. Available at www.guardian.co.uk.

———. 2007b. "Climate Change and Shortages of Fuel Signal Global Food Crisis." *The Guardian Weekly,* September 11: 3.

———. 2008. "Billions Wasted on UN Climate Programme." *The Guardian Weekly,* May 30-June 5: 1.

———. 2010. "How Food and Water are Driving a 21st-Century African Land Grab." *The Observer,* March 7.

———. 2011. "Bolivia Enshrines Rights of Mother Nature." *The Guardian Weekly,* April 15: 7.

Wacker, Corinne. 1994. "Sustainable Development Through Women's Groups: A Cultural Approach to Sustainable Development." In *Feminist Perspectives on Sustainable Development,* edited by Wendy Harcourt. London: Zed.

Wade, Robert. 2010. "Reply to Martin Wolf." *Financial Times,* July 26.

Walker, Richard. 2004. *The Conquest of Bread: 150 Years of Agribusiness in California.* New York: New Press.

Wallach, Lori. 2003. "What the WTO Didn't Want You to Know." Available at www.iatp.org.

Wallach, Lori, and Michelle Sforza. 1999. *Whose Trade Organization? Corporate Globalization and the Erosion of Democracy.* Washington, DC: Public Citizen.

Wallach, Lori, and Patrick Woodall. 2004. *Whose Trade Organization? A Comprehensive Guide to the WTO.* New York: New Press.

Wallerstein, Immanuel. 1974. *The Modern World-System.* New York: Academic Press.

———. 1988. "Development: Lodestar or Illusion?" *Economic and Political Weekly,* 23(39): 2017–2023.

Walton, John, and David Seddon. 1994. *Free Markets & Food Riots: The Politics of Global Adjustment.* Oxford, UK: Blackwell.

Warde, Ibrahim. 2008. "Are They Saviours, Predators or Dupes?" *Le Monde Diplomatique,* May: 1–2.

Waring, Marilyn. 1988. *If Women Counted: A New Feminist Economics.* San Francisco: Harper & Row.

Watkins, Kevin. 1991. "Agriculture and Food Security in the GATT Uruguay Round." *Review of African Political Economy* 50: 38–50.

———. 2002. "Money Talks." *Guardian Weekly,* May 9–15: 21.

———. 2006. "The Forgotten Other India." *The Guardian,* October 3. Available at www.guardian .co.uk.

Watts, Jonathan. 2005–2006. "Rivals Awake to a Giant in Their Midst." *Guardian Weekly,* December 23–January 5: 36.

———. 2010. "Greatest Shoppers Ever?" *The Guardian Weekly,* 16 July: 25–27.

———. 2011a. "China Counts Cost of Breakneck Growth." *The Guardian Weekly,* 7 January: 10.

———. 2011b. "Rich in China Get Richer Only Faster." *The Guardian,* July 11.

Watts, Michael. 1994. "Life Under Contract: Contract Farming, Agrarian Restructuring, and Flexible Accumulation." In *Living Under Contract: Contract Farming and Agrarian Transformation in Sub-Saharan Africa,* edited by Peter D. Little and Michael J. Watts. Madison: University of Wisconsin Press.

Weber, Heloise. 2004. "The 'New Economy' and Social Risk: Banking on the Poor?" *Review of International Political Economy* 11(2): 356–386.

Weis, Tony. 2007. *The Global Food Economy.* London: Zed Books.

Weiss, R. 2008. "Firms Seek Patents on 'Climate Ready' Altered Crops." *Washington Post,* May 13.

Weissman, Robert. 1991. "Prelude to a New Colonialism: The Real

Purpose of GATT." *The Nation,* March 18: 337.

Wessel, James. 1983. *Trading the Future: Farm Exports and the Concentration of Economic Power in Our Food System.* San Francisco: Institute for Food and Development Policy.

Wheatley, Alan. 2010. "Water Crisis Threatens Asia's Rise." *International Herald Tribune,* October 12: 24.

White, Richard E., and Gloria Eugenia González Marino. 2007. "Las Gaviotas: Sustainability in the Tropics." *World Watch* 20(3): 18–23.

Widmer, Rolf, Heidi Oswald-Krapf, Deepali Sinha-Khetriwal, Max Schnellmann, and Heinz Böni. 2005. "Global Perspectives on E-Waste." *Environmental Impact Assessment Review,* 25: 436–458.

Williams, Austin. 2009. "Dongtan: The Eco-City That Never Was." *Spiked,* 1 September. Available at www .spiked-online.com/index.php/site/ printable/7330/.

Williams, Gwyneth. 1981. *Third-World Political Organizations: A Review of Developments.* Montclair, NJ: Allenheld, Osmun & Co.

Wilson, Elliot. 2010. "Billions Pour in for India's Superclass." *The Guardian Weekly,* May 14: 17.

Wittman, Hannah. 2009. "Reworking the Metabolic Rift: La Vía Campesina, Agrarian Citizenship and Food Sovereignty." *The Journal of Peasant Studies,* 36(4): 805–826.

Wolf, Eric. 1969. *Peasant Wars of the Twentieth Century.* New York: HarperCollins Paperbacks.

———. 1982. *Europe and the People Without History.*

Berkeley, CA: University of California Press.

Wolf, Martin. 2010a. "Three Years on, Fault Lines Threaten the World Economy." *Financial Times,* July 14: 7.

———. 2010b. "Why the West Faces a Harsher Future." *Financial Times,* July 12.

Wolfensohn, James. 2000. "Rethinking Development—Challenges and Opportunities." *UNCTAD* meeting, Bangkok, February 16. Available at www.iatp.org.

Wong, Edward. 2010. "As China Aids Labor, Unrest Is Still Rising." The New York Times, June 21.

Wood, Robert E. 1986. *From Marshall Plan to Debt Crisis: Foreign Aid and Development Choices in the World Economy.* Berkeley: University of California Press.

Woodall, Pam. 1994. "War of the Worlds: A Survey of the Global Economy." *The Economist,* Special Supplement, October 1: 24.

Woods, Ngaire. 2006. *The Globalizers. The IMF, the World Bank, and Their Borrowers.* Ithaca: Cornell University Press.

Worden, Scott. 2001. "E-Trafficking." *Foreign Policy,* Spring. Retrieved from www.foreignpolicy.com/ issue_marapr_2001/gnsprint.html.

World Bank. 1998–1999. *World Development Report.* Washington, DC: World Bank.

———. 2000a. *World Development Report.* Washington, DC: World Bank.

———. 2000b. *Voices of the Poor.* New York: Oxford University Press.

———. 2003. Press Release, Foreign Investment, Remittances Outpace Debt As Sources of Finance For

Developing Countries: World Bank No. 2003/266/S. Available at http://go.worldbank.org/1RE2ADYFF0.

———. 2007. *World Development Report*. Washington, DC: World Bank.

———. 2010. *Rising Global Interest in Farmland: Can It Yield Sustainable and Equitable Benefits?* Washington, DC: World Bank.

———. 2011. World Bank. http://go.worldbank.org/NPD630TRR0.

World Institute for Development Economics Research. 2006. *The World Distribution of Household Wealth*. Helsinki. Available from www.wider.unu.edu.

Yardley, Jim. 2007. "China Says Rich Countries Should Take Lead on Global Warming." *The New York Times,* February 7: A9.

Yumkella, Kandeh K., and Leena Srivastava. 2010. "Energy for All." *Making It,* 2, April: 23–29.

Yunus, Muhammad. 2011. "Sacrificing Microcredit for Megaprofits." *The New York Times,* January 15: A19.

Zalik, Anna, 2004. "The Niger Delta: 'PetroViolence' and 'Partnership Development.'" *Review of African Political Economy* 31(101): 401–424.

Zalik, Anna and Michael Watts. 2006. "Imperial Oil: Petroleum Politics in the Nigerian Delta and the New Scramble for Africa." *Socialist Review,* April. Available at www.socialistreview.org.uk/article.php?articlenumber=9712.

Glossary/Index